The Diplomats 1919-1939

EDITED BY

GORDON A. CRAIG

AND

FELIX GILBERT

VOLUME I: THE TWENTIES

ORIGINALLY PUBLISHED BY
PRINCETON UNIVERSITY PRESS

ATHENEUM

NEW YORK   1963

TO THE MEMORY OF

THEODOR ERNST MOMMSEN, 1905-1958

AND

FRANK MANSFIELD CRAIG, 1882-1952

Published by Atheneum
Reprinted by arrangement with Princeton University Press
Copyright 1953 by Princeton University Press
All rights reserved
Printed in the United States of America by
The Murray Printing Company, Forge Village, Massachusetts
Bound by The Colonial Press, Inc., Clinton, Massachusetts
Published in Canada by McClelland & Stewart Ltd.
First Atheneum Edition

ACKNOWLEDGMENTS

THE EDITORS and contributors wish to express their gratitude to:

Theodor Ernst Mommsen, for having first suggested to the editors the usefulness of a symposium on interwar diplomacy, and Datus C. Smith and Joseph R. Strayer for having seconded the suggestion so enthusiastically;

the Research Committee of Princeton University, the Rutgers University Research Council, the Board of Directors of the American Philosophical Society, and Edward F. D'Arms and the Board of Directors of the Rockefeller Foundation for grants in aid of research and assistance in meeting necessary travel and conference expenses;

Bernard C. Noble and Bernadotte Schmitt of the Division of Historical Policy Research, the Department of State, for permitting the use of certain papers bearing on the Japanese problem; the Swedish Foreign Office for allowing one of the contributors to have access to its files; and Herman Kahn, Director of the Franklin D. Roosevelt Library, Hyde Park, N.Y., for assistance and advice to several of the contributors;

Alexis Saint-Léger Léger and Joseph Clark Grew for their interest and counsel; and Walter Johnson and the Directors of Houghton Mifflin Company for having made available to the editors the proofs of Mr. Grew's *Turbulent Era: A Diplomatic Record of Forty Years,* which has now been published under the editorship of Professor Johnson;

Allen Macy Dulles, for information included in his unpublished Princeton B.A. thesis on the British Foreign Office; and Robert B. Glynn, for permitting the use of his unpublished Harvard honors thesis on Nevile Henderson;

Fred Aandahl, Gerald Aylmer, Cyril E. Black, Percy Corbett, Edward Mead Earle, Carl Hillger, Leonard Krieger, Philip Noel Buxton, E. S. Passant, Raymond J. Sontag, Jacob Viner, John W. Wheeler-Bennett and Sir Llewellyn Woodward for information and advice; and

Elizabeth D'Arcy and Mrs. Benton Schrader of Princeton, N.J., Joan Connolly of Bryn Mawr College, and Patricia and Gordon Decato of Keene, N.H. for typing, and retyping, the manuscript; and Harriet Anderson for seeing it through the press.

For the shortcomings of the book, none of the individuals or institutions mentioned above can be held accountable; but, if this volume makes any contribution to our knowledge of the recent past, they deserve much of the credit.

ACKNOWLEDGMENTS

CONTENTS

INTRODUCTION

THERE are few extended discussions of diplomacy in which the author does not, sooner or later, get around to quoting Sir Henry Wotton's definition of the diplomat as "an honest man sent to lie abroad for the good of his country," and it would be a pity to violate a tradition so firmly established. However hackneyed by use, this seventeenth century conceit does at least convey a sense of the atmosphere of suspicion which has always surrounded the diplomatic profession. It is not surprising that diplomats are the object of some distrust in the countries to which they are accredited. They are, after all, aliens, representing the interests and ambitions of their own nations, seeking information which will be of advantage to their own governments, and protected—as they pursue their not necessarily friendly activities—by international codes and conventions that transcend local law. But diplomats are apt also to encounter suspicion in their native lands and to discover that, among their fellow citizens, there are many who disapprove of men who spend most of their life abroad, or dwelling on affairs abroad, and who believe that facility in strange tongues and intimacy with foreign statesmen must lead inevitably to "secret deals" at the expense of the nation. In this atmosphere, the diplomat becomes a kind of wanderer between two worlds, in neither of which he is wholly accepted.

The intensity of the suspicion with which the diplomat is customarily regarded might be understandable if his role in the international politics of our time were more decisive than it obviously is. But the fact of the matter is that the age in which diplomats held the fate of nations in their hands lies definitely in the past; and, for the last century and more, their influence has been subject to a process of marked diminution.

I

Diplomacy, as we know it, had its origins in the period in which the modern sovereign state emerged in Europe—that is, the period from the sixteenth to the eighteenth century—and its forms and conventions still reflect the social and economic conditions of that age. The characteristic feature of the period in which diplomacy arose was the absolute state—the state which was governed by a ruler with virtually unlimited powers and which was, moreover, completely identified with the personality, the ambitions, and even the whims of that ruler. In the age of absolutism, the men who were sent on missions abroad were in a real sense personal representatives of their prince and, during their tours of duty, they consorted exclusively with other princes or with royal representatives whose positions corresponded to their own. As trusted agents of their sovereign, they were given a high degree of freedom of action —a privilege which was in any case made necessary by the primitive state of long-distance communication—and they were expected to display judgment and initiative in the conduct of their sovereign's affairs. Their duties in this respect, however, were facilitated by the fact that the European states of this period were autarchical entities and that the factors that determined their international behavior and their intercourse with their neighbors—such things as political ambition, economic power, and military resources—were, or seemed to be, easily calculable. With the essential facts at their disposal, and provided further with such time-honored rules of thumb as *ragione di stato* and balance of power, the diplomats possessed a conceptual framework within which they could move with confidence.

The diplomatic practices and conventions which emerged in this situation persisted in the subsequent period, although the conditions that shaped them were profoundly altered. If the eighteenth century was the classical age of diplomacy, the nineteenth century marked the beginning of the process by which the diplomat's freedom was restricted and his functions transformed. Technical invention made communication between foreign capitals both easier and more rapid. The ambassador's long summary reports to his sovereign, carried by courier over dangerous routes and often arriving long after the described conditions had changed or the projected actions had been executed, were replaced by telegraphic dispatches and, eventually, by telephone conversations. When this happened, the age of the "great ambassadors," who were perforce policy-makers in their own right, was over. Only in the most remote regions was independent action along the line of eighteenth century diplomacy possible or necessary. The policies of the Great Powers were now closely controlled by the administrative agencies of the home governments, and the Foreign Offices in particular began to play an important role as the protectors of system and continuity in the conduct of foreign policy.

At the same time, the position of the diplomat was affected by the remarkable economic changes which were ushered in by the industrial revolution and the era of free trade. As intercourse between nations expanded in the private economic sphere, the number of people who could claim to be well-informed about conditions in countries other than their own increased; the monopolistic position of the diplomat was broken, and he became much more exposed to competition and criticism. Simultaneously, the nature of his functions changed and their scope was enlarged, for he was now expected to provide information on economic and military questions of the most highly technical nature. His staff grew in numbers and was divided into functional departments; he became increasingly dependent upon his experts; and, although he was still apt to regard diplomacy as an art which could, and should, be professed by a chosen few, this contention was patently contradicted by the facts of his daily existence.

But the most important change in the position of the diplomat was brought about by developments in the constitutional sphere, and, specifically, by the collapse of absolutism and the rise of democratic institutions. The spread of democracy and the growing belief in the necessity of democratic control of foreign policy challenged one of the characteristic features of traditional diplomacy: its secrecy. The secret character of diplomatic negotiation could not, of course, be lightly abandoned in deference to democratic sentiment, for all nations do not enjoy the same degree of political enlightenment, and practices which seem reprehensible to some are considered indispensable by others. Since negotiation is a process in which—if success is desired—some regard must be given to the conditions imposed by the opposite party, secret diplomacy did not disappear with the speed demanded by advocates of democratic control; and this fact in itself enhanced, in some countries, the suspicion with which diplomats were regarded. Nor was this the only respect in which the impact of democracy was felt. As governments became more dependent on the expressed wishes of the electorate, the whole concept of rational power calculation was jeopardized. What might seem to the diplomat's mind as a shrewd stroke of policy—a Hoare-Laval Pact, for instance—could be abruptly and indignantly rejected by an aroused public opinion; and, in consequence, the most difficult problem confronting the diplomat in the new age was that of reconciling reason of state with popular desire.

Finally, the emergence of democratic government undermined a basic assumption of the diplomatic profession: the idea, namely, that the diplomat was the personal representative of the sovereign. In large part, the prestige and the effective action of the diplomat depends upon the maintenance of this fiction; but the fact that it has been maintained, and with it the ceremonial, the punctilio, and the observance of social hierarchy and custom which the role involves, has strengthened the popular impression that the diplomat is something of an anachronism, forming part of a social tradition that belongs to the past. In a world of ordinary citizens and forthright and industrious businessmen and workers, the diplomat seems to stand out as the man with top hat and monocle—as indeed he is, or was until recently, portrayed in neon tubing over a restaurant in the shadow of the old State Department building in Washington.

The contrast between the traditions of the diplomatic profession and the world of modern industrialism and democracy developed slowly throughout the nineteenth century. The first great climax in the conflict came with the outbreak of the first world war. By many people in the Western states in particular, this catastrophe was laid at the door of the professional diplomat; and "secret diplomacy" was widely regarded as one of its primary causes. The demand for a New Diplomacy, as a first step toward attaining a better and more peaceful world, was now heard on every hand.

The new techniques and methods which were introduced into diplomatic practice in the attempt to satisfy this demand, and the resultant strains and confusion of purpose which ensued, will be discussed in the pages below. But the search for New Diplomacy was not the only, or even the most important, development in the period which followed the war. From the turmoil engendered by the conflict, new forms of political organization emerged, and the democratic states found themselves confronted with totalitarian powers—the Soviet Union, Fascist Italy, and Nazi Germany—which denied the laws and the values which they themselves recognized. When this happened, the anomalies of the diplomat's position were further heightened. If sent to represent his country's interests in a totalitarian society, he found himself, curiously enough, in a situation not dissimilar to that which faced the diplomat of the eighteenth century when he was accredited to another country; that is, if he was to be successful, he had to ignore the political, economic, and social strata which democratic opinion insisted were important and to concentrate his energies upon the task of establishing a personal relationship with the despot and his immediate aides. In his relations with his own government, on the other hand, he was forced to adjust his methods to the requirements of democratic sentiment or suffer the consequences. With the totalitarian states professing a newer—or older—diplomacy than the New Diplomacy demanded in the democracies, the position of the professional diplomat was, to say the least, uncomfortable.

II

This book is concerned with the diplomacy of the period between the two world wars, and its pattern is necessarily determined by the events of the period. Thus, it deals successively with the reorganization of the European system which took place at the end of the first world war; the first stirrings of dissatisfaction with the Peace Settlement, and the beginnings in the 1920's of the movement known as revisionism; the totalitarian onslaught against the Peace Settlement which was inaugurated in the 1930's; and the weak and hesitant response which this challenge met among the founders and guardians of the existing order. The focus throughout is primarily European, since Europe was still clearly the decisive area in world politics; but, in the concluding chapters of the book, an attempt is made to describe the shift to non-European forces which terminated this period of world history.

But, although this book deals with the development of foreign affairs from 1919 to 1939, it does not pretend to provide a complete chronological account of the period. This is a book about diplomats—the envoys in the field and the officials in the Foreign Offices—and the events of the period are considered from their point of view, rather than from a more general perspective. As the events of the period are described, the reader is invited to concern himself, neither with the figures whose names appeared most frequently in the headlines—Stresemann and Briand, Hitler and Mussolini—nor with such forces for historical change as economic potential, demographic tendencies, or ideological zeal, but rather with the actions and the problems of the diplomats who helped to formulate national policies and who conducted the negotiations by which they were implemented. To be more concrete, the basic problem with which this book is concerned is that of the significance which traditional diplomacy possessed in a period in which its institutions were assailed from the democratic, as well as from the totalitarian, side but during which—and this must be emphasized—it continued to be employed by all Powers as an instrument for attaining national objectives.

These remarks may serve to explain the selection of the individual diplomats whose work is discussed in these pages. Here again the pattern has been influenced by the events of the period, and an attempt has been made to choose, for extended treatment, men whose influence or actions were important at decisive moments in the history of these years. Three other considerations have also, however, been taken into account here. In the first place, diplomats, like other people, have personalities of their own, and their reactions to problems are influenced by individual attitudes and idiosyncrasies. An effort has been made, then, to illustrate this personal element in diplomacy, and to show how some of the diplomats, like Rumbold and Schulenburg, responded instinctively to new problems by invoking the traditional canons of their profession, while others, like Dirksen and Nevile Henderson, sought desperately to launch themselves upon what they believed to be the wave of the future.

In the second place, in discussing an age in which the tenets of traditional diplomacy were being questioned, it would be unwise to neglect the role of the Foreign Offices of the various Powers. It was, after all, the permanent officials of these establishments who stood as the custodians of diplomatic system and propriety; and it has consequently seemed advisable here to discuss the typical problems which they experienced as their methods and principles were challenged, in the democratic societies, by the champions of open diplomacy and, in the totalitarian, by arrogant amateurs like Ribbentrop and Ciano.

Finally, the struggle between the old and the new diplomacy assumed new and interesting forms in those countries which, because they were new creations, possessed no diplomatic tradition or, because they were aggressively revolutionary, recognized none. Thus, a Benes, who created a tradition for his country, and a Chicherin, who succeeded in convincing the Bolshevists that the aristocratic diplomatic tradition had at least defensive uses, have a place in a book of this kind also.

Granted all this, the choice of the men who have been included in this volume will probably seem arbitrary to some readers. Why, after all, when such permanent officials as Berthelot and Bernhard von Bülow are treated at length, is there no fuller discussion of Vansittart, whose influence was as great as, and perhaps more protracted than, theirs? Why, when Undén and Arthur Henderson and Beck have chapters of their own, are Titulescu and Nansen omitted? Why are Franco's diplomats neglected, and why the short but noisy career of Curtius? The answer to these questions must be twofold. If all those who justly deserve a place in a discussion of the diplomacy of the interwar years were included here, this book would become an unmanageable dictionary, rather than an admittedly selective treatment. Furthermore, in the case of the most notable omission here—Vansittart—it was thought wiser to defer an appraisal of his diplomacy until the documents bearing on the period of his greatest influence have been published, as they will be, presumably, in the near future.

A further word should perhaps be spoken on the question of availability of material. The publication of the files of the British, German, and Italian Foreign Offices is now under way, although it has not yet advanced far enough to give more than fragmentary coverage of the period as a whole. The volumes which have appeared are of essential importance to the diplomatic historian, but it need hardly be pointed out that he cannot afford to rely upon them solely. In general, the dispatches published do not reflect the factors that shaped the policies set forth in them; and the British editors have warned their readers that they have not tried to present "a complete record of the processes of formulation of policy as distinct from execution," since reasons of constitutional propriety forbid the publication of "discussion and divergencies of view in the Cabinet and between Departments and individuals." In other countries as well, much that went on behind the scenes does not appear in the published correspondence. To discover the details of the discussions and conflicts which preceded policy decisions, the historian is forced to rely upon other materials, and particularly upon memoirs and diaries written by participants. The existence or nonexistence of such materials has not been the least important of the factors which have determined the organization of this volume.

III

This is a book without a hero. In it, there appear honest men and evil men, fighters for lost causes and enthusiastic gravediggers, fools and knaves, men with whom we sympathize and men whom it is difficult to regard without contempt, men who lived according to the values and traditions in which they were educated and men who lost or abandoned their principles and their faith—but few men, if any, who are likely to be regarded by future generations as great historical figures.

This point is made lest the reader of these pages conclude that we have intended to make a hero, if not of any individual official or envoy, then of the professional diplomat as a type. This impression may, indeed, seem to be borne out by the fact that the different chapters of this book, however much they vary in content and approach, do stress certain problems in which the professional point of view is treated sympathetically. Again and again in the chapters that follow, there will be references to the tendency of the political leaders of the state to prefer "diplomacy by conference" to the technique of negotiation by note and official exchange of views—a preference which had unfortunate results on many occasions. Again and again, the reader will find the professionals excluded from important discussions and the advice of trained observers in the missions abroad neglected in favor of the intuitive judgments or chance impressions of tourists who possess the ear of the political ministers. He will notice also frequent references to the custom in this period of entrusting matters which could have been performed perfectly well by embassy staffs to special and extraordinary missions, headed by politicians with dubious qualifications and negligible experience in foreign affairs. And he will certainly detect a note of criticism in the accounts of the growing tendency of home governments to give attention, and preferment, to those diplomats who reported what their superiors wanted to hear rather than to those whose analyses of the developing situation have been justified by history.

Despite the emphasis placed upon these aspects of interwar diplomacy, it should not be concluded that this book is intended as a defense of the professional diplomat or, further, that it seeks to advance the view that the world would have become a happier and more peaceful place if only the professionals had been given their heads and permitted to arrange matters in their own way. It has no such thesis. It is quite apparent that the professional diplomats would not have lost their former privileges and prerogatives if they had not, in fact, been somewhat out of step with the prevailing forces of the day and if, indeed, there had not been a good deal of truth in the frequently reiterated charge that they had failed adequately to adjust their thinking and their methods to the requirements of modern society.

Nevertheless—and if the book must have a thesis, this is it—it is dangerous to carry distrust of professional diplomacy to the point where you always insist upon doing what the professionals say must not be done and always refuse to do what they describe as necessary. Too many of the interwar political leaders succumbed to this kind of perverseness, with odd, and sometimes fateful, results. Surely they would have been better advised to make the necessary reforms in the machinery of diplomacy, so that it might, while becoming once more an effective means of promoting the national interest, have also been able to operate again—in the words of Sir Robert Peel—as "the great engine used by civilized society for the purpose of maintaining peace."

It need hardly be added that the problem of adjusting the machinery and the methods of diplomacy to the needs of contemporary society is still of importance, not least of all to the United States of America. This nation has been projected into a dominant role in world affairs with a suddenness and finality which has still not been fully appreciated by many of its citizens. In addition, it approaches its new problems and responsibilities with a tradition that is deeply opposed to that of international diplomacy. In the circumstances, a book which shows how dangerous suspicion of the conventions and practices of diplomacy can be, if it is not modified by an earnest desire to make use of those aspects of the diplomatic art which have been proven by time and experience, may serve a useful purpose.

Nelson, N. H.   G.A.C.
    August, 1952   F.G.

A NOTE ON ABBREVIATIONS

The most frequently cited collections of printed diplomatic correspondence and other documents are consistently referred to in the footnotes by short titles. For the convenience of the reader, the abbreviated title employed and the full titles of the collections follow.

BRITISH DOCUMENTS. *Documents on British Foreign Policy, 1919-1939*, edited by E. L. Woodward and Rohan Butler (London, H. M. Stationery Office, 1949 and continuing).

CONSPIRACY AND AGGRESSION. *Nazi Conspiracy and Aggression* (8 vols. and 2 supplements, Washington, Government Printing Office, 1946-1949).

DEGRAS. Jane Degras, ed., *Soviet Documents on Foreign Policy*, Volume I, 1917-24 (Oxford, 1951); Volume II, 1925-32 (Oxford, 1952).

DIRKSEN PAPERS. Ministry of Foreign Affairs of the USSR, *Documents and Materials Relating to the Eve of the Second World War*. Volume II, Dirksen Papers, 1938-1939 (Moscow, 1949).

DOCUMENTS AND MATERIALS. Ministry of Foreign Affairs of the USSR, *Documents and Materials Relating to the Eve of the Second World War*. Volume I, November 1937-1938 (Moscow, 1949).

DOCUMENTI ITALIANI. Ministero degli Affari Esteri, *I Documenti Diplomatici Italiani* (Rome, La Libreria dello Stato, 1952 and continuing).

FOREIGN RELATIONS. *Foreign Relations of the United States* (Department of State, Washington).

GERMAN DOCUMENTS. *Documents on German Foreign Policy, 1918-1945: From the Archives of the German Foreign Ministry* (Washington, Government Printing Office, 1949 and continuing).

NAZI-SOVIET RELATIONS. *Nazi-Soviet Relations 1939-1941: Documents from the Archives of the German Foreign Office*, edited by R. J. Sontag and J. S. Beddie (Washington, 1948).

POLISH WHITE BOOK. Republic of Poland, Ministry for Foreign Affairs, *Official Documents concerning Polish-German and Polish-Soviet Relations, 1933-1939* (London, 1940).

TRIAL OF MAJOR CRIMINALS. *The Trial of the Major War Criminals* (42 vols., Nuremberg, 1947-1949).

TRIALS OF WAR CRIMINALS. *Trials of War Criminals before the Nuernberg Military Tribunals under Control Council Law No. 10* (14 volumes, Nuremberg, 1946-1949).

VORGESCHICHTE. *Dokumente zur Vorgeschichte des Krieges*, herausgegeben vom Auswärtigen Amt der deutschen Regierung (Basel, 1940).

All other works are cited by their full title on the first reference in any chapter. Thereafter, short—but, it is to be hoped, easily recognizable—titles are used.

1

The British Foreign Office from
Grey to Austen Chamberlain

BY GORDON A. CRAIG

"THE FOREIGN OFFICE," said the Marquess of Londonderry in the House of Lords in March 1944, "is the pivot of the Government, and the Foreign Secretary should be the most dominant personality in the Cabinet after the Prime Minister.... It may be a harsh thing to say that the Foreign Office has not existed since the days of Sir Edward Grey."[1]

It was, indeed, a harsh thing to say in a chamber whose membership included three men who had served as Secretaries of State for Foreign Affairs, as well as three former Permanent Under-Secretaries for Foreign Affairs;[2] but there was more than a modicum of truth in Londonderry's statement. There can be little doubt that the prestige and authority of the Foreign Office during the postwar period was much less than that which it enjoyed in the period before 1914; and it is not difficult to demonstrate that, on numerous occasions, its influence on British policy was so negligible that its existence as the agency constitutionally charged with the conduct of British foreign relations seemed to have become more formal than real.

In the years before 1914, the formulation of British foreign policy in its broadest outlines was the responsibility of the Cabinet, as it was also their responsibility to explain and defend it before Parliament. Within the Cabinet itself, however, the Foreign Secretary was "the most important person who shape[d] the policy of [the] country."[3] He, after

---

[1] Parliamentary Debates: Lords, 5th series, CXXXI (1943-1944), 363.

[2] The Lord Chancellor, Viscount Simon, had been Foreign Secretary from 1931 to 1935, Viscount Templewood (Sir Samuel Hoare) in 1935, and the Earl of Halifax from 1938 to 1940. Lord Hardinge of Penshurst had served as Permanent Under-Secretary in the Foreign Office from 1905 to 1910 and from 1916 to 1920, Lord Tyrrell from 1925 to 1928, and Lord Vansittart from 1930 to 1938.

[3] Earl Grey of Falloden at the first annual dinner of the Royal Institute of Inter-

all, was in the best position to be informed of the plans and ambitions of other governments, thanks to the reports of his agents abroad and his conversations with foreign representatives in London; and he alone had, in the Foreign Office, an expert staff which made systematic and continuous studies of the foreign situation and—especially after the Foreign Office reforms of 1906[4]—advised him concerning the course Britain should take in given contingencies. The Cabinet itself was too cumbersome and too busy to devote much time to the details of policy. When pressing matters were brought before them, they were generally inclined to follow the Foreign Secretary's lead, and, for the rest—the normal day-by-day policy decisions—to trust to his discretion. It was realized, as J. A. Spender has written, that the ever pressing domestic concerns of the Cabinet, as well as the normal business of the Foreign Office, would be hopelessly disrupted if the Foreign Secretary found it "necessary to consult the Cabinet on more than a few urgent questions; and needlessly to multiply these was one of the sure signs of a bad Foreign Secretary."[5]

Before 1914, then, the right of the Foreign Secretary and the permanent officials in the Foreign Office to consider themselves as the chief advisors of the Cabinet in matters of foreign policy was never seriously questioned; and, although there were occasions when their advice was rejected by the Cabinet, such action was never taken lightly or without careful consideration of the Foreign Office point of view. Similarly, it was generally recognized that the *execution* of foreign policy decisions—discussion with foreign Powers and the varied tasks of negotiation— was the prerogative of the Foreign Secretary, his aides in the Foreign Office and the diplomats in the field; and necessary departures from this rule were made only after the Foreign Office had been informed and consulted.[6]

After the first world war, this state of affairs changed radically. In

national Affairs, July 16, 1930. See *Journal of the Royal Institute of International Affairs* (later *International Affairs*), IX (1930), 579.

[4] On these reforms, which strengthened the advisory functions of the staff of the Foreign Office, see Sir John Tilley and Stephen Gaselee, *The Foreign Office* (London, 1933), pp. 156ff.; Sir John Tilley, *London to Tokyo* (London, 1942), pp. 69-70; F. Ashton-Gwatkin, "Foreign Service Reorganization," *International Affairs*, XXII (1946), 58ff.

[5] J. A. Spender, *The Public Life* (2 vols., New York, 1925), II, 42. Mr. L. Amery in *The Observer* (London) of April 18, 1934 pointed out that, in the unwieldy Cabinet, "there is very little Cabinet policy on any subject."

[6] This applied even to the visits of foreign envoys to the sovereign. Canning had successfully insisted that "constitutional" doctrine made it the duty of the Foreign Secretary to be present at such meetings. See Algernon Cecil, "The Foreign Office," *Cambridge History of British Foreign Policy* (3 vols., Cambridge, 1923), III, 556.

matters of policy, Foreign Office advice was frequently ignored and often shrugged aside with an indifference which the Cabinet would not have dared to evince toward the views, let us say, of the Admiralty or the War Office.[7] Not only were policies adopted by the Prime Minister which ran counter to those advocated by the Foreign Secretary and his staff, but, on numerous occasions, the nature of these policies and the reasons for adopting them were not communicated—or were communicated belatedly and imperfectly—to the Foreign Office. Meanwhile, in the sphere of diplomacy proper, functions formerly reserved to the professional diplomats were farmed out to other departments of the government, while important tasks of negotiation were taken over by political leaders whose new-found enthusiasm for foreign affairs was generally unguided either by training or experience. In consequence, postwar British diplomacy came to be characterized by dangerous defects of coordination, as well as by a high degree of amateurishness, imprecision, and feckless opportunism. These faults of technique were directly related to the inadequacies of British policy in the interbellum period, a period which, it need hardly be added, is in little danger of being regarded by future historians as one in which British statesmanship distinguished itself.

The flouting of the Foreign Office, the dislocation of the processes of policy administration, and the supersession of the diplomatic corps by the political leaders and their private agents reached their height in the 1930's, and there will be occasion to revert later in this book to their consequences in the Munich period. But even in the days when the chief beneficiary of Munich was still an obscure German politician, these tendencies were manifesting themselves in Great Britain, and precedents were being established for the kind of diplomacy which was to guarantee his victory in 1938. It is of some importance, then, to consider the position and the problems of the British foreign service in the first decade of the postwar period.

I

The decline of the authority of the Foreign Office began with the coming of war in 1914. It was inevitable that, with the outbreak of the conflict, the Prime Minister and the Cabinet as a whole should have assumed a greater degree of responsibility for the daily decisions of policy. This development need not, however, have deprived the Foreign Office of its position as technical adviser to the government on international relations; and the fact that it tended to do so is probably due to

[7] See Harold Nicolson in *The Spectator*, December 29, 1944.

the character and methods of Sir Edward Grey and Mr. Asquith. The Foreign Secretary was inclined to believe—as his autobiography demonstrates[8]—that diplomacy did not count for much in wartime, and he was, in addition, temperamentally unfitted to fight for the prerogatives of his office against such confident and aggressive personalities as Churchill, Kitchener, and Lloyd George. Mr. Asquith, whose last years in office were marked by a fatal habit of indecision and a willingness to allow administrative problems to solve themselves, raised no objections as Grey abdicated his functions to the War Office and the Admiralty, and showed a similar degree of unconcern when those departments performed the assumed tasks spasmodically and with indifferent success. The resultant lack of system and direction did not contribute to the success of the war effort, although it did have a sensible effect in the chain of events which led to the fall of the Asquith government in December 1916.[9]

The substitution of Lloyd George for Asquith did not, however, improve the position of the Foreign Office. The new Prime Minister sought to increase the efficiency of the war effort by abolishing the old cabinet system and establishing a War Cabinet of six members who were relieved of all departmental duties so that they might devote their entire energies to the direction of the war. The new Foreign Secretary, Lord Balfour, was not a member of this body, but he was permitted to attend when he wished to do so, as was the Permanent Under-Secretary, Sir Charles Hardinge.[10] Theoretically, this should have assured the Foreign Office of a proper degree of influence in all policy matters. In actuality, the Foreign Office representatives were, with increasing frequency, placed in the position of approving decisions which had already been made by other agencies. The War Cabinet was, for instance, provided with a Secretariat under the direction of Sir Maurice Hankey, which was designed originally to prepare memoranda and perform liaison duties for the Cabinet, but which became, over the course of the years, an official general staff for the Prime Minister and a means by which—as one critic wrote—he could "conduct foreign policy without the inconveniences of Foreign Office intervention."[11] Lloyd George furthermore established a private

[8] Viscount Grey of Falloden, *Twenty-Five Years, 1892-1916* (New York, 1925), pp. 157ff. and especially p. 159.

[9] On these developments, see Eustace Percy, "Foreign Office Reform," *The New Europe*, XI (1919), 53ff.

[10] Hardinge of Penshurst, *Old Diplomacy* (London, 1947), p. 205; Blanche E. C. Dugdale, *Arthur James Balfour, First Earl of Balfour* (2 vols., New York, 1937), II, 176.

[11] *The Nation* (London) October 14, 1922. See also Sir Maurice Hankey, *Diplomacy by Conference, Studies in Public Affairs, 1920-1946* (London, 1946), pp. 61-82.

Secretariat which, under the leadership of Philip Kerr (later Lord Lothian), took up quarters in temporary huts erected in the garden of 10 Downing Street. This "Garden Suburb," or "Downing Street Kindergarten," also cultivated a taste for dabbling in matters of high policy, for its members tended to be contemptuous of the Foreign Office mind and Kerr himself once expressed the conviction that that department "had no conception of policy in its wider sense."[12]

Lord Balfour's biographer has denied that these developments disturbed the Foreign Secretary,[13] and this is probably true, since Balfour, as was perhaps befitting a philosopher, was not accustomed to resist things which he felt were inevitable and since, in any event, he subscribed to a policy of "a free hand for the Little Man." Her further statement, however, that no important steps in foreign policy were taken without Balfour's knowledge[14] is largely meaningless. The Foreign Secretary was always informed, but often too late for him to be able to influence decisions; and his acquiescence in this state of affairs could not help but have a deleterious effect upon Foreign Office morale and efficiency. With the two Secretariats arrogating to themselves more and more advisory and executive functions in foreign policy, the Foreign Office—as a contemporary critic noted—"came increasingly to feel that it had no adequate channels of communication with the War Cabinet; that it was at any given moment imperfectly acquainted with the Prime Minister's intentions, and that it could never be certain that any advice which it might have to tender on any matter would reach the Cabinet in the proper form. It relapsed more and more into the position of a rubber stamp."[15] Nor was this all. The Prime Minister soon began to interfere in an irresponsible manner with diplomatic appointments, and usually without consulting the Foreign Secretary or his staff in advance. In 1917, he attempted to recall Sir George Buchanan from St. Petersburg and to replace him with Arthur Henderson, a plan which was checked only by Henderson's realization, once he had reached Russia, that the change would be ill-advised;[16] and his attempt in the same year to force Lord Bertie out of the Paris Embassy—a scheme which Hardinge believed was hatched in the private Secretariat and never communicated to Balfour—would prob-

[12] Lord Riddell, *Intimate Diary of the Peace Conference and After* (London, 1933), p. 219. For an eye-witness account of the "Garden Suburb," see Joseph Davies, *The Prime Minister's Secretariat, 1916-1920* (Newport, 1952).
[13] Dugdale, *Balfour*, II, 175.
[14] *ibid.*
[15] Eustace Percy in *The New Europe*, XI (1919), 53ff.
[16] Mary Agnes Hamilton, *Arthur Henderson: A Biography* (London, 1938), pp. 125-128.

ably have succeeded if it had not been for spirited protests in *The Times*.[17]

More evidence of the declining influence of the Foreign Office was provided when the war drew to an end and the nations prepared to go to the Peace Conference at Paris. It had been assumed in the Foreign Office that, during the peace negotiations, the professional diplomats and official advisors of the government would be brought back to the center of the stage; and plans had been made to provide expert studies of the principal questions at issue and to select a qualified staff of negotiators, well-briefed and able to carry on discussions in French. But, as Balfour's Permanent Under-Secretary has written, Lloyd George "insisted on employing a staff of his own unofficial creation, who had no knowledge of French and none of diplomacy, and the Foreign Office organization was consequently stillborn." In the British delegation that went to Paris, the Foreign Office had only eighteen members, while the contingents from the War Office, the Admiralty, the Board of Trade and the Colonial Office numbered some 200, with an additional clerical staff of 200 more.[18] These figures are perhaps unimportant, since, in the last analysis, Lloyd George became wearied of the advice of experts from whatever department they might be drawn and, closeting himself with Wilson, Clemenceau, and Orlando, undertook to solve the problems of the conference by his own intuition. It is worth noting, however, that, while the Foreign Office experts were relegated to tedious and unrewarding labors on the various territorial committees,[19] Lloyd George's private aides were often permitted to indulge themselves with the exciting tasks of high-level negotiation and policy formulation. This was true, for instance, of the Prime Minister's private secretary, Philip Kerr, who on one occasion at least was empowered to engage in delicate negotiations with French and American representatives concerning the possibility of British participation in the postwar occupation of the Rhineland;[20] and who was furthermore reported to have been the sole author of the Allied reply to the German objections to the Peace Treaty.[21]

[17] Hardinge, *Old Diplomacy*, p. 214. Bertie was, however, replaced in April 1918 by Lord Derby after protests by Hardinge and some expressions of surprise and disagreement by the French ambassador in London, Paul Cambon. *Ibid.*, p. 226.

[18] *ibid.*, pp. 229-230. For other expressions of concern over the composition of the British delegation, see *The History of "The Times"*, IV (London, 1952), Part I, 463.

[19] On the frustrations suffered by those who served on the territorial committees, see especially Harold Nicolson, *Peacemaking 1919* (New York, 1939), pp. 124-131.

[20] House of Commons Sessional Papers, 1924, XXVI: Cmd. 2169, "France No. 1 (1924). Papers Respecting Negotiations for an Anglo-French Pact," pp. 59-69.

[21] A. L. Kennedy, *Old Diplomacy and New* (London, 1922), p. 307.

The degree of authority which Kerr was permitted to exert seems finally to have ruffled even the usually imperturbable Foreign Secretary. On one occasion, when Balfour asked Kerr whether Lloyd George had read a certain memorandum, the private secretary answered, "I don't think so, but I have." "Not quite the same thing is it, Philip—yet?," Balfour remarked.[22] The Foreign Secretary might have been excused a much stronger expression of irritation than this, for, before the conference was over, he had occasion to discover that Kerr was privy to secrets not disclosed to him. Even in such an important matter as the treaty in which Great Britain and the United States guaranteed to come to France's aid in the event of future German aggression, Balfour was not consulted; and he was informed of its contents by Kerr only after it had been drafted in accordance with the Prime Minister's personal instructions and had been approved by Wilson and Clemenceau.[23]

Even before the end of the Peace Conference, Lloyd George's cavalier treatment of the Foreign Office and the Diplomatic Service had begun to arouse some alarm among responsible observers. In a series of articles written in 1919, *The New Europe*, the well-informed journal of international affairs which was edited by R. W. Seton-Watson and George Glasgow, drew attention to the dangers implicit in the Prime Minister's policy, and it continued to revert to the subject until its unfortunate demise in 1920. Pointing out that foreign policy should not be allowed to grow "like Topsy in the sanctities of No. 10 Downing Street, out of the brains of miscellaneous informants and secretaries," it insisted that the Foreign Office must once more be made "capable of bearing the full responsibility for the formulation of advice on foreign policy through the Foreign Secretary to the Prime Minister" and must once more become the "recognized and accredited center into which all kinds of information about foreign countries shall flow." It recognized that the first step toward the restoration of the department's lost authority must be a thoroughgoing reform of the foreign service as a whole. Early in 1919, as a result of recommendations made earlier by the Royal Commission on the Civil Service, certain reforms had been carried through. The artificial separation of the Foreign Office and the Diplomatic Service had been abolished, and the two services had been amalgamated. The property qualification for candidature for the foreign service had also been eliminated, a step which presumably would open the career to the talents.[24] What was needed now, *The New Europe* insisted, was further

[22] Dugdale, *Balfour*, II, 199.   [23] Hardinge, *Old Diplomacy*, p. 241.
[24] On the partial reforms of 1919, see "Changes in the Organisation of the Foreign and

progress in the same direction: a greater systematization of promotion to bring talent to the fore; administrative improvements capable of encouraging initiative and extirpating the "vagueness" and "hand-to-mouth opportunism" which had often been apparent in the department; a more careful system of diplomatic appointments, which would assure the sending of the right men to the right places;[25] and, finally, careful coordination of the work of the foreign service with that of the newly established League of Nations. But such reforms would be useless unless the usurpation of the functions of the foreign service by irresponsible agencies and institutions was stopped. The journal cited in particular one wartime development—the establishment of a Commercial Diplomatic Service, administered by the Department of Overseas Trade which, in its turn, was responsible to the Foreign Office and the Board of Trade conjointly. In practice, this arrangement had led to the progressive absorption of commercial intelligence by the latter department, and the Foreign Office had much less influence in the economic and commercial aspects of diplomacy than it had before the war. If this, and similar developments caused by "departmental jealousy," were not checked, the administration of British foreign affairs would become increasingly chaotic and ineffective.[26]

These were reasonable views, but they elicited very little response in 1919. Even in normal times Foreign Offices do not enjoy much popularity in democratic states, where foreign affairs seem to be a dangerous distraction from the true business of the nation and where the officials who make a career of dealing with foreign affairs are apt to be viewed with grave suspicion. "On n'aime pas," Jules Cambon has written, "ces porteurs de secrets que sont les ambassadeurs."[27] And in 1919 the unpopularity of the British foreign service was at its height. Recent revelations concerning the nature and methods of prewar statesmanship had convinced large sections of the public that "secret diplomacy" had been the principal cause of the war and that, in consequence, the professional diplomats were among the major war criminals. This belief conditioned the thinking of several highly vocal groups which advocated the shack-

---

Diplomatic Service," *British Year Book of International Law* (1920-21), pp. 97-108. The Consular Service was not included in the amalgamation.

[25] *The New Europe* was generally critical of diplomatic appointments made in this period. See XII (July-October 1919), 209ff.

[26] *The New Europe*, XI (1919), 77ff., 102ff., 128ff., 147ff. See also the article by E. J. Davis, *ibid.*, XIV (Jan.-Apr. 1920), 73ff.

[27] Jules Cambon, *Le Diplomate* (Paris, 1926), pp. 10-11.

ling, if not the outright abolition, of the diplomatic agencies of the government.

Typical of these groups was the Union of Democratic Control, which had been founded in 1914 by E. D. Morel, whose *Morocco in Diplomacy* (1912) was one of the first revelations of the nature of prewar diplomacy,[28] Ramsay MacDonald, the leader of the Labor party, Norman Angell, the author of the widely read book *The Great Illusion,*[29] and Arthur Ponsonby, Charles Trevelyan, and Philip Snowden, who were to become leading lights in the Labor party.[30] The U.D.C. called for an end to "balance of power" politics and secret diplomacy and demanded, among other things, that, in the postwar world, there should be open and frequent declarations of policy by the government, submission of all treaties and engagements to Parliament, periodic revision of treaties, the forbidding of military conversations with other Powers except with parliamentary sanction and the establishment of a parliamentary committee on foreign affairs to keep the Foreign Secretary in touch with public opinion and to prevent the country from being confronted with *faits accomplis.*[31]

For this program there was doubtless much to be said, but members of the U.D.C., and of other Labor and Liberal groups, often went beyond it and expressed the belief that the professional diplomats as a class were socially and temperamentally unfitted to conduct Britain's foreign relations in the postwar world. It would be a mistake, one writer warned, to leave " 'the whole of that industry of protocolling, diplomatising, remonstrating, admonishing and having the honour to be' in the hands of the British Junkers."[32] The professional caste, said another, is discredited by "its methods, its archaic outlook upon life, its complacent self-sufficiency in face of shattering exposures of ignorance and incompetence" and by the patent fact that it is "a conscious aristocratic instrument . . . the last barrier interposed by Providence between the English governing

[28] On Morel, see F. Seymour Cocks, *E. D. Morel, The Man and His Work* (London, 1920) and his own numerous articles in *Foreign Affairs,* the journal of the Union of Democratic Control.

[29] On Angell's role in the movement, see *After All: The Autobiography of Norman Angell* (London, 1951), pp. 191-193.

[30] Trevelyan and Ponsonby were among the Labor party's "experts" on foreign affairs. Ponsonby served as Under-Secretary for Foreign Affairs in the first MacDonald government. Snowden was Chancellor of the Exchequer in both Labor Ministries.

[31] See, for instance, Arthur Ponsonby, "The Democratic Control of Foreign Affairs" in Organisation Centrale pour une Paix Durable, *Recueil de Rapports sur les différents points du Programme-Minimum,* deuxième partie (La Haye, 1916), pp. 252-261.

[32] J. H. Hudson, "Labour's Greatest Menace: The Foreign Office," *Foreign Affairs,* January 1920.

[23]

classes and the rising tide of world democracy."[33] "What can Labour do?" asked a third. "It is pledged, when it comes to power, to sweep the Foreign Office clean."[34]

This atmosphere of suspicion of, and social antagonism toward, the Foreign Office and the Diplomatic Service was reinforced by the muddled optimism of the many people who, regardless of party affiliation, seemed to believe that, in the postwar world, there would be no need for the traditional agencies and techniques of foreign affairs, which would presumably be replaced by new methods and organizations. This type of thinking was doubtless encouraged by the exhortations of the President of the United States, who had promised a world in which "diplomacy shall proceed always frankly and in the public view." It was conditioned also by the fervent hopes entertained for the new League of Nations. And it was probably not uninfluenced by flights of oratory in the House of Commons, like that of the member who declared in 1918: "After the war, the old diplomacy of Court and upper classes will be, in the eyes of most people, obsolete and inadequate. In fact, what is the whole idea of the League of Nations except the substitution of open and popular diplomacy for the old system? The idea is that difficulties between nations should no longer be settled in conclaves of Ambassadors, but by public, international discussion, and by arbitration of a public kind."[35]

In this situation, few people were receptive to the idea of making the Foreign Office once more an organization "capable of bearing the full responsibility for the formulation of advice on foreign policy" and fewer still became very interested in proposals of constructive reform for that office and the Diplomatic Service. As a result, none of the administrative reforms suggested by the writers of *The New Europe* or by men like Sir Robert Cecil were put into effect. There was no systematization of promotion; there were no real attempts to improve coordination between departments engaged in foreign policy functions. Even the awkward arrangement concerning the Department of Overseas Trade, which had tended to deprive the Foreign Office of its commercial and financial functions, was allowed to continue. This, as Sir William Tyrrell said during the second world war, "was a great weakening of that Office, [and] it also had a psychological effect. . . . It had, perhaps subconsciously the effect of leaving the members of the Foreign Office more and more disinterested in any of those questions"; and, apart from this, it succeeded

---

[33] Harold Grenfell, "Behind the Veil in Diplomacy," *ibid.*, May 1920.

[34] A. E. Mander, "Secret Diplomacy," *ibid.*, January 1921.

[35] Parliamentary Debates: Commons, 5th series, CIV (1918), 846.

ultimately in removing from the domain of the Foreign Office one of the most important problems of the 1920's, the problem of reparations, which was as much a political as a financial question, but which was handled for the most part by other departments.[36]

In addition, the unpopularity of the diplomatic agencies—which continued with some variations of intensity throughout the interwar period[37]—doubtless had an unfortunate influence on the quality of the personnel recruited by those agencies. Despite the amalgamation of the services and the abolition of the property qualification in 1919, the idea persisted that talent and initiative were less valuable to aspirants to a diplomatic career than aristocratic birth and private means;[38] and this idea was strengthened by contemporary studies of the services.[39] It seems likely that many promising candidates for the Civil Service preferred to find their way in the Treasury or other departments rather than to risk frustration and disappointment in diplomacy. The extent of this is difficult to estimate, but it was probably a not unimportant factor in reducing the over-all effectiveness of the diplomatic corps in this period.

Finally, the unpopularity of the Foreign Office and the Diplomatic Service was admirably designed to remove any hesitation which Lloyd George may have felt about continuing the course which he had set during the war and at the Peace Conference. The Prime Minister yielded to no man in his contempt for the professionals; and he was now encouraged to follow his natural bent and to provide the British people with a new type of diplomacy, which they apparently expected and desired.

II

In the summer of 1919, when the Peace Conference finally finished its labors, Lord Balfour resigned as Foreign Secretary and was replaced by the Marquess Curzon of Kedleston. This change was welcomed by those who were most critical of Lloyd George's methods. Curzon had held offices which were among the most exalted which the state had to offer;

[36] Parliamentary Debates: Lords, 5th series, CXXVI (1942-1943), 970. See also the speech of the Earl of Perth, *ibid.*, CXXXIV (1944-1945), 287-288; the remarks of Sir Walford Selby at a discussion at Chatham House on October 11, 1945, *International Affairs*, XXII (1946), 170; and his article on "The Foreign Office," in *The Nineteenth Century*, July 1945.

[37] The criticisms of the Diplomatic Service made after the second world war, for instance, are a mere repetition of those made in 1919. See House of Commons Sessional Papers 1942-1943, XI: Cmd. 6420, "Misc. No. 2 (1943). Proposals for the Reform of the Foreign Service," p. 2.

[38] Tilley and Gaselee, *The Foreign Office*, p. 195.

[39] See, for instance, George Young, *Diplomacy Old and New* (London, 1921), Chapter I, "Diplomacy and Personnel."

he had been Viceroy of India from 1898 to 1905 and a member of the Cabinet since 1915. He was a man of great abilities, strong convictions, and intense personal pride; and it was difficult to believe that he would "play the part of a mere figurehead or allow the effacement of the Foreign Office to continue."[40] He was no stranger to that organization, for he had served as Lord Salisbury's Under-Secretary in the years from 1895 to 1898; he had a proper appreciation of the role assigned to it in the business of the nation; and he respected the ability of the men who were to be his chief aides in the Foreign Office and the Diplomatic Service.[41]

With regard to the last point, it may be added that he had reason for this respect. Despite the critical tone of contemporary writing concerning it, the British foreign service in 1919 compared favorably with that of any other country in Europe. In the Foreign Office itself, the post of Permanent Under-Secretary was filled—after Sir Charles Hardinge went to the Paris Embassy at the end of the year[42]—by Sir Eyre Crowe, who was to continue in office until his death in 1925. Crowe has been described by Harold Nicolson as "the perfect type of British civil servant—industrious, loyal, expert, accurate, beloved, obedient and courageous."[43] He had served in the Foreign Office since 1885, had been the leading spirit in the administrative reforms of 1905-1906 and had, as chief of the Western Department, written that well-known memorandum of January 1, 1907, which, perhaps for the first time, laid bare the true nature of the German threat to British interests.[44] Since 1912 he had been Assistant Under-Secretary of State, had done notable work on the Ministry of Blockade during the war and had been a member, with the rank of Minister Plenipotentiary, of the British delegation to the Paris Conference. People meeting Crowe for the first time were sometimes repelled by his

---

[40] *The New Europe*, XIII (October 1919-January 1920), 59-60.

[41] On Curzon, see especially Harold Nicolson, *Curzon: The Last Phase, 1919-1925* (new ed., New York, 1939) and Earl of Ronaldshay, *The Life of Lord Curzon, being the Authorized Biography of George Nathaniel Marquess Curzon of Kedleston, K.G.* (3 vols., London, 1921). For shorter, but perceptive, accounts see Viscount d'Abernon, *An Ambassador of Peace* (3 vols., London, 1929-1930), I, 48-52; Winston Churchill, *Great Contemporaries* (rev. ed., London, 1938), pp. 273-288; J. D. Gregory, *On the Edge of Diplomacy* (London, 1928), pp. 245-255; Harold Nicolson, *Some People* (Boston, 1927), pp. 187-213; and Tilley, *London to Tokyo*, pp. 91-92.

[42] Hardinge had also been Viceroy of India, a circumstance which promised to create awkwardness, and there had also been differences between Curzon and him during the war. He was due for retirement but Curzon refused to take advantage of this and offered him the Paris post. See Hardinge, *Old Diplomacy*, pp. 243-244.

[43] Harold Nicolson, *Portrait of a Diplomatist* (New York, 1930), p. 239.

[44] The memorandum is printed in G. P. Gooch and Harold Temperley, eds., *British Documents on the Origins of the War, 1898-1914* (London, 1926-36), III, 397-420.

rigidity and the punctilio of his official manner, but there were few, on closer acquaintance, who did not admire his industry and his breadth of view.[45]

Crowe was assisted by a staff of more than ordinary talents. Sir William Tyrrell, who had been Grey's Private Secretary, a man who was "intuitive, conciliatory, elastic and possessed [of] a remarkable instinct for avoiding diplomatic difficulties,"[46] was Assistant Under-Secretary; the Assistant Secretaries included Sir John Tilley, Eric Phipps, and Victor Wellesley; while among the Senior Clerks were R. G. Vansittart and Alexander Cadogan, who were in time, like Tyrrell, to become Permanent Under-Secretaries. That the chief posts in the Diplomatic Service were also in good hands was admitted even by journals normally critical of diplomatic appointments.[47] Hardinge was at Paris; Sir George Buchanan, after years of distinguished service in St. Petersburg, was at Rome; Sir Auckland Geddes was on his way to Washington. The new and possibly crucial posts at Prague and Warsaw had been filled by Sir George Clerk and Sir Horace Rumbold, who quickly justified their appointments; and, when relations with the former enemy countries were resumed, the Berlin Embassy was occupied by Viscount d'Abernon, one of the most adroit and perspicacious British diplomats of the interwar period.[48]

But, if the competence of his subordinates was gratifying to the new Foreign Secretary, it did not weigh very heavily with the Prime Minister. For the professional diplomats Lloyd George had—as has already been indicated—very little respect; and his disregard extended even to their methods, especially to their penchant for exchanges of views by means of formal correspondence and carefully drafted notes. "I wish the French and ourselves never wrote letters to each other," Lloyd George said in 1920. "Letters are the very devil. They ought to be abolished altogether. . . . If you want to settle a thing you see your opponent and talk it over with him. The last thing you do is write him a letter."[49] Moreover, the Prime Minister was firmly convinced that it did no good to leave the

---

[45] *The Times*, April 29, 1925. See also Gregory, *On the Edge of Diplomacy*, pp. 255-261.

[46] Nicolson, *Portrait of a Diplomatist*, p. 239.

[47] See, for instance, *The New Europe*, XII (July-October 1919), 209ff.

[48] D'Abernon was not of the career service, having formerly been president of the Ottoman Bank in Constantinople, and initially there was some opposition in the Foreign Office to his appointment. See Hardinge, *Old Diplomacy*, p. 249, and the speech of Lord Vansittart in Parliamentary Debates: Lords, 5th series, CXXXIV (1944-1945), 295.

[49] Riddell, *Intimate Diary*, p. 206. For a very similar opinion, expressed by Aristide Briand, see below Chapter 10, § IV.

talking-over to the professional diplomats. "Diplomats were invented simply to waste time," he said during the war. "It is simply a waste of time to let [important matters] be discussed by men who are not authorized to speak for their countries."[50]

These last words were not idly spoken. Lloyd George believed—and his belief was doubtless strengthened by his awareness of the popular distrust of "old diplomacy"—that the great questions of foreign policy should be negotiated, not by career diplomats, but by men who possessed mandates from the people; and his was the strongest influence in carrying the methods which had been inaugurated at the Paris Conference over into the years that followed and in making the period subsequent to 1919 a period in which "diplomacy by conference" took precedence over the techniques of traditional diplomacy.[51] Thanks to him, the first years of peace were filled with elaborate confabulations between the political leaders of Great Britain, France, Italy, Germany, and other countries, conferences at which the problems created at the Paris meetings—reparations, security, the economic plight of Europe, relations with Soviet Russia, and the like—were debated in a white glare of publicity. These conferences were held in charming and unconventional places, far from the beaten paths used by orthodox diplomacy—at Cannes and San Remo and Spa and Genoa—but, even when they found their locations in national capitals, the professional diplomats did not bulk large in their councils, if, indeed, they were invited at all. Diplomacy by conference was Lloyd George's response to the popular demand for a "new diplomacy," and he was not inclined to have the effect spoiled by the obtrusive presence of members of the suspected caste. Even the Foreign Secretary, who came in time to detest these *omnium gatherums*, was often ignored in the selection of the British delegations. This was true, for instance, at the time of the Genoa Conference of 1922, of which Curzon wrote: "When I reflect that the P.M. is alone at Genoa, with no F.O. to guide him ... I can feel no certainty that we may not find ourselves committed to something pregnant with political disaster here."[52]

This deliberate neglect of the resources and the experience of the British foreign service was reflected immediately in the paucity of results

[50] Kennedy, *Old Diplomacy*, pp. 364-365.
[51] "The French Prime Minister, Millerand, looked forward ... early in 1920 to the resumption of normal diplomatic methods of negotiation, but the multiplicity of issues and the personal aptitudes of the British Prime Minister combined to compel the continuance of the conference method." W. M. Jordan, *Great Britain, France and the German Problem, 1918-1939* (London, 1943), p. 58.
[52] Nicolson, *Curzon*, p. 245.

attained by Lloyd Georgian diplomacy in the years from 1919 to 1922. The record of the Prime Minister's peripatetic activities, indeed, does much to justify Nicolson's statement that diplomacy by conference is "perhaps the most unfortunate diplomatic method ever conceived."[53] Because Lloyd George disliked writing letters, the conferences often assembled without any prior agreement concerning agenda and procedure and generally without any precise formulation of the issues which could be expected to arise for discussion. Because Lloyd George and his foreign colleagues could not, as the political leaders of their countries, remain long absent from their capitals, the conferences were apt to be seriously restricted in time, a fact which, in view of the absence of preliminary agreement and consultation, made it virtually impossible to achieve positive results. Finally, because it was important to Lloyd George and his colleagues to *seem* to have achieved positive results, since they had generally aroused a high degree of public expectation, they became adept at concluding their most inconclusive meetings with the publication of eloquent formulas, which hinted at agreement and progress but which in actuality disguised genuine and acute differences of opinion among the Powers.[54] It can scarcely be argued, for instance, that the twelve international conferences which were held on the reparations question made any progress toward achieving a reasonable solution of that troublesome problem. It would be more accurate to say that their principal result was a series of public clashes between British and French policy, awkwardly smoothed over by compromises which satisfied no one and which finally produced, in England, an unreasoning suspicion of France and, in France, a degree of exasperation which found its ultimate expression in the fateful occupation of the Ruhr in 1923.[55]

Some of the conferences got completely out of hand and produced unforeseen results which embarrassed the British and French participants. This was notably the case at the Genoa Conference of 1922, a meeting convoked, despite French reluctance, as a result of Lloyd George's insistence that it was time to face up to the Russian problem and that, by doing so, the Powers would be able to solve all of Europe's outstanding

---

[53] *ibid.*, p. 397.

[54] Lloyd George's latest biographer speaks almost approvingly of this aspect of the Prime Minister's diplomacy. "Failure to reach agreement or to do no more than expose divergencies to the world could, as a rule and for the moment, be veiled in intentional obscurity by drafting a dextrous formula, an art in which his secretaries became proficient." Thomas Jones, *Lloyd George* (Cambridge, Mass., 1951), p. 180. For a contemporary criticism of this practice, however, see "Is There a New Diplomacy?" *Fortnightly Review*, CXI (1922), 709-725. See also d'Abernon, *An Ambassador of Peace*, I, 163.

[55] See Jordan, *Great Britain, France and the German Question*, p. 59.

economic problems.[56] The conference failed signally to live up to its advance publicity, and its only tangible result was the dramatic rapprochement of Germany and Soviet Russia at Rapallo.[57] Nor was this event—which foreshadowed a significant shift in the European balance and which, at the same time, widened the rift in the Entente—uninfluenced by the deficiencies of Lloyd George's diplomatic methods. There had been much talk of "open diplomacy" and "the mobilization of world opinion" before the conference opened; and provision was made to keep the international public fully informed of the discussions of the various commissions into which the conference was divided. But after this concession to democracy had been made, the political commissions in particular found that they had very little to do, while secret talks, from which many of the participating states were excluded, were conducted between an intimate group in Lloyd George's villa on the one hand and—through various devious channels—the Russians on the other. The Germans were not admitted to these talks and, since they feared a Russian arrangement with the Entente at their expense, they were amenable to the suggestions made to them by Chicherin.[58] The resultant *débacle* justified Lord Grey's gibe, earlier in the year, that there was "both too much limelight and too much secrecy" in Lloyd George's diplomacy.[59]

But it was not only in his attempt to supplant the professional diplomats in the field of negotiation, that Lloyd George's methods had unfortunate results. Even more serious was his willingness to make important decisions on policy and far-reaching commitments to foreign governments without prior consultation with the Foreign Office or with its chief. This became apparent as early as 1920, at the time of the war between Poland and Russia. The dramatic reversal of Polish fortunes in that conflict and the beginning of the Russian advance upon Warsaw coincided with the assembling of the Spa Conference of July to consider

[56] On the Genoa Conference, see *inter alia*, J. Saxon Mills, *The Genoa Conference* (New York, 1922); Viscount Swinton, *I Remember* (London, 1946), pp. 17-25; A. J. Sylvester, *The Real Lloyd George* (London, 1947), pp. 80-98; Amedeo Giannini, *Saggi di storia diplomatica, 1920-1940* (Firenze, 1940), pp. 27-50; Degras, I, 287-318; Louis Fischer, *The Soviets in World Affairs* (new ed., 2 vols., Princeton, 1951), I, 318-354; Harry Kessler, *Walter Rathenau, His Life and Work* (New York, 1930), pp. 304-340; and *The History of "The Times"*, IV, Part II, 662-677.

[57] On the eve of the conference, Lloyd George gave the British press copies of a memorandum circulated at Paris in 1919, warning of the dangers of driving Germany into the arms of Russia. Fischer, *Soviets*, I, 323. This was, however, part of his attempt to induce the French to treat with the Soviets rather than an expression of a belief that a Russo-German treaty was imminent.

[58] See Kessler, *Rathenau*, pp. 319-20, 322-23.

[59] *The Times*, January 28, 1922.

the question of German coal deliveries; and it was at Spa that the Polish minister Grabski approached Lloyd George and pleaded for aid. The Prime Minister upbraided Grabski for the follies of his government and insisted that Polish forces must be withdrawn to positions 125 miles behind those they presently occupied; but, having done that, he went on to promise that, if the Poles retired and if the Russians then crossed the new line which he had sanctioned, "the British Government and their Allies would be bound to help Poland with all the means at their disposal." In any circumstances, this would have been an extraordinary commitment for a British Prime Minister to make; but its most remarkable feature was that it was made without the authorization of the Cabinet and without any attempt to consult the Foreign Office. Indeed, the Foreign Office was not informed of the nature of the Prime Minister's declaration until after he had returned to London, a fact which placed Sir Horace Rumbold, Britain's minister in Warsaw, in the humiliating position of being unable for three days to verify or deny press accounts of the Spa declaration.[60]

Worse was to follow, for the Russians did cross the line approved by Lloyd George, and the validity of his promises was immediately put to the test. He responded to this, not with the kind of determined action pledged at Spa, but with a series of equivocal public speeches in which he said that only "the most imperative call of national honour, national safety and national freedom can justify war." When the Poles, finding no comfort in this sort of thing, sued for an armistice, and when the Russians offered terms, Lloyd George seized upon these eagerly and, characteristically, approved them at once without asking the opinions of the men trained to analyze documents of this kind. It would be difficult to find a more revealing description of the haphazard nature of Lloyd George's diplomacy than the note concerning this episode which appears in the diary of his confidant Lord Riddell, the press magnate. "Golf with L. G. at St. George's Hill. . . . Before we left, a message arrived announcing that the Russian Government were prepared to grant the Poles an armistice and that instructions had been sent to the military commander to make the necessary arrangements. L. G. in a high state of glee. When we arrived at the golf-club he sat down in the dressing room and wrote out a message to his secretary at Downing Street, instructing him what documents to issue to the press. A very precise little document."[61] It was not until considerably later that the Prime Minister

---

[60] On these events, see especially Nicolson, *Curzon*, pp. 202-208 and Kennedy, *Old Diplomacy*, pp. 314-338.
[61] Riddell, *Intimate Diary*, p. 225.

was convinced, and persuaded to announce publicly, that his enthusiasm had been premature and that the Russian terms were, in fact, incompatible with the independence of Poland. By that time, however, it was too late to repair the damage which these vacillations had inflicted upon British prestige in Central Europe; and the Poles, who had meanwhile been saved by vigorous French measures before Warsaw, were left feeling that Britain was an unreliable friend in time of trouble.

To Lord Curzon, who regarded British prestige as an asset which must be maintained at all costs, this episode was a painful one. Even more painful was the accumulating evidence that it was not an exceptional case, that the Prime Minister was in fact incorrigible, that he would go on making policy at his breakfast table and neglecting to inform the Foreign Secretary of his decisions, that he would go on preferring the advice of his secretaries to that of the Foreign Office (and sometimes even permitting them, rather than the Foreign Office staff, to draft important notes to foreign governments),[62] and that he would continue to avoid the orderly channels of diplomatic communication in favor of casual conversations, or even sly intimations to foreign representatives, of which no written record was kept. Curzon could not help but be aware that the department over which he presided was being deprived of its constitutional functions and that the process by which this was being effected was making his country's policy seem confused and unreliable. Why, then, did he submit to these practices?

This problem has been considered by both of Curzon's biographers and they are generally agreed in their conclusions. Curzon's only weapon against the Prime Minister was the threat of resignation. It was a weapon which could easily be turned against him, for Lloyd George, after all, might be disposed to accept an offer of resignation. It was precisely that possibility that deterred Curzon. He knew that he was not a popular figure, but he hoped that he was a respected one; and he was "morbidly sensitive to the effect which his resignation might have upon the estimation in which the public held him,"[63] especially if (as was quite possible) they did not understand the principles which prompted his action. Resignation, moreover, would probably mean the end of his public career. Curzon remembered too clearly the long years in which his talents had been neglected by the party leaders after his retirement as Viceroy of India in 1905 to hope that he would be allowed to return to

---

[62] Sir Valentine Chirol, "Four Years of Lloyd-Georgian Foreign Policy," *Edinburgh Review* (January 1923), p. 4.
[63] Ronaldshay, *Curzon*, III, 255.

high office if he retired voluntarily again;[64] and that, of course, would mean sacrificing his last chance to become Prime Minister. Nor was he deterred only—or even primarily—by these personal factors. In all fairness to the Foreign Secretary, it must be emphasized that he was convinced that his resignation would remove the last restraints upon Lloyd George and deliver the country over to a personal diplomacy which would be disastrous.[65] And it should be added that many of his friends and professional colleagues shared this view and urged him to remain at his post, even at the cost of personal humiliation.[66]

In these circumstances, the hope entertained by the friends of the Foreign Office when Curzon first became Foreign Secretary—namely, that he would stop the decline of that department—was bound to be disappointed. His attitude made inevitable the continuation of the system which he himself described in October 1922, in a letter drafted for, but not sent to, the Prime Minister:[67] "a system under which there are in reality two Foreign Offices, the one for which I am for the time being responsible, and the other at No. 10—with the essential difference between them that, whereas I report not only to you but to all my colleagues everything that I say or do, every telegram that I receive or send, every communication of importance that reaches me, it is often only by accident that I hear what is being done by the other Foreign Office. . . . This condition of affairs has reached such a pitch that not only is it a subject of common knowledge . . . but it is known to every journalist in London . . . the Foreign Office and myself in particular having been held up to contempt for having abdicated our functions, or allowed them to be stolen away."

Neither the accuracy of this picture, nor the dangers implicit in the situation described, were realized by the general public. This was again due to the continued unpopularity of the diplomatic caste, but certainly also to the peculiar character of the House of Commons which had emerged from the Khaki Elections of 1918, a body which contained only a handful of men who had any understanding of foreign affairs or any critical standards concerning the way in which they should be administered.[68] As a result, it was not until the autumn of 1922, when Lloyd George's methods had brought the country uncomfortably close to war

[64] Nicolson, *Curzon*, pp. 24, 28-31.

[65] He wrote on one occasion that he stayed on "in the certain knowledge that if I were to go my place would be taken by the ——— combination, which I regarded as a great national peril." Ronaldshay, *Curzon*, III, 256.

[66] Nicolson, *Curzon*, p. 23.

[67] Ronaldshay, *Curzon*, III, 316-317.

[68] See the comments in "A Farewell Survey," *The New Europe*, XVII (1920), 50.

in the Near East, that anything in the nature of a public awakening was achieved.

The chain of events which led to the Near Eastern crisis of 1922 will be discussed later in this book.[69] Here it need only be said that the crisis was the result of Turkish opposition to the terms of the Treaty of Sèvres and of the disunity of the Entente Powers in face of that opposition. The deterioration of Anglo-French cooperation, in turn, had been caused in large part by Lloyd George's great admiration for the Greeks and his firm conviction that, in return for territorial advantages in Asia Minor, they would assume the chief burden of enforcing the Sèvres provisions upon the Kemal government. This belief was weakened neither by the remonstrances of his Foreign Secretary, who believed that the Greek government was incapable of preserving order five miles outside the gates of Salonika, nor by the obvious dissatisfaction of the French and Italian governments with the tendencies of his eastern policy; and it was persisted in even after it had become clear that those governments were entering into private arrangements with Kemal and moderating their previous objections to his ambitions. The importance of this defection became clear at the same moment that Curzon's doubts were justified. In August and September Kemal's armies drove the Greek forces headlong into the sea; and the British people made the unpleasant discovery that an isolated British force at Chanak was all that stood in the way of a Turkish surge across the Straits and into the lost Turkish provinces beyond. And when, on September 15, a group within the Cabinet—including Lloyd George and Winston Churchill, but not including Curzon—issued an appeal to the Dominions for aid, war seemed a very real possibility.

In the end it did not come to that, thanks to Kemal's realization that war might compromise a victory already virtually won and thanks to Curzon's success, in a series of hurried talks in Paris, in effecting a renewed semblance of Anglo-French cooperation. But the crisis did bring down Lloyd George. The convolutions of his policy since 1919 were attacked in the press of the right and of the left. *The Nation* described his methods as having "all the faults of the old [diplomacy] and none of its superficial virtues";[70] *The Times* declared roundly that his government had "made a treaty and departed from it . . . dallied with Bolshevism and supported campaigns against it . . . coquetted with Germany and played fast and loose with France . . . dragged from Conference to Conference their failure to face the reparations issue . . . [and

---

[69] See Chapter 6, §§ 11, III below.   [70] *The Nation*, October 7, 1922.

finally come] to the verge of an armed conflict in the Near East, the course and outcome of which no man could foretell. As a result of their inconsistencies, the word of England lost currency throughout a great part of the world as the word of an upright land."[71] Attacked by the Liberals for indulging in "the improvisations of an intermittent and incalculable dictatorship"[72] and repudiated by the Conservatives upon whose support his retention of office depended, Lloyd George yielded his place in the center of the political stage to the less dynamic personalities of Bonar Law, Stanley Baldwin, and Ramsay MacDonald.

III

The crisis of 1922 freed the foreign service of the eccentricities of Lloyd George; but this did not mean that the conditions under which the Foreign Office and the Diplomatic Service had operated before 1914 were in any sense restored. If anything, the war scare tightened the restrictions imposed upon those agencies and increased the difficulties under which the professional advisers on policy and the representatives abroad had to work. For one thing, it revitalized the old campaign against "secret diplomacy." The elections of November 1922, which were strongly influenced by the events in the Near East, brought back into the House of Commons some of the most inveterate opponents of the Foreign Office. Among the increased Labor representation, for instance, were seventeen members of the Executive and General Council of the Union of Democratic Control, including such stalwarts as Morel, Trevelyan, Ponsonby, and MacDonald. To this group the Chanak crisis was proof, not only of Lloyd George's deficiencies as a diplomat, but also of the dangers of orthodox diplomacy as such. They began almost at once to gather support for a Parliamentary resolution stipulating that no act of war against a foreign state should be committed, no treaty ratified, no diplomatic arrangement or written or verbal agreement involving military obligations concluded, and no military or naval staff talks held, without express authorization of Parliament—a bill of particulars so all-embracing and yet so ill-defined that, if passed, it would seriously have handicapped intercourse with other Powers.[73] At the same

---

[71] *The Times*, October 30, 1922.

[72] Asquith at Dumfries, October 6, 1922. See Ronaldshay, *Curzon*, III, 318.

[73] In the summer of 1923 a draft resolution of this kind was sent, together with a letter signed by 100 Labor and Liberal members of Parliament, to members of the Dominions Parliaments, who were asked for advice and support. See *Foreign Affairs*, V (1923-1924), 23-24. During the first MacDonald government, when the Lausanne Treaty was laid before Parliament, the government announced that henceforth all treaties would be laid

time, they entertained, and publicly expressed, the strongest possible suspicion even of the normal processes of diplomacy. As early as December 1922, Ronald McNeill, the Under-Secretary for Foreign Affairs, was forced to answer so many questions concerning recent visits of Lord Curzon and Sir William Tyrrell to Paris that he complained that the Opposition was always talking of "sinister rumours" and was apparently wholly convinced that secret deals and dark conspiracies were being hatched on all sides by their officials.[74]

This in itself need not have been a matter of much consequence. But the Chanak crisis had helped to reinforce in public opinion generally an atmosphere which Sir Alfred Zimmern has described as being compounded of "dull anxiety, of feverish suspicion, of reckless inquisitiveness."[75] Tired of war and troubled by grave economic problems, the English people were in no mood for foreign adventures; they were more interested in disarmament than in prestige; and they were fearful of commitments which might lead to more dangerous Chanaks. This popular temper had a perceptible, and not altogether fortunate, effect upon the policy of the governments that ruled England in the years that followed. The Bonar Law-Baldwin government of 1922-1924, the Mac-Donald government of 1924, and the Baldwin government of 1924-1929 all tended to follow rather than to lead public opinion in foreign affairs, to satisfy the immediate desires of the electorate rather than the ultimate interests of the nation,[76] to make foreign policy the prisoner of domestic politics rather than to seek to pursue a farsighted independent course and to carry the public with them step by step.[77] This preoccupation with public opinion made it seem necessary for the Prime Minister and the Cabinet as a whole to intervene in the details of policy to a greater extent than in the past and to exercise a stricter supervision over

---

before the House of Commons for a period of 21 days before ratification. Arthur Ponsonby declared at the same time that the government would enter no secret agreements and that it favored Parliamentary discussion of all agreements and understandings with foreign Powers. *Ibid.*, 216. The U. D. C. resolution was submitted to Commons during the second Baldwin Ministry but failed of passage, after a debate in which Charles Trevelyan warned that the Labor party would recognize as binding no agreement which had not been sanctioned by Parliament. *Ibid.*, VI (1924-1925), 233. On July 1927, however, Sir Austen Chamberlain declared in Commons that "there is nothing secret about British policy. There are no engagements or undertakings that are not known to the House of Commons and [the Government will] undertake no future engagements on behalf of our country without submitting those engagements to Parliament and having the approval of Parliament for them." Parliamentary Debates: Commons, 5th series, CCVIII (1927), 1775.

[74] Parliamentary Debates: Commons, 5th series, CLIX (1922), 3343.

[75] Sir Alfred Zimmern, *The League of Nations and the Rule of Law* (London, 1936), p. 485.

[76] See Nicolson, *Curzon*, p. 185.   [77] Zimmern, *League of Nations*, p. 485.

the executants of policy; and, not infrequently, it led them, because of shifts in the popular temper, to indulge in abrupt and awkward reversals of policy, even in the course of delicate negotiations for objectives previously agreed upon.

All of this made the tasks of the professional diplomats infinitely more difficult. Lord Curzon, who continued to serve as Foreign Secretary until 1924, discovered this during the conference which met at Lausanne in January and February 1923 to arrange a definitive treaty with the Turks. With an adroitness and an authority which won the admiration of his foreign colleagues, Curzon dominated the conference and succeeded, not only in winning all his principal objectives—although this achievement was not confirmed until after he had retired from office—but in laying the basis for the reestablishment of friendly relations between Turkey and Great Britain. His successes, however, were won in the face of a fearful, and at times bitterly critical, public opinion, and of a Cabinet which on more than one occasion threatened to withdraw its support. "I found Bonar," Curzon wrote at the beginning of the conference, "longing to clear out of Mosul, the Straits and Constantinople, willing to give up anything and everything rather than have a row, astonished at the responsibility I have assumed at Lausanne and prepared for me to back down everywhere."[78]

Another instance of the same sort of thing—but with a less happy result—came during the Corfu crisis later in the year. In face of this first attack by Mussolini upon the public law of Europe, Sir Robert Cecil in Geneva was originally instructed to mobilize the forces of the League of Nations. At the critical moment, however, this policy was reversed, and he was ordered to refer the dispute to the Conference of Ambassadors in Paris, which promptly gave in to the Duce's terms. The reasons for this change of front are not entirely clear, but it was probably not uninfluenced by the campaign being currently conducted by the *Daily Mail* and other newspapers, which were accusing Curzon, Cecil, and the Foreign Office of "war-mongering."[79]

Deference to public opinion was, during Ramsay MacDonald's first ministry, coupled with deference to party opinion; and, on at least one

---

[78] Ronaldshay, *Curzon*, III, 332. After Baldwin had become Prime Minister, Curzon wrote to him: "I must confess I am almost in despair as to the way in which Foreign Policy is carried on in this Cabinet. . . . We must act together and the P.M. must see his F.S. through." G. M. Young, *Stanley Baldwin* (London, 1952), p. 50.

[79] On this, see G. P. Pink, *The Conference of Ambassadors* (Geneva Research Center: Geneva Studies, XII, Nos. 4-5, 1942), pp. 207-246; Viscount Cecil, *A Great Experiment* (London, 1941), pp. 150-151; Nicolson, *Curzon*, pp. 368-371. See also Chapter 7, § IV, below.

occasion, MacDonald's obedience to his party's demands led him to overrule the Foreign Office and indulge in what might almost be described as diplomatic chicanery. The conspicuous example of this was during the negotiations for an Anglo-Russian agreement in 1924. These negotiations were held in London, and they stretched over a period of four months before it became clear that the Russians had not the slightest intention of making any compensation for the debts repudiated, and the British property confiscated, by them during the revolution. Since this was the chief issue of the talks, the Foreign Office announced that the negotiations would be broken off. At this point, however, a deputation from the Labor party, which had been conducting parallel talks with the Russian delegation—in itself a rather dubious procedure—protested to Arthur Ponsonby, MacDonald's Under-Secretary for Foreign Affairs. They argued that it would be fatal to the reputation of the Labor party if the conference disbanded without a result; and they submitted a compromise which they felt would be satisfactory to both parties. This was a formula quite as vague as those which Lloyd George's Secretariats had been so adept at producing; it covered irreconcilable differences between the parties with a veil of amicable platitudes; but the government nevertheless accepted it and gravely announced the conclusion of a treaty. Coming from a party which talked so much about the way in which the old diplomacy had deceived the British people, the conclusion of this bogus agreement was a curious procedure; and it was promptly turned against its authors, becoming one of the most important issues in the elections of October 1924 which turned Labor out of office.[80]

To the pressure of national and party opinion must be added that of public opinion in the Dominions. Before the war this had been an inconsiderable factor in the conduct of British foreign relations. This was no longer true. Curzon had explained to the French ambassador in December 1921 that "British foreign policy was now not the policy of the Cabinet in Downing Street alone, but was the policy of the Empire, and the points of view of the Prime Ministers of our distant Dominions had also to be seriously considered."[81] If there was any doubt about the importance of this, it was removed by the effects of the Chanak crisis of 1922 upon the Dominion governments. The famous telegram of September 15, which had asked whether the Dominions would send contingents

---

[80] On the Russian agreement, see especially Philip Viscount Snowden, *An Autobiography* (2 vols., London, 1934), II, 680-686.

[81] Cmd. 2169 (1924), p. 111.

to the Near East, had been the first intimation made to them of trouble in that quarter; and it was received with surprise and, especially on the part of Australia and Canada, with resentment.[82] From this time on, the Dominions were increasingly vigilant concerning steps taken by the British government which might involve them in troubles in Europe or in other areas in which they were not vitally interested, and British cabinets tended to become increasingly attentive to Dominion opinion. From the very beginning of his term as Foreign Secretary in the second Baldwin government, Austen Chamberlain stressed the importance of this factor in the conduct of British foreign relations. "The first thoughts of any Englishman on appointment to the office of Foreign Secretary," he said in his first public address after taking office, "must be that he speaks in the name, not of Great Britain only, but of the British Dominions beyond the seas, and that it is his imperative duty to preserve in word and act the diplomatic unity of the British Empire. Our interests are one. Our intercourse must be intimate and constant, and we must speak with one voice in the councils of the world."[83]

The difficulty here was that intimate and constant intercourse with the Dominions was virtually impossible to maintain, given the state of communications in the 1920's. Interchange of views was possible at Imperial Conferences, but these were held infrequently, and in the seven years ending in December 1926 there were only three plenary meetings of the Imperial Prime Ministers. Problems arose and solutions were demanded too suddenly for the British government always to consult the Dominions;[84] yet none of the governments of this period was willing to take a firm line in European affairs which might be repudiated by members of the Empire at a subsequent date. Their natural inclination, therefore, was to be tentative and hesitant in matters of crucial European importance, a fact which increased the difficulties of British negotiators abroad and which, in some European quarters, led to criticisms of British indecision and unreliability.

[82] See A. J. Toynbee, *The Conduct of British Empire Foreign Relations since the Peace Settlement* (London, 1928), pp. 47ff.; Gwendolen M. Carter, *The British Commonwealth and International Security: The Role of the Dominions, 1919-1939* (Toronto, 1947), pp. 84-90; *The History of "The Times"*, IV, Part II, 734; and Bruce Hutchison, *The Incredible Canadian: a candid portrait of Mackenzie King* (Toronto, 1952), pp. 89-97.

[83] Sir Austen Chamberlain, *Peace in Our Time: Addresses on Europe and the Empire* (London, 1928), pp. 1-2. See also his speech at Chatham House on February 4, 1930 in which he spoke of the "new distribution of executive power in the Empire [which] must profoundly affect the conduct of foreign affairs." *International Affairs*, IX (1930), 182.

[84] On attempts to solve this problem, see Toynbee, *British Empire Foreign Relations*, pp. 72-74.

The combined impact of national and Dominions public opinion upon the formulation of British foreign policy is seen perhaps most clearly in the question of European security in general and Britain's relations with the League of Nations in particular. Enthusiasm for the League of Nations was widespread in Great Britain and, to a somewhat lesser degree, in the Dominions, and no British government would have dared to ignore that organization in the conduct of its policy. Faith in the League was not, however, generally combined with an understanding of its machinery, or of the obligations which Britain had assumed in adhering to the Covenant; nor was the enthusiasm for the League as a moral cause matched by equal enthusiasm for efforts to strengthen League machinery so that it could, by compulsory arbitration or military sanctions, enforce the cause of peace against potential aggressors. As one historian has written, the notion of collective security "remained an alien on English soil throughout the decade which followed the war";[85] and many people believed that even to think seriously about the question of sanctions was unwholesome and possibly destructive of peace. For their part, the Dominions were disinclined to become involved in responsibilities in Europe and were, consequently, opposed to Britain's assuming new obligations under a strengthened Covenant.

In these circumstances, the governments which ruled Britain from 1923 to 1929 elected to follow a dual course, proclaiming on the one hand that their "whole policy" rested on the League but resisting, on the other, attempts to solve the security question by strengthening the Covenant. The two constructive efforts made to repair the gaps in the Covenant were rejected—the Draft Treaty of Mutual Assistance by the MacDonald government, the Geneva Protocol by the Baldwin government that succeeded it.[86] The reasons given in the two cases were similar: the plans were subversive of the true purpose of the League and would promote rather than prevent war; they would discourage disarmament and hence weaken the best assurance of peace; they were too complicated and, conversely, too logical for the British temperament; and they would not be supported by the Dominions. Britain preferred to confine her contribution to a solution of the security question to a regional pact in that part of Europe in which she had vital interests and did so by accepting the Locarno Treaties in 1925.

It is not possible to state with any degree of assurance what the attitude of the expert advisers in the Foreign Office was to these developments.

[85] Jordan, *Great Britain, France and the German Question*, p. 206.
[86] See Chapter 4, § III and Chapter 10, § I below.

In the case of the Draft Treaty, it seems likely that Foreign Office opinion was not very important. Mr. MacDonald was his own Foreign Secretary, a circumstance which seems at times to have persuaded him that it was unnecessary for him to keep in close touch with his department.[87] Moreover, the Prime Minister's views at this time carefully reflected those of the pacifist wing of his party; he was irreconcilably opposed to the Draft Treaty and was almost temperamentally incapable of discussing it rationally.[88]

In the case of the Geneva Protocol, the only Foreign Office memorandum which is available is one written in February 1925 by the Historical Adviser, Sir James Headlam-Morley.[89] This is a document which raises grave doubts as to the advisability of adopting an attitude of blank negation towards continental attempts to repair the gaps in the Covenant. Headlam-Morley argues that Britain cannot separate herself from the troubles of Europe; that the contention that the Dominions do not desire involvement in European affairs should not determine Britain's position; that the danger point in Europe is not the Rhine but the Vistula; and that, consequently, no security pact will be effective if it is not European, rather than regional, in scope. The author intimates further that, for the above reasons, the Geneva Protocol should not be rejected but revised.

To what extent this represented Foreign Office opinion in general is not known. Headlam-Morley's arguments may have had some influence on Austen Chamberlain, for at the outset at least he was not unalterably opposed to the Protocol.[90] But speculation on this point is neither helpful nor important. In the event, the decision on the Geneva Protocol was made by the Cabinet as a whole, which deferred to what it considered to be public opinion and—perhaps unnecessarily—to the desires of the Dominions[91] and which, after deciding on outright rejection of the

---

[87] Certainly the confusion during the affair of the Zinoviev letter betrays a lack of any effective liaison between MacDonald and the Foreign Office. There is, moreover, other evidence. MacDonald's Under-Secretary was at times so out of touch with his chief that he employed Norman Angell to communicate his views to MacDonald (Angell, *After All*, p. 239); and the Foreign Office, and everyone else, seems to have been excluded from the conversations between MacDonald and Herriot at Chequers, with resultant confusion. Snowden, *Autobiography*, II, 667.

[88] See the damaging account of Angell's discussion of this matter with MacDonald and H. M. Swanwick of the Union of Democratic Control. Angell, *After All*, pp. 240ff.

[89] Sir James Headlam-Morley, *Studies in Diplomatic History* (London, 1930), pp. 171ff., 187.

[90] Wickham Steed, *The Real Stanley Baldwin* (London, 1930), pp. 114-115. See, however, Sir C. Petrie, *Life and Letters of the Right Hon. Sir Austen Chamberlain* (2 vols., London, 1939-1940), II, 258.

[91] Carter (*British Commonwealth*, p. 121) believes that the objections of the Dominions were not insuperable.

Protocol, entrusted the drafting of the note explaining the British position, not to the Foreign Office or even to the Foreign Secretary, but to Lord Balfour.[92] And this step, once taken, was irrevocable, for, after the Baldwin Cabinet had, with some misgivings,[93] sanctioned the negotiations which led to the Locarno Treaties, and after those treaties had been signed, it steadfastly refused to countenance any further consideration of the security question.

IV

"The art of diplomacy," declares a British White Paper of 1943, "consists in making the policy of His Majesty's Government, whatever it may be, understood and, if possible, accepted by other countries."[94] To have made the British attitude on security explicable and palatable to other members of the League in the years after 1925 would have required a British representative possessed of great gifts of persuasion, understanding, and tact. Austen Chamberlain undertook to serve as that representative himself.

There is a story to the effect that Chamberlain was once, earlier in his life, considered as a possible candidate for the Paris Embassy; and that Paul Cambon, asked about this, said: "Ce cher Austen! Quel brave homme! Ce n'est pourtant pas un article d'exportation!"[95] The observation, if it is not apocryphal, was shrewd. For the direction of a difficult set of negotiations, Chamberlain possessed all the requisite qualities, as he demonstrated by the skillful manner in which he conducted the Locarno negotiations—working in close cooperation with his ambassadors in Paris and Berlin, clearing away misunderstandings and narrowing the issues by the exchange of written notes, and holding the crucial meetings only after a firm basis for agreement had been reached.[96] He was less well equipped, however, with those gifts which a representative of his country abroad should always possess—balance, perspective, humor and personal charm, the ability to state his country's position without alienating his hearers, the willingness to give a fair hearing to their point of view and to indicate that he understands the reasoning that informs it even when he cannot accept it.

[92] Sir Alfred Zimmern has described the argument against unhealthy preoccupation with sanctions, which Balfour wrote and Chamberlain read to the League Council in March 1925, as a "cheerful recommendation to adopt a policy of Couéism." *League of Nations*, p. 358.

[93] See Petrie, *Chamberlain*, II, 264.   [94] Cmd. 6420 (1943), p. 2.

[95] Steed, *Stanley Baldwin*, p. 110.

[96] See Petrie, *Chamberlain*, II, 260, 264, 272, 281, 286-88; and Sir Victor Wellesley, *Diplomacy in Fetters* (London, 1944), p. 31.

Chamberlain began by impressing and ended by irritating his fellow members in the League. His attempts to convince them that they must, in approaching European problems, abjure the use of reason and logic, since these would only render their efforts suspect in English eyes, succeeded only in bewildering them—while causing extreme discomfort to those Englishmen who had also to listen to these arguments.[97] His manner before the Assembly was never entirely free from the faintest suggestion of condescension, and occasionally he was betrayed into verbal lapses in which he spoke of "your League" as if Britain was not willing to admit her membership.[98] When British policy was criticized, he was apt to grow shriller and to indulge in astonishing philippics against his foreign colleagues; and one such performance on his part was paraphrased by a British observer to read: "We are perfect. We are British. And yet you, you dagoes, dare to come here and criticize US!"[99] Nor is it to be imagined that his frequent argument that Great Britain had entire faith in the League but believed that its progress must be slow, like the imperceptible evolution of the British constitution, aroused much enthusiasm among continental statesmen or much confidence in Britain's willingness to aid in the solution of European problems.[100]

Chamberlain also attracted a certain amount of criticism because of a development which was probably unavoidable. The conclusion of the Locarno Pact foreshadowed the entrance of Germany into the League of Nations. In the interval before that could be effected, however, collaboration among the Locarno Powers had already become so close that there was a good deal of resentment in the corridors at Geneva over what was termed "the Locarno cabal."[101] These feelings were not allayed by the tactics pursued by Briand and Chamberlain during the Special Assembly of March 1926, tactics which seemed designed to settle the future composition of the League Council by private conversations and secret deals carried on behind the Assembly's back and which succeeded only in creating a major crisis which did not help the League's international reputation.[102] Moreover, even after Germany had made good her claim to a

---

[97] "No intelligently patriotic Briton can feel anything but shame at being guyed by the Foreign Secretary before the whole world as a man who will not think or plan, who scorns logic and relies on muddling through." *Foreign Affairs*, VII (1925-1926), 93.

[98] See, for instance, the account of his speech at the Eighth Assembly in F. P. Walters, *A History of the League of Nations* (2 vols., London, 1952), I, 346.

[99] Steed, *Baldwin*, p. 129.

[100] On this see Cecil, *A Great Experiment*, pp. 190-191.

[101] Jordan, *Great Britain, France and the German Question*, pp. 98-100.

[102] On this crisis, see G. Scelle, *Une Crise de la Société des Nations* (Paris, 1927); Cecil, *A Great Experiment*, pp. 177-178; Walters, *History of the League*, I, 316-325; and Chapter 3 below.

permanent seat on the Council, the "cabal" did not dissolve. There was doubtless good reason for this, for the Locarno Powers were forced to discuss among themselves questions which were not of immediate interest to the League. Unfortunately, however, they often arrogated to themselves other matters which did belong properly within the competence of the Council; and it sometimes appeared that their intention was to extend this practice further, leaving to the Council only "such weighty matters as the appointment of the governing body of the International Cinematographic Institute at Rome."[103] All things considered, Chamberlain's role as a charter member of the "cabal" did not improve his personal stature, or his country's reputation, at the seat of the League.

But quite apart from all this, it is doubtful whether Chamberlain's decision to represent his country at Geneva was a wise one. He was Foreign Secretary of a large country, a position which imposes a crushing burden upon its incumbent at any time. His position as Britain's representative on the Council not only greatly increased his labors but necessitated frequent absences from London, for, after Germany's entrance into the League, the Council met four times a year. He was left little time to supervise the administration of his department and none to institute reforms, the need for which had been recognized since 1919. And, inevitably, the added weight of work sapped his energies and reduced his overall efficiency, and was probably responsible for actions for which he was much criticized during his last three years of office.

Certainly much of the prestige which he had won by his careful management of the Locarno negotiations was dissipated by what appeared to be his bungling of the Geneva Naval Conference of 1927. That meeting, between representatives of Great Britain, Japan, and the United States, was reminiscent of the conferences of the Lloyd George period. It was convened without adequate diplomatic preparation; it began with a public meeting at which delegates hurled widely divergent plans at each other's heads; and it ended—after weeks of futile wrangling, and after an attempt at compromise had been indignantly repudiated by the British Cabinet under the inspiration of Mr. Winston Churchill—in total failure.[104] A year later, Chamberlain's reputation was damaged by an even more serious diplomatic *gaffe*. On July 30, 1928, the Foreign Secretary announced in the House of Commons that a compromise in regard to the

---

[103] Felix Morley, *The Society of Nations* (Washington, 1932), p. 385.

[104] The most succinct and penetrating discussion of the technical deficiencies of this conference is that of Sir Arthur Salter, "The Technique of Open Diplomacy," *Political Quarterly*, III (1932), 64-65.

limitation of naval armaments had been reached with France, that it had been communicated confidentially to the United States government, but that it could not yet be made public. This public avowal of the existence of a secret was a curious procedure;[105] and it aroused a good deal of irritable speculation. In the end, it transpired that Britain and France had agreed on a plan similar to one already rejected by the United States; and their rather feeble attempt to bring pressure on that country succeeded only in antagonizing American public opinion. But it appeared further—as the *Manchester Guardian* deduced from inspired articles in the French press—that, in order to reach agreement with France, concessions had been made to her in the pending question of land armaments, and there was evidence that the government was now inclined to accept the French point of view that trained reserves should not be included in estimates of national military strength which would be used in future schemes for disarmament. "If [this] principle . . . has been abandoned," declared *The Guardian*, "it is more than a concession: it is a betrayal!"[106] British public opinion, which was firmly wedded to the idea of disarmament, agreed, and a howl of criticism went up in which all of the old charges of "secret diplomacy" and "conspiracy with France" were revived.

These examples of diplomatic maladroitness—and they are recognized as such even by Chamberlain's biographer[107]—had repercussions in the general elections of 1929 which brought the Labor party back to power. Their wider significance, perhaps, is that, because of them, the first postwar decade ended, as it had begun, with a good proportion of the British public entertaining grave suspicions of British diplomacy and, inevitably, of the diplomatic establishment—that is, the Foreign Office and the Diplomatic Service. Had Chamberlain's personal prestige remained undiminished, it might have had some effect in enhancing the popular reputation of the Foreign Office. This was not the case.

The British foreign service was still regarded, at the end of this decade, as a last stronghold of aristocratic privilege and a preserve for Etonians and Harrovians who were inadequately prepared to meet the problems of modern democratic society.[108] The complete failure of the Conservative governments to entertain any suggestions of internal reform served only to reinforce this idea. In addition, there was a strong suspicion in

---

[105] See Salter's comments, *ibid.*, p. 66.
[106] *Manchester Guardian*, August 3, 1928.
[107] Petrie, *Chamberlain*, II, 324-325.
[108] See, for instance, R. Nightingale, *Personnel of the British Foreign Office and Diplomatic Service* (Fabian Tract No. 232), (London, 1930).

the ranks of Labor that the Foreign Office was a center of political reaction and that it had, in fact, been primarily responsible for the fall of the Labor government in 1924. This belief was based on the rather shaky thesis that the Foreign Office publication of the famous Zinoviev letter, which figured so largely in the 1924 elections, had been designed deliberately to embarrass the Prime Minister,[109] whereas the step seems to have been taken to anticipate publication in the press.[110] Still, the belief was a stubborn one and, in 1928, it was strengthened, when a Foreign Office official whose name had figured in the Zinoviev affair became involved in a Treasury inquiry into speculation in foreign exchange by civil servants, a circumstance which led the press to revive popular memory of the "Red letter plot."[111]

To this atmosphere of awakened distrust, the failures of Austen Chamberlain's diplomacy made their contribution. One of the by-products of the breakdown of the Geneva Naval Conference, for instance, was the resignation from the Cabinet of Lord Robert Cecil, who had served as one of the British negotiators in the naval talks. Cecil's action was the end result of a series of disagreements with his colleagues which dated back to the days of the Draft Treaty;[112] and his differences with Chamberlain at the time of the Special Assembly of 1926 had come close to precipitating a break at that time. His resignation now caused a public sensation, during which it was rumored that he had fallen prey to reactionary officials in the Foreign Office.[113] With the ground thus prepared, it was very easy, during the disclosures of the abortive arrangement with France in the following year, for critics on the left to assume that those reactionary officials were now firmly in the saddle and that "secret diplomacy" was again to be the order of the day unless the people—as

---

[109] In a speech at Dundee on October 25, 1924, E. D. Morel said: "The whole thing has an ugly look. . . . The work of world pacification which Labour has taken in hand must not be allowed to be jeopardized by certain highly-placed permanent officials in the Foreign Office. . . . If there has been a plot—and I am inclined to think there has—that plot has been hatched in the interests of the Tory Party, and its instigators will be found in the triangle of Fleet Street, the City and the Foreign Office." *Foreign Affairs*, VI (1924-1925), 129.

[110] On this affair, see, *inter alia*, Fischer, *Soviets*, II, 493-498; Snowden, *Autobiography*, II, 714-715; Gregory, *On the Edge of Diplomacy*, pp. 215-231; Young, *Baldwin*, pp. 85-88.

[111] Parliamentary Debates: Commons, 5th series, CCXV (1928), 47-106.

[112] Cecil, *A Great Experiment*, pp. 358-363.

[113] Cecil himself shared the belief in the influence of such officials on Chamberlain. See *ibid.*, p. 163. Later when he became one of Britain's representatives to Geneva during the second MacDonald government, he was given an office in the Foreign Office. Of that period, he has written: "I will say nothing of the permanent officials of the Foreign Office and the Cabinet Offices except that they were all very competent and some of them helpful." *Ibid.*, p. 201.

Norman Angell wrote in October 1928—took the control of foreign affairs away from "the expert, which means too often the Foreign Offices, the old-time diplomats, the devisers of secret treaties."[114]

V

If, in the above pages, emphasis has been placed on the question of the popularity of the Foreign Office and the Diplomatic Service, this has been done deliberately. Administrative and executive agencies which enjoy the respect, or at least the confidence, of Parliament, press, and public do not generally have to concern themselves about the protection of their powers and prerogatives. In democracies, however, this happy state is rarely attained by the Foreign Offices, and this fact is probably the chief reason why unwise and disruptive invasions of their legitimate sphere of activity are so frequent.

In an interesting book on the conduct of foreign relations in the inter-war period, Sir Victor Wellesley has declared that "British diplomacy is no longer master in its own house," and he has listed the "fetters" which in recent years have bound British diplomacy and prevented it from performing effectively the functions for which its personnel are trained: tighter parliamentary control over foreign affairs; the complication of consulting the Dominions; the pressure of an inquisitive, demanding, but often ill-informed public opinion; the failure of proper coordination between the work of political, military, and economic agencies of the government; and others.[115] Reference has been made to these factors above. But certainly the gravest disadvantage under which the British diplomatic establishment had to operate in these years was the persistent suspicion in which it was held by large sections of the British public. It was essentially this, for instance, which made possible Lloyd George's carefree, but always dangerous, flouting of the normal processes of diplomacy and the introduction, into the administration of British policy, of faults of coordination which were never entirely corrected before 1939.

The most flagrant abuses of the Lloyd George period were, of course, discontinued in the years which followed his dismissal from office; and Austen Chamberlain was never forced to feel the humiliation and the impotence which had been the experience of Lord Curzon. But as long as the public attitude toward the Foreign Office and the Diplomatic Service remained unchanged—and it did remain substantially unchanged

---

[114] *Foreign Affairs*, XI (1928-1929), issue of October.
[115] Wellesley, *Diplomacy in Fetters*, p. 7 and *passim*.

throughout the decade discussed—there was no assurance that Lloyd George's methods might not be employed in the future by other political leaders as confident and as self-willed as he. The precedents had been established. In the 1930's—with no apparent objections from a public which was bewildered by the sudden deterioration of the international situation—they were to be improved upon, first by Ramsay MacDonald and later, and more disastrously, by Neville Chamberlain.

2

The French Foreign Office:
The Era of Philippe Berthelot

BY RICHARD D. CHALLENER

THE FRENCH FOREIGN OFFICE, though not without its faults or its critics, emerged from the first world war and the Peace Conference with its prestige undimmed. There were, to be sure, not a few Frenchmen who were dissatisfied with the final terms of Versailles or who regretted such results as Clemenceau's decision to abandon French claims for a Rhineland buffer zone in favor of an Anglo-American treaty of guarantee which never materialized. But at the same time the Quai d'Orsay did not become the target for the attacks of well-meaning dilettantes who regarded the professional diplomat as an expendable luxury and the Foreign Office as an institution of questionable merit.

There was, after all, no nation more conscious than France of the fact that both her European and her international position depended upon a viable foreign policy. The British might once again come to look upon many phases of Continental politics with characteristic, pre-1914 aloofness, and the Americans could believe it sound policy to retire behind the Atlantic, but no Frenchman could approach international affairs with a similar spirit of quixotic detachment. As a people the French were acutely conscious of their geographic exposure to invasion, of their limited population and of their industrial backwardness. They all knew, though at times some French leaders might act as if they had forgotten, that their recent military triumph had been possible only because they had been members of a grand alliance. Nor were the French sure of the permanence of their victory—to a Poincaré, ever fearful of a revival of German military power, it was a truism that "Time, in passing, has already worked against us." Hence, if the fruits of victory were not to wither on the vine, the Quai d'Orsay would have to develop a foreign policy which would guarantee the French triumph and maintain the security of the nation.[1]

Nor did the French, unlike the Americans or the British, have many regrets about their prewar diplomacy. To a small minority their wartime President became known as "Poincaré la Guerre," but on the whole Frenchmen believed passionately and virtually unanimously in German war guilt. Because the French knew they could not have avoided defeat without their allies, they considered the diplomacy by which the Entente of 1914 had been formed as a necessary and brilliant policy which had saved their country; it was by no means a heinous "secret" diplomacy which had committed the French people to a war which could have been averted. And, above all, as a result of their victory the French had regained Alsace-Lorraine, the two "lost provinces" whose recovery had been the basic objective of French diplomacy since the war of 1870-1871. Small wonder, then, that the historical movement known as "revisionism" found in France the slimmest foothold of all. Typical was the verdict of Joseph Barthélmy, noted jurist and for many years a member of the Chamber Committee on Foreign Affairs: "It was thanks to secret diplomacy that France recovered from the state of isolation and weakness in which the disasters of 1870 had left her, by means of the Franco-Russian alliance, the Entente Cordiale, and the friendly attitude of Italy."[2]

As a result, the Foreign Office, though not without its critics, survived the first decade of the postwar period with surprisingly few changes. Indicative of the French temper was the fact that, at a time when the professional diplomat was regarded with suspicion in most democratic countries, the French immediately after the war moved not to attack but to strengthen the position of the professional element in the Quai d'Orsay. "May our diplomats, better recruited, better selected, better known and better loved, be worthy of our soldiers—our soldiers of yesterday, our soldiers of tomorrow," was the conclusion of a Chamber of Deputies report in 1920. Significantly, too, the only major change in Foreign Office organization in the 1920's was the creation in January 1920 of the post of permanent Secretary General. It was to be his function to direct all phases of French diplomacy and to coordinate all of the many activities of the Quai d'Orsay.[3] Back of this reform was the idea—

[1] For evidence of the awareness among French political leaders of the need for a successful foreign policy see, in particular, the reports of the Chamber of Deputies committees which examined the Quai d'Orsay budgets in 1920 and 1921. *Journal officiel, Chambre des Députés, Documents*, 1920, No. 802, pp. 855ff. and 1921, No. 2020, pp. 309ff.

[2] Joseph Barthélmy, *Le Gouvernement de France* (Paris, ed. of 1919), p. 119.

[3] Emmanuel de Levis-Mirepoix, *Le Ministère des affaires étrangères* (Angers, 1934), pp. 132-133.

concurred in although never formally approved by the Chamber of Deputies—that the frequent changes in French cabinets made it mandatory to have a permanent official of the highest rank, serving directly under the responsible minister, whose presence would assure the continuity of French foreign policy. It was also felt that the tendency for the Premier to hold the post of Minister of Foreign Affairs made it all the more necessary to have such a permanent official at the Quai d'Orsay. Hence, although a Foreign Minister might be in office for only a few months and, in addition, might be unable to give full-time attention to foreign affairs, the Secretary General would preserve the traditions of French diplomacy and prevent French policies from fluctuating with each passing ministry.[4]

The possibility of preserving continuity in French diplomatic policies was further enhanced by the fact that in the immediate years after Versailles many of the career personnel of the prewar era retained their positions and much of their authority. Paul Cambon, who as ambassador to Great Britain had been so influential in building the Entente of 1904, remained in London until the end of 1920, while his equally famous brother Jules presided over the Paris meetings of the Council of Ambassadors for some years after that. Camille Barrère, whose diplomatic talents had smoothed Franco-Italian relations, retained his post in Rome until 1924, and Jules Jusserand, once the confidant of Theodore Roosevelt, continued to represent the Third Republic at Washington until the same year. To be sure, the advice of these older diplomats was not always followed. Paul Cambon, for instance, resigned his post in part because he felt that the postwar French political leaders had an incomplete understanding of the need for close ties with Britain and seemed willing to disregard the traditions established in the years after 1871.[5] But at the same time the presence of these pre-1914 diplomats, many of whom had been the associates of Delcassé in the building of the French alliance system, helped to prevent any sharp break with the past, and these men

[4] *Journal officiel*, 1921, No. 2020, p. 317 and 1920, No. 802, p. 870. The *rapporteur*, M. Noblemaire, insisted upon the need for such a permanent official but at the same time expressed his preference for the British system of a permanent Under-Secretary of State. What Noblemaire hoped for was an official, not subject to removal with each ministerial change, who would act as liaison agent between the Foreign Office and the legislature rather than as director of the Quai d'Orsay itself. No action was ever taken to comply with his views.

[5] Paul Cambon, *Correspondance, 1870-1924* (Paris, 1946), III, 387. The attitude of the new French leaders would, Cambon felt, produce a new Fashoda and a new set of diplomatic disasters.

could be counted upon to represent the traditional attitudes and practices of the Foreign Office.[6]

The development of French political life in the decade of the 1920's was in itself another factor which helped to preserve the prestige of the Quai d'Orsay and to prevent frequent deviations in foreign policy. In the latter stages of the war and during the Peace Conference the figure of Georges Clemenceau had, of course, been dominant in French affairs. His Foreign Minister, Stephen Pichon, had occupied a purely subordinate position and had possessed a minimum of authority or independence; however, his willingness to accept Clemenceau's leadership had averted friction and disagreement.[7] But from the end of the Clemenceau ministry early in 1920 until April of 1925, the Premier always assumed for himself the office of Minister of Foreign Affairs. While this political development had the disadvantages already noted, it was also a clear indication of the importance which French leaders attached to foreign policy and, furthermore, served to preserve the stature of the Foreign Office itself. Above all, in direct contrast to the unhappy British experience with Lloyd George and Curzon, this tendency to unite the two offices in the hands of one man effectively prevented competition and jealousy from arising between the chief of the Cabinet and the minister responsible for the conduct of foreign relations.

Moreover, whereas France had between 1920 and 1930 no less than fifteen different ministries and ten different Premiers, there were only six individuals who served at the Quai d'Orsay. Of these six, Millerand and Leygues were in office only in 1920, and du Prey was a transient who held his post for a mere five days in June 1924. Actually, despite the chronic French ministerial instability, from January 1921 until March 1932—with the exception of two short interludes when Herriot was at the Foreign Office—French foreign policy was in the hands of but two men, those inveterate rivals, Raymond Poincaré and Aristide Briand.[8]

Raymond Poincaré, whose ministry was characterized by an attempt to give France an independent foreign policy, was a man of strong convictions and a legalistic outlook who took his stand upon the letter and the

[6] See, for example, the familiar article by Jules Cambon, "The Permanent Bases of French Foreign Policy," reprinted in Hamilton Fish Armstrong, *The Foreign Affairs Reader* (New York, 1947), pp. 103ff. Jules Cambon argued that, regardless of changes in forms of government, public opinion or the conduct of diplomacy, the principal foreign policy objectives of any great nation remained constant.

[7] Paul Cambon, *Correspondance*, III, 297, 303, 367.

[8] These statistics based upon the charts in F. L. Schuman, *War and Diplomacy in the French Republic* (New York, 1931), Appendix B.

law of the Versailles Treaty. His favorite device was to go into the French countryside on Sunday afternoons and, usually while dedicating a memorial to the war dead, deliver a long oration in which he insisted that Germany could and must pay every franc of her reparations obligations. Well before 1914 Poincaré, a representative spokesman of the Conservative-Nationalist tradition in French politics, had been convinced of Germany's aggressive intentions; after the war he continued to typify all those Frenchmen who believed that the "hereditary enemy" across the Rhine must be "kept down" by a program of treaty enforcement, military alliances with the new states of Central Europe, and a strong army. He deeply resented any and all Anglo-American attempts to conciliate the Weimar Republic as well as any diplomatic gesture by his own country which appeared to endanger any of France's treaty rights. When, at the Cannes conference in 1922, Briand appeared willing to concede on reparations in order to work more harmoniously with Britain, Poincaré participated in the campaign which drove Briand from the Foreign Office and shortly afterwards replaced him as Premier and Foreign Minister. During the next two and a half years, despite Anglo-American pressure, he went ahead with his policy of strict treaty enforcement, a program highlighted by the controversial occupation of the Ruhr. Although Poincaré frequently spoke of the need for close alliance with England and even continued negotiations begun by Briand, his policy, in reality, was an attempt to show the rest of the world that France could conduct an independent foreign policy.

Aristide Briand, on the other hand, was a man of more flexible disposition who was deeply devoted to the preservation of European peace. An orator rather than a thinker, a pre-1914 Socialist who had gradually abandoned most of the tenets of the left, Briand had his greatest successes on the platform and seemed to possess an uncanny ability to grasp the mood of his audience. His speeches at the League of Nations, particularly the one heralding the entry of Germany into the Geneva councils in which he proclaimed, "Arrière les canons, arrière les mitrailleuses," made him the spokesman of the French moderates and the Left as well as of the international peace movement. Though Briand was actually as "security-conscious" as Poincaré and never as idealistic as his enemies charged, the policies which he put into practice were diametrically opposed to those of his rival on many fundamentals. After the experiences of the first world war, Briand came to feel that French security depended upon cooperation with the League of Nations, closer ties with Great Britain and, ultimately, upon Franco-German rapprochement. His greatest days came after 1924 and after the failure of the Poincaré experiment. Then, through the Locarno pacts and the close collaboration in the League Council between Austen Chamberlain, Gustav Streseman, and himself, it seemed that Europe was about to enter a new era of peace and good will in which the "spirit of Geneva" would infuse international relations.

The rivalry between these two schools of thought on French foreign policy—the "côté Briand" and the "côté Poincaré"—lasted until the mid-1920's. From early 1922 until the elections of 1924, a period of two and a half years, Poincaré was in control; he enjoyed the support of public and parliament and, although there were dissidents, opposition was in large measure over his tactics rather than his aims. Then came the electoral victory of the Cartel des gauches in 1924, a dramatic reversal of French political fortunes which accurately reflected popular dissatisfaction with the economic disorders resulting from the Ruhr occupation and with Poincaré's policy of "going it alone." Shortly thereafter Briand began a "reign" at the Quai d'Orsay which lasted for seven consecutive years from 1925 until 1932. His unprecedented tenure of office was interrupted only once and then for a mere twenty-four hours. During this time Briand enjoyed a popularity with both the Chambers and with the public which was unmatched by any Foreign Minister since the era of Delcassé. Although his appointment in 1925 was a direct result of the recent electoral victory of the Left, he continued to be the only acceptable Foreign Minister long after the Cartel des gauches, broken on the rack of monetary problems, was but a faint political memory.

Indeed, from 1926 to 1929 Briand served as Minister of Foreign Affairs in a centrist ministry headed by Poincaré. The combination of these two former rivals was a necessary consequence of the facts of French political life after the abandonment of the Ruhr occupation and the failure of the Cartel to solve the financial difficulties of the Republic. After the "fall of the franc" both the public and the Chambers demanded a domestic program of conservative economics—this meant Poincaré. But at the same time, after the failure of the policy of strict and unilateral treaty enforcement, they also demanded a foreign policy based upon more liberal lines—and this meant Briand. Thus, although Poincaré had not changed his own views on French foreign relations, he and his followers could no longer hope to make their opinions prevail and had no choice but to accept Briand as head of the Quai d'Orsay and also to follow his policies. Popular and parliamentary support for the Briand program—strikingly confirmed by the next elections of 1928—meant that in the long run he remained at the French Foreign Office while a succession of ministries tried with varying success to cope with domestic problems.[9] And, regardless of the specific political complexion of these cabinets, Briand was to have a relatively free hand in carrying out his policies, at least until the depression began to produce its disrupting effect upon European relations at the end of the decade.

Although both Briand and Poincaré were able to put their respective policies into effect with popular and parliamentary support and though "secret diplomacy" was never the issue in France that it was in Anglo-Saxon countries, nonetheless there was a noticeable increase of interest on the part of both legislative houses and of the public to supervise the work of the Quai d'Orsay in the years after the war. In pre-1914 France there had been rather general agreement upon the orientation of French diplomacy and little parliamentary interest in restricting the Foreign Office. During the years when Delcassé was transforming the bases of French diplomacy, his policies had provoked almost no discussion in the Chamber of Deputies.[10] It was an aphorism of French politics that a ministry did not fall over an issue of foreign policy, a belief which, while exaggerated, contained more than a modicum of truth.[11] However, after Versailles the French legislature was no longer content to remain indifferent on foreign policy issues and expected that its views would be given some consideration by the Foreign Minister and his staff of permanent officials.

Early in 1921, for instance, the Chamber gave a strong indication of its outlook when a ministry fell from power over a question of foreign policy. In January of that year the Leygues Cabinet was overthrown when the Deputies refused to grant the Premier immunity from questions about the course which he intended to follow at the forthcoming London Conference. Similarly, eight years later, Briand, then serving as both Premier and Foreign Minister, fell after interpellations concerning French policies at the international conference to be held at The Hague. In both instances it was quite clear that the Deputies desired information in advance about the policies which their government would pursue at these conferences. Yet, despite these signs of a parliamentary willingness to enforce its views on the Quai d'Orsay, the examples of Leygues and Briand were unique in the 1920's. Moreover, both Cabinets were already

[9] For an exceptionally interesting contemporary analysis, see Charles Seignobos, "La signification historique des élections françaises de 1928," *L'Année politique*, III (July, 1928), 257-282.

[10] Bertha R. Leaman, "The Influence of Domestic Policy on Foreign Affairs in France, 1898-1905," *Journal of Modern History*, XIV (December, 1942), pp. 449-451.

[11] A. Soulier, *L'Instabilité ministérielle sous la Troisième République* (Paris, 1939), p. 203.

in dire difficulties over domestic and other questions; it is not inconceivable that the Chamber majority seized upon an issue of foreign policy as a means of disposing of an unpopular cabinet. Furthermore, what was denied to Briand and to Leygues was conceded to others on at least a half dozen occasions when the Chamber flatly admitted the right of the government to pursue its own foreign policies without being bound to any specific legislative program.[12] When, for instance, in 1919 a resolution was introduced into the Chamber calling upon the government to insist at the Peace Conference that Germany should have no military organization whatsoever, the presiding officer ruled that the proposal was an unwarranted and illegal interference with the freedom of the executive to conduct diplomatic negotiations.[13]

More famous was the sudden and dramatic resignation of Briand in 1922 during the negotiations at Cannes. Finding Millerand, the President of the Republic, Poincaré, at that time leader of the Senate Committee on Foreign Affairs, and even members of his own Cabinet opposed to his attitude on reparations and an Anglo-French alliance, Briand returned abruptly from the meetings with Lloyd George. After outlining his policies to the Chamber, he unexpectedly resigned without bothering to request a formal vote of confidence. Whether Briand could have secured a favorable response on such a vote remains an unanswered question although it is certain that his parliamentary majority was fast decreasing in the face of mounting criticism of his foreign policies. His opponents felt that he was becoming a pawn for Lloyd George. Among the evidence cited by Briand's critics was a widely-publicized newspaper photograph in which the British Prime Minister appeared to be giving him golf lessons. Here, his enemies charged, was proof that Briand not only engaged in frivolous activities when serious problems were at stake but also was completely under the influence of the Englishman. Parisian newspapers used the opportunity to launch bitter attacks against Briand and his policies.[14] Yet even though Briand's parliamentary position was decidedly

[12] John E. Howard, *Parliament and Foreign Policy in France* (London, 1948), pp. 57, 65-73, a complete analysis of these two situations. The earlier chapters contain a useful summary of the constitutional position of the Foreign Minister and the pre-1914 precedents.

[13] Henry Kittredge Norton, *Foreign Office Organization* (Philadelphia, 1929), p. 3. (Supplement to Volume CXLIII of the *Annals of the American Academy of Political and Social Science.*)

[14] There are a number of interesting accounts of this disastrous golf game. Among the more readable is A. J. Sylvester, *The Real Lloyd George* (London, 1947), pp. 71-74. It appears also that Briand was in real need of instruction in golf. Having never held a club in his hands before, he had great difficulty hitting the ball and spent a good portion of the afternoon in the rough. Though he wandered from the fairway, his precise location

unfavorable, the political complexities and personal animosities involved were such that, at least in retrospect, Briand's resignation appears a highly particularized incident rather than a point of new departure in legislative control of foreign policy.[15]

These examples of ministries forced from office over issues in which foreign affairs were a basic point of contention indicate that during the 1920's the French legislature exhibited a new found interest in maintaining checks upon the conduct of the Quai d'Orsay. However, as a general rule, the extent and effectiveness of this parliamentary control was and remained somewhat limited. In the first place, the examples already cited were not always clear-cut instances. Moreover, neither the Chamber nor the Senate ever succeeded in controlling the details of policy formulation. During the period from 1919 to 1924 the legislature was successful in establishing certain broad boundaries beyond which no Foreign Minister could go. For instance, the Chambers made it impossible for any ministry to remain in power if it did not insist upon complete fulfillment of German reparations. But how this was to be accomplished remained, in general, for the Foreign Minister to decide.[16] And after 1925, with the popularity of Briand and the altered composition of the Chamber, even this broad legislative control was less effective than during the earlier period. An indication of the relative weakness of the Chambers was, for instance, the fact that although the postwar governments submitted far more treaties to the Chambers for ratification than had been the rule prior to 1914, nevertheless such important agreements as the 1924 treaty with Czechoslovakia or the Franco-Belgian military convention were neither placed before the legislature nor, for that matter, even adequately described to the Deputies and Senators.

In the 1920's neither the Chamber nor Senate Committees on Foreign Affairs emerged as the masters of the Quai d'Orsay. They remained, in the words of an English historian, "channels for information about foreign policy rather than agents in the making of it."[17] Neither commit-

---

could always be charted by the flow of Gallic profanity emerging from the sand traps and other obstacles.

[15] See the complete analysis in Soulier, *L'Instabilité ministérielle*, pp. 203-204, 271-274. It is worth noting that the British ambassador in Paris, Lord Hardinge, reported to London during the Cannes negotiations that Briand was in grave danger of being overthrown by the Chamber of Deputies. House of Commons Sessional Papers, 1924, XXVI. Cmd. 2169, "France No. 1 (1924). Papers Respecting Negotiations for an Anglo-French Pact," p. 126.

[16] Howard, *Parliament and Foreign Policy*, pp. 144ff.

[17] David Thomson, *French Foreign Policy* (Oxford Pamphlets on World Affairs, No. 67, 1944), p. 11.

tee ever sought or obtained the power to alter or amend the terms of treaties submitted for ratification and, in this respect, fell far short of the achievement of the similar body in the United States Senate. As Louis Barthou somewhat ruefully observed when the Versailles Treaty came before his committee, the members were virtually compelled, whatever their personal opinions, to ratify a *fait accompli*. And although the principal powers of the legislative committees related to their authority to interrogate the Foreign Minister, it was a standard complaint of the members that both Poincaré and Briand neglected to keep them informed of their policies.[18] Moreover, throughout the 1920's members of parliamentary committees constantly felt that there was an incomplete liaison between themselves and the Quai d'Orsay particularly on matters which interested the legislators, a complaint which, like the others, was another indication of the relative weakness of the legislative branch as an effective controlling agent.[19]

It appears, then, that despite the interest of postwar Deputies and Senators in supervising the Quai d'Orsay, the agents of French diplomacy nonetheless continued to enjoy a wider latitude in carrying out their policies than their confrères across either the Channel or the Atlantic.

The Quai d'Orsay was itself an organization in which the highest positions, both in Paris and abroad, were staffed by professional members of the foreign service and in which consular and diplomatic services had been at least partially assimilated into a unified organization.[20] A decree of 1916 had, moreover, specifically reserved the top positions in the central administration to men who had worked in foreign service posts outside France. Henceforth a successful career in the field was to be virtually a *sine qua non* for promotion to a policy-making position in Paris. Since 1907 diplomatic and commercial affairs had been channeled through the same Paris divisions. Although fusion between the two services was not as effective in posts abroad as at the Quai d'Orsay, the French appear to have minimized competition between the two branches of their

[18] See the excellent discussion of the problems and powers of the Chamber committee by Joseph Barthélmy, himself a member during the 1920's. *Essai sur le travail parlementaire et le système des commissions* (Paris, 1934), pp. 257-266. Also useful is R. K. Gooch, *The French Parliamentary Committee System* (New York, 1935), pp. 241-247.

[19] *Journal officiel, Sénat, Documents*, 1933, No. 264, p. 327, report of the committee which examined the Foreign Office budget for 1933.

[20] Discussions of the structure of the Foreign Office in the 1920's are at best incomplete and sketchy, and there is a particular dearth of memoir material. Best are the two parliamentary reports already cited, Nos. 802 of 1920 and 2020 of 1921. Competent though brief surveys are to be found in Schuman, *War and Diplomacy*, pp. 28-45 and Norton, *Foreign Office Organization, passim*. An unreliable and journalistic work is Paul Allard, *Le Quai d'Orsay* (Paris, 1938) which does, however, contain some interesting material.

foreign service.[21] Throughout both services, in Paris and outside France, the major posts were held by career officials. There were, of course, occasional exceptions. The Foreign Minister was free to make political appointments at the ambassadorial level, and in 1924, for instance, the Cartel des gauches rewarded Jean Hennessy, a member of the Chamber of Deputies, with the post of ambassador to Switzerland. But although there were such incidents, by far the vast majority of the top diplomatic positions in the French foreign service were held by career men.[22]

The dominance of professionals even extended to the special corps of assistants appointed to serve the Foreign Minister as his own cabinet. These men, personally chosen by the minister, were to form a staff of advisers unconnected with the professional bureaucracy. In theory they were to provide the politically responsible Minister of Foreign Affairs with the opportunity to have as his immediate associates a group of men whose opinions would not reflect the opinions of the professional diplomats. But, in fact, the ministerial cabinet was normally composed of foreign service officers chosen from the diplomatic corps. With a change in ministry they simply returned to their former positions in the Foreign Office. It would seem also that, instead of representing a separate advisory staff, this group by and large reflected the attitudes and opinions of the career officialdom.

Although during the 1920's there was a minimum of discussion of possible defects or deficiencies in the Quai d'Orsay and no effective pressure for organizational reform, later criticisms suggest that even at this time the French Foreign Office was operating under a number of handicaps. There was, in the first place, a wide range of problems which were financial in character. The permanent personnel, like the vast majority of the *fonctionnaires*, were hard hit by the decline in value of the franc. In the long run only those who enjoyed a private income or who came from well-to-do families could afford the luxury of a diplomatic career. And, although the Foreign Office, unlike the other bureaus of the French government, was able to maintain its prestige and its attractiveness, never-

---

[21] The question of fusion of diplomatic and consular services had been an issue in France since at least 1876. It was at least partially resolved by the creation of tables of equivalent grades, the possibility of transfer from one service to the other, and by the merger, at the Paris level, of the highest positions. See Schuman, *War and Diplomacy*, pp. 43-45.

[22] Walter Sharp, *The French Civil Service: Bureaucracy in Transition* (New York, 1931), pp. 326-327. The high degree of professionalism in the French diplomatic corps particularly, and for good reason, impressed American observers. Norton, making his study in 1930, claimed that there was but one noncareer man then occupying a major post in the French foreign service. Norton, *Foreign Office Organization*, p. 43.

theless the recruitment of new personnel was adversely affected.[23] The system whereby officers in the foreign service were recalled to positions at the Quai d'Orsay did not work out as well in practice as in theory. For, while such personnel assigned to work in Paris retained their previous status with regard to rank and promotion, their salaries depended upon the jobs to which they were assigned in the central administration. It thus happened that recall to Paris and a more responsible position frequently involved a net loss in income. This situation, noted by parliamentary critics as early as 1921, was still only partially remedied by the first reforms of the Quai d'Orsay undertaken in 1932.[24]

It was also claimed, probably not without considerable justification, that the Foreign Office continued throughout the 1920's to function in the style and manner of prewar years and that its horizons were limited by traditional practices. In its daily routine the Quai d'Orsay frequently seemed to regard the typewriter as a new-fangled instrument and the telephone and telegraph as gadgets whose usefulness had not as yet been fully demonstrated. Diplomatic personnel abroad, it was said, all too often learned of decisions taken in Paris not through regular channels but rather through the medium of the press in the country in which they were stationed. Nor was the documentation or information furnished by the Quai d'Orsay always sufficient. Particularly galling to those who felt that the Foreign Office still lived in a pre-1914 world was the minimum budget and minimum attention devoted to overseas information and propaganda services.[25] Moreover, within the central administration itself, the system of departmental organization—in which items of major im-

---

[23] Sharp, *French Civil Service*, p. 145. See also Schuman, *War and Diplomacy*, pp. 44-45.

[24] For more than perfunctory criticism of the Foreign Office one must refer to documents of the Senate and Chamber published in 1933 when the question of departmental reorganization had at last become a live issue and an interministerial council was working on the problem. This and following paragraphs rely heavily upon the abundant materials in *Chambre des Députés, Documents*, 1933, No. 1535, pp. 494ff. and particularly pp. 510-511 and *Sénat, Documents*, 1933, No. 264, pp. 326ff. These reports, incidentally, placed considerable credence upon articles written for *Le Temps* and *Le Figaro* by the political and diplomatic commentator, Wladimir d'Ormesson. It is interesting and also somewhat disconcerting to compare the parliamentary reports of 1933 with those of 1920-1921 and to observe how many problems mentioned at the earlier date remained still unsolved in the 1930's.

[25] Both of the parliamentary reports of 1933, already cited, devoted by far the bulk of their criticisms to the insufficiency of the French propaganda services. The Chamber reporter even appended a long and useful bibliography on the subject. Joseph Paul-Boncour, who as Minister of Foreign Affairs in the early 1930's had much to do with the reorganization of the Quai d'Orsay, mentioned only the reform of these propaganda and information services when he discussed this period in his memoirs. Joseph Paul-Boncour, *Entre deux guerres* (Paris, 1945), II, 398ff.

portance were handled by various desks representing geographical areas of the world—not infrequently led to duplication of effort and to inefficiency.

Later critics contended that the Quai d'Orsay devoted insufficient attention to the economic aspects of foreign policy and to the affairs of the League of Nations. The parliamentary reports of the early 1930's, reflecting these sentiments, stressed the idea that modern diplomacy, like modern war, had become "total"—or, to put it another way, that the Foreign Office, to achieve success, would have to be concerned with the whole range of human activities and not merely with the traditional legal-political relationships between states. To be sure, in the postwar decade much of what these observers desired had already been accomplished. A functioning French embassy, like that in Berlin, had a special section devoted to financial questions and a whole battery of experts who studied and reported the conditions of the German economy; François-Poncet, the ambassador after 1931, had been selected for the post because of his knowledge of business and finance, and the director of the political section of the Berlin embassy was a career diplomat who had previously spent eight years in the economic and commercial services of the Paris administration.[26] Similarly, the French Foreign Office had always taken the League of Nations seriously. The councils of Geneva, even during the heyday of Poincaré and the nationalists, had always included as representatives of the Third Republic men who were not only important figures in French diplomacy but also firm friends of the League itself: Léon Bourgeois, even in pre-1914 years an advocate of international organization, Joseph Avenol, for more than a decade second in command to Secretary General Drummond, and, of course, Joseph Paul-Boncour and Aristide Briand. Moreover, although it was the French Left which showed the most devotion to Geneva, conservatives and nationalists, despite considerable skepticism about the capabilities of the existing organization, were always interested in transforming the League into an agency capable of providing a thorough and rigorous system of collective security.[27] Nevertheless, despite these signs of the broadening activi-

---

[26] See the interesting account of the Berlin embassy at work, reprinted from the newspaper *Petit Parisien*, in Alfred Zimmern, *The League of Nations and the Rule of Law, 1918-1935* (London, 1936), pp. 488-491.

[27] There is no need to elaborate upon the many projects, such as the Treaty of Mutual Assistance or the Geneva Protocol, which engaged the attention of the Quai d'Orsay in the 1920's and which were seriously sponsored by the French. For a convenient summary of the French attitude, see Zimmern, *League of Nations*, pp. 324-326, and for an estimate of the interest of French conservatives in the Geneva organization, Arnold Wolfers, *Britain and France between Two Wars* (New York, 1940), pp. 157-160.

ties of the French Foreign Office, the officials who directed French commercial relations and League of Nations affairs tended to occupy a subordinate position in the central administration. Their work, until the reforms of the 1930's, was improperly coordinated with that of the all-important *Direction politique*. Thus, although the Quai d'Orsay was expanding its functions and interests, it was less successful in integrating these newer concerns with economic affairs and the League with the familiar political services.[28]

If the continuation of certain "traditional practices" hampered French diplomacy after Versailles, mention should also be made of the perpetuation of what might be called "traditional prejudices" which arose from the social and educational background of the men in the French foreign service. Prior to 1914 many French diplomats had been recruited from the ranks of the aristocracy—for while most aspects of the Third Republic were anathema to these families, the foreign service, like the army, had continued to be an "acceptable" career for those descended from the aristocracy. After the war, however, one of the notable changes in the composition of the French foreign service was its infiltration by the sons of the upper middle class.[29] The foreign service, in a very real sense, became a blend of the old aristocracy with the newer representatives of big business and finance. Thus, for instance, while the French ambassador in Great Britain in the early 1920's bore the distinguished name of the Comte de Saint-Aulaire, the change was symbolized by the fact that such representatives of the business-financial world as André François-Poncet and Jean Herbette went to the embassies in Berlin and Moscow. Moreover, as noted earlier, both the low salary scales and the need for an advanced and costly education tended to prevent any influx of new foreign service personnel from the other strata of French society.

But whatever the social background of the French diplomats, by far the majority of them were the product of at least one common mold— the *École libre des sciences politiques*, a specialized school founded shortly after the Franco-Prussian war to provide the young Republic with a corps of trained administrators. The extent to which this "school of diplomats" had an educational monopoly is shown by the fact that of

[28] The reorganization of 1932-1933 suggested that the *fonctionnaires* directing commercial and League affairs should be put on a par with the officials who were in charge of the various "area desks" organized on a geographical basis within the *Direction politique*. It was suggested that they be given the status of assistant directors of the political section as a means of improving policy coordination. *Journal officiel, Chambre*, 1933, No. 1535, p. 510.
[29] Norton, *Foreign Office Organization*, p. 32.

the 192 men appointed to diplomatic or consular vacancies between 1907 and 1927, a total of 153 held diplomas from the *École libre*.[30] Instruction was admittedly less specialized than that in the law faculties of the various French universities, and, in addition to the standard courses in history and international relations, students could take courses in a wide variety of fields—economics, administration, public law, geography. Indeed, in the 1920's one of the more noticeable trends in the education and selection of new foreign service personnel was the extent to which the *École libre* taught and the Quai d'Orsay expected candidates to be informed about the economic and geographical aspects of international relations instead of the purely legal or diplomatic factors.[31] However, despite the new emphases in education, it seems quite possible—though documentation of this point is fragmentary—that the training of French diplomatic personnel remained somewhat narrow and academic. The *École libre*, in the words of Bertrand de Jouvenal, "fashioned minds which were not only specialized in their knowledge *mais presque dans leurs âmes.*"[32] And as Jules Cambon—himself a great ambassador who distrusted the tendency to select the future members of the diplomatic corps on the basis of formal education and examinations—cautioned, the art of diplomacy required many skills and sensitivities which "aren't learned in school."[33]

Another aspect of French diplomacy which close observers began to notice in the postwar decade was the ever-increasing tendency for major decisions to be made in Paris and, in particular, by the officials who formed the permanent staff of the Quai d'Orsay. This development, which had its serious consequences in the 1930's, had several facets. In the first place, the French diplomats abroad were frequently neither consulted nor heeded, and they themselves played an ever-decreasing role in both the formulation and execution of policies. Secondly, it was the professional element in Paris which tended to become the masters of policy. Moreover, these career officials began to become more and more a "closed corporation," a self-perpetuating body of advisers which surrounded the politically responsible Foreign Minister. These officials, it might be added, had not only long since completed their own period of

[30] Sharp, *French Civil Service*, p. 112.

[31] *ibid.*, pp. 111-112, 147-148. Another brief but not too helpful discussion of the education of foreign service personnel is to be found in Louis Eisenmann, "The Study of International Relations in France," League of Nations, *Educational Survey*, III (March, 1932), 44-52.

[32] Bertrand de Jouvenal, *Après la défaite* (Paris, 1941), p. 50.

[33] Jules Cambon, *Le Diplomate* (Paris, 1926), p. 63.

service abroad but also had no desire to abandon the Quai d'Orsay for an embassy outside France.[34] In the words of a parliamentary investigating commission, established after the second world war to discover the reasons for the French defeat of 1940: "Our foreign policy thus became almost exclusively the work of the central administration of the Quai d'Orsay. . . . All too frequently the (foreign) ministers were informed of events occurring abroad only through the medium of the *fonctionnaires trop sédentaires* of their cabinet or of the various services. There existed, in fact, in the midst of our diplomatic personnel a group of bureaucrats who made their careers almost exclusively within the offices of the Quai d'Orsay and who came between our ministers and their diplomats abroad."[35]

Although these tendencies were certainly present, their extent and seriousness, at least during the 1920's, can be exaggerated. Joseph Paul-Boncour, himself prominent in French foreign affairs between the wars, has cautioned against the prevalent tendency to blame most of the ills of French diplomacy on the permanent staff of the Quai d'Orsay and to overlook the responsibility of the various Foreign Ministers.[36] Moreover, the process by which diplomatic decisions were focused in Paris— in part simply the result of improved communications—was not without its advantages. Paris, able if it so desired to gain information from a foreign capital at a moment's notice, was frequently better equipped

---

[34] See the pertinent discussion by Senator Bérenger, chairman of the foreign affairs commission of the French Senate in his report on the Foreign Office budget for 1933, *Journal officiel, Sénat* (1933), No. 264, p. 327. Both he and the Chamber *rapporteur* felt that the Quai d'Orsay did not sufficiently consult or rely upon its ambassadors in foreign countries. The report recommended the institution of regularly-scheduled meetings between the Minister of Foreign Affairs and all of his top-ranking ambassadors. The tendency for promising young officials to be recalled to Paris early in their careers and kept there indefinitely was noted by Sharp, *French Civil Service*, p. 331. For some interesting comments on the declining importance of the ambassador, see Jules Cambon, *Le Diplomate*, pp. 118ff. After the second world war all of these questions were raised once again in the course of a monumental parliamentary investigation into the causes of the French disaster of 1940. See, in particular, the testimony of Jean Dobler, from 1931 to 1937 the French consul-general in Cologne. *Assemblée nationale, 1946, Commission d'enquête parlementaire. Les événements survenus en France de 1933 à 1945 Témoignages et documents* (Paris, 1951), II, 469ff. Dobler was a witness with an ax to grind and, although the great bulk of his testimony pertained to events after 1933, it is clear that he believed that many of the failings which he observed at that time had been prevalent a decade earlier. He complained bitterly that the central administration had paid scant attention to the reports of French agents abroad and that the career officials in Paris were responsible for this. Unfortunately, when the investigating commission questioned other prominent diplomats, like François-Poncet or Coulondre, these issues were not pursued further. However, Dobler's testimony did make considerable impression upon the investigating commission and was specially noted in the final report written by the Deputy, Charles Serre.

[35] *Commission d'enquête, Rapport*, I, 86-87.

[36] Paul-Boncour, *Entre deux guerres*, II, 125.

to formulate policies. And with decisions centered at the level of the central administration, there was also a better chance to assure continuity and consistency in foreign policy. However, as would become more evident in the years after Hitler's rise to power, there was also the distinct disadvantage that the advice and reports of the diplomats on the spot would be ignored, that the decisions of the Paris career officials would be based upon inaccurate appraisals, and that French foreign policy would be the loser.

II

Although Briand and Poincaré were the political figures who dominated French foreign affairs in the first postwar decade, the Secretary General of the Quai d'Orsay, Philippe Berthelot, quite possibly left a more indelible mark upon French foreign policies and the conduct of French diplomacy. Although twenty years have passed since his retirement, one does not yet write with great confidence about the specific influence of Berthelot. He remains, at best, something of an enigma. Furthermore, since Berthelot destroyed his personal papers and published no memoirs—something as unique among French public officials as among contemporary American generals—it seems unlikely that the full and true measure of his role will ever be known.[87]

Philippe Berthelot prided himself on being the discreet *fonctionnaire*, the inscrutable civil servant whose own personality would never appear as part of the diplomatic record. Even the documents already published by the French and British Foreign Offices shed but little light upon his ideas, his character, or his influence. His name appears high on the list of French personnel at nearly every important international conference in the 1920's, but only rarely did he take part in the discussions or, from

[87] To date there is but one biography of Berthelot, that of his lifelong friend and admirer, Auguste Bréal: *Philippe Berthelot* (Paris, 1937). It is, however, noncritical and, though valuable, largely a series of anecdotes. Perhaps the best estimate of the Secretary General is to be found in Georges Suarez, *Briand, sa vie . . . son œuvre* (Paris, 1941), Vol. v, *passim*. It carries the story only through 1923 and, because of the death of Suarez, remains uncompleted. Of the greatest value are three short sketches by another of his friends, the poet-ambassador, Paul Claudel. These essays, originally written in 1937, are reprinted in Paul Claudel, *Accompagnements* (Paris, 1949), pp. 182-209. There is also some information of value in Allard, *Quai d'Orsay*, pp. 52ff. and a useful sketch, largely distilled from Bréal, in Robert Lengerle, *Nos grands chefs* (Paris, 1945), pp. 162ff. Periodical literature on Berthelot is also limited, but see Louis Dumont-Wilden, "Une grande figure de la diplomatie française," *Revue Bleue*, LXXV (October, 1937), 618-623 and "Philippe Berthelot" in *L'Asie nouvelle*, XXXV (December, 1934), 318ff. London and Paris dailies carried extensive death notices in their editions of November 22 and 23, 1934; of these the most valuable is the appraisal of Berthelot by Wladimir d'Ormesson in the November 23, 1934, issue of *Le Figaro*. See also Charles de Chambrun, *Traditions et souvenirs* (Paris, 1952), pp. 117-118.

the record, appear to have influenced the decisions which were reached. Furthermore, in the biographies and memoirs of the various European statesmen of the postwar decade—whether those of Paul-Boncour, Stresemann, or Austen Chamberlain—Berthelot is never a central figure and not infrequently is only casually mentioned as if he were a person of incidental importance.

To his admirers, however, Berthelot was the animator of French diplomacy, the one official who assured the continuity of French foreign policy and a man of such competence and broad vision that his advice, if followed at all times, would have spared his country most of its postwar diplomatic errors. Jean Giraudoux, the playwright-novelist who himself pursued an active career in the press and information services of the Quai d'Orsay, once made Philippe Berthelot the hero and Raymond Poincaré the villain of a particularly successful political novel, *Bella*. In the Giraudoux novel, Berthelot was ". . . the only plenipotentiary at Versailles, except Wilson, who would have reconstructed Europe generously, and the only one, without exception, who would have done it competently."[38] To the author of *Bella*, one of Berthelot's few lifelong friends, the Secretary General was not only the diplomat who had set Central Europe on its feet but also a statesman whose particular strength was his knowledge of man as a political animal: "Men, it may be, he did not know, but great men he knew to perfection. He knew the habits, the strength and weakness of the international tribe which spends its life, if not above, at any rate just outside the law. He even knew their special anatomy. He knew how to fatten and how to thin them down, and what food and drink raised their political genius to its highest point."[39]

Others, less inclined to worshipful praise, found something sinister in the regime of Berthelot at the Quai d'Orsay. In their eyes he was an all-powerful and irremovable permanent official who manipulated the political heads of the Foreign Office as if they were but puppets. "Some individuals," a French journalist observed, "go so far as to claim that the Minister of Foreign Affairs is only the *nominal* chief of the Quai d'Orsay and that, even if the man who holds the portfolio is Briand, the true minister is Philippe Berthelot."[40]

Midway between these extremes was the opinion that whatever his merits or failings, the Secretary General was simply unfathomable. André Géraud, political commentator for *L'Echo de Paris*, was a prolific writer

[38] Jean Giraudoux, *Bella* (Paris, 1926), p. 7.   [39] *ibid.*, p. 13.
[40] Allard, *Quai d'Orsay*, pp. 48-49.

who, as Pertinax, could fill two thick volumes with detailed accounts of the gravediggers of France, but despite his best efforts, he could never find a satisfactory answer to the riddle of Berthelot. The Secretary General, wrote Géraud, "was a strange man. He boasted that while paying tribute to the Geneva institution in high-sounding words, he knew how to safeguard the long-tested concepts and precedents of French foreign relations. That man has always baffled me. Whether he was more than an exhibitionist addicted to perpetual paradoxes, an opportunist, and a questionable connoisseur of exotic antiquities remains a riddle."[41]

The reign of Berthelot, from 1914 until the end of 1932, coincided with the years in which France exerted her greatest influence in European affairs since the time of the first Napoleon. Paradoxically, it terminated just at the date at which French diplomacy was beginning its abrupt slide into the trough of futility and French influence was falling toward its nadir. Philippe Berthelot, whose principal concern had been to find a viable solution to the German problem, retired at the very moment when Adolf Hitler came to power and initiated the series of diplomatic and military maneuvers which quickly put an end to the years of French hegemony in Europe.

The future Secretary General entered the foreign service in the closing years of the nineteenth century, but although his rise in the Paris administration had been rapid, he did not achieve prominence until the summer of 1914. During the crisis which preceded the outbreak of war he enjoyed a rare and unexpected opportunity to influence the course of events, and his conduct and initiative during those critical days were such that he immediately achieved a commanding position in the Quai d'Orsay. When the threat of a general European war suddenly arose in late July, the French President, Poincaré, the Premier and Foreign Minister, Viviani, and the foremost permanent official of the Quai d'Orsay, de Margerie, were all absent from Paris on their famous mission to Russia. Bienvenu-Martin, Minister of Justice in the Viviani Cabinet, had been chosen to serve as acting Premier and acting Foreign Minister, but he was a complete novice in the handling of foreign affairs. Berthelot, then the assistant director of European political affairs, was the only official of high rank and experience remaining on duty at the Quai d'Orsay and had been temporarily placed in charge of the political affairs division. Thus, until the French government returned to Paris, it was Berthelot who, as Bienvenu-Martin's principal adviser, had a

---

[41] André Géraud, "Diplomacy Old and New," reprinted from *Foreign Affairs* in Armstrong, *Foreign Affairs Reader*, p. 404.

large share in formulating French policies and in determining the initial replies of the Quai d'Orsay when Austria and Germany attempted to persuade France to keep hands off the pending Austro-Serbian conflict.[42]

Berthelot, it appears, was from the outset of the crisis suspicious of Austro-German intentions and felt that the two Powers, while not desiring war at any price, would certainly at the last instance not shrink from fighting. He believed that both Germany and Austria sought a brilliant diplomatic victory and hoped to frighten France into putting pressure on Russia to remain quiet while the Dual Monarchy disposed of the Serbs on its own terms. Determined to avoid what he regarded as a German trap, Berthelot therefore would not agree that his country should intervene at St. Petersburg to restrain the Russians unless Germany would exert similar pressure upon Vienna, and at the same time he studiously avoided giving any impression to the public, as the German ambassador desired, that France and Germany were working in close harmony to maintain Europe peace.[43] In addition to his refusal to put pressure on Russia, Berthelot advised the Serbians to play for time by conceding to Austria on all points which did not compromise their sovereignty and by making an appeal to the Great Powers to mediate the dispute. And, since the Serbian reply to the famous Austrian ultimatum hewed close to the line suggested by Berthelot, it was later claimed—though the charge is baseless—that the entire note was "inspired" by the French diplomatist.[44] This, incidentally, was the first but not the last time that he was accused of exercising secret influences far beyond the confines of the Quai d'Orsay. But, in any event, it was Berthelot's handling of these initial phases of the crisis which won for him the commanding position in the Foreign Office which, with but two brief exceptions, he was to hold for almost thirty years afterwards.

Throughout the course of the war Berthelot was considered by foreign diplomats as the official who was best-informed about French policies and the man to know if one desired to discover the objectives of French diplomacy. Though he was an important figure in most inter-Allied con-

[42] On the situation in the French Foreign Office, see Bienvenu-Martin's own account, "Mon intérim de chef de gouvernement," *La Revue de France*, XIII (August, 1933), 639-652. In this article Bienvenu-Martin expressly stated that Berthelot's advice had been of the greatest assistance to him.

[43] On Berthelot's general views, see Sidney B. Fay, *The Origins of the World War* (New York, ed. of 1931), II, 388. On his reaction to the initial Austro-German *démarches* designed to persuade France to remain on the sidelines, see, particularly, Pierre Renouvin, *The Immediate Origins of the War* (Eng. ed., New Haven, 1928), pp. 84-86, 102-104.

[44] Renouvin, *Immediate Origins*, pp. 93-94.

ferences, his influence remained unobtrusive. Only the initiated knew of it, and Berthelot himself remained virtually unknown to the French public.

Berthelot had expected that in recognition of his wartime services he would be named to head the French delegation at the Paris Peace Conference. He was, however, disappointed. For reasons which still appear uncertain Clemenceau passed over him and appointed instead an obscure diplomat, Dutasta, then the French ambassador at Berne, to be the principal French negotiator. Apparently "the Tiger" never fully trusted or admired Berthelot, and, as he always preferred to run his own show, wanted as chief of the French delegation some one who would be willing to accept a subordinate status.[45] Berthelot, however, was not a negligible figure at the Peace Conference. He represented France in the commission which concerned itself with the establishment of the new states of Central Europe that emerged from the debris of the now defunct Austro-Hungarian Empire. At the same time within the hierarchy of the Quai d'Orsay his importance continued to increase; when de Margerie accepted the Brussels embassy, Berthelot succeeded him as director of the Foreign Office's all-important division of political and commercial affairs. Furthermore, although there is again no direct evidence, it seems clear that Berthelot, who enjoyed close personal relations with Dutasta, was consulted on all major issues of the Peace Conference and shared at least indirectly in all of the territorial decisions made by the French representatives. At any rate Berthelot himself apparently believed that he had played a part in writing the Versailles Treaty which was larger than the one to which he had been officially assigned. For when Lloyd George asked him to explain just exactly what his role in the French delegation had been, Berthelot replied with a smile, "Everything . . . and nothing."[46]

Within a short period after the Peace Conference, however, Berthelot had become the most important of the permanent officials at the Quai

[45] Bréal, *Berthelot*, pp. 188-189. To Bréal the nomination of Dutasta appeared "incredible" and, unable to find a logical reason for Clemenceau's action, he concluded, "Let's not even try to explain it." Claudel, *Accompagnements*, pp. 198-199 could find no reason other than the caprice of Clemenceau. Poincaré, however, in his wartime diary indicated in an entry of December 29, 1918, that at this time there was considerable intrigue among the officials of the Quai d'Orsay, some of it involving Berthelot. His somewhat cryptic entry in his diary does not add much to the above account except to indicate that Berthelot was very disappointed and may possibly have been involved thereafter in efforts to have de Margerie removed from his position as director of the political affairs division. Raymond Poincaré, *Au Service de la France* (Paris, 1932), X, 459.

[46] Bréal, *Berthelot*, p. 195.

d'Orsay. As early as the autumn of 1919 he had unofficially reached the top; at that time Paul Cambon, the French ambassador in London, noted that as a result of the lethargy and illness of Pichon it was Berthelot who was "the real Minister of Foreign Affairs."[47] His career was officially climaxed when in September 1920 he was appointed to direct all phases of the Foreign Office's activities as its permanent Secretary General. In December of the same year he was given the rank of ambassador. From then until his retirement at the end of 1932, with the exception of a three-year interlude, Berthelot was the ranking permanent official at the Quai d'Orsay and considered by all observers as the animator or "motor" of French diplomacy.

But from 1922 to 1925 Berthelot was out of office and in disgrace. A special disciplinary council, over which Premier Poincaré had personally presided, suspended him from the foreign service for ten years and had, for all practical purposes, read him out of the Quai d'Orsay forever. Berthelot was accused of using the influence of the Foreign Office to try to avert the collapse of the Banque Industrielle de Chine, a personal intervention which appeared particularly culpable since his own brother was the managing director of the bank. As in most cases of this nature, there was certainly more involved than the official charges. Berthelot himself admitted that he had intervened in the bank crisis without bothering to notify Briand, then the Foreign Minister, but he also felt that Poincaré had for both personal and political reasons desired to have him removed from office. There is, indeed, some substantiation for his view. Poincaré was committed to the policy of forcing Germany to fulfill her treaty obligations, while Berthelot—as will shortly be noted—was even at this time of the opinion that France should reach some accommodation with the Weimar Republic. Furthermore, Poincaré, like Clemenceau, was a man of strong and forceful temperament who wanted to run his own diplomatic show without interference from a career official of independent mind; significantly, during the thirty months which Poincaré held the Foreign Ministry, he never bothered to fill the vacant post of Secretary General. At any rate, Berthelot was restored to his former position in 1925 when Herriot rescinded the verdict of the disciplinary council and, in the presence of Berthelot, had all of the records pertaining to the "case Berthelot" destroyed.[48] His restoration at this time was of course a logical result of

[47] Paul Cambon, *Correspondance*, III, 365.
[48] The best account of the whole scandal is to be found in Suarez, *Briand*, V, 108ff. Both Bréal and Claudel are inclined to minimize the affair and charge it up to Poincaré's

the fact that the Cartel des gauches now controlled the political destinies of France. It was widely believed that Berthelot had suffered primarily because of his political differences with Poincaré; to reverse the earlier verdict was considered an act of political justice. But more important was the fact that Berthelot returned to his post as permanent director of the Quai d'Orsay just at the moment when the French were in the process of making an abrupt switch from a policy of coercing Germany to one of trying to conciliate her.

If Philippe Berthelot appears difficult to understand, it is in large part because of his personality. Through rigorous self-discipline he appeared always imperturbable, always the master of his emotions. His wit was barbed and pointed, and, as Géraud noted, he rejoiced in cynicism and paradox. Human beings, he once wrote, preferred to fight in civil wars rather than in foreign wars because "they know the people they are killing."[49] The Polish leader Pilsudski he once described as a man with a furtive expression who looked as if he always expected something unpleasant to happen to him.[50] Intellectually brilliant, Berthelot had few close friends and was one of those men who were feared rather than respected. That he should not dominate and rule was, to Berthelot, obviously unthinkable. He was, after all, both by birth and accomplishment one of the intellectual elite of the Third Republic. Son of Marcellin Berthelot, one of the founders of modern chemistry, Philippe had from his earliest years lived on terms of easy familiarity with the small group of republican intellectuals and political leaders who had made the Republic in the years after 1871. Social position and the influence of his noted father had in his youth opened all doors to him—in particular, the door of the Quai d'Orsay—and all of this he had considered as but his due. Small wonder, then, that Berthelot impressed others as dominating, if not domineering.

Though Philippe Berthelot gained his entrée into the foreign service through the influence of his father, he was far more than a mere dilettante. Indeed, it seems that almost from the moment he entered the Quai d'Orsay he deliberately set out to reach the top by making himself indispensable. He drove himself at top speed and showed an ability

---

vindictiveness. Most interesting is the fictionalized account of the Berthelot-Poincaré feud which is in Giraudoux' *Bella* and serves as the central theme of the novel. Giraudoux stresses the personal aspects also: Poincaré appears as a narrow-minded legalist determined to have his own way whatever the cost, while Berthelot is pictured as a man of flexible, generous disposition and breadth of vision whose superior talents naturally stirred up the resentment of his opponent.

[49] Bréal, *Berthelot*, p. 103.
[50] Hardinge of Penshurst, *Old Diplomacy* (London, 1947), p. 256.

to work endless hours without rest; like the hero of the typical success story, he was the first to enter the Quai d'Orsay in the morning and the last to leave at night. Berthelot made it his business to see every bit of correspondence, every document which went through the Foreign Office and to know everything that happened. Moreover, he remembered virtually all that he read or heard, for he was gifted with an almost encyclopedic memory. Thus over the years he gradually and intentionally drew all the many threads of French diplomacy to his own person. And though in later years there were not a few in French political life who would have liked to have him replaced, it was not as easy to find another man capable of performing his functions as it was to keep him in office—he had become, in fact, the "indispensable man" he had set out to be. These traits and this desire to reach the top, incidentally, suggest that Berthelot's disagreements with men like Poincaré and Clemenceau were not one-sided. These two "strong men" of twentieth century French politics must have sensed that they were in the presence of a man whose ambition to rule and control was not only as fierce as their own but also a threat to their own supremacy.

Berthelot's long period of ascendancy at the Quai d'Orsay was quite probably not without its disadvantages. He was frequently accused of "empire building" and, in particular, of filling the press and information services of the Foreign Office with his own favorites until that organization became a sort of Noah's ark in which men of first-rate talents worked alongside those of "the seventeenth order."[51] It is certain that he had a natural affinity for diplomats with literary or artistic skills. Both Jean Giraudoux and Paul Claudel were particular favorites whose careers Berthelot fostered; it was the Secretary General who put the former in charge of the French overseas information service after the Armistice and who in 1924 secured the latter's appointment as ambassador to the United States.[52]

More serious is the fact that it was during Berthelot's reign that, as earlier noted, there was an increasing tendency for Paris to make most

---

[51] Suarez, *Briand*, v, 125-126.

[52] Berthelot had become Giraudoux's "protector" even before 1914 and thereafter watched over his career; *Bella* was, in a very real sense, Giraudoux's revenge against Poincaré for firing his friend, and, incidentally, the novel provoked the Foreign Minister into assigning Giraudoux to a job which kept him so busy he had almost no time to write. Paul Morand, *Adieu à Giraudoux* (Paris, 1944), pp. 25-34. On Berthelot's long interest in Claudel, see Charles Benoist, *Souvenirs* (Paris, 1934), III, 278-279 and Paul-Boncour, *Entre deux guerres*, II, 376, as well as the frequent references to Berthelot in *The Correspondence between Paul Claudel and André Gide, 1899-1926*, edited by Robert Mallet (London, 1952).

of the basic diplomatic decisions. Indeed, throughout the 1920's the power and importance of the office of Secretary General steadily grew, frequently at the expense of good administration. Since Berthelot sought and assumed responsibilities far beyond those which any man should have attempted, there was a noticeable failure during his years in office to delegate responsibility throughout the various echelons of the Foreign Office.[53] Likewise it was during these years also that the career personnel who never left Paris began to exercise increasing authority at the expense of French representatives abroad—Berthelot himself, it might be noted, had not served outside the walls of the Quai d'Orsay since the early years of the century. It is quite possible, however, that the Secretary General, himself gifted with a sense of detachment from his immediate surroundings, realized what was happening. Shortly after his retirement he was visited by Jean Dobler, French consul-general at Cologne, who complained that no one in the Quai d'Orsay bothered to read his dispatches warning of the growing strength of Hitler. Berthelot told his visitor that he should go directly to the Foreign Minister and tell his story to him in person. When Dobler protested that this was impossible, Berthelot replied with his usual bland smile, "His cabinet chief isn't a career man . . . You have a chance."[54]

Philippe Berthelot, though essentially a man of the Left, always distrusted politicians and throughout his long career avoided political life. Presented with a chance to run for election to the Chamber, he spurned the opportunity. Briand supposedly offered to back his candidacy and argued that within a short time after election as a Deputy Berthelot could himself become the Foreign Minister. But Berthelot was not interested. In part this was because he was a poor speaker, ill at ease before large groups, and, by contrast, fully effective only around the conference table. But his scorn for politics was more likely a question of temperament. Aware of his own talents and abilities, Berthelot simply felt that the conflicts and compromises of political life were beneath a man of his stature. Typically, when he testified before the foreign affairs commission of the Chamber, he impressed the Deputies with the wealth of his knowledge and his mastery of detail, but at the same time he made them feel not only that he did not like to appear before the commission

---

[53] Wladimir d'Ormesson in *Le Figaro*, November 23, 1934.

[54] *Commission d'enquête, Témoignages et documents*, II, 501. Dobler, despite his bitter criticisms of most Paris career officials, was quite moderate in discussing Berthelot. Though Dobler thought that Berthelot had probably not been immune to the usual ailments of the sedentary bureaucrat, at the same time he felt that Berthelot's judgment had always been saved by his "incomparable intelligence."

but also that he had come "only because the Minister had told him to do so."[55] Furthermore, Berthelot avoided political life because he preferred to remain the civil servant who worked behind the scenes and who would not lose his office with a shift in ministries. As a permanent *fonctionnaire* he felt no doubt that he actually possessed more power and authority than the responsible minister. As a hostile yet discerning critic observed, Berthelot preferred the substance of power to its semblance.

It is, unfortunately, still not possible to say with finality where Berthelot stood on all of the great and troubled diplomatic issues of the 1920's. André Géraud appears to have come closest to the mark when he pointed out that the Secretary General believed that his own contribution was to try to bridge the gap between the old and the new diplomacy. That is, Berthelot felt that he succeeded in enabling France to adjust to the new era of diplomacy by conference and through the League of Nations without at the same time sacrificing any of the traditions or methods of the pre-1914 era. It is indeed certain that he had a deep sense of the history and of the traditions of his country and that these sentiments possessed a living reality for him.[56] Certainly, too, he was always a bit skeptical of the League of Nations. Even though he worked in close association with Briand and was "his man," Berthelot was never able to place quite as much faith in Geneva as his chief. The Secretary General, from 1919 until his retirement—and even during the heyday of the League in the mid-1920's—always doubted if the League could produce effective results, for he felt that a system of alliances, like that of pre-1914 Europe, was more in accord with the unchanging nature of man.[57] Likewise, the idea of "diplomacy by conference" was not pleasing to the Secretary General. Diplomacy, he felt, was a job for specialists. He preferred the meetings of experts behind closed doors, meetings carefully prepared by advance negotiations and conducted without fanfare or publicity. And the tendency for the public figures of the day to try to settle complicated international problems during informal chats while they played golf or sat on the banks of a river struck Berthelot as the negation of diplomacy.

Although Poincaré began the process of building alliances with the new states of Central Europe, it was Philippe Berthelot who was responsible for much of France's postwar interest in these countries. Indeed, it appears that Berthelot was throughout the 1920's "the most

[55] Barthélmy, *Essai sur . . . le système des commissions*, pp. 266-267.
[56] Suarez, *Briand*, v, 127.   [57] Bréal, *Berthelot*, pp. 214-215.

consistent artisan" of the new alliance system which bound France to the states which had been created from the wreckage of the Hapsburg Monarchy.[58] His interest in Central and Eastern Europe, moreover, antedated the Peace Conference. During the war he had become convinced that the survival of the Austro-Hungarian Empire was a political impossibility and he had entered into negotiations with Central European statesmen, like Benes, who were trying to obtain political independence for their peoples. Thus, as early as January of 1917, when Woodrow Wilson asked the Allies to clarify their war aims, it was Berthelot who edited the reply which stated that one of France's major objectives was to secure the liberation of the Czechs.[59] At the Peace Conference Berthelot, as the sole French representative on the subcommission which considered the problem of the new states, worked assiduously in behalf of the Poles, the Czechs, and the Yugoslavs as well as of the other peoples who had claims against the defeated Powers. It was the French diplomat, for instance, who was largely responsible for the fact that the Poles were able to keep many of the portions of Upper Silesia which were still in dispute after the famous plebiscite, for he drew up the partition scheme which was eventually accepted by Lloyd George and the British Foreign Office. His work during the war and at the Conference in behalf of the Czechs was, it might be noted, always remembered by the leaders of that country. When in 1927 Berthelot paid a visit to Prague, he was given a particularly warm welcome by Czech officials, and, at a banquet in his honor, Benes paid glowing tribute to him for the assistance which he had given the Czechoslovakian cause before and after the Armistice.

Berthelot's interest in the new Central European states was, however, not simply the result of any passionate devotion to the Wilsonian principle of nationalities. Indeed, according to Paul Claudel, Berthelot always felt that the old Austro-Hungarian Empire, whatever its faults, had at least provided Central Europe with an economic and geographic unity which was sorely missed when the new states were created in its stead.[60] But at the same time he believed that these countries could and should be won as the friends of France because they would be valuable partners in the job of holding Germany in check. In other words, Berthelot, as a diplomat who believed in France's traditional policy of

[58] Bertrand de Jouvenal, *D'Une guerre à l'autre* (Paris, 1940), I, 213. For an extended though superficial discussion of Berthelot's interest in the new European states, see Allard, *Quai d'Orsay*, pp. 44 ff.

[59] Bréal, *Berthelot*, p. 218; Claudel, *Accompagnements*, pp. 199–200.

[60] Claudel, *Accompagnements*, p. 200.

having allies to the east of Germany and who hesitated to put full faith in the League, prized these new states as potential military allies who would help to keep Germany from attempting to rupture the Versailles settlement. Significantly, when in 1925 France came to an agreement with the Weimar Republic which supposedly settled the Franco-German frontier for all time, it was Berthelot who persuaded Briand that a French treaty of mutual assistance with Czechoslovakia should be made an integral part of the Locarno pacts.[61] Thus, even when he was engaged in promoting a Western European settlement, Berthelot thought also in terms of France's allies to the east and wished to include them as partners in the agreement.

Berthelot was not, of course, at the Quai d'Orsay during the occupation of the Ruhr. He was, however, opposed to Poincaré's scheme to collect reparations at the point of a bayonet. To his friend, Auguste Bréal, he wrote early in 1924 that ". . . the new year is not pleasant because it is always raining and the government remains strong. It is true that the franc is steadily declining, but the public believes that this is the result of the jealousy of the rest of the world and of a conspiracy by our former allies and not the consequence of the policies being followed. Everything is thus for the best."[62] In Berthelot's case there is no doubt that his views were colored by his personal dislike of Poincaré. It was, after all, the Minister of Foreign Affairs who had presided over the council which had suspended him, and as long as the Lorrainer remained as head of the government, there was no possible chance for Berthelot to return to the Quai d'Orsay.

However, Berthelot's opposition to the Ruhr occupation was not founded solely upon personal pique. Even at this early date he had decided that, somehow or other, Germany and France must manage to live together in the same European system. His ideas were not based upon any love for the German or upon the belief that reparations were wrong. He continued to be suspicious of German intentions even though he advocated reaching an understanding with the Weimar Republic—indeed, it was at Berthelot's instigation that in the late 1920's the successive French consul-generals at Cologne were specifically instructed to act not merely as commercial agents but also as political observers and to report their findings to the Quai d'Orsay.[63] Berthelot's desire for a Franco-German rapprochement was based rather upon what he believed was a realistic estimate of the situation. Germany, he felt, could not forever

[61] Allard, *Quai d'Orsay*, p. 46.   [62] Bréal, *Berthelot*, p. 205.
[63] *Commission d'enquête, Témoignages et documents*, II, 470.

be maintained in a position of inferiority; furthermore, when the defeated nation recovered, her political and military potential would far outweigh that of France. Would it not then be more intelligent, thought Berthelot, to attempt a rapprochement rather than to continue a policy of coercion?

Equally important in Berthelot's dislike for the Poincaré policy of the *main au collet* was the fact that he was convinced that France had been a victor in 1918 only because she had possessed allies at her side. As a matter of principle he opposed any policy, which like that of Poincaré, threatened to disrupt the Anglo-French entente and to place his country in the position of taking unilateral action which none of the other major powers would support. It was a basic point of Berthelot's diplomacy to maintain France's ties with England—during the war he had done much to improve relations with Great Britain, shortly afterwards he supported Briand's attempt to secure a Franco-British military and political alliance, and in 1934, just a few days before his death, he made a special trip to England to deliver a speech at a banquet promoting Anglo-French friendship. Thus, because the Poincaré program threatened the maintenance of the entente with England, Berthelot strongly disapproved of the occupation of the Ruhr and the attempt to keep Germany down by force.

As early as January of 1922, soon after his own removal from office, Berthelot wrote a letter to Briand in which he supported the policy of Briand, himself shortly to fall from power, to seek an alliance with England even to the extent of modifying the French stand on reparations. "Your logic remains intact," Berthelot wrote, "and the facts will soon show that without a firm Anglo-French entente we will encounter the gravest difficulties not only in our foreign policies but also in our domestic affairs as well."[64] Twelve months later, just two weeks after French troops had occupied the Ruhr, he again sent Briand a summary of his views on French foreign policy, and the opinions expressed in this letter contained the germ of Locarno two years before the event:

"It cannot be forgotten that if we are today the strongest and will remain so for another dozen years, in a period of from twenty to fifty years the weight of seventy million organized, hard-working men will end up by being heavier than that of thirty-eight million Frenchmen.

"If, then, we don't try to create a German republic hostile to war, we are doomed. So far, instead of gaining ground with German democratic opinion, we haven't ceased to stir up hatred of ourselves.

[64] Suarez, *Briand*, v, 408.

"Even admitting that we will succeed in making Germany yield by our pressure on the Ruhr, the policy which immediately follows should be very generous and should very possibly even sacrifice the very objectives of our action. However, I don't believe that any German government can yield now that the Anglo-Saxon world is more separated from us than it appears and that Italy is only waiting for the chance to declare herself against us."[65]

Aristide Briand shared many of these views. He, too, believed it necessary to try to work with Germany rather than against her and hoped to make the Weimar Republic a viable government. Like Berthelot he believed that, in pursuing this goal, France could not afford to disregard the attitude of Great Britain. It was upon such assumptions that Locarno was founded. And it was also upon these same assumptions that Briand and Berthelot began to work together in 1925.

Despite certain differences of approach and of opinion the combination of Briand and Berthelot appears to have been a successful working arrangement in the years from 1925 to 1932. To be sure, the Foreign Minister probably never shared his deepest thoughts with his Secretary General. What went on at Thoiry, when Briand and Stresemann dreamed beautiful dreams of future Franco-German cooperation, was apparently never fully revealed to Berthelot.[66] And the latter, as noted, had less confidence than his chief in the League. But on the whole their seven-year collaboration seems to have been successful. Unlike the 1930's, when Alexis Léger assumed Berthelot's position, the Briand-Berthelot period was not a time during which the Secretary General felt that he was being called upon to execute policies with which he was in fundamental disagreement. And parenthetically, it might be noted—as the chapter on Léger will indicate[67]—that Léger himself, then serving as Briand's *chef du cabinet*, regarded his years at the Quai d'Orsay immediately after Locarno as the happiest of his career and felt that during this period the views of the responsible political leaders harmonized with his own.

Berthelot regarded his own association with Briand as a partnership in which he provided the essential facts and wrote many of the basic state papers, while the Foreign Minister, with his ease and facility as a speaker, won the support of the Chambers and of the public. The two men, in a real sense, complemented each other—it was Berthelot, for instance, who conducted the intricate diplomatic preliminaries which led

[65] *ibid.*, p. 429.   [66] Géraud, "Diplomacy Old and New," p. 410.
[67] See below, Chapter 12, §1.

[78]

to Locarno,[68] while it was Briand who gained the approval of the French public with his speeches. Berthelot never ceased to marvel at the way his chief, even though unprepared, could grasp the essentials of any given problem within a matter of moments and then deliver a speech in which he appeared to possess knowledge that resulted from years of study. The difference between Poincaré and Briand, he is supposed to have remarked with his customary cynicism, was that "The one knows everything but understands nothing; the other knows nothing but understands everything."[69]

III

It is not yet possible, on the basis of the evidence available, to write more than a tentative estimate of Philippe Berthelot as a diplomat. What makes the task difficult is the fact that for the crucial years after 1925 there is but little information at hand. It is at least possible to trace the main lines of Berthelot's thought up to that point: his faith in established diplomatic practices, his belief in the Anglo-French entente, his desire for Franco-German rapprochement and his insistence upon Continental alliances. But, paradoxically, we know the least about Berthelot in the years after Locarno when he was acting as Briand's collaborator and when many of the policies which he had himself previously advocated were now the policies of the French government. To be sure, since he returned to the Quai d'Orsay just at the moment when the French were making an abrupt switch to the line which he had recommended and since he was essentially "Briand's man," it is logical to assume that he agreed with the program that Briand put into effect during his long stay at the Foreign Ministry. But any final estimate of Berthelot will have to wait until we know in some detail how he reacted to the specific events and policies of those years—was he, for instance, a convinced believer in the Briand approach or was he perhaps a traditional diplomatist who followed Briand hoping only that the Foreign Minister's policies would achieve a part of his goals? And since the Secretary General destroyed his personal papers and left no memoirs, the answers, unfortunately, may always be tentative.

There is, however, almost unanimous agreement on one point: that Berthelot was particularly adept and successful in conducting diplomatic negotiations whatever their difficulty or complexity. His grasp of detail and his encyclopedic memory made him an exceptionally able negotiator.

[68] Paul-Boncour, *Entre deux guerres*, II, 161.
[69] There are many versions of this remark, see Suarez, *Briand*, v, 128.

He once surprised Lord Curzon by conducting an entire meeting without either notes or aides while the British Foreign Secretary, himself no mean diplomatist, had felt it necessary to come well supplied with both documents and assistants. Nearly all of Berthelot's contemporaries—even those who personally disliked him—were agreed on his competence. Lord Hardinge, who regarded Berthelot as no friend of Britain, was of the opinion when Berthelot was removed from office in 1922 that "France could not long dispense with the services of such a very able and remarkable man."[70] And even Poincaré, when he heard that Dutasta and not Berthelot was to be the chief French negotiator at the Peace Conference, noted in his diary that the latter would certainly have fulfilled the assignment with greater competence.[71] Similarly a friend like Paul-Boncour, himself a Foreign Minister in the interwar years, wrote of Berthelot's "unequaled mastery" of the art of diplomacy; Harold Nicolson, whose familiar criticism of the Peace Conference emphasized the lack of organization, maintained that the negotiations would have proceeded far more smoothly had Berthelot been in charge; and Lloyd George, with whom it was never easy to associate, indicated that the French Secretary General ". . . was a good man to do business with because he understood that agreement meant a comprehension of what the other side were after and a readiness to concede to their point of view details which did not give away the substance of one's own objective."[72]

But was Berthelot more than just a skilled negotiator? Even his lifelong friend, Paul Claudel, wrote that there was little point in examining his general ideas or his guiding theories, for the Secretary General's real forte was in the conduct of the everyday, practical details of diplomacy. And Claudel went on to observe that throughout his life Berthelot had loved to gamble, first at cards, later at dominoes. His patience, his attention, and his skills, Claudel thought, may well have been the result, at least in part, of these interests: "Who knows if these games didn't serve as the veritable *Kriegsspiel* of the diplomat?"[73] But Claudel's estimate leaves the faint suspicion that Berthelot, who loved to operate behind the scenes, was perhaps a skillful manipulator who may well at times have played the diplomatic game for its own sake, *pour le sport* as it were, without sufficient realization of the con-

[70] Hardinge, *Old Diplomacy*, pp. 251-252.

[71] Poincaré, *Au Service*, X, 459.

[72] Paul-Boncour, *Entre deux guerres*, II, 339; Harold Nicolson, *Peacemaking, 1919* (New York, 1939), pp. 119-120; David Lloyd George, *The Truth about the Peace Treaties* (London, 1938), II, 1104.

[73] Claudel, *Accompagnements*, pp. 186-187.

sequences. Such a verdict, of course, without documentation cannot be proven, but whoever attempts a final estimate of Berthelot will at least have to consider this facet of his make-up.

In estimating the worth of Berthelot's policies it is important to remember that he resumed his post at the Foreign Office just at the point when French foreign policy was switching from one tactic to another. In the preceding three years the French under Poincaré had tried to conduct an independent policy—that is, to handle Germany on their own terms without regard for the views of their wartime allies. This program had, for a variety of reasons, become impossible and the French had caved in. At home there was rising discontent because the Ruhr occupation had led to the famous and disastrous "fall of the franc," and Poincaré's political opponents, though for some time slow to make use of this situation, eventually claimed that his foreign policies had provoked the French financial plight. At the same time both Great Britain and the United States exerted tremendous pressure upon France to come to a final and viable settlement with Germany, above all to put an end to the Ruhr occupation and to settle the troubled reparations question. Even Poincaré, although he had forced Germany to agree to full compliance with his policy and, literally, had the Germans on the run, had felt it necessary to yield to this pressure; considerably before the elections of 1924 he agreed to the meeting of what became the Dawes commission. It was, of course, the electoral victory of the left in 1924—ultimately bringing Berthelot and Briand to the Quai d'Orsay—which made it thenceforth impossible to continue the Poincaré foreign policy. And it was under these circumstances and after these events that the Locarno accords were reached and the opportunity presented to carry out the policy of Franco-German rapprochement and Anglo-French cooperation that Berthelot had advocated since at least 1922.

Locarno, however, whatever the insights of its creators, no longer appears the brightest page in the diplomatic history of the 1920's. Some if not all of the bloom is off the rose. Before the second world war, writers frequently referred to the Locarno era as the "years of hope"; today they seem more likely to have been "years of illusion." For—and there are innumerable reasons, ranging from the premature death of Stresemann to the coming of the world depression, which we cannot pause to explore—Locarno never led to a permanent settlement of Franco-German difficulties or established the bases of a lasting reconciliation. If Locarno and the various decisions which followed it left many Frenchmen dissatisfied, there were also on the other side of the Rhine, as the memoirs of Dirksen and Weizsäcker bear more than adequate testimony, many more Germans who likewise remained unconvinced.

More important, however, is the fact that Locarno, in essence, meant that France had knuckled under to Great Britain. She had, by yielding to the British demand to evacuate the Ruhr and by bringing in the British as guarantors of the Franco-German frontier, completely abandoned any hope of an independent policy or of any return to it. Furthermore, immediately afterwards the British, as well as the supposedly isolationist Americans, began to exert full pressure on the French to agree to disarmament conferences. The British argued at great length that, since the French now had the security pact which they had been clamoring for since Versailles, the time had now come to investigate the chances of reducing armaments, in particular, French armaments. All of this, in the setting of the 1920's, appeared to be Anglo-French cooperation or collaboration, but it really boiled down to French subservience to the wishes of England. The fact is that, after the end of the Ruhr experiment and after the signing of the Locarno pacts, the French never again would act alone; they had, indeed, lost a large part of their nerve, had caved in before English pressure and thereafter followed closely behind a British lion whose roar was frequently not very loud. Thus Berthelot's program of close Anglo-French cooperation, in other times and in other circumstances, was to make French policy a prisoner of the British. It was, indeed, a first and important step on the road to Munich.

It can, of course, be argued that Berthelot and other French diplomats tried to avoid this pitfall by keeping France's eastern alliances as the other theme of their foreign policy. But here again a number of difficulties were involved. In the first place, the British would never associate themselves with this program. They would never agree to an "Eastern Locarno" or permit themselves to be drawn in as even silent partners in France's continental alliance system. In Austen Chamberlain's paraphrase of Bismarck, "For the Polish Corridor, no British government ever will or ever can risk the bones of a British grenadier." England's idea of European—and French—security stopped with the Rhine, and what happened in Central or Eastern Europe involved faraway countries with which Britain was little concerned. Furthermore, and this is of course a story in itself, France's Eastern alliances were themselves insufficient. Individually the nations were weak, and they never learned, despite French prompting, to work together; no military implementation of the French alliances was ever worked out, and the defensively-oriented French army, after the mid-1920's, would have been of little value to these allies. Above all, the French alliance system had been built up in an era which assumed not only German disarmament but also the demilitarization of the Rhineland. When Hitler built up his armed forces and moved into the Rhineland, France's Eastern system almost overnight became valueless.

Perhaps, though, no French foreign policy could have been long successful. Many of France's difficulties in the 1920's appear in retrospect to have been almost inevitable. French power after the first world war was after all essentially artificial; it depended not only upon the continuing weakness of Germany but also upon the exclusion of Russia from European affairs. Certainly French hegemony could not long withstand the recovery of those states. Moreover, any attempt to conciliate Germany was fraught with unknown perils and imponderables almost beyond measure. It was impossible for France to enlist Britain as an ally in the East; on the other hand it was impossible to get along without England. But to follow her meant that French ties with Central Europe were increasingly worthless, while to rely on continental allies alone was to have no real strength. French foreign policy, in short, whether following the strategy of a Poincaré, a Briand or a Berthelot was throughout the 1920's caught on the horns of a dilemma for which there was no simple solution, and for which, quite possibly, there was none at all.

Perhaps the virtue of Philippe Berthelot was simply that he was always conscious of this dilemma and that he was not merely a doctrinaire advocate of Anglo-French collaboration or rapprochement with Germany. He was, it seems, not merely another Holstein who failed to realize that the policies which he had long advocated would, in turn, create new difficulties when they were put into operation. The clue to this—and it is admittedly only a clue—is furnished by the testimony of Paul Claudel. If Claudel is correct, Philippe Berthelot put the Locarno program into effect and between 1925 and 1932 went along with Briand not so much because he believed in the policy but simply because he could envisage no alternatives. Though he had himself recommended the course which led to Locarno and had strongly believed in working closely with Britain and in trying to conciliate Germany, he very quickly realized, once this strategy was attempted, that it was no panacea and that it led to new and grave difficulties for which no solution was in sight. Thus, although Berthelot implemented the policies which followed Locarno, he did so with no confidence and solely because his own analysis indicated that there were no alternatives. Moreover, under the impact of this bitter realization—and here we have an indication of why it is so difficult to learn much about the Berthelot of these later years—he isolated himself more and more in the accomplishment of his purely routine, administrative tasks.[74] Thus, after nearly thirty years of guiding French foreign policy, Berthelot recognized the impasse which confronted his nation, and, finding that the program which he himself had recommended was far from a complete success, took refuge in the routine of the Quai d'Orsay.

IV

Philippe Berthelot, after his retirement, lived long enough to witness the first signs of the collapse of the security system which he had tried to construct. With an increasingly bitter awareness, he understood that the structure of the postwar world was coming apart at the seams. And he feared that no one could solve the deepening crisis.

During the first world war Berthelot had been famous for his optimism. Even in the darkest days of 1917 he had never been without hope. Foreign diplomats, in need of consolation, frequently sought him out when they wanted a cheering word. But in the 1930's Berthelot was unnerved. Declining health may have deepened his natural skepticism. Possibly, too, the man who believed himself indispensable naturally felt that those who succeeded him were incapable of continuing the diplomatic struggle. But, in any event, those who had known him all their lives and who saw him in the months before his death in November of 1934 were struck by the pessimism with which Berthelot regarded the future.

Wladimir d'Ormesson, himself a one-time diplomat and writer for Parisian dailies, remembered that in his last interview with Berthelot, the former Secretary General's face was grave as he spoke cruel words about the pettiness of the politicians who were throwing away French security. d'Ormesson felt that Berthelot actually suffered to see what he regarded as his life's achievements being compromised amid the domestic turmoil in France.[75] Upon hearing of the assassination of Alexander of Yugoslavia, Berthelot wrote to a lifelong friend, "Destiny is against France. The death of the king of Yugoslavia annuls the only really good card in our game." And a little later: "Life more and more imitates the movies, and the law of the gangsters is being imposed everywhere. The

[74] On Berthelot's loss of faith in Locarno and his increasing tendency to turn inwards the only reference is Claudel, *Accompagnements*, p. 203.
[75] d'Ormesson in *Le Figaro*, November 23, 1934.

brigands have more energy than the honest men. Meanness, idiocy and dishonesty are rampant."[76]

Events after 1934 were to prove Berthelot was right—the gangsters and brigands did have more energy than the honest men. Thus Philippe Berthelot, in his last days, joined the ranks of the many clairvoyant European diplomats who sensed the gathering of the storm but who knew themselves powerless to avert its course.

[76] Both cited in Dumont-Wilden, in *Revue Bleue*, LXXV, 618.

3

Sweden: The Diplomacy of Östen Undén

BY ERIK LÖNNROTH

[THE CONGRESS OF VIENNA was the first international body to distinguish formally between Great Powers and lesser powers. The distinction was sharply challenged at the time and has been frequently debated since;* but, however insecure its legal basis may be, it has without a doubt been validated by international practice over the course of the years. One of the most notable—and, in the eyes of many thoughtful students, most fateful—developments of the nineteenth century was the increasing domination of European politics by the five states which were generally recognized as Great Powers: Great Britain, France, Germany, Austria-Hungary, and Russia; and it was clear, even before the coming of the first world war had helped to prove it, that the lesser states had lost that ability to exert a moderating and balancing influence in international affairs which they had possessed and exerted in earlier centuries.

For a brief period after the first world war, it appeared that this development might be checked, or even reversed. At the Peace Conference at Paris, a large number of new states were created which were not, perhaps, Powers of the first rank, but some of which—Poland, for instance, or Czechoslovakia—did not seem to be markedly inferior in strength to self-styled Great Powers like Italy or doubtful quantities like revolutionary Russia.[1] Moreover, the principle of equality of all states was now vigorously asserted, and a new international body, the League of Nations, was established to give it effective expression. In the decade that followed, the newly created states, and the lesser Powers

---

* At Vienna, the representative of Holland remarked that "of this newly invented term, 'the Great Powers,' he understood neither the precise meaning nor the intention." C. H. Hazen, "Le Congrès de Vienne," *Revue des études napoléoniennes,* xv (1919), 69. See also Federico Chabod, *Storia della politica estera italiana dal 1870 al 1896: I. Le premesse* (Bari, 1951), 154 and notes.

[1] See Arnold Toynbee, *The World after the Peace Conference* (London, 1925); and, as an introduction to the problems of the Scandinavian countries, *Survey of International Affairs, 1939-1946: The World in March 1939* (London, 1952), pp. 157-162.

in general, had a natural interest in the organization and development of the League, for it seemed to offer them both an assurance that their voices would not be unheard when questions of European importance were being determined and a possible means of restraining the dangerous ambitions, and appeasing the dangerous passions, of their greater neighbors.

The hopes entertained with regard to the League were not, in the end, realized; it succumbed to the domination of the Great Powers, and its activities and purposes were shaped in accordance with their desires. It would be misleading, however, to see the story of the League as a tragedy in which the vices of the Great Powers triumphed over the virtues of the lesser. For the small Powers too had special interests which restricted and determined their actions at Geneva. They could no more follow a course of pure idealism or internationalism than could the Great Powers. They too, in formulating policy, had to yield to the dictates of their national tradition and the requirements of their national security.

One of the most instructive examples of the conflict between internationalism and national interest, as it affected the smaller Powers, is the so-called League crisis of 1926,[2] a crisis which arose when the question of Germany's entry into the League precipitated a general scramble for seats on the Council and released animosities which threatened to rip the Covenant asunder. The decision of the Swedish government to sacrifice Sweden's seat in the interests of general pacification seems to offer one of the most shining examples of an altruistic policy which can be found in the 1920's.[3] As this chapter reveals, closer analysis indicates that Sweden's conduct in this affair was always guided by a careful regard for the requirements of national interest, and provides an instructive illustration of the limits within which the lesser Powers were confined in their support of the new world organization. *The Editors.*]

I

During the first world war, Sweden was transformed from a constitutional monarchy to a full parliamentary democracy. The change had

[2] A brief account will be found in F. P. Walters, *A History of the League of Nations* (2 volumes, London, 1952), I, 316-327. See also G. Scelle, *Une crise de la Société des Nations* (Paris, 1927); and Chapter I, §IV above.

[3] An English journalist wrote in 1926: "It is important to understand that Sweden's concern was for the League only and that, not for the first time, she set aside all claims of separate interests for the sake of that concern." H. M. Swanwick, "Anarchy at Geneva," *Foreign Affairs* (London), VII (1925-1926), 286.

an immediate impact on the course of Swedish foreign policy, and was reflected in the abandonment of a policy which, while officially neutral, had been somewhat pro-German in tendency, in favor of a policy based upon the League of Nations.

The reality behind the constitutional transformation was an electoral reform which took place in 1918 and which completely changed the character of the first chamber or Senate of the Swedish *Riksdag*. In contrast to the second chamber, which was elected by universal and equal suffrage, the Senate had before 1918 been elected by a voting system in which the right to vote was dependent on the voter's economic status. The Conservatives, who had a large minority in the second chamber, could, under this system, always be sure of a majority in the first chamber and were thus able to check their Liberal and Social Democratic opponents. After the reform of the first chamber in 1918, however, the Conservatives could form no government without the support of the Liberals; and it became impossible to carry out a foreign policy that was not in accord with public opinion as expressed in the *Riksdag*.

The interwar years represent the highpoint of parliamentary power in Swedish history. During the second world war, a renewed concentration of power in the hands of the Executive was to take place and was, especially in the sphere of foreign policy, to limit public debate and parliamentary influence again. But this development was not foreseen, and would have seemed quite unlikely, during the 1920's and early 1930's when Sweden was generally ruled by weak minority governments which had no strong control over parliament as a whole. It is symptomatic of the influence of the parliament on foreign policy that, in 1921, a committee of the *Riksdag* was created for the purpose of discussing foreign affairs with the King and the government. Though this committee never seriously interfered with the actions of the government, its existence clearly demonstrated the claim of the *Riksdag* to control over Sweden's foreign policy. Between 1919 and 1939, no Swedish Foreign Minister dared to disregard the views of the parliamentary majority—with one exception. In 1923, the Conservative Foreign Minister Hederstierna made a speech recommending an alliance with Finland, but the newspapers expressed such strong opposition to the suggestion that he was forced to resign a few days later.

In the period between 1919 and 1932, there was little stability in Swedish politics; governments changed every two years and sometimes at shorter intervals. Alternating coalitions of Liberals, Conservatives, and Social Democrats succeeded each other and it was not until after 1932, when the Social Democrats began their cooperation with the Farmer's party, that there was greater stability. Nevertheless, even in the 1920's, during the period of greatest instability in domestic policy, Sweden's foreign policy kept a steady course. This can partly be explained by the fact that no strong partisan feelings were aroused by the issues of foreign policy once the conservative line of policy had been abandoned; although it might have been expected that the ideological differences of the parties would find some reflection in foreign policy, this was very seldom the case. During the interwar years, most of the Swedish Foreign Ministers were prominent lawyers, and party divergences were overbalanced by professional conformity in their approach to foreign affairs. Moreover, the departmental tradition in the Foreign Office seems to have been very strong.

The Swedish diplomats of the 1920's were professionally trained officials recruited from upper-class families; and the key posts in Paris, London, Berlin, Moscow, and Rome were still held by members of the nobility. Some of the diplomatic representatives had risen to prominence in party politics. Baron Palmstierna, the Minister in London, had been Minister of Foreign Affairs in the first Social Democratic cabinet; Count Ehrensvaerd in Paris had held the same post in a prewar Liberal cabinet; and Baron Ramel in Berlin was to serve as Foreign Minister for the Liberals in the early 1930's. But even if they owed their positions to their connections with political parties, they were aristocrats and had the same background as the other Swedish representatives abroad. The diplomats in the field and the staff of the Foreign Office in Stockholm formed a close unit, with the Cabinet Secretary—i.e. the permanent secretary of the Foreign Office—and the head of the Political Bureau as key figures. The diplomats were responsible for gathering the news about political developments in the outside world which touched on Sweden's interests and for its analysis and interpretation. In the conduct of Swedish foreign policy, therefore, the Foreign Minister and the government could rely on the work done by men who were all guided by the same professional "esprit de corps"; and the Foreign Office, with its officials at home and abroad, thus constituted a collective power of considerable importance. Its influence was not much mentioned in the political discussions of the day, but it can be seen in the continuity of Swedish foreign policy in this period, and, occasionally, in differences of opinion between the Foreign Minister on the one hand and his Cabinet colleagues on the other.

II

The most outstanding figure among the Swedish Foreign Ministers of the interwar period was Östen Undén. Born in 1886, he had been appointed to the chair of Civil Law at the University of Uppsala in 1917. When he had been an undergraduate at Lund University, he had joined the Social Democratic party. In 1917, when for the first time, the Social Democrats entered the government in a coalition with the Liberals, the young professor became a member of this coalition Cabinet. In 1920 when the first purely Social Democratic government was formed, Undén became Minister of Justice; and, in the Cabinets of 1924-1926, he served as Minister of Foreign Affairs, first under Prime Minister Hjalmar Branting and, after Branting's death in 1925, under Richard Sandler.

Undén had worked for the Foreign Office as an expert on international law from 1921 to 1924, and consequently was more the specialist than the politician when he became Foreign Minister. He had, indeed, never been a member of the *Riksdag* before he appeared there as a member of the Cabinet. He was a respected, but not a very popular, political personality; his way of thinking, his speech and general behavior were precise and rather formal. His legal education, combined with a certain natural stiffness and shyness, tended to keep others at a distance. On the other hand, his ability and will power enabled him to become a strong head of his department and to assert his influence within the government as the expert on foreign policy. By the parties and press of the opposition who tended to think of him as a rigid, somewhat ineffectual doctrinaire, he was on the whole underestimated.

In the 1920's, the activity of a Swedish Foreign Minister centered on the League of Nations which Sweden had joined in 1920. Two years later, Sweden had been elected member of the Council of the League, where she was given an opportunity to act in her natural role as the leading member of a group of small states, chiefly ex-neutrals, who worked to form a counterweight against the dominating influence of the Great Powers. Within this group, the three Scandinavian countries constituted a natural inner circle by virtue of their geographical proximity, their close cultural relations and linguistic kinship, and their common interest in peace and in moderating European tensions. There was close cooperation among them. They held common views on the chief issues discussed at Geneva; and Sweden, in her position as member of the Council, acted as their spokesman.

From the outset, the Scandinavian countries opposed the use of mili-

tary sanctions by the League. In the early 1920's, the Swedish government stated frequently that, considering the weakness of the League
structure, the employment of military sanctions would be a risky adventure. In the Swedish view, the victors of the first world war were now
the leading Powers in the League, and the use of military sanctions would
involve sacrifices for a system of security that these Powers had established but that Sweden regarded as by no means perfect. The Swedish
alternative to sanctions was compulsory arbitration in international conflicts, an alternative that reflected a belief that arbitration alone could
guarantee real impartiality in international conflicts, and which corresponded to that faith in the paramount importance of law which was
deeply rooted in the Swedish national tradition. Undén, the former law
professor, was a born champion of this cause; and during the League
Assembly of 1925, he formally proposed that compulsory arbitration be
accepted as a basic principle of League activity. The failure of the Geneva
Protocol had stimulated search for other means to strengthen the efficiency of the League, and the committee in which Undén's suggestion
was discussed showed great interest in his proposal, although the Assembly, in its resolution of September 25, 1925, confined itself to a recommendation in its favor.

The Swedish prescription for the solution of international disputes
obtained a significant success in the Mosul question.[4] In the solution of
this problem, Sweden played a leading role; and the Swedish member
of the Council acted as *rapporteur* during the hearings. The actual issue
here was the drawing of a frontier between Iraq and Turkey, but since
Great Britain championed Iraq's cause, Britain and Turkey were the real
antagonists. Branting, the Swedish delegate, was responsible for the
proposal to invite Turkey to participate in the meetings of the Council
in which the Mosul question was to be discussed, and his motion, which
was accepted, can be regarded as providing the basis for the successful
solution of the conflict. Branting also drew the provisional demarcation
line, the so-called Brussels line, which was accepted by both parties and
prevented military clashes during the negotiations.

After Branting's death, Undén succeeded him as *rapporteur*. Experts,
meanwhile, had worked out a solution stipulating that all territory south
of the Brussels line should go to Iraq, provided that Iraq, for the purpose of protection of the minorities, would remain a British mandate.
Britain and Iraq agreed to this solution, but Turkey refused and
declared that the Council of the League was not competent to make

[4] On this problem see Walters, *History of the League*, I, 305-310.

a decision. The Swedish Foreign Ministry, where the issue had been thoroughly discussed, recommended a solution *ex aequo et bono*. After Undén's attempts to persuade the Turks to accept the mediation of the Council had failed, he asked the Permanent Court to rule on the nature of the powers which the Council could exercise. The ruling of the Court established the competence of the Council and the Council subsequently gave a decision in agreement with the recommendation of the experts. The caution and precision with which Undén established the legal rights of the Council in this case was an important factor in the peaceful outcome of the conflict and in the strengthening of the idea of arbitration.

III

The final months of the Mosul conflict saw the emergence of another issue, which was of much more vital importance to the League and in which all the great European Powers and the entire European balance of power was involved. Germany's entry into the League and her claim to a seat on the Council inaugurated a thoroughgoing discussion of the whole problem of Council membership and reorganization. Here again Sweden played a prominent role; and it may be said that Undén's handling of this problem represents his main achievement as Foreign Minister. Under his direction, Sweden appeared as a star performer in the Geneva theatre. In the action which Sweden undertook, idealistic internationalism and national interest worked hand in hand and spurred each other to action.

On October 16, 1925, the Treaty of Locarno was signed. Germany was accepted as a member of the European family of states, in return for which she renounced all claims to a revision of her western boundary as laid down in the Treaty of Versailles. Germany, however, did not guarantee her eastern boundaries; her claims to a revision of the Polish frontier, especially with respect to the so-called Polish corridor between Eastern Prussia and the Reich, remained. In recognition of this, France tried to compensate her Polish ally by means of a guarantee against German aggression, but the British government gave no promises to the eastern allies of France, and, because of this, Poland especially could be regarded as the injured party in what was otherwise regarded as a notable peace settlement.

Locarno was only the first step on Germany's way to the full recognition of her title as Great Power. She had now to enter the League of Nations and to receive a permanent seat on the League Council. There could be no doubt that this second move would accentuate Poland's embarrassment. Could Poland and her powerful ally France permit these developments without making a countermove to offset Germany's growing influence? And, if they made such a countermove, would it not weaken Germany's willingness to adopt a policy of international collaboration? In the German *Reichstag*, the Nationalists, the Nazis, and the Communists had voted against the ratification of the Locarno Treaty, and there was considerable popular opposition to it. Any serious blow to Stresemann's policy of understanding with the West might well give the upper hand to the opposition parties.[5]

Sweden had one central interest in the developments on the international scene: pacification of the Baltic. The tension between Germany and France reached into this area: Poland was the ally of France, and had in the early 1920's sought to extend its influence to the north by trying to conclude an alliance with Finland, a development most unattractive to the Swedes. Germany and the Soviet Union, on the other hand, were linked by the Treaty of Rapallo. Together with Denmark, Sweden controlled the entrance to the Baltic, but in a war between the contending Powers in which one of them claimed passage through Öresund, Sweden and Denmark might become involved in a major conflict. If, on the other hand, Germany entered the League of Nations and could be won for peaceful cooperation with the Western Powers, the Rapallo front would be split, and the tension in the Baltic area considerably relieved. In the fall of 1925, things seemed to hang in the balance; the Swedish Foreign Office was receiving indications that Russia, dissatisfied with Germany's moves towards the Western Powers, was doing her best to stir up German opposition. The democratic Weimar Republic was popular in Sweden, and the restoration of Germany's international position was regarded as a question of justice and common sense. But the calculations of the Swedish Foreign Office were not determined by sentimental considerations. The line which Swedish foreign policy pursued was dictated by her position as a small neutral Power in the Baltic area, and by the wish to strengthen the true spirit of peace and collaboration in the League of Nations.

On November 4, 1925, the Polish plenipotentiary in Stockholm asked for Undén's views concerning an eventual Polish claim to a seat on the League Council. A permanent seat, Undén answered, was hardly possible. He even doubted the desirability of a nonpermanent seat; this would be in the interest neither of Poland nor of other countries, because

---

[5] See Gustav Stresemann, *His Diaries, Letters and Papers*, edited and translated by Eric Sutton (New York, 1937), II, 505-507.

a simultaneous entry of Germany and Poland into the Council would involve the risk of serious friction between these two Powers.

Two weeks later, on November 21, the German plenipotentiary came to Undén and expressed his concern about rumors of a Spanish claim to a permanent seat, and referred to reports that the Spanish government would make this a condition of her consent to Germany's membership in the Council. Undén was seriously disturbed by this information and, in December, decided to discuss the matter with the British Foreign Secretary, Austen Chamberlain.[6] Chamberlain informed him that the British government had decided to support the Spanish claim, but had not yet made up its mind how to handle the Polish case. Chamberlain's words, however, seemed to suggest that he personally had no objections to the Polish aspirations. Undén was so anxious to change Chamberlain's views about the Polish case that he expressed exaggerated hopes of Polish moderation, but he did not convince Chamberlain, who remained skeptical.

Undén seemed to be working wholeheartedly in the German interest, with the idea of giving Germany a seat on the League Council and refusing entry to that body to any other Power. The line of policy which he pursued in this regard had been previously formulated in agreement with all the Scandinavian Powers and was based on the principle that only really Great Powers should have permanent seats, the temporary seats circulating among the other nations. This program was inspired by the idea of making impossible the formation of permanent combinations of satellite Powers within the Council. But, in this fight for principle, Undén was spurred on by interests of a more concrete nature; the entire Locarno policy seemed to him endangered and he wanted to keep Germany on the course of cooperation with the West. To gain these aims, Undén mobilized all the resources of Swedish diplomacy.

On January 21, 1926, the Swedish Foreign Minister directed an appeal to the governments of Norway, Denmark, the Netherlands, Finland, Switzerland, and Belgium. Undén explained that probably Spain, and possibly Poland, would claim permanent seats on the League Council; and that Spain had already been assured of British support. Compliance with the aspirations of these states would, however, endanger the fundamental principles which determined the distribution of permanent and nonpermanent seats on the Council. The Swedish view was that, in addition to those Great Powers who already held permanent seats, there were only three Powers who could justly claim permanent seats, namely Ger-

---

[6] For Chamberlain's attitude, see Walters, *History of the League*, I, 317.

many, Russia, and the United States. At the coming meeting of the Council, therefore, Sweden was inclined to oppose claims from any other Power. Undén asked whether the governments to which he addressed his appeal could be counted upon to join Sweden in this attitude.

The various governments had answered by February 8. Norway, Finland, and Switzerland expressed agreement with the Swedish position without reservation. Denmark also accepted the Swedish point of view, but was skeptical about the outcome of the projected action; these doubts were influenced by the fact that Denmark possessed information about additional claims: namely, claims of Brazil to a permanent seat. The Belgian government was willing to join Sweden, but Paul Hymans, the Belgian delegate at Geneva, had little hope that the small Powers could hold out if the Great Powers agreed on a definite line of policy. The Dutch government shared Sweden's views about the undesirability of enlarging the Council, but had not yet decided whether to take a stand or to declare itself "disinterested."

As a result of Undén's appeal, therefore, he was in a position, in presenting the Swedish view on the organization of the Council, to act as spokesman for the group of small Powers. But because he acted on the basis of principle, he was forced to deal with the politically innocuous claims of Spain and Brazil on the same level as with the highly significant and explosive claim of Poland. Nevertheless, from now on, Sweden was bound by the principle which Undén had enunciated.

The outcome of the question depended essentially on Great Britain, who held the key position; and Sweden made her main diplomatic efforts in London. The task of dissuading Austen Chamberlain from supporting the Polish claim was given to Baron Palmstierna, the Minister in London. Palmstierna had a personal interest in this question because he was in full sympathy with Undén, who had succeeded him as Foreign Minister in a Social Democratic government, and he went about his task with commendable energy. Palmstierna was in close touch with those groups in England who shared the Swedish opposition to an enlargement of the Council; in particular, he sought the advice of Ramsay MacDonald. The minister was fully aware that opposition against Chamberlain in this question was strong in Britain, and was shared even by members of the Baldwin Cabinet. Palmstierna set his hopes on the combination of the two Social Democratic Foreign Ministers, Undén of Sweden and Vandervelde of Belgium, with the Labor party leader MacDonald. Joint action by Belgium and Sweden, he believed, might stop the project which had by now been submitted to the League Council; and his reports to Stockholm encouraged the Swedish government to put up a fight in the Council. Throughout the League crisis, Palmstierna exerted great influence on the course of Swedish policy, particularly when, in February 1926, a change in Chamberlain's formerly announced position seemed to justify his earlier optimistic evaluation of the situation. At that time Chamberlain seemed willing to delay decision over the Spanish claim and stated that the British government had made no commitments with regard to the claims of Poland and Brazil. It thus appeared, temporarily, that the Swedish attitude corresponded to Britain's real intentions.

This view was shared by the German Foreign Minister, Stresemann, who was in constant contact with Undén, whom he tried to make a whole-hearted champion of Germany's interests within the League and on the Council. Stresemann actually claimed that the British government desired Sweden to take responsibility for opposing all claims for additional seats on the Council, with the exception of that of Germany. This argument may have affected Undén, although he tried to keep somewhat aloof from Germany and emphasized the independence of Swedish policy. It was not easy to do this, given the nature of Undén's instructions. For these directed him unequivocally to support the German claim to a seat, while opposing any further enlargement of the Council. In drawing up these instructions, the Swedish government seem not to have realized how far they were sticking their necks out and how exposed Sweden's position was really to be.

Their main error of judgment lay in their analysis of Chamberlain's attitude. In moderating his previous position, the British Foreign Secretary seems to have been motivated by a desire to counter any German threat to abandon the League of Nations and the Locarno policy. He apparently feared that, if Germany made out of this issue a question of prestige, any compromise between the German and the Franco-Polish interests would become impossible. He was perfectly willing, therefore, that Sweden should come forth as the chief opponent of the Polish claim, for the dispute then became one of principle, rather than an issue of national prestige and political rivalry; and it was in Britain's interest to keep the discussion on a somewhat abstract level. But, in taking an uncompromising line of opposition to the Polish claim, Sweden seemed to be acting for Germany, which threw doubts upon her true motives.

In the first days of March 1926, therefore, rumors began to spread that Chamberlain had changed front again and was now preparing a compromise. Simultaneously, the Polish government, which had been very critical of Sweden's position, suddenly adopted a different tone and expressed understanding and sympathy for the Swedish attitude.

Undén found himself in Geneva in a very difficult situation. His first task was to explain that Sweden was not acting on behalf of Germany but was following an independent line. But Undén was isolated. Vandervelde informed him that, if the question of the enlargement of the Council led to a showdown, Belgium could not vote against France and Britain. With the exception of Germany, which was still debarred from the League, no other Power shared Sweden's flat refusal to consider any compromise.

When Brazil and Spain presented their claims for permanent seats on the Council, Undén resisted strongly and remained firm even when Chamberlain attempted to influence him to take a less uncompromising line. Then Spain gave way, and the Brazilian delegate consented to ask for new instructions from home. On March 12, then, Undén seemed to have won out and to have prevented the enlargement of the Council. The true crisis came, however, when Vandervelde proposed the establishment of a new, temporary seat for Poland. This suggestion could not be reconciled with Unden's instructions or with the German point of view; but Sweden and Germany had now been placed in a most awkward position. If they remained adamant, they would appear to be the only obstacles to an agreement, for all the other Powers were willing to make concessions. Under the influence of representations by Vandervelde, Undén began to search for a way out of the dilemma. He asked Prime Minister Richard Sandler about the possibility of new instructions; he suggested a plan, which he had already mentioned in January to the Polish Minister in Stockholm. Sweden would resign her own nonpermanent seat in favor of Poland, thus appeasing Polish sensibilities without permitting an alteration of the constitution of the Council. Undén found little understanding in Stockholm. The Swedish press was strongly in favor of Germany's entry into the League, but was equally convinced of the correctness of the attitude of the small Powers in objecting to an enlargement of the Council. Public opinion in Sweden had no understanding of the change in atmosphere to which Vandervelde's compromise proposal had led; and the government refused to amend Undén's instructions.

Meanwhile, the clouds had darkened in Geneva. The Swiss Foreign Minister Motta recommended that the Swedish delegation make concessions. At the same time, in a secret meeting of the Council, Aristide Briand declared that France could not permit Germany to impose conditions for entering the League. If, as a result of German maneuvers, Poland was refused a Council seat, Briand declared, he would return to Paris and resign as Foreign Minister; and the Locarno policy would be at an end.

Under this pressure, Undén gave way as much as his instructions permitted. He promised to consult the German delegation about the situation, a suggestion which was eagerly accepted by the other members. It was clear that, if Germany too could be persuaded to favor a compromise, Sweden would appear to be more papal than the Pope in resisting any possible arrangement; and the Swedish government might in these circumstances agree to a change of Undén's instructions.

Undén had thus to work along two different lines. He had, in the first place, to get the permission of the Swedish Cabinet to resign the Swedish seat in the Council, so that Poland could enter the Council without enlargement of this body. For two days, telegrams of a truly dramatic character went back and forth between Geneva and Stockholm. But, in addition to his difficulties with his own government, Undén had to secure the German agreement. On March 15 the Germans expressed their willingness to accept Undén's suggestion on the condition that either Belgium or Czechoslovakia would join Sweden in resigning from the Council. Since Benes of Czechoslovakia was prepared to cooperate in order to save the situation, Undén, in reporting to Stockholm, informed his government that he now took it for granted that all obstacles to Sweden's abandonment of her Council seat were removed. The Cabinet gave way. The crisis was over, but it was followed by an anticlimax. Brazil declared her intention of insisting upon receiving a permanent seat in the Council; and the German entry into the League had after all to be postponed until the fall of 1926. But there was no longer any doubt that the real issue had been solved and that Germany would be able to take her seat. The question had been freed from those aspects which were politically explosive and had been reduced to the technical question of the constitutional structure of the League.[7]

Swedish public opinion had still not grasped the twofold aspect of the issue and did not realize that, if Undén had not achieved full victory, he had made an important contribution to European pacification. Swedish public opinion had been interested chiefly in the principle of maintaining the present size of the Council, and Brazil's stubbornness had won out over this principle at the last moment. Sweden's sacrifice of her Council seat seemed therefore to have been made in vain; Undén had diffi-

---

[7] On the negotiations, see Walters, *History of the League*, I, 323-325.

culty in defending himself against the Conservative opposition in the *Riksdag*; and, when the Cabinet resigned in May 1926, his personal popularity had quite obviously been diminished.

Undén's policy in the League of Nations crisis of 1926 can be correctly evaluated only if it is seen as an attempt to relieve the tension among the Great European Powers and to make Locarno a success. It can probably be said that the memory of the events of 1926, when he worked for an understanding among the Great Powers, had its influence in shaping the line which Undén has taken during recent years in the United Nations.

But it is important to note that, in his policy of 1926, Undén was not a starry-eyed idealist. He pursued a subtle policy, perhaps too subtle to be understood in all its implications by the Swedish people and the Cabinet. He was constantly aware of the relationship between European peace and Sweden's national interest in peace in the Baltic area. He did not embark on a new course, but continued the traditional line worked out by the professionals of his department. If Undén's performance seemed new and startling, the reason may be sought more in the personal qualities of this resolute, stubborn, and courageous man than in the contrast between a foreign policy of parliamentarism and a foreign policy of professionals.

4

Czechoslovakia: The Diplomacy of
Eduard Benes

BY PAUL E. ZINNER

IN THE ANNALS OF DIPLOMACY covering the period between the two world wars, Eduard Benes is likely to command a fair amount of attention. He belonged to a small group of statesmen who represented the lesser Powers of the Continent and who left an imprint on the European political scene—a group which also includes Nicolas Politis, Take Ionescu, and Nicolae Titulescu. But of all of these men Benes perhaps stands out as the one who was most often and most intimately involved in events of European significance, and the one on whom world attention was focused at crucial junctions in the post-Versailles period of Europe. The creation of Czechoslovakia, in which Benes shared top honors with Thomas G. Masaryk and Milan R. Stefanik, was symbolic of the introduction of a new, more democratic international order in Europe. The destruction of Czechoslovakia in 1938 in turn symbolized the breakdown of this order and the bankruptcy of Allied diplomacy.

Just how history will evaluate the diplomatic achievements and failures of Eduard Benes, remains to be seen. It is almost certain, however, that he will be recorded as one of the more controversial statesmen of his era. Indeed, no man who was as close to so many of the diplomatic skirmishes of the interwar period and who, in the last analysis, was responsible for such portentous decisions as Benes could possibly avoid being controversial. His judgments and decisions and the policies he advocated and tried to implement were often questioned and frequently censured by his contemporaries. Few people remained indifferent to him or to his policies, and he was either admired or hated by those who knew him. To date no unbiased biography of Benes exists.[1] In fact, there is no penetrating and

---

[1] The following, however, are useful: P. Crabites, *Benes, Statesman of Central Europe* (London, 1935); Radim N. Foustka, *Zivot, dilo a priklad Dr. Edvarda Benese (The Life, the Accomplishments and the Example of Dr. Eduard Benes)* (Praha, 1946);

reliable analysis and evaluation of his real significance in, and influence on, European politics. One of the difficulties in penetrating beyond the façade of his activities stems from his own secretiveness. He left nothing approaching an intimate journal of his daily doings and personal reflections on the affairs of the world.

With the exception of T. G. Masaryk, Benes never had any really intimate associates. Those who worked closely with him might have gleaned what they thought to be his intimate thoughts. It is questionable, however, if Benes ever directly confirmed their assumptions. But even those who worked closely with him and could possibly throw some light on his activities have thus far remained silent. In his own published statements, of which there are many, the subjective element is masterfully concealed. He intended, or so he said, eventually to publish his account of the events preceding the Munich debacle. It was to be an integral part, the first volume in fact, of his memoirs, which he began publishing in 1947.[2] But with characteristic taciturnity, he first published the second volume of reminiscences, which dealt with a less controversial period. The Communist coup, of course, intervened and disrupted whatever plans he might have had for additional volumes. His death in September 1948 postponed perhaps indefinitely the publication of such of his "intimate papers" as might have been preserved. The sketch presented here, therefore, does not purport to be an exhaustive and authoritative account of Benes' long diplomatic career. It will limit itself to a treatment in broad outline of the salient features of Benes' career as Foreign Minister of Czechoslovakia and statesman of international renown.

It is perhaps appropriate to open a discussion of Benes' diplomatic career by stating that it was in almost every respect *sui generis*. Few men, whatever their official position in the government of their particular country, were as intimately connected with the very existence of their native land as was Benes. Moreover, few representatives of small nations tried as assiduously and consistently to play the "great game" of inter-

---

Edward B. Hitchcock, *Benes, the Man and Statesman* (London, 1940); Godfrey Lias, *Benes of Czechoslovakia* (London, 1940); Compton Mackenzie, *Dr. Benes* (London, 1946); Jan Opocensky, ed. *Eduard Benes: Essays and Reflections Presented on the Occasion of his Sixtieth Birthday* (London, 1945); Jan Papousek, *Dr. Edvard Benes: Sein Leben* (Praha, 1937); J. Werstadt and others, *Dr. Edvard Benes, Sbornik Stati* (Dr. Eduard Benes: A Collection of Essays) (Praha, 1924) and *Edvard Benes, Filosof a Statnik* (Eduard Benes, Philosopher and Statesman) (Praha, 1937). Benes' own contributions to our knowledge of his life are cited in the notes below. His major speeches from 1924 to 1933 are collected in a mammoth volume of some 800 pages under the title *Boj o Mir a bezpecnost statu* (The Struggle for Peace and Security of the State) (Praha, 1934).

[2] Edvard Benes, *Pameti* (Memoirs) (Praha, 1947).

national politics traditionally reserved for the major Powers. Benes was imbued with a compelling sense of national and international mission. In his mind, as in that of his mentor and friend T. G. Masaryk, nationalism and internationalism were not competing but complementary doctrines and beliefs and the fulfillment of Czech national aspirations was equated with the attainment of the exalted aims of pan-humanism.[3] More concretely, Benes clearly saw that the welfare of a democratic Czechoslovakia coincided with the maintenance of a stable and peaceful Europe. In Benes, as in Masaryk, high moral purpose and the recognition of obvious national self-interest blended to such an extent that it was difficult if not impossible to determine the primacy of one or another as the underlying motive for policies they advocated. Both high moral purpose and national self-interest, however, required a "European" or internationalist orientation of Czechoslovak foreign policy and the confluence of two such powerful motivating elements must be held responsible for the presumptuous prerogative which Benes often exercised in meddling in the affairs of the Great Powers with an intent to steer them to the adoption of policies frequently unacceptable and sometimes distasteful to them.

Benes' heterodoxy is poignantly demonstrated by his education in the art of diplomacy and the unfolding of his career as a diplomat and statesman. He was certainly no "professional diplomat" in the full and traditional sense of the word. He was not "born" to be a diplomat, nor did he learn his *métier* by slow and easy stages in the service of a tradition-laden Foreign Office. He entered on a diplomatic career fortuitously at the somewhat advanced age of 31 years, and the first position he held was that of *de facto* Foreign Minister without, of course, a ministry to command or even a country to represent. His first "diplomatic mission" was to "sell" the Allied Powers on the desirability of establishing an independent Czechoslovak state.[4] It was a self-imposed task which he discharged with admirable skill and eminent success.

His greatest accomplishment was to extract from French, British, and Italian statesmen recognition of Czechoslovakia as a state even before the conclusion of an armistice with Austria-Hungary. The fact that Benes was invited to attend the plenary meeting of the Supreme War

[3] For a recent essay on Masaryk which stresses this aspect of his thinking, see "Thomas Masaryk, Maker of Czechoslovakia," *The Times Literary Supplement*, March 3, 1950.

[4] For an exhaustive account of Benes' activities during the first world war see his *Svetova valka a nase revoluce* (The World War and Our Revolution) (3 vols., Praha, 1927 and 1928). A much abbreviated English version is *My War Memoirs* (London, 1928).

Council on November 4, 1918, and was able to participate in the armistice negotiations was a triumph of incalculable moral and material benefit to him. None other of the so-called "succession states" could boast a similar achievement. The significance of the commitment the Allies had undertaken vis-à-vis Czechoslovakia particularly strengthened Benes' hand in setting forth the political and territorial demands of his country at the ensuing Peace Conference.[5] With this, his first diplomatic mission, Benes was launched on a lifelong career as Foreign Minister and it is not an exaggeration to call him Foreign Minister by profession. He held the portfolio of foreign affairs in the Czechoslovak government for seventeen years without interruption. When he relinquished it, it was only to step up to a higher office, the Presidency of the Republic. But even as President, Benes retained firm control over the conduct of his country's foreign affairs.

Benes combined some of the talents, prerogatives, and propensities of professional diplomat, statesman, and scholar. Obviously he was neither a professional diplomat in the traditional sense of the word, nor could he be identified with the type of "amateur" diplomat-statesman frequently encountered on the political scene of post-Versailles Europe. He shared the professional diplomat's expert knowledge derived from continual exposure to international affairs, and he also showed a marked inclination for secret negotiations and that most effective weapon of international diplomacy, the *fait accompli*. However, he was not unalterably opposed to "open diplomacy" which he found an effective means to plead the cause of a small country. What he had in common with the "amateur" diplomat-statesman of his era was a general disdain for expert advice and a penchant for informal diplomacy.

It is possible, in fact, to identify Benes as the exponent and practitioner *par excellence* of that personal diplomacy which became so popular in the 1920's and 1930's. Disregard for expert advice was in his case perhaps less disastrous than in the case of men like Lloyd George or Neville Chamberlain. Moreover, the circumstances of Benes' early career clearly imposed on him the practice of personal diplomacy. While working to promote the independence of Czechoslovakia in Paris during the first world war, he had no public opinion to consult. He could not even be identified with a known geographic or historical entity. Czechoslovakia at that time existed only as a projection of the personality and ideas of

---

[5] The reader may refer to the thoughts of a not altogether favorably inclined critic on this matter by consulting David Lloyd George, *Memoirs of the Peace Conference* (New Haven, 1939), pp. 601ff. For Benes' evaluation of the significance of his success see his *Problemy Nove Evropy* (Problems of the New Europe) (Praha, 1924), p. 10.

Masaryk and Benes. But, in subsequent years the habit of working alone
without benefit of consultation, of making decisions on his own and assuming full responsibility for them, persisted; and Benes continued to practice
personal diplomacy when it was perhaps no longer imperative and, possibly, had even become detrimental to him and to his country. Nevertheless, if Benes shared the "amateur" diplomat-statesman's passion for
personal diplomacy, he did not share the "allures" and pretensions of the
"great" European statesmen. His general mannerism was that of a permanent under-secretary of state. His speeches lacked lustre and were devoid of emotional overtones. They were dry, dull, painfully long, and
full of facts and closely reasoned argumentation. Finally, he retained the
true scholar's method of work. He was an avid student of international
affairs who kept himself informed on every possible political development
the world over. He sought to project pragmatic problems against a well-
defined and unalterable philosophical frame of reference. To him the
practice of politics, especially of international politics, without a firm
philosophical foundation was unimaginable.

Benes' prerogative to run Czechoslovakia's foreign affairs virtually at
will was never seriously challenged. Immediately after the foundation
of the Republic, of course, there was no one else with sufficient ability and
necessary familiarity with international affairs to plead the Czechoslovak
cause abroad. So complete was Benes' sway in foreign affairs that he did
not bother to return to Prague for consultation with the government and
the "Revolutionary National Assembly," although to most of the Czechoslovak political leaders he was at that time not personally known. He had
left Prague in 1915 as a little-known university lecturer who had not cut
a swath in politics at all. Nevertheless, Benes remained at Paris where
his headquarters had been during the war and made policy on the spot
without benefit of advice from his government. He did not return to
Prague until September 1919. Meanwhile, the Cabinet and the National
Assembly at Prague refrained from any action on foreign affairs. The
fate of the newborn Republic was in Benes' hands.[6] His influence in
foreign affairs was only slightly modified as time went by. Strictly speaking, he was free from the formal constitutional controls governing
Cabinet members and was also largely free from the rigid party controls
which shackled every other Cabinet member and parliamentary deputy.
This is not to say that Benes openly circumvented his constitutional

---

[6] See Ferdinand Peroutka, *Budovani Statu* (Building the State) (Praha, 1934), II,
1308ff. This is a monumental work totaling four volumes and giving an excellent documented account of the formative years of the Republic.

responsibility or flouted the consensus of the more powerful political leaders on crucial issues. In the case of Russia, he repeatedly postponed recognition of the Soviet regime because of the opposition of his conservative critics.[7] However, Benes guided public opinion rather than being led by it. His views found ready acceptance among the people, and even the political leaders usually deferred to his judgment, although his ideas were not always popular with them.

Benes reported to the foreign affairs committee of the House and Senate and to the full assembly of both Chambers often and at great length. As exposés of the unfolding international scene, his parliamentary speeches were masterly for the manner in which individual events were put into their historical perspective. But they seldom revealed anything of importance concerning the inner secrets of international diplomacy; and because the approach was often abstract, the dramatic immediacy of specific problems facing Czechoslovakia was obscured. Finally, Benes' speeches acquainted the National Assembly only with past events and actions. Rare was the occasion on which he consulted with members of the House or Senate in advance of diplomatic moves which he contemplated, and the same can be said of his relationship with members of the Cabinet and the chairmen of the political parties. His decisions were made alone or in consultation and agreement with Masaryk.

Benes' autocratic direction of Czechoslovakia's foreign policy had ad-

---

[7] Conservative elder statesmen were nettled by Benes' obviously privileged position in the Republic as one of the founders of the state and as T. G. Masaryk's closest friend, protégé and heir-apparent to the Presidency. Despite his undeniable merits in forging Czechoslovakia's independence, Benes was considered by the "elders" of Czechoslovak politics as an upstart on whom they did not want to bestow the same honors and privileges they had accorded to Masaryk. Benes' efforts to stay out of party politics, as Masaryk had done, and thus to groom himself for the role of the charismatic, benevolent philosopher-king (President) so perfectly played by Masaryk did not meet with the approval of the party chiefs who sought to exercise overriding influence in the country. It is safe to say that only Masaryk's staunch support saved Benes from being dismissed on a number of occasions, and only Masaryk's stubborn insistence brought about Benes' election to the Presidency in 1935. Political and personal opposition to Benes centered in the Agrarian party, which was the most powerful Czechoslovak party from the early 1920's until 1938, and which exercised overwhelming influence in domestic affairs. Benes was also bitterly opposed by Karel Kramar and Jiri Stribrny. The former was an arch-conservative Russophile, who had originally hoped to install a Russian prince as monarch in Czechoslovakia and whose hatred of the Soviet regime bordered on the pathological. The latter was a disgruntled member of the National Socialist party (a non-Marxist reform socialist party), which Benes finally joined and which was not big enough to contain the opposing views of these two men. Stribrny's career culminated in his leadership of a small but noisy "fascist league." The reader will find reference to Benes' difficulties with his domestic opponents in several of the biographic studies about him. See especially Mackenzie, *Dr. Benes, passim* and Hitchcock, *Benes*, pp. 200ff. For his own account of these difficulties see *Pameti, passim*, and his *Sest let exilu a svetove valky* (Six Years of Exile and World War) (Praha, 1946), pp. 22ff.

vantages as well as disadvantages. His long and uninterrupted tenure in office and his integrated approach to international affairs imparted both a stability and a unity and purpose to Czechoslovakia's foreign policy which it otherwise would certainly have lacked. Judging by the nature of the Czechoslovak government coalition, which never consisted of less than five political parties representing fundamentally opposing views, it is difficult to see how the Cabinet as a body, or for that matter any individual not enjoying Benes' unique status, could have devised and carried out a clear-cut policy. Compromise was the essence of Czechoslovak politics, and each party outdid the other in shirking responsibility. For this reason, the rougher the going, the more willing was Parliament to defer to Benes and to let him shoulder the heavy responsibilities of policy making. However, Benes' failure to take political leaders into his confidence left him relatively isolated. Consequently, domestic and foreign policies were not always as closely coordinated as they might, and indeed should, have been, for in the case of Czechoslovakia domestic and foreign problems were inextricably linked.[8]

Benes' reluctance to draw people into his confidence was also reflected in his relations with the staff of the Ministry of Foreign Affairs.[9] He showed little concern with the organization and personnel of the Ministry and made no serious effort to pack it with people carefully chosen because of their ability and their loyalty to him. He had a small coterie of loyal underlings, some of whom served as his personal secretaries at one time or another and then were rewarded with more exalted posts in the foreign service. His closest collaborator was Kamil Krofta, who succeeded Benes as Foreign Minister in 1935, and who, like Benes, was university professor by vocation.

The Ministry under Benes did not become a training school for capable diplomats, and since the country possessed no hereditary aristocracy with a "corner" on diplomatic assignments, Czechoslovakia's career diplomats were essentially run-of-the-mill civil servants with limited responsibilities and corresponding ability. Top diplomatic posts were originally occupied by individuals who had in one way or another

---

[8] Benes did, of course, take a much more active hand in the direction of domestic affairs after he became President.

[9] For a general survey of Czechoslovak foreign policy and the organization and functioning of the Ministry of Foreign Affairs, see Ministerstvo Zahranicnich Veci (Ministry of Foreign Affairs), *Deset let ceskoslovenske zahranicni politiky* (Ten Years of Czechoslovak Foreign Policy) (Praha, 1928). With the exception of this authoritative but somewhat arid source, details of Benes' relations with his staff and his direction of the Ministry can be gleaned only from personal conversation with his former associates.

collaborated in the Czechoslovak liberation movement abroad. Changes in top personnel were extremely rare. For example, Stefan Osusky held the post of minister at Paris from 1920 to 1939. There is no evidence that Czechoslovak representatives abroad, whatever their status, were entrusted with truly weighty matters. Nor is there any indication that their reports, judgments, and opinions were particularly heeded by Benes. Some of them substituted for Benes at international conferences (Osusky at Geneva, Veverka at Geneva and at meetings of the Little Entente, Fierlinger at Stresa), but all gatherings of importance were attended by Benes himself. He rarely delegated authority to any one, and while correspondence between the Ministry and the "field" was lively, it seemed for the most part limited to routine matters. Benes was not only Foreign Minister but served as a sort of roving ambassador of his country, traveling from one European capital to another, in an attempt to deal with the responsible European statesmen personally on the scene of action whenever possible. He became known as peripatetic journeyman and especially during the 1920's spent as much time away from as in Prague. Geneva was virtually an alternate seat of the Czechoslovak Foreign Ministry.

II

The foreign policy which Benes pursued with singular consistency reflected an immutable conviction concerning the interrelatedness between the continued welfare of Czechoslovakia and the maintenance of the Versailles *status quo*. Not that Benes unalterably opposed the re-admission of the defeated Powers to the international community. But he resolutely combated "revisionism" under any guise and fought against upsetting the balance of power created at Versailles. He realized that if the defeated Powers were permitted to challenge the Versailles order rather than being gradually absorbed into it, a new contest for supremacy in Europe would develop in which Czechoslovakia, having been carved out of the Habsburg Monarchy and embodying sizable national minorities, would be a primary target for attack. He also realized, more keenly than his contemporaries, that an attack on Czechoslovakia would not be an end in itself but would be the start of a far broader revision of the European balance of power. As he put it: "Our state is the key to the whole postwar structure of Central Europe. If it is touched . . . the peace of Europe [is] seriously infringed. . . . It is for that reason that . . . our international position and our internal stability are a matter of great interest equally to France and the Soviet Union, equally to England

and Italy and to the Little Entente, as they ought to be to Germany, and Poland."[10] In the last analysis his view of European politics was correct, for the resurgence of the defeated Powers, notably Germany, coupled with the growth of aggressive fascism in several European countries, resulted in the gradual whittling away both of the form and substance of the Versailles peace settlement, causing not only the destruction of Czechoslovakia but terminating the hegemony on the continent of the great democracies who first yielded to the onslaught of the dictatorships of the Right and then, as a consequence of the second world war, receded before the Soviet Union.

The interrelationship between Czechoslovakia's welfare and the maintenance of the Versailles *status quo* provided a convenient platform for an integrated approach to the specific problems facing Czechoslovakia and the general problems of the international community. Essentially, Benes' foreign policy can be summed up as a continual search for security through complementary systems of bilateral and regional agreements, on the one hand, and a general scheme of arbitration and pacific settlement of disputes on the other. The chosen instrument for the latter was the League of Nations whose moral and political prestige Benes tried assiduously to increase.[11]

The system of regional and bilateral security agreements engineered by Benes suffered from an obvious weakness. It rested solely on solemn treaties with "third" Powers, i.e. states that were either geographically remote or were not directly exposed to the same immediate threats as was Czechoslovakia.[12] Benes was unable to settle on a permanent basis the differences between Czechoslovakia and its potential enemies Germany, Hungary, and Poland, all of which coveted Czechoslovak territory. Benes' inability to conclude lasting agreements with any or all of Czechoslovakia's predatory neighbors was often held against him by his domestic critics—notably the Agrarian leadership—who would have favored a less "cosmopolitan" and more "utilitarian" foreign orientation, including a rapprochement with Germany at the expense of solidarity

---

[10] Edouard Benes, *La lutte pour la sécurité collective en Europe et la guerre Italo-Abyssine. Sources et documents Tchecoslovaques* No. 29 (Praha, 1935), p. 59.

[11] It was perhaps Benes' efforts in this respect which led a distinguished historian of the League to describe him as "the cleverest, the best-informed, and for many years the most successful of European ministers." F. P. Walters, *A History of the League of Nations* (London, 1952), II, 116.

[12] The cornerstone of Czechoslovakia's bilateral security system was its mutual defense treaty with France, signed in January 1924. The other pillars of its defense system were treaties with Rumania and Yugoslavia within the framework of the Little Entente, and an assistance treaty with the Soviet Union signed in May 1935.

with France. The failure to come to terms with any of its potential enemies, of course, left Czechoslovakia in a precarious political and military
position in which defense against aggression without considerable outside help was at best a tenuous proposition, and, as is generally known,
Czechoslovakia's paper alliances were of little tangible benefit to it at
the time of greatest need. It is questionable, however, if an alternate
course of action by Benes, for instance, a settlement with one or more of
the neighboring states, would have been crowned with greater success.
It seems highly unlikely that a settlement in good faith could have been
effected without forswearing the birthright of the Republic.

The dispute over Czechoslovakia's frontiers and the sizable ethnic
minorities incorporated in the country was one of a number of perennial
fundamental issues which apparently could not be solved rationally. Lest
Czechoslovakia's relations with its neighbors be misunderstood, it should
be said explicitly that they were not uniformly bad. Only with Hungary
was there virtually constant tension[13]—the result of many factors of
historical as well as contemporary origin. Outstanding among them were
the obstinate refusal of the Hungarian regime to acquiesce in the outcome of the first world war and to relent from continual revisionist agitation, and the genuine fear of the Czechoslovak government that a Hungarian assault—diplomatic or military—against the "soft underbelly" of
the Republic might be crowned with success. In the case of Germany and
Poland, acute friction was preceded by a period of quiescence and normalcy. It was only in the 1930's, when Nazism triumphed in Germany
and when Poland showed a marked shift toward totalitarianism, that
Czechoslovakia's relations with these countries entered the crisis stage.
By then, of course, opposing philosophies of state further obstructed the
possibility of reaching an understanding between Czechoslovakia, on the
one hand, and either Germany or Poland on the other.

The system of collective security envisaged by Benes was no less "unrealistic" than were the regional and bilateral agreements he concluded.
It seemed to take too little cognizance of the very real possibility of a
breakdown as a result of clashing interests and interpretations of the
good of the international community, and it was devoid of precautions
against the eventuality of a crisis. Of course, the ultimate aim of his
system of collective security was to obviate international crises; as he
put it, "European peace and collective security" were indivisible.[14] Benes

[13] For a fuller treatment of Czechoslovakia's difficulties with Hungary see, *inter alia*,
Felix J. Vondracek, *The Foreign Policy of Czechoslovakia 1918-1935* (New York,
1937).
[14] Benes, *La Lutte*, p. 11.

readily admitted that a workable system of collective security could not be reached overnight but only step by step. Nevertheless, he often appeared to act as if that distant goal had already been achieved.

Benes was inclined to vest too much authority in the League of Nations, which he regarded all too obviously as a democratic forum where differences between great and small nations—based primarily on power —would be minimized. Conversely he was resolutely opposed to a European directorate of Great Powers. Following up on the premise of the small Powers' prerogative to take an active part in determining the good of the international community, the Czechoslovakian statesman sometimes went to considerable length to induce the Great Powers to subscribe to his concept of balance of power in Europe and to undertake commitments which they were not necessarily willing to risk. Fundamentally, he attempted to preserve the wartime alliance between France and England and sought to obtain a British guarantee of the security of Germany's eastern neighbors. He also strongly advocated bringing Soviet Russia into the European community as an antidote to resurgent German power and an "indispensable factor of peace in Europe." He attempted, in short, to achieve a synthesis of East and West, with Czechoslovakia—not only because of its geographic position but because of its racial, cultural, social and political heritage—as a bridge or unifying factor between them. The role he thus assigned to his country and to himself was an ambitious one, for it entailed navigating extremely hazardous waters and, indeed, spanning unbridgeable chasms. In his endeavor to reconcile basically irreconcilable points of view, Benes developed into an exponent of the middle course or "solution moyenne" as he called it.[15] In principle, the middle course is always a commendable one, for it presumably embodies the virtues of democratic parliamentarism. In practice, the middle course is more often than not difficult to maintain. Benes' efforts to play both ends against the middle were not successful for the simple reason that few if any of the European nations were willing to desist from playing power politics; and the inevitable result of the assiduous practice of power politics was the polarization of European political forces. Czechoslovakia, caught in the middle of this process, was one of its early victims.

Benes' propensity for "making" international policy was not always graciously received by the exponents of Great Power supremacy, although his critics were by no means limited to this quarter. Various aspects of

---

[15] For an excellent essay on Benes' "solution moyenne" or "midway philosophy" see Felix Weltsch, "A critical optimist," in Opocensky, *Eduard Benes*, pp. 118-156.

his concept of collective security and of his *modus operandi* at one time or another irritated virtually all of the Great Powers. His unorthodox views, coupled with his efforts to play the "great game" of international diplomacy traditionally thought to be reserved for the major Powers, contributed to his unpopularity in British conservative circles.[16] But the Soviet regime also found cause to be critical of him. For, despite his professed friendship for the Soviet Union, he lagged cautiously behind the Western European countries in extending *de jure* recognition to the Communist regime.[17]

III

Benes' long career in the field of diplomacy was at its height in the early 1920's when the lofty ideals bandied about at the Peace Conference had not yet completely vanished and the new international order created at Versailles had not yet been seriously challenged. At the Peace Conference itself, Benes was not a central, nor even an important figure. He concentrated on staking out Czechoslovakia's territorial and political claims and in this endeavor was singularly successful. He pleaded his cause earnestly with ant-like diligence, flooding the delegations of the Great Powers with elaborately detailed memoranda and statistics properly garnished with professions of adherence to the noblest democratic principles. The impression he created was that of an interminable and perhaps somewhat irritating speaker. Harold Nicolson, a junior member of the British delegation at the time, described him as a "competent, plausible little man."[18]

By concluding a series of commercial treaties and making political

---

[16] His unpopularity in the 1930's hardly needs comment. However, even in the 1920's, when Benes was generally acclaimed for his work at Geneva, acid overtones of criticism could be detected from the direction of London. Without assailing him directly, Conservative spokesmen warned incessantly against the dangers of the kind of "visionary efforts" in which he indulged. In September 1924, for instance, at a time when the Draft Treaty of Mutual Assistance and the Geneva Protocol were still very live issues, the *Times* declared: "The League and its best friends have . . . grounds for some uneasiness as to the course of its present deliberations. The extravagant oratory with which the League was exalted at its birth, and before its birth, has misled many of the lesser States and the masses in some of the larger States as to its real authority. . . . It is to be hoped, in the interest of the League itself, and of the principles for which it stands, that no illusions on this head will be entertained in the present session. The League, it seems, feels constrained to apply itself to the vast political problems of security and disarmament instead of confining its labors to the less ambitious subjects of a practical and administrative order, for which it has shown itself to be particularly well fitted. . . . *The lesser states may exercise, and do exercise, in the League a very great moral influence, but it is vain for them to aspire to more. . . .*" *The Times*, September 2, 1924. Italics mine.

[17] *De jure* recognition was extended to the Soviet Union on June 9, 1934. See Max Beloff, *The Foreign Policy of Soviet Russia* (2 vols., London, 1947-1948), I, 131.

[18] Harold Nicolson, *Peacemaking 1919* (London, 1933), p. 240.

alliances designed to reopen the clogged channels of diplomatic intercourse and to strengthen the newly created international order, Benes
successfully placed Czechoslovakia on firm footing in the international
community and quickly turned to broader issues. Under his guidance
the new state soon became a pillar of stability and strength in Central
Europe. Benes himself rapidly became established as a veteran statesman, although his tenure in office had hardly begun and his experience was still meager. However, he learned fast and indeed comported
himself as one of the charter members of the European diplomatic community. His understanding of international problems and the scope of
his vision clearly distinguished him from the run-of-the-mill representative of a small country.

His efforts during the first four or five years after the Peace Conference centered on consolidating Central Europe. He was the spiritual
father of the Little Entente, a coalition of Czechoslovakia, Rumania, and
Yugoslavia, dedicated originally and primarily to the containment of
Hungarian revisionist aspirations.[19] The Little Entente, however, was
not an exclusively defensive alliance. Its positive aims centered on political and economic integration in Central and Southeastern Europe, although the idea of a confederation was not on Benes' agenda. Progress
along constructive international lines at any rate was slow and halting.
In Benes' conception, the Little Entente served essentially as an instrument for dominating Central Europe. It was a safeguard against en-
croachments on the independence of action of the small victorious Powers
in this area. It not only guarded against the resurgence of Hungarian
power, or the restoration of the Habsburg Monarchy in one form or another, but was also intended to keep the Great Powers—both friendly
and unfriendly—at a respectable distance from the Central European
domain. Finally, through the medium of the Little Entente, its individual members could magnify their influence in international deliberations,
for when speaking and voting *en bloc* they came close to equaling the
status of a "Great Power." The most striking demonstration of the possibilities inherent in joint action was at the Genoa Conference in 1922,

---

[19] On the Little Entente, see especially Florin Codresco, *La Petite Entente* (Paris,
1930), a doctoral dissertation which is the most meticulous factual account on the
activities of the Little Entente in the 1920's; Aurel Cosman, *La Petite Entente* (Paris,
1926); J. O. Crane, *The Little Entente* (New York, 1931); Robert Machray, *The
Little Entente* (London, 1929) and *The Struggle for the Danube and the Little Entente,
1929-1938* (London, 1938); Albert Mousset, *La Petite Entente* (Paris, 1923); and
Bojidar Sarich, *La Petite Entente, Facteur de Paix en Europe* (Paris, 1933), another
doctoral dissertation.

where the Little Entente as such was asked to designate representatives to the various committees deliberating on the fate of Europe.

While Benes was busily laying the foundations of the Little Entente, he also tried to regulate his country's relations with its immediate neighbors. He showed considerable astuteness in establishing good relations with Austria, for the prevention of an *Anschluss* was as much a matter of concern to him then as it was in 1938. The assumption underlying his policy toward Austria was that, by preventing its economic collapse, which was indeed imminent in the early 1920's, the political independence of that country could also be saved and the integrity of Central Europe preserved. Benes approached the economic rescue of Austria both directly and through the good offices of the League of Nations. Direct negotiations with Karl Renner, the Austrian Chancellor in 1920, resulted in the conclusion of a commercial treaty and the extension of a Czech loan to Austria the following year. In December 1921 a treaty was negotiated between the two states establishing the bases of general cooperation and arbitration of disputes. In 1922, when Austria was again in dire financial straits, Benes was approached with a request for help. He took the matter to the League of Nations as the agency best designed to help Austria and simultaneously to request from her government a guarantee of her continued will to independent political existence. A general guarantee of the political independence of Austria was, of course, much more to Benes' liking than any direct deals he could have made with that country, for he realized that by taking a direct hand in settling Austria's affairs he was bound to evoke the jealousy, fear, and antagonism not only of the Central European countries but also of Italy, who followed Austria's development with considerable attention and not unselfish interest. In October 1922 a treaty was signed by Great Britain, France, Italy, Czechoslovakia, and Austria under League auspices, whereby the signatory Powers undertook to respect the political independence and territorial integrity of Austria and to refrain from compromising its sovereignty by imposing undue and unusual economic or financial burdens on it. A new loan to Austria negotiated through the League in 1923 was underwritten by several states, including Czechoslovakia who, along with Great Britain and France, guaranteed 24.5 per cent of the loan. By assisting Austria in overcoming her economic difficulties Benes undoubtedly made a major contribution to the stability of the Central European area in the 1920's.

In sharp contrast with the trend of Czechoslovak-Austrian relations was the air of tension that constantly hung over Benes' dealings with

Hungary. No sooner had Czechoslovakia ceased to fight off an armed invasion by Hungarian troops of the territory she had claimed and received at the Paris Peace Conference than the first threat of Habsburg restoration was raised at Budapest. The fall of Bela Kun's Red regime in the summer of 1919 was followed by the rise of Archduke Joseph to a commanding post in the country. This, in Benes' view, foreshadowed the possibility of Habsburg restoration, and he requested the Supreme Council of the Allies to intercede in order to exclude the Archduke from political activity, a request which was acted upon satisfactorily. In March 1921, the ex-Emperor-King Charles made an attempt to seize power at Budapest. His effort, although only halfheartedly supported by the regime of Admiral Horthy, elicited a frantic response from Benes. The Czech statesman considered the incident a *casus belli* and sent an ultimatum to the Hungarian government, demanding the immediate departure of the ex-ruler—an action taken, incidentally, before Benes had received replies to the requests for aid which he had simultaneously sent to the Western Powers and his allies in the Little Entente. A further attempt by Charles in October 1921 evoked an even sharper reaction from Benes, who served the Hungarian government with another ultimatum threatening armed intervention unless his conditions concerning the definitive settlement of the Habsburg question, and the adherence of Hungary to the terms of the Trianon Peace Treaty, were met. Charles was duly removed from the scene; but the rest of Benes' demands were not fulfilled and relations with Hungary remained strained. The revival of Hungarian revisionist agitation in 1927, the subsequent rapprochement between Hungary and Italy, and a number of incidents, such as the large scale counterfeiting of Czechoslovak (and French) banknotes in Hungary allegedly for the purpose of financing subversive activities in Czechoslovakia, kept the two countries at loggerheads.

As to Germany, the conclusion of a commercial treaty with that country in 1920 was considered something of a "coup" for Benes. Although the treaty did nothing more than to regulate trade between the two countries and specify certain questions pertaining to transportation and transit traffic of goods in and out of Czechoslovakia, it was an important symbolic step toward the restoration of "normalcy" in Central Europe. Among other things, the clarification of her transit rights through Germany was essential for Czechoslovakia in order to avoid virtual economic strangulation, for the bulk of her trade with Western Europe and with overseas areas had to be transported on German railroads or rivers.

Turning to broader European issues, Benes soon found himself mediating fundamental differences of opinion between France and Great Britain. The unsettled state of European economy gave considerable cause for worry to Great and small Powers alike. By 1921, Great Britain, hard hit by the general slump, showed particular interest in improving the general economic situation and took the initiative in convoking a general economic conference for that purpose. The British plan called for restoring equality at least in the commercial field between victor and vanquished on the Continent, and for inviting Soviet Russia to participate in the deliberations as a prelude to the resumption of normal trade relations with that country. The French government was somewhat balky at the suggestion, for it was still preoccupied with problems relating to its security and was trying—unsuccessfully—to draw Great Britain into a close military alliance. France was less worried about European trade than she was over the resurgence of German military and industrial power, over the possibility of a German-Russian rapprochement, and over attempts to revise the provisions of the peace treaties which might arise if equal status were granted to the defeated Powers. Preliminary conferences held between French and British statesmen at Cannes at the beginning of 1922, however, paved the way for a joint approach to the problem and set the stage for an international economic conference at Genoa.

The distant rumblings of a possible rapprochement with Russia naturally aroused Benes' keen interest, for he had long advocated such a course of action. He immediately initiated a meeting of the Little Entente which convened at Belgrade. There, a joint plan of action was decided on by the three Central European countries. Benes then proceeded to Paris and London, not only to make his and the Little Entente's views known, but also to iron out serious differences of opinion that had arisen anew between Great Britain and France as a result of the fall of Briand, who had been responsible for the Cannes commitments, and the succession of Poincaré as Premier.[20] Poincaré disliked conferences as a matter of principle, and he now posed again many of France's original doubts as to the wisdom of a European-wide conclave. Moreover, he also resisted *de jure* recognition of Communist Russia.

This is where Benes stepped in. He succeeded in associating himself both with the British position, championed by Lloyd George, and with France's reservations concerning treaty revision and a possible alteration of the European power balance. Having consulted with both the French and British governments, he produced a compromise plan which in-

[20] On the change-over from Briand to Poincaré, see Chapter 2, §1, above.

corporated Poincaré's proviso that neither reparations nor the peace treaties should be discussed at the conference and that participation of the Russian delegation should not imply *de jure* recognition of the Soviet government. He then went on to satisfy Lloyd George's views on the resumption of trade with Russia and the desirability of concluding a nonaggression convention. His efforts at mediation brought about a meeting between Poincaré and Lloyd George at the end of February at Boulogne, where the Genoa Conference was agreed upon.

The conference itself, as is known, ended in fiasco, not only because six days after its opening, on April 16, 1922, the Germans and Russians surprised the world by announcing the conclusion of a bilateral treaty (the Rapallo treaty), but because the Russian delegation, headed by Chicherin, was immovable in its refusal to acknowledge the responsibility of its government for prewar debts and for compensating foreign owners of nationalized property in Russia, a particularly hard blow at France. But although the conference failed, Benes utilized the opportunity afforded by its sessions to contact Chicherin and succeeded in negotiating a trade treaty with the Russian delegate. As a matter of diplomatic discretion, the treaty was not signed until June 5 at Prague. The terms of the treaty were not altogether favorable to Czechoslovakia, since she received no compensation for property previously held in Russia. On the other hand, the Soviet government gave up its previous *conditio sine qua non* concerning *de jure* recognition and the extension of credits, and agreed furthermore to respect the safety and freedom of Czechoslovak citizens and to cease propaganda in Czechoslovakia. The treaty also included a pledge of neutrality in the event of an attack on either one of the two countries by a third Power, and contained a diplomatic and consular agreement.[21]

Meanwhile, Benes also began to make his influence felt at Geneva. He embarked on what turned out to be a long and generally fruitless struggle to strengthen the League Covenant, to enlarge the scope of the League's jurisdiction over international disputes, and to extend the moral sanction of the League to regional and bilateral treaties. It was with the last mentioned of these projects that Benes opened his campaign to strengthen the peace in Europe. He proposed the amendment of Article 21 of the Covenant in order to "encourage regional conferences or conventions as an essential complement to universal agreements

---

[21] On the Genoa Conference, see the works cited above in Chapter 1, note 56. A text of the Soviet-Czechoslovak commercial treaty will be found in Papousek, *Dr. Benes*, p. 231.

which must necessarily be very general and ill defined in scope." Soon afterwards he plunged headlong into a far greater endeavor, that of elaborating a comprehensive system of arbitration, security, and disarmament.

The impulse for a general treaty of mutual guarantee had resulted from negotiations relating to the possibility of achieving European disarmament. In 1923, Lord Robert Cecil had prepared a draft treaty in line with a previous resolution of the League Assembly, which had expressed the view that disarmament must be conditional upon a defensive treaty of mutual guarantee, open to all, and ensuring that its signatories would receive prompt assistance from their cosignatories in the event of aggression. From the Cecil draft, amended in discussion with other Powers, arose the famous Draft Treaty of Mutual Assistance which the League considered in 1923 and 1924.[22]

To the idea of such a treaty Benes responded warmly, although he was at the same time one of the Draft Treaty's most thoughtful critics. He was concerned over the provision which required unanimity in the Council of the League before sanctions could be taken against an aggressor, recommending that a majority vote should suffice. He also objected to the procedural steps which must precede any action, for he felt that, in any instance involving sanctions, prompt action would be of paramount importance and that this was not sufficiently provided for. Moreover, he felt that the success or failure of any general security pact depended on the degree of perfection of a compulsory mechanism for the pacific settlement of disputes: without such mechanism, disarmament and a security pact would not eliminate the possibility of aggression. "To endeavor to prevent wars by the reduction or limitation of armaments is to mistake the means for the end, thus committing a fundamental error. The employment of the means—even with a large measure of success—in no way implies that the goal has been attained."[23] Nevertheless, although Benes did not consider the treaty an effective enough instrument, he guided its passage through the League, for then as on subsequent occasions, schemes advancing the concept of collective security, no matter how imperfect they might have seemed to him, received his enthusiastic support.

Benes' biggest hour came in 1924, when, after the Draft Treaty had

[22] Walters, *History of the League*, I, 223-228.
[23] Benes' reply to the League concerning the draft of the Treaty of Mutual Assistance circulated for comment among the members. See League of Nations, Official Journal, Supplement No. 26 (Geneva, 1924), pp. 247ff.

failed to secure the assent of the major Powers,[24] a fresh start was made to effect a system of "Arbitration, Security and Reduction of Armament." Benes, who had been elected to the League Council the year before, was rapporteur for the so-called Third (Armament) Committee. The introduction of the Protocol for the Pacific Settlement of International Disputes (better known as the Geneva Protocol) at the Fifth Assembly of the League in 1924 and the reception which was accorded to it was in a sense a personal triumph, for Benes had worked untiringly to satisfy as many divergent views as possible without sacrificing the general principle he aimed to achieve, the prohibition of aggressive war. Work on the Protocol was started as a result of a joint resolution submitted by Mac-Donald and Herriot. However, as a chronicler of the League puts it, the origins of the idea "could be traced to the skillful hands of Benes—Benes, of whom more than of any other European Minister it could be said that he knew exactly what he wanted and that what he wanted was in full harmony with the purposes of the League."[25]

The Geneva Protocol went further than the Draft Treaty, and satisfied Benes' objections to that instrument, by providing definitely for the pacific arbitration of disputes and by making refusal on the part of any Power to submit to such arbitration an offense punishable by the general application of sanctions against it. This ambitious scheme was greeted with enthusiasm, not only by Benes and Politis, who shared honors in its preparation, but by the entire Assembly. In the midst of the festive atmosphere accompanying the presentation of the Geneva Protocol, Benes declared that the Assembly was "in the presence of a system the adoption of which may entirely modify our present political life."[26] His hopes were quickly dashed, for a change in government in Great Britain brought the Conservative party back to power and it, presumably yielding to Commonwealth interests, torpedoed the Protocol.[27]

After this failure, Benes had to satisfy himself with the far less comprehensive system of security guarantees which was embodied in the Locarno treaties. The arbitration treaty signed by Czechoslovakia and Germany at this time was a far cry from the security system for which Benes had worked so hard, and the comfort Czechoslovakia could derive from strengthening its mutual security treaty with France was only partial compensation for the loss of general guarantees. Nevertheless,

[24] See Chapter 1, §III above.
[25] Walters, *History of the League*, I, 271-272.
[26] League of Nations, Official Journal, Supplement No. 26, p. 207.
[27] See Chapter 1, §III above.

Benes was able to go before the Czechoslovak National Assembly with words of praise for the Locarno treaties and encouragement for the prospect of international peace. At the same time, he expressed hope that, before long, "another Locarno might be achieved where Europe would come to terms with Russia," thereby contributing to the welfare of both Russia and Europe.

In the late 1920's Benes continued to work unceasingly on his favorite project of general security and arbitration. His standing in the League of Nations was unimpaired. He was repeatedly elected to the Council and was its rapporteur for security matters. In 1926 Germany's imminent entry into the League, combined with bids by Spain, Brazil, and Poland for permanent tenure of the League Council, caused a considerable scramble for Council seats. The Special Assembly of March 1926 failed to resolve the controversy. In order to help untie the Gordian knot that apparently hindered the unraveling of this delicate situation, Benes—like his Swedish counterpart Undén[28]—placed his seat at the disposal of any or all seekers. His magnanimous gesture, while not of immediate effect, contributed to the final solution and certainly raised his reputation at Geneva and in Europe generally. In September 1926, when new elections to the enlarged Council took place, Benes was restored to the seat he had vacated. In the following year, he won a further success when the League adopted two of his proposals making it obligatory for League members to facilitate meetings of the Council and improve and expedite the functioning of the organs of the League in time of emergency. Simultaneously, an Arbitration and Security Committee was formed with Benes as chairman; and in 1928, he presided over a session of a sub-commission of this committee which worked out sample types of arbitration and guarantee treaties. These were approved by the Assembly as a means for calming areas in Europe where disputes were still in progress and which were not included in the Locarno treaties. As Benes' stature increased, so did that of his country, or at least his claims with regard to it. Thus, in 1928, when the Kellogg-Briand Pact was being prepared for signature, Benes could claim special consideration for Czechoslovakia, arguing, not only that it was a signatory of the Locarno Treaties, but that it was a state which necessarily had an interest in all matters pertaining to European security.

IV

Although his efforts were only partially successful, Benes' diplomatic

[28] See Chapter 3 above.

labors in the 1920's, and especially his work at Geneva between 1924 and 1929, earned him widespread, if not unreserved, respect and recognition. With the turn of the decade, international developments took a definitely disadvantageous turn as far as he was concerned. Geneva now ceased to be, if it ever had been, the center in which the great decisions were made. When the long awaited Conference on Disarmament was finally convoked in 1932, it was overshadowed by impending events in Germany. At that Conference, Benes played his customary energetic role and, as rapporteur of the General Commission, was largely instrumental in formulating the draft resolution which was accepted by the majority of the delegations in July 1932. This resolution was, however, decisively rejected by Germany and by the Soviet Union, and subsequent events were to prove that it, and the work of the Conference as a whole, had no real significance.[29] Benes continued to seek compromises which would reconcile the divergent interests of the participating Powers, but it was clear now that his old gifts had little relation to the realities of the new age of power politics which was opening.

Necessarily, therefore, Benes was forced to return to the more traditional methods of diplomacy.[30] In the first years after Hitler's rise to power, he had two principal objectives: first, to prevent the establishment of a Great Power directorate which might reduce Czechoslovakia's European role; and, second, to strengthen his country's existing treaty system and, in particular, to improve the cohesion and power of the Little Entente. In pursuance of the first of these, he was a bitter opponent of the Four Power Pact which Mussolini had initiated in the spring of 1933. Before Ramsay MacDonald went to Rome to discuss the Pact in March 1933, Benes warned him against it; and his subsequent agitations in Warsaw and Paris, supported as they were by the Little Entente as a whole, had an undoubted effect in the watering down of the Pact which took place before its signature and which, essentially, rendered it an innocuous engagement.

With respect to his second objective, his prospects of success appeared, until 1935, to be quite favorable. His cordial relations with Alexander of Yugoslavia and Foreign Minister Barthou of France seemed to promise that the Little Entente would not only be maintained but would be the center around which a new security system for eastern Europe was established. This hope was further supported by Russia's rapprochement with

---

[29] On the Conference on Disarmament, see below Chapter 10, §IV and Chapter 13, §II.
[30] For a summary account of Benes' diplomacy between 1932 and 1938, but not including the Munich crisis, see his *Pameti*, pp. 1-73.

the West and her entrance into the League in 1934, which Benes, as chairman of the League Council, helped to effect, and by the subsequent conclusion of a mutual assistance treaty between Czechoslovakia and the Soviet Union, an engagement coordinated with Czechoslovakia's existing ties with France.

These hopes were quickly disappointed. Between 1934 and 1938, the Little Entente disintegrated rapidly. The assassination of Alexander and Barthou in 1934 and the dismissal of Titulescu of Rumania in the following year removed three of its most ardent supporters, and Italy succeeded in detaching Yugoslavia from the partnership through Ciano's treaty with Stojadinovic in the first months of 1937.[31]

Benes' attempts to buttress his security system were weakened further by the fact that Barthou's successors failed fully to exploit their new relationship with the Soviet Union and, simultaneously, developed doubts about the advisability of maintaining the integrity of Czechoslovakia against the threat of external aggression. Benes was, therefore, in a highly exposed position when, in the spring of 1938, Hitler inaugurated the openly aggressive phase of his policy.

In the absence of direct testimony from Benes, who was the suffering protagonist in the dramatic events of the summer and early fall of 1938, it would be difficult, if indeed not unfair to him, to attempt a critical evaluation of his behavior. The testimony of available documents is clear on one point. Neither France nor Britain treated Czechoslovakia as if moral right were on her side. The two Western Powers appeared to be anxious to "steamroll" Czechoslovakia, first, into concessions to the Sudeten German Nazis of such far-reaching nature as to impair the sovereignty of the country and, subsequently, into capitulation to Hitler's demands. The representatives of Great Britain and France showed an *a priori* hostile disposition toward Benes and toward his slow deliberations concerning the course his government should follow.[32] Their impatience with Benes and the peremptory manner in which

---

[31] See below Chapter 16, §11.

[32] This hostility sometimes took curious, but revealing, forms. See, for instance, the private letter written immediately after Munich by the deputy-editor of *The Times*, R. M. Barrington-Ward, a convinced and influential member of the appeasement school. Referring to Benes, Barrington-Ward wrote: "I am sorry for him but . . . I regard him—along with Clemenceau, Poincaré, Austen, Barthou and others—as one of the most active architects of disorder in Europe. No one battled to maintain the disastrous artificialities of the French 'system' with greater diligence and ability than Benes. No one was more adept in using the language of the League to consecrate the *status quo*." *The History of "The Times"*, IV, Part II, 944-945.

they treated him was in glaring contrast to the esteem he had been accorded on earlier occasions.

Confronted with this crisis, Benes did not seem to be in full possession of his diplomatic skill. It was difficult for him to deviate from a principle to which he had adhered most tenaciously, namely that the question of the ethnic minorities in Czechoslovakia was an internal matter not subject to international consideration. It was also difficult for him to realize that the Western Powers—especially France—would actually abandon Czechoslovakia in a showdown. For a long time, Benes indeed seemed to hesitate as to the right course of action. His hesitation, which was interpreted by his Western critics as willful obstinacy, was rather due to his honest inability to face reality and choose to "go it alone" as an alternative to capitulation. In the precarious circumstances in which he found himself, the only tangible offer he seemed to have made consisted in suggesting that any litigation between Czechoslovakia and Germany take place within the framework of the arbitration treaty the two countries had concluded in 1925. In a broadcast to the Czechoslovak people at the height of the crisis he bade them to be calm, for he had "a plan." What his plan was has not been authoritatively revealed. Some people claim that he hoped somehow to weather the first onslaught of German demands and to come to terms with Poland and Hungary in order to free his country's exposed flanks from the danger of attack. It is questionable whether Benes could have carried out his plan successfully under any circumstances. Events, however, moved too rapidly and the efficacy of the plan was not tested.

At Munich, where the fate of the Czechoslovak Republic was sealed, neither Benes nor his emissaries were permitted to participate in the deliberations. In sharp contrast with the beginning of his career, when he managed to secure representation in high international councils without having a state behind him, Benes now had to suffer the humiliating experience of having his country's destiny decided without benefit of consultation with him. It was an ignominious end to a diplomatic career that had begun so brilliantly.

Diplomats and Diplomacy in the
Early Weimar Republic

BY HAJO HOLBORN

THE GERMAN DIPLOMATIC SERVICE could not pride itself on as old a tradition as the French or English services. In the strict sense a corps of German diplomatists came into existence for the first time after the founding of the North Germanic Confederation of 1867. Broadly speaking, only two generations had served in the new Foreign Office when the Bismarckian empire collapsed in military defeat and internal revolution. But even if we consider the German Foreign Office a mere continuation of the Prussian Foreign Office, the German foreign service would not gain a very long or great history. The old Habsburg empire had always trusted the diplomatist's art as much as military valor, and it had picked its diplomatic representatives from among the high nobility of the Holy Roman Empire, Hungary, Italy, and the Austrian Netherlands. Prussia's rise to a Great Power position in Europe was the work of her soldiers and, in a less conspicuous way, of her internal administrators. For these careers Prussia's eighteenth century kings had trained the uncouth scions of the Prussian gentry. The Diplomatic Service was subordinate to the major departments of state activity. A good many Huguenots and Italians were used by Frederick II as diplomatic agents because they had linguistic ability and social versatility.

Diplomacy became a more important business in Prussia during the age of Napoleon, but it was historically significant that before Bismarck's day no Prussian diplomat ever rose to the highest office in the monarchy, as for example Metternich did in Austria. His Prussian colleague at the Congress of Vienna, Hardenberg, was undoubtedly an accomplished diplomat, but he had made his career in domestic administration. Even after 1815 the Prussian Diplomatic Service did not attract outstanding talents, nor was the timid Prussian foreign policy, conducted by reactionary officers and bureaucrats, a school for diplomats.

The chief example of new forces in Prussian diplomacy was Otto von Bismarck, who proved to the Prussians and Germans what great diplomacy could achieve. He defined the place of the diplomats in the pseudo-constitutional system of the new German empire and became the real father of the German Diplomatic Service.

In addition to all the intricacies of the constitutional life of the second German empire, two major problems existed in the formulation of German foreign policy. The army remained the greatest power in the state and, as in the past, was not under civilian supervision. It exercised a strong influence on the conduct of foreign policy.[1] In both the wars of 1866 and of 1870 Bismarck fought bitter fights with the military leadership over war policies. As long as Moltke was chief of the Prussian general staff these conflicts did not extend in a serious manner into the peacetime relations of the civilian and military authorities, though cases of friction occurred, which arose chiefly from the insubordination of the military attachés in the German diplomatic missions.[2] They increased once Moltke's influence was superseded by younger men like Count Waldersee and worsened even more with the appearance of Admiral von Tirpitz' ambitious naval attachés. During the first world war the army under Ludendorff's ill-starred leadership emerged not only as dominating the course of German foreign policy but also as the master of German internal affairs.

But the impact of the constitutionally independent position of the armed forces on German foreign policy cannot be discussed without considering at the same time the power that Bismarck had laid in the hands of the emperor-king. The Chancellor was appointed by the monarch and executed officially the policy of the emperor. It was Bismarck's belief that the emperor would normally support the policy framed by his experienced minister with the assistance of an expert staff, the foreign service. William I lived up to these expectations though at times violent

[1] Cf. on the relations between military and civilian leadership most recently Gerhard Ritter "Das Verhältnis von Politik und Kriegführung im bismarckischen Reich" in *Deutschland und Europa, Festschrift für Hans Rothfels*, ed. by Werner Conze (Düsseldorf, 1951), pp. 69-97. For the older literature see Hajo Holborn "Moltke and Schlieffen" in *Makers of Modern Strategy*, ed. by E. M. Earle (Princeton, 1943), pp. 172-205.

[2] A number of cases are illustrated by Albrecht Mendelssohn Bartholdy, in *Diplomatie* (Berlin-Grunewald, 1927), pp. 51-77. For a historical analysis see Gordon A. Craig, "Military Diplomats in the Prussian and German Service: the Attachés, 1816-1914" *Political Science Quarterly*, LXIV (1949), 65-94.

clashes occurred between Chancellor and emperor over issues of foreign policy, as in 1866 with regard to the peace and, in 1879, to the alliance with Austria. But while William I was malleable, his grandson proved eccentric and untractable, and there was no obstacle in the Bismarckian constitution against direct monarchical government. Differences on foreign policy were not of major importance in the dismissal of Bismarck in 1890, but the personal regime of William II immediately went on the rampage in foreign affairs.

The damage inflicted by the preposterous speeches and ill-considered actions of the emperor on Germany's position in the world was enormous, but William II was too deficient in imagination and consistency to become the exclusive director of German foreign policy. Apart from the management of the routine operations, the Foreign Office retained a considerable measure of policy-making authority. What endangered this authority, however, more than purely personal gestures and interventions was William's propensity to accept the advice of his military and naval chieftains. The determined and reckless machinations of Admiral von Tirpitz overpowered William II, and since Tirpitz was in addition to his diplomacy a master of popular propaganda, the Foreign Office lost the decisive role in the molding of Anglo-German relations. Between 1890 and 1914 the political influence of the German Foreign Office declined rapidly from the height that it had attained under Bismarck.

The first world war completed the breakdown of the policy-making authority of the German Foreign Office. The invasion of Belgium, that made the entry of Britain into the war inevitable, had already been conceded to the military before 1914. But every demand raised by Hindenburg and Ludendorff in the course of the war was granted by the Chancellor and the Foreign Office. The proclamation of a Polish Kingdom in 1916, which killed all possibility of separate peace negotiations with Russia, and the opening of unlimited submarine warfare in 1917, which made the United States declare war on Germany, present only two illustrations of the eclipse of the German Foreign Office. But Ludendorff, protected by Hindenburg's popularity and assisted by Tirpitz' wily gift of mass manipulation, threw the full power of the army behind a program of annexations that only a military victory over all the enemies of Germany could have realized. Moreover, once Hindenburg and Ludendorff had been given supreme command of the German army, they dictated the policies of the civilian government as well. In July 1917 the military leaders forced William II to dismiss Chancellor von Bethmann-Hollweg; in July 1918 they brought about the resignation of the Secretary of

Foreign Affairs, Richard Kühlmann. In these months the personal regime of William II was buried, but so were the last vestiges of Foreign Office authority. The virtual dictatorship of Ludendorff came to an end only when he had to admit defeat in late September 1918 and suddenly demanded a parliamentary German government to conclude an armistice and peace. Then, the German Foreign Office could recover somewhat from the lowly place to which it had fallen.

Whether the German Foreign Office would have provided Germany with a more intelligent foreign policy if it had retained under the reign of William II some of the power that it wielded in Bismarck's days, nobody can say. Undoubtedly, there existed in the German Foreign Office at all times persons who on account of their familiarity with conditions in other countries were conscious of the need for moderation. But though a few of them were ready to take the risk of resignation, none of them showed the willingness to fight for a radical revision of the Bismarckian constitutional system.

This was not surprising. Diplomats are the last people to man barricades, though revolutionaries have often become good diplomats. But the German diplomatic corps that Bismarck created after 1871 was composed of people who supported his constitutional system. Bismarck took great care to make the new German foreign service representative of the new empire. The selection of the German ambassadors to the Great Powers illustrates his policy most clearly. The post in St. Petersburg was in the hands of the Prussian general Hans Lothar von Schweinitz from 1876 to 1893, while Prince Chlodwig Hohenlohe, Bavarian prime minister in the founding days of the German empire, became in 1874 ambassador in Paris. Count Georg Münster, the son of the British-Hanoverian minister who in 1814-15 had restored the kingdom of Hanover, was sent in 1873 as German ambassador to London. A younger son of one of the small reigning princely families of Germany, Prince Henry VII Reuss represented Germany at the Austrian court from 1878 to 1894. When in the 1880's Prince Hohenlohe was made regent of Alsace-Lorraine, Count Münster went to Paris and was followed in London by Prince Paul Hatzfeldt. In Constantinople Joseph M. von Radowitz, the first German specialist on Oriental affairs, attended to German interests.

Each of these six men set a standard of diplomatic performance that compared favorably with that of any ranking member of the older foreign services of other countries. It was obvious that Bismarck tried successfully to expand the Prussian into a German foreign service.[3] Indeed, Swabians and Bavarians were quite numerous in German diplomacy after 1871. There was a European air about Bismarck's ambassadors. By ancestry or marriage many of them were related to the nobility of other countries, and their German national patriotism was tempered by their sense of European responsibility. Up to a point Bismarck also cherished people of independent judgment. He always admonished his diplomatic emissaries to feel themselves not only attorneys of German national interests but also pleaders of the case of the foreign governments to which they were accredited. Bismarck was conscious of profiting from their personal reactions and disregarded, therefore, a certain amount of deviationist opinion. Count Münster, a grandseigneur of stubborn individual convictions, caused him particular worries by his staunch opposition to German colonial acquisitions. On the other hand, none of Bismarck's ambassadors was fully initiated into the arcana of the chancellor's over-all policy. After Bismarck's resignation in the debate over the renewal or nonrenewal of the German-Russian reinsurance treaty, all of them sadly missed the decisive points of Bismarckian foreign policy since they were familiar only with the special problems of their particular posts.

In the Diplomatic Service of the Second Empire a sharp distinction existed between the "political" diplomats and the rest of the Diplomatic Service. Nobody was accepted in the political Diplomatic Service who did not enjoy a private income that was comparable to a high official's salary. Without it he might perhaps be accepted in the consular service or become a legal councillor of the German Foreign Office, but could not normally hope to receive a diplomatic post or enter the political section of the German Foreign Office. In theory at least a separation was maintained among the three sections of the German Foreign Office—the political, the economic, and the legal sections and their dependent diplomatic and consular careers. In practice the distinction often proved surmountable. Quite a few people who started as dragomans in the oriental field went through the consular into the Diplomatic Service. The first Under-Secretary of the German Foreign Office, Dr. Clemens Busch, and the last imperial Foreign Secretary, Dr. Solf, were examples of such advancement. There were also in Bismarck's Foreign Office, as distinct from foreign posts, some special experts who enjoyed the confidence of the Chancellor. The most important personality in this connection was

[3] A good description of the German Foreign Office and foreign service in the Bismarckian period is contained in Joseph Maria von Radowitz, *Aufzeichnungen und Erinnerungen*, ed. by Hajo Holborn (Stuttgart, 1925).

Lothar Bucher, the friend of Karl Marx, who was brought back from his English exile and served Bismarck in the political division of the Foreign Office chiefly as councillor in charge of Western European affairs. As a rule, however, members of the political foreign service in rotation served in the political division of the German foreign service, though also in cases like that of Baron Friedrich von Holstein members never returned from the central office to posts abroad.

A strange dichotomy can be noticed in Bismarck's activities as an organizer and educator. He was very conscious of his responsibility as the founder of the German Diplomatic Service and took endless pains to help its members perfect their performance. He never tired of warning them that Germany's role was not that of Europe's policeman or schoolmaster. But he went as well into more special problems of diplomatic conduct. Thus he once remonstrated when at a conference one of his ambassadors had apparently let pass a public pronouncement that spoke contemptuously, with reference to Bulgaria, of the machinations of a small nation undermining European peace. "Our judgment and our vote," Bismarck wrote, "have more weight before Europe the more calmly and dispassionately they are presented. Such an expression weakens the impression that German policy is not exclusively the product of cool reasoning but rather of some sort of touchy sentiment . . . the more I agree politically with your Excellency's interpretation and treatment of the situation the more I would wish that also the form of its expression should be colored by the gentleness and benevolence that we do not inwardly cherish but whose outward appearance will act as the oil in the machine and will not increase the anger of others beyond an unavoidable measure."[4] Admonitions of this type went out to the German diplomats continuously.

Yet at the same time Bismarck wanted to leave the direction of German politics to a young generation imbued with pride in Germany's international position and faith in the worth of Germany's semi-absolutist order. He contributed greatly and deliberately to inflating the autocratic sentiments of Prince William, whom he wished to immunize against the liberal tendencies of his father, Emperor Frederick III, and his mother, the daughter of Queen Victoria. The same policy was noticeable in the 1880's in his selection and preferment of the younger members. His own son, Prince Herbert Bismarck, who was his father's chief assistant in diplomatic affairs during the last years of his reign, already represented a new type of German diplomat, less individualistic and more adaptable to the wind that blew from highest quarters, on the other

---

[4] J. M. von Radowitz, *Aufzeichnungen und Erinnerungen*, II, 256-257.

hand more assertive in international dealings. Herbert Bismarck was profoundly loyal to his father and the Foreign Office tradition that the latter had initiated, but other young members of the service had their eyes on the coming ruler.

Even under William II a good many men of original character and high competence could be found in the German foreign service. Count Paul Wolff-Metternich, German ambassador in Britain, proved his statesmanlike qualities in his long political duel with Admiral von Tirpitz. During the first world war Count Johann Heinrich Bernstorff in Washington and Richard von Kühlmann fought with similar fortitude for the recognition of their own ideas. But none of them prevailed in correcting the course of German foreign policy, and altogether there were too few independent men left in the high places of the German Foreign Service to maintain the distinctive level of the first period. The Foreign Office was internally divided by the factions which were the result of the personal schemes of Baron Friedrich von Holstein, who made himself the actual governor of the office between 1890 and 1906 and drove many of the Bismarckian old guard into the wilderness of peripheral posts or retirement. William II on his part liked people of personal wealth who could glamorize the social functions of diplomacy. He encouraged drastic language and sharp demands if incidents occurred that could be construed as reflections on German national honor. But the emperor paid little attention to the advice of highly experienced diplomats. Dashing smartness and languid servility were rewarded instead, and an atmosphere of mediocre cleverness settled over the *Wilhelmstrasse*. Though the average German diplomat in the age of imperialism was not lacking in self-consciousness, his sense of importance occasionally paled when he had to admit that in the competition with the military and naval coteries for the nod of the imperial majesty, the German Foreign Office more often than not failed to succeed, till during the world war it found itself on the side-lines. "Politics must keep its mouth shut during the war until strategy allows it to talk again," William II proclaimed.[5]

II

When Dr. Wilhelm Solf became Foreign Secretary in the Cabinet of Prince Max of Baden on October 4, 1918, the German Foreign Office was charged with the melancholy mission of concluding an armistice and opening peace negotiations after the war had been lost. At least it was no longer seriously hampered in its task by the army. When Luden-

[5] Otto Hammann, *Bilder aus der letzten Kaiserzeit* (Berlin, 1922), p. 128f.

dorff reversed his political attitude late in October and proposed to break off the armistice negotiations in view of the Allied demands, the new government could depose him without incurring opposition. But the Foreign Office had to cope with the influences emanating from the political parties. Matthias Erzberger, who had led the catholic Center party into the coalition with the Progressive and Social Democratic parties, became the chief German armistice delegate and affected German foreign policy during the whole period very profoundly.[6]

Solf was a liberal and convinced that only democracy could offer Germany a better future. He was a man of considerable learning, wide interests, and foreign experience. Temperamentally he was well-equipped to fit the German Foreign Office into a democratic state. But the November revolution not only swept away the monarchical institutions but also placed the chances of a democratic development into grave jeopardy. After November 10 the executive and legislative power fell into the hands of a council of people's delegates formed by three members of each of the Majority and Independent Socialist parties. The Majority Socialists under Ebert and Scheidemann saw in the council only a temporary authority to be abolished as soon as democratic elections for a national assembly could be held. Meanwhile they were anxious to see the old bureaucratic agencies of the federal government, among them the Foreign Office, carry on under their general supervision. The bulk of the Independent Socialists was not fundamentally but only partly in disagreement with these aims. They, too, wanted a national assembly, but at a later date in order first to gain through revolutionary action more positions of economic and political power. In this connection they took also a far more critical, and even at times hostile, view of the professional civil servants, a feeling naturally reciprocated by the latter.

But under the wings of the Independent Socialist party there also existed extremist groups, which pressed revolutionary action forward and which were willing to do so even in alliance with the so-called Spartacus group, the incipient communist movement of Germany, then under the leadership of Karl Liebknecht and Rosa Luxemburg. In the local workers' and soldiers' councils and on the streets the radical and bolshevist groups displayed formidable strength. In the absence of a properly functioning central authority they could embarrass and possibly even overthrow the moderate elements in the council of people's delegates. The struggle, that went on in Germany in the three months after No-

[6] For the general history, see Arthur Rosenberg, *The Birth of the German Republic* (New York, 1931) and Harry R. Rudin, *Armistice* (New Haven, 1942).

vember 9, 1918, was fought in the first place for domestic ends, but it had from the outset the strongest possible foreign implications.[7] Adherence to democratic forms would mean the creation of a national government that would have the strongest moral right to speak for the whole German people and could take fullest advantage of the democratic principles that Wilson had promised would guide the peacemakers. A democratic Germany, as an equal among the Western democratic nations, could save not only her national unity but also most of her disputed possessions, such as parts of her Polish and Alsatian provinces and perhaps even some of her African colonies. If such a convenient peace could be achieved the internal German conflict would be eased. The democratic principle would protect the continued existence of a strong German national state. It would simultaneously shield the moderate forces from the accusations of the parties on the Right that the Left had been the gravedigger of the Reich. It would equally help to quiet criticism from the socialists that no bourgeois group had ever done anything under the empire to stop official German foreign policy from building up growing anger against Germany among the nations of the world. The first American diplomatic observer, Ellis Lorring Dresel, who visited Germany after the armistice at the end of December 1918, wrote quite correctly: ". . . there is a strong wish to take up relations again with the United States at the same point where they were before the war, and the hope is cherished that the events of the war will be overlooked and condoned and that by the help of America, Germany will be enabled to rehabilitate herself."[8]

It was with such beliefs and hopes that liberals like Solf placed themselves behind Ebert and the Majority Socialists and appealed for the support of the German bourgeoisie through the founding of the new German Democratic party, which on January 19, 1919, polled about a third of the nonsocialist vote.[9] But before these elections took place the whole democratic program appeared endangered by the growing might of the radical forces in Berlin as well as by Ebert's seeming unwillingness to free himself from the embrace of the sinister Independent Socialists and to put down the terror of the street by force. On December

[7] Cf. Hajo Holborn, *La Formation de la Constitution de Weimar*, *problème de politique extérieure* (Paris, 1931) (Dotation Carnegie, Bulletin 6).

[8] The interesting reports of the first Dresel mission are printed in *Foreign Relations: Paris Peace Conference*, II, 130-172.

[9] In the national elections of January 19, 1919, the Majority Socialists received 37.9, the Independent Socialists 7.6, while the Center party received 19.7, the Democratic party 18.6, the German People's party 4.4, and the German Nationalist People's party 10.3 per cent of the national vote.

9, 1918, Solf appeared at a meeting of the council of people's delegates and caused a scene by accusing Hugo Haase of collusion with the Russians. Both the moment and the target for such an attack were ill-chosen. Haase had no sympathy with Lenin and had readily assented to the continued exclusion of a Soviet diplomatic representation from Germany. But even if Haase had not taken an anti-Soviet stand, Ebert at this stage could not have afforded an open break with the Independent Socialists. He hoped to outvote them easily at the elections and was preparing to meet any attempts at disturbing the elections or refusing to accept their verdict by the use of military force. Solf's sally came too early and he consequently had to be dropped as Foreign Secretary. As his successor the people's delegates selected Count Ulrich von Brockdorff-Rantzau, who was obviously anxious to direct German foreign policy and whom the delegates considered the finest horse in the stable of professional German diplomats.

Brockdorff-Rantzau was undoubtedly one of the best bred among the old-time German diplomats. Descended from an old noble family of Holstein, which in former centuries had seen many of its sons serve in high places in Denmark, and at German courts—in the seventeenth century a Rantzau even had become *maréchal de France*—the count was an unyielding individualist. The artist George Grosz in one of his satirical cartoons of the early 1920's depicted him with his short moustache, cold eyes, and disdainful look as the model of the aristocrat contemptuous of the democratic mob. (See illustrations.) During the first world war Brockdorff-Rantzau as minister to Denmark had seen to it that Germany respected the neutral rights of its small northern neighbor. Since the German legation in Copenhagen by the end of the war had become one of the most important among the few remaining German missions abroad, the minister had been able to acquaint himself with the broad aspects of German foreign policy.

Naturally, Count Brockdorff-Rantzau had been brought up as a monarchist, but he became a critic of German policies under William II. The emperor's flight to Holland in early November 1918 had in his opinion wrecked the moral reputation of the Prussian-German monarchy forever and he used to speak thereafter of William II as "the deserter of Doorn." On the other hand, his twin brother and most intimate confidant, Count Ernst Rantzau, acted in the days of the Weimar republic as the administrator of the large estates and possessions of William II in Germany. Brockdorff-Rantzau was free from a blind chauvinism, prone not to overrate military power in international relations, and a resolute hater of generals meddling in foreign affairs. Apart from a burning German patriotism Brockdorff-Rantzau was motivated by cool reason rather than by sentiment. The Russian and German revolutions impressed him with the strength of the masses and, though he was no genuine democrat, he considered the introduction of democracy as inevitable and as the only bulwark against bolshevism. As conditions of his assumption of office he demanded from the people's delegates the suppression of the power of the revolutionary councils and the earliest possible election of a democratic national assembly. He also wanted to be heard in internal questions and to be assured that in certain circumstances he would have the support of the government if he refused to sign the future peace treaty.[10] From the beginning it was his belief that a united public opinion had to be built behind the official policy at the peace conference in order to impress the Allies and to keep them from imposing humiliating and unbearable conditions. Still Brockdorff-Rantzau did not gain a marked influence on the evolution of Germany's domestic situation even after he had become German Minister of Foreign Affairs in the first republican Cabinet approved by the German national assembly in February 1919. When the critical phase of the peace negotiations arrived in May and June 1919, Brockdorff-Rantzau's policy failed to command sufficient support at home.

Brockdorff-Rantzau realized that he could not become a German Talleyrand. The vanquished Germany could not hope like the defeated France of 1814-15 to safeguard her position as one of the Great Powers by diplomatic finesse. The thought of diplomatic maneuver, in particular between the United States and the European nations but also between Britain and France, was, of course, by no means entirely absent from the minds of German diplomats, but the German peace strategy was fundamentally built upon the loud appeal to world public opinion, which it was confidently hoped would compel the governments of the West to adopt a most liberal interpretation of the Wilsonian peace program. "Open diplomacy," as first practiced in a telling way by Trotsky at Brest-Litovsk and then officially promulgated by Wilson,[11] was to become the chief medium of German diplomacy. The Germans expected that now after the Fourteen Points had been declared as the guiding principles

[10] See his letter and memorandum to Scheidemann of December 9, 1918, in Graf Brockdorff-Rantzau, *Dokumente und Gedanken um Versailles* (3rd ed., Berlin, 1925), pp. 29-35. Obviously, Scheidemann must have been in contact with Brockdorff-Rantzau before the actual Solf crisis.
[11] On the historical background of the idea of "open diplomacy" see Hajo Holborn, *The Political Collapse of Europe* (New York, 1951), pp. 80 and 104-105.

of peacemaking they would have an equal voice in debating and settling the application of these principles to the concrete issues.

German diplomacy chose to place an interpretation on the Fourteen Points that favored German claims everywhere. This attitude was understandable if taken at the opening of the great debate, but rather dangerous if maintained to the bitter end. The actual meaning of the Fourteen Points was not easily defined. By and large national self-determination was most strongly emphasized, but certain ideas about free trade and access to the sea were also considered valid. Considerations of national security, too, were not entirely excluded from the Wilsonian peace proposals, and in what form a balance between the various elements of thinking could be struck remained uncertain.

But even with regard to specific problems the quest for the exact sense of the Fourteen Points required more than an abstract philosophical acumen. Point 13 said: "An independent Polish state should be erected which should include the territories inhabited by indisputably Polish populations, which should be assured a free and secure access to the sea and whose political and economic independence and territorial integrity should be guaranteed by international covenant." Broadly speaking, the German-Polish settlement of Versailles, though unnecessarily harsh in details, could be depended on as a fair execution of Point 13. The passionate German assertions that Point 13 excluded the cession of the major part of the province of West Prussia that became the Polish corridor and the creation of the free city of Danzig were untenable. One can indeed go so far as to sympathize with the position that the Poles took even after 1919 when they complained that the Versailles treaty did not give them "secure" access to the sea. Already in the summer of 1920, when Russian armies approaching Warsaw threatened the very existence of the new Polish state, Danzig refused to let arms shipments from the West go through its port. All this is not to say that the German-Polish settlement was not open to criticism on other grounds. It was very questionable whether it was practical policy to impose provisions of this sort upon Germany so long as the Western Powers were not determined to maintain as close a watch over the Vistula as over the Rhine. But such an argument has no direct connection with the search for a correct interpretation of Wilsonian political ideals.

German foreign policy and propaganda under Count Brockdorff-Rantzau represented the Germans as the true champions of pure and politically unadulterated Wilsonianism. The Germans failed to appreciate that their erstwhile enemies would rub their eyes when they saw the

Germans appear in the white garb of liberalism and would become greatly suspicious if the Germans were in any way to twist Wilsonian principles. Their failings in this respect weakened their case with Wilson especially. The German Foreign Office had entertained great hopes that the United States, not having special interests in Europe, would moderate the war aims of her European allies. But the Germans lacked any understanding of the peculiar political circumstances in which Wilson had to pursue his policy.

Wilson's peace program, which embodied the aspirations of the liberal sections of the American people, clashed sharply with the war aims of the European allies, as expressed in the secret treaties. An uneasy compromise between the United States on one side and Britain, France, and Italy on the other had been achieved at the time when Germany urged the conclusion of an armistice. As a matter of fact the German intelligence service, which in contrast to Germany's foreign press analysis was very efficient in this period, had somehow managed to get hold of the key document of these negotiations, the so-called "official" American commentary to the Fourteen Points of October 1918.[12] The document was presented by Colonel House to Clemenceau and Lloyd George to illustrate what the American government considered the practical meaning of Wilson's program as it was to be applied at the conference. It was clear that in all cases the United States would take as benevolent a view of the interests of her wartime allies as was compatible with the letter of Wilson's declarations on peace aims. Nobody, for example, with any political judgment could assume that Wilson's ideas on the reform of the colonial system would be deemed applicable to the colonies of America's European allies. Lloyd George and Clemenceau had agreed to accept the American principles as regulating the future peace settlement with the defeated Central Powers, but not the internal problems of the British and French empires.

Yet the execution of the agreement, reached only under great difficulties, depended to a large extent on the development of the internal political scene. The loss of control over Congress in the November elections of 1918, the fight about American partnership in a League of Nations, and the relative indifference of the American public to all the details of the German settlement narrowed Wilson's freedom of action.

[12] The document was printed in Charles Seymour, ed., *The Intimate Papers of Colonel House* (Boston, 1928) IV, 192-200. I first mentioned in my *Kriegsschuld und Reparationen auf der Pariser Friedenskonferenz von 1919* (Leipzig-Berlin, 1932, p. 18n.), that the document had fallen into German hands, a fact later on broadcast by Hjalmar Schacht, "Germany's claim for Colonies," *Foreign Affairs*, xv (1937), 223-34.

Equally grave was the collapse of British liberalism in the British December elections both in its effects on Lloyd George's own policies and on the cooperation between the Prime Minister and the President. Brockdorff-Rantzau did not display a clear insight into the political situation on the Allied side and Count Bernstorff, the former German ambassador in Washington who headed the bureau in the German Foreign Office charged with the preparations for the Paris conference, apparently did not correct Brockdorff-Rantzau's notions.[13] The German diplomats had made a certain attempt to define priorities among the German national interests that they proposed to defend at the conference. They did not wish to put up a fight for Alsace-Lorraine or for Poznania and were prepared to make concessions to Denmark in North Schleswig, but they intended to insist on the retention of the Rhineland, including the Saar, and of all the eastern territories except Poznania. On Austria and what was at a later date called Sudetenland, the Germans were to reserve their claims, but they were not ready to push them too far, since they feared that the merger of Austria with Germany was likely to give the French a chance to demand the whole left bank of the Rhine. Brockdorff-Rantzau also realized that most and possibly all of the German colonies would be lost.

Officially the decision to accept the Allied decision to limit the future German army to 100,000 men was made by the German Cabinet and not by Brockdorff-Rantzau. General Hans von Seeckt, who was the chief military member of the German delegation at Versailles, attacked Brockdorff-Rantzau for making the German army an object of diplomatic barter.[14] And though it is true that the German Cabinet, chiefly under the influence of Matthias Erzberger, adopted this policy, there is no indication that Brockdorff-Rantzau disapproved of the move that was intended to avoid the appearance of German militarism and instead place the restoration of Germany's economic position first. At the last stage of the peace negotiations the German government even went so far as to offer to forego the building of all the battleships that the draft treaty had left to Germany in order to achieve the revision of other sections of the treaty. In addition to the territorial integrity of the German Reich within the limits already mentioned a reasonable settlement of the reparation issue was made the major aim of the diplomatic strategy of the German

[13] On the organization of the German preparations for the peace conference see Alma Luckau, *The German Delegation at the Paris Peace Conference* (New York, 1941), pp. 27-53.
[14] The event was the origin of the enmity between Seeckt and Brockdorff-Rantzau; see Friedrich von Rabenau, *Seeckt, Aus seinem Leben 1918-1936* (Leipzig, 1940), pp. 159-186.

Foreign Office. Also, the immediate participation of Germany not only in the League of Nations but also in the drafting of its constitution was considered a highly desirable end.

In itself this program would not have been unrealistic if it had not been followed through in a doctrinaire spirit. German policy was overrating its chances to defend Germany's eastern frontiers. Its desire to partake in the drafting of the League's covenant was hopeless, the more so since the German proposals aimed at turning the League from a federation of governments into an assembly of peoples, ideas that would have made it even more difficult for Wilson to get acceptance of the League of Nations in the United States. But under Brockdorff-Rantzau the original program was adhered to with the utmost determination and, when it began to meet resistance, German diplomatic tactics became stiff and tough-voiced. It should not be forgotten for a moment that the Allies never tried to take cognizance of natural German pride and feeling. The denial of oral negotiations and the humiliating conditions in which the Germans were placed at Versailles were insulting. Still, it is most doubtful whether Brockdorff-Rantzau did a good service to the German cause when he set the style of all subsequent German diplomatic presentations by the tone of his first speech at Versailles on May 7, 1919. It was probably not so important that he remained seated on that occasion as that he purposely used an aggressive language.[15] It was strange to say: "At this conference, where we alone, without allies, face the large number of our opponents, we are not without protection. They themselves have brought us an ally, the law that is guaranteed to us by the agreement on peace principles." While this undiplomatic way of addressing the future partners of negotiations, who had granted Germany the benefit of the Fourteen Points, could perhaps be psychologically explained as an outbreak of honest emotion, other remarks show a rather demogogic attitude. "The hundred thousands of non-combatants, who perished since November 11 on account of the blockade, were killed with cold determination after our opponents had achieved and secured victory. Of this you ought

---

[15] The incident of the German representative remaining seated in his reply to Clemenceau has been interpreted in many different ways. See for example D. Lloyd George, *Memoirs of the Peace Conference* (New Haven, 1939), pp. 453-454. This author believes that Brockdorff-Rantzau's neglecting to get up was the result of his extreme nervousness at that moment. But the count always supported the myth that he had acted this way deliberately and thereby gave belated justification to the understandable annoyance of the conference. That the German representatives were themselves divided concerning the character of this first German speech before an international audience is shown by the discussion that took place on the evening before among the members of the German peace delegation. See Luckau, *The German Delegation*, pp. 63-65, 213-220.

to think when you talk about guilt and atonement."[16] Now, it was true that the armistice of November 11, 1918—and it was an *armistice* and not a peace—had continued the blockade, but by February 1919 the Allies had agreed to lift the blockade and the further delay was as much due to German unwillingness to employ her idle ships and pay for food imports with her own gold as to Allied hesitation to grant credits.[17] These events were fully known to the German minister, and it was not surprising that his speech caused resentment at Paris.

Obviously, Brockdorff-Rantzau felt even at the beginning of the peace negotiations that he would have to use the threat of the German refusal to sign the peace treaty, and no doubt this was the only weapon left to the Germans at the time. But the minister entertained highly exaggerated notions about the possible effects of such a policy. It required a strong and unified popular support in Germany, and it presupposed on the Allied side lack of confidence in the righteousness of their position. Various means were employed to produce both, but most important and, as we may add, most fallacious in its immediate political results was use made of the war guilt question. It was certainly a futile German hope that Allied opinion on Germany's war guilt, the centerpiece of all war propaganda, could be shaken or modified by German arguments, particularly at the very moment when victory had blessed the cause of justice.

On the German side the war guilt question logically became a moral and political issue at the time of the collapse of imperial Germany. The Germans in their vast majority had also been convinced during the war that the others had been responsible for starting the war. The bellicose nature of the pan-Slavism of Tsarist Russia and of British imperialism was singled out for special condemnation. Even most of the German Social Democrats, who before the war had always denounced war as the evil fruit of capitalism and castigated the armaments policy of the German empire, joined in the general German attitude. They justified their own support of the German war effort by the thesis that war had been forced upon Germany by the other Powers and that a socialist party was bound to play its part in the defense of its own national community. Once committed to this new line, however, they had not only made a full contribution to the German defense effort but had also tolerated the

---

[16] See Brockdorff-Rantzau's speech in Brockdorff-Rantzau, *Dokumente und Gedanken*, pp. 70-73. Also in Luckau, *The German Delegation*, pp. 220-223.

[17] W. Arnold-Forster, *The Blockade, 1914-1919* (New York, 1939). Also D. Lloyd George, *Memoirs of the Peace Conference*, pp. 192-199; John M. Keynes, *The Economic Consequences of the Peace* (New York, 1920) and his article on Dr. Melchior in *Two Memoirs* (London, 1949).

disregard displayed by the government for limited war aims. Not even the peace treaties of Brest-Litovsk and Bucarest of 1918 had aroused the Social Democratic party to forceful protestations. The tolerant and conniving policy of the majority of the party with regard to the nationalistic wartime policy of the imperial government had led in 1917 to the secession of a group of Social Democratic members who formed the Independent Socialist party. They asserted that no socialist party ought to forget in its support of national wartime defense its international and social responsibilities. War was a result of capitalistic competition and likely to feed imperialism. It was the sacred duty of the leaders of the socialist workers' movement to oppose with all the force at their disposal imperialistic war aims. Thus the Independents became the only party that voted in the *Reichstag* against the Brest-Litovsk treaties and maintained a sharply critical opinion of German foreign policy before and during the war.

Armistice, revolution, and the ensuing struggle between the Majority and Independent Socialists inevitably brought these problems to the fore and the Independent Socialists endeavored to demonstrate not only the imperialistic character of German wartime policies but to find evidence for the culpability of the German imperial government for the outbreak of war in 1914. The most eminent Marxist scholar of the time, Karl Kautsky, was to devote himself to the perusal of the documents of the German Foreign Office pertaining to the diplomatic crisis of July 1914. In Bavaria, where the revolution had unleashed strong regionalist tendencies, the criticism of the foreign policy of the German empire was presented with an anti-Prussian bias. It was Berlin that since Bismarck's days had falsified the course of German history through the Prussian centralization of German resources and their reckless use for militaristic purposes. Backed by such popular sentiment Kurt Eisner, an independent socialist of doctrinaire complexion whom the foaming Munich revolution had made the temporary master of Bavaria, could open his campaign for a frank German confession of war guilt as the first step toward the purification of German life from the sins of militarism as well as toward the restoration of international confidence in Germany. A repentant democratic Germany could hope to receive from Wilson a just and democratic peace. Eisner did not confine his agitation to public oratory but also began to publish secret diplomatic documents bearing on German policy in July 1914, and he demanded that the Foreign Office be purged of personnel.

The Bismarckian constitution of 1871 had retained Bavaria's right to maintain diplomatic missions abroad, which enabled Eisner to send Professor Friedrich Wilhelm Foerster, one of the few German intellectuals who was a sincere absolute pacifist and a radical critic of the German *Machtstaat*, as Bavarian minister to Berne in Switzerland. Foerster succeeded in making contact with George D. Herron, an American professor who served as an emissary of President Wilson. Nothing seems to have come of all these transactions. Herron apparently was not received by Wilson in Paris, and it is doubtful whether in any event Wilson would have been interested in this approach.[18]

While the war guilt was hotly debated in Germany and used to defame the monarchical system and to criticize the moderate political parties for their lukewarm opposition to the vagaries and excesses of German foreign policy in the past, popular sentiment in the victorious countries was running high with expression of indignation about the responsibility of the imperial German government for the war of 1914 and for many violations of international law in the course of the war. It was said that retribution for the wrongdoers ought to form the chief objective of the forthcoming peace conference. This whole trend was highlighted by the furor of the British election campaign, which also showed that this emotionalism could shift governmental policies away from the original agreement on peace principles. The promises suddenly made by Lloyd George and his ministerial colleagues about reparations were certainly not in harmony with the pre-armistice agreement. Internal and external developments thus conspired to fill the German policy makers with dark forebodings about the political significance of the war guilt question. Within Germany it was an instrument to press the revolution further and to drive a wedge between the radical parties on one side and the moderate as well as the old conservative parties on the other. It also threatened, as Eisner's Independent Socialist and separate Bavarian foreign policy proved, the unity of German foreign policy. Yet even worse was the danger that the war guilt accusation would be employed by the Allied governments to supplant the Fourteen Points in the drafting of the peace treaty. On November 29, 1918, Solf sent a note to the Allied governments proposing to turn over the examination of the causes of the world war to a neutral commission whose members should be given free access to the archives of all the Powers.[19] The proposal met with the rejection of all the Allied governments, who found that it was unnecessary to explore what was self-evident.

[18] Mitchell Pirie Briggs, *George D. Herron and the European Settlement* (Stanford, 1932).

[19] *Foreign Relations: Paris Peace Conference*, II, 71-75.

This result did not allay German fears. In particular democratic groups felt that the political use of the war guilt accusation would have a pernicious effect on the moral resistance of the German people and the foundation of a just international peace. The great German sociologist Max Weber, whose influence on the establishment of the Weimar republic was strong, was also most active in condemning the assertions of a German war guilt raised at home and abroad. A group of democratic political and academic figures, the Heidelberg Association for a Policy of Law,[20] began to address the general public in early February 1919 with manifestos on the question of war guilt. After that the Germans became more and more preoccupied with the expectation that the Allies would base their demands on the allegation of a German war guilt.[21] Such a belief seemed to be confirmed beyond all doubts when the German government came into the possession of a report of a committee of the Paris peace conference dealing with the "authorship of the war." Count Brockdorff-Rantzau consequently did not hesitate at the meeting of the peace conference on May 7, with the big treaty still lying unopened before him, to talk out: "The demand is made that we shall acknowledge that we alone are guilty of having caused the war. Such a confession in my mouth would be a lie."[22]

The Germans when they examined the treaty were apparently not puzzled about the fact that it contained no statement on the German war guilt where one might have expected it most, in a preamble to the treaty, or to the League of Nations, or in Section v, covering the German disarmament, or in Section vii, dealing with war crimes. A reference to German war guilt could be discovered only in Article 231, which opened Section viii, the reparation section of the treaty. This article was now quickly considered to be the result of the already mentioned committee report and thought to demand from Germany the recognition of her war guilt.

Actually the German delegation was mistaken both with regard to the historical origins and the intended legal meaning of Article 231. The committee "for the responsibilities of the authors of the war and sanctions" had considered but, chiefly under American and English influence,

[20] On the Heidelberg Vereinigung see Luckau, *The German Delegation*, pp. 46-53. Also Max Weber, *Politische Schriften* (Munich, 1921), pp. 381ff., 394ff., 485ff.

[21] See the report by the representative of the Foreign Office to the committee for peace negotiations of the Weimar national assembly on April 15, 1919, in Luckau, *The German Delegation*, p. 187f.

[22] *ibid.*, p. 220.

rejected a recommendation for the inclusion of an article on war guilt.[23] They were content to write a summary report on the origins of the war of 1914, the very report that came into German hands. But this was only an opinion and no further official action followed from it. The reference to war guilt slipped into the draft treaty of Versailles unintentionally during the discussions of German reparations by the Reparation Commission and the Council of Four. The drafting of the provision for German reparations started from the conditions of the Lansing note of November 5, 1918, which specifically stated that Germany would make compensation "for all damage done to the civilian population of the Allies and their property by the aggression of Germany by land, by sea and from the air." But French and British opposition against this formula was strong, since public opinion in Britain and France expected, and had been made to believe by their governments, that Germany could be forced to make much larger payments than this definition permitted. Lloyd George was also anxious to find a settlement that would give Britain a higher percentage share of the future German reparations than the Lansing note would have made possible. Consideration of Germany's capacity to pay, however, indicated that the actual sum would remain far below popular French and British hopes and be in practice closer to figures that could be derived from the Lansing note.

In order to protect Lloyd George and Clemenceau against the wrath of their parliaments it was decided after long and intricate discussions[24] not to set a final sum that would only cause disappointment. It was also resolved to open the reparations section with a statement that Germany was theoretically responsible for all the loss and damage that the Allies had suffered. But after thus appeasing popular sentiment in Article 231, recognition was taken in Article 232 of Germany's capacity to pay and finally the Lansing formula was reestablished as the ruling principle for eventual German payments and deliveries. However, the appendix to this article, which spelled out the categories of these reparations, expanded the German obligations in an extravagant way by adding war pensions and other items.

Article 231, the first article of the reparations section of the Versailles treaty, was not intended to be a war guilt clause.[25] It was not designed

[23] The minutes of this committee were published by Albert de Lapradelle, *La paix de Versailles*, III: *Responsabilités des auteurs de la Guerre et Sanctions* (Paris, 1930).

[24] They are excellently narrated and documented in Philip M. Burnett, *Reparation at the Paris Peace Conference* (New York, 1940).

[25] This opinion was first expressed by R. C. Binkley and A. C. Mahr, "A New Interpretation of the 'Responsibility' Clause in the Versailles Treaty," *Current History*, XXIV

to pass moral judgment on the foreign policy of Germany before 1914, but was meant to affirm a liability of Germany for damages which she was not requested to repair. These exceeded, however, those contained in the Lansing note; and the wording of Article 231 by people who were all convinced of Germany's war guilt could not avoid moral undertones.

The whole difficulty rested with a single word. Article 231 read: "The Allied and Associated Governments affirm and Germany accepts the responsibility of Germany and her allies for *causing* all the loss and damage to which the Allied and Associated Governments and their nationals have been subjected as a consequence of the war imposed upon them by the aggression of Germany and her allies."[26] The insertion of the word "causing" changed what would otherwise have been only a financial liability into a causal responsibility. Thereby "aggression," a word that in the Lansing note (and in Article 232) described only military actions after the outbreak of the war, could change its meaning so as to include events and plans prior to the war.

The German peace delegation read it in this sense, and in their nervous obsession with the war guilt question their German translation of the fateful sentences placed the accent entirely on the moral issue. Their passionate pleas with the Allies against the acceptance of this article produced stern rebuttals. The Allies would probably never have attached to the article the sense of a moral war guilt had it not been for the German remonstrance. In a very strict sense not even the Allied notes dealing with German war guilt linked it with Article 231, but they avoided a denial of such connection and since they expressed the Allied conviction of Germany's guilt with heated acrimony, they were taken by the world as proof that the German interpretation was largely correct. It was impossible for the Allied statesmen to retreat, once they were challenged by the Germans. The article had been written to cap a delicate political compromise among themselves which would have been endangered if they had disavowed its text. Moreover in public they would have

---

(1926), 398-400; then again, with better material, in Binkley's "The 'Guilt' Clause in the Versailles Treaty," *ibid.*, XXX, 294-300. Shortly before the Lausanne Conference of 1932 that buried the reparations problem, two eminent French historians gained wide publicity by their study of the problem. Camille Bloch and Pierre Renouvin, "L'Article 231 du Traité de Versailles. Sa Genèse et sa signification," *Revue d'Histoire de la Guerre Mondiale*, X (1932), 1-24. Cf. also my treatment in *Kriegsschuld und Reparationen auf der Pariser Friedenskonferenz*. A well-balanced and thorough modern historical statement is found in the introduction of Burnett, *Reparation at the Peace Conference*.

[26] Italics mine.

appeared as betraying a main tenet of common faith. For everybody in the Allied camp was convinced of Germany's war guilt.[27]

The German Foreign Office could not, of course, have known what had been going on behind the scenes of the conference of the Allies in Paris. But even if the German reading of Article 231 was bound to be different from what the Allied reparation experts had primarily intended to put into it, the German delegation approached the problem in a frame of mind that was conditioned by the singular circumstances of a Germany in revolution and defeat. It was no doubt desirable to set into motion an objective study of the causes of the world war. But the mills of historical research grind slowly and do not easily produce a standardized result. Moreover it takes a long time to acquaint the general public with the findings of historians who in most cases tend to agree rather on the complexity of the issues raised by the past than on their absolute meaning. From the German point of view, however, it was enough to have made it clear that historical problems could not be settled by simple moral verdicts of a victor and that historical truth, at least in a world that recognized the freedom of the human spirit, was not the monopoly of any single Power.

It was, however, a different matter to make the war guilt issue the hub of a radical fight against the acceptance of the peace treaty. Any cool examination of the treaty was bound to show that the practical provisions, including those for reparations, would have been identical with or without Article 231. Obviously, the treaty of Versailles had been drafted by people who believed in Germany's responsibility for the outbreak of the war of 1914, but they were not likely to change their opinions from one day to the other because of German protests. If Count Brockdorff-Rantzau decided upon making Article 231 the official test case of the sincerity of the Allied nations to conclude a democratic peace, he felt confident that by declaring the article a despicable attack upon German national honor the government could rally the great majority of the German people to resist the acceptance of what soon became known in Germany as "the peace of infamy." Even at Versailles, Brockdorff-Rantzau spoke incorrectly of Article 231 as imposing on Germany the *sole* guilt, and Chancellor Bauer repeated this statement from the rostrum of the national assembly in Weimar.[28]

The fight against the war guilt did, indeed, bring the mass of the Ger-

---

[27] See for example Charles Seymour, *Intimate Papers of Colonel House*, IV, 392, 409.

[28] Brockdorff-Rantzau, *Dokumente und Gedanken*, p. 70; *Stenographische Berichte der verfassunggebenden Nationalversammlung*, CCXXXVII, 1115.

man people together, but it united them on a very dangerous platform. All the German parties with the exception of the reactionary parties and the Spartacus group had been quite irresponsible in their expectations of what a peace on the basis of the Fourteen Points would be like. The government failed to enlighten them before the beginnings of the Versailles discussions about the true feelings of the Allied countries towards Germany. The American diplomatic observer in Germany, Dresel, wrote on May 10, 1919: "The entirely insincere belief that the armistice was only concluded on condition that President Wilson's peace program, as interpreted for the benefit of Germany, would be enforced, had become general. The people had been led to believe that Germany had been unluckily beaten after a fine and clean fight, owing to the ruinous effect of the blockade on the home morale and perhaps some too far-reaching plans of her leaders, but that happily President Wilson could be appealed to, and would arrange a compromise peace satisfactory to Germany."[29] The announcement of the peace conditions was, therefore, a terrific blow to practically everyone in Germany. It could be said now that the introduction of democracy had not saved Germany from a grim fate and that the imposition of the war guilt made it necessary for the Germans to defend their national past. Such at least was the impact of these events on the many bourgeois people who immediately after the revolution had given their vote to the new Democratic party, since they hoped that democracy would protect them against bolshevism at home and foreign nationalism. The Democratic party left the government before the signing of the Versailles treaty, but its power was spent. In the national elections of 1920 the party lost almost half of its members and declined steadily thereafter. The German bourgeoisie went back to the old parties of the Right, the more easily since the spectre of Bolshevism had lost in the course of 1919 much of its terror after the new German armed forces, the so-called "free corps," had established order.

Count Brockdorff-Rantzau hoped through the appeal to German national honor to gain the approval of the nation. This policy was unrealistic. The threat that Germany would not sign the treaty was a practical political device. Lloyd George foresaw the high cost that further or even total occupation of Germany would entail. It might kill the chance of ever getting reparations from Germany and it was certain to reopen all the political issues just laboriously settled with France. The British Prime Minister became the champion of considerable treaty modifications. The most important concessions that the Germans wrested

[29] *Foreign Relations: Paris Peace Conference*, XII, 119.

from the Allies were a plebiscite in Upper Silesia and a number of adjustments with regard to the German-Polish frontier which actually foreshadowed subsequent British support to German claims in this field during the postwar period. Other valuable promises of a more anticipatory nature, like the early accession of Germany to the League of Nations, were added to the final reply of the Allies to Germany.

Still it was entirely unwarranted to assume that Germany could have improved the treaty conditions if it had rejected the Allied ultimatum. It was wishful thinking on the part of the German peace delegation to urge in their final report the refusal of signing the treaty, because, as Brockdorff-Rantzau expressed it, "if our enemies execute their threat and apply force against us, though we are willing to fulfill all their just demands, we are convinced that the progressive peaceful development of the world will give us soon the objective tribunal before which we shall demand our right."[30] It was an optimism born of despair, but with no basis in fact. We know today what would have happened. The Allied armies would have marched into Germany and have occupied northern Germany as far east as the Weser River, cut off southern Germany, and established contact with Czechoslovakia.[31] Most of the German army had dispersed after the armistice and the revolution. After January 1919, however, new troops had been organized on a voluntary basis and the military balance of power vis-à-vis Poland, though not the West, favored Germany. Allied forces had been depleted between November 1918 and June 1919 from 198 to 39 divisions. General Foch was, however, confident that this force was adequate for the occupation of Germany up to the Weser, an estimate in which the German generals fully agreed.[32] For a push beyond the Weser to Berlin Foch demanded additional troops and the authority to conclude armistices with individual southern and western German states.

There is no question that a final German refusal to sign the Versailles treaty would have meant the end of the unity of the German empire. Military resistance, Hindenburg and Groener admitted, was of no avail. In such circumstances a policy of refusing to sign the treaty would have been suicidal. Direct cooperation with the Soviet Union might have changed the German position to some extent. In this case Germany ought

[30] Brockdorff-Rantzau, *Dokumente und Gedanken*, pp. 116-117.

[31] See the discussions of the Council of Four in *Foreign Relations: Paris Peace Conference*, VI, 501-550. On German military estimates, cf. Rabenau, *Seeckt, Aus seinem Leben*, pp. 181-187. Also a book for which its author received much information from General Groener, E. O. Volkmann, *Revolution über Deutschland* (Oldenburg, 1930).

[32] Volkmann, *Revolution über Deutschland*, pp. 278-279.

to have publicly renounced the treaty of Brest-Litovsk and withdrawn her troops from the territories of the prewar Russian empire. This could have opened the way for some sort of diplomatic cooperation between Germany and the Soviet Union that might have impressed the Western Powers. Instead German troops remained in the Baltic states fighting Bolshevism and created a deep gulf between Germany and Russia. Still it was highly doubtful how much assistance Germany could have derived from the economically disorganized and exhausted Russia. The new Russian rulers in 1919 thought in terms of world revolution, and Germany was in their opinion the country that had to be won over first. Lenin would probably have supported with all his might and with all the resources at his disposal a Germany fighting the capitalistic countries with revolutionary means. This, however, would have required a radical workers' government in Germany which would soon have drifted into complete dependency on Moscow. Brockdorff-Rantzau was certainly not planning to promote such a political combination, but for that matter nobody in Germany except the communists and a few adventurers of the extreme Right was willing to take this path. Not even most Independent Socialists were prepared to turn to the East. They denounced the Brockdorff-Rantzau policy of resistance as a revival of German nationalism at the expense of the suffering masses who needed peace and bread.

But would there be peace and bread if the treaty was signed? Did not the treaty contain many provisions which could be used by the victors to commit further hostile acts against Germany, and was not the limitless demand for reparations an absolute block to any economic recovery? And finally would it be possible under such conditions to build a democracy in Germany? These were, indeed, questions that could make any German falter, but there were certain points which could inspire a modicum of confidence. First of all, the unity of the empire was preserved; second, after a respite one could hope to restore the greatest treasure of the nation, the capacity for hard work. Beyond this one might trust that other countries would learn to appreciate the fact that Europe could not recover if Germany did not regain a reasonable prosperity and that if one wished to talk of a comity of democratic nations, Germany could claim the protection of liberal principles.

This belief won out in the councils of the German Social Democratic and Center parties. After the revolution the Center party had come under the leadership of its democratic wing. Matthias Erzberger dominated, and this former Swabian village teacher, who had a quick, if glib mind, became the chief opponent of Brockdorff-Rantzau on the German political scene. As the chairman of the German armistice delegation he had been in contact with Allied representatives since November 11, 1918.[33] Erzberger converted the Center party to the acceptance of the treaty. In the Social Democratic party the sober advice of Hermann Mueller finally prevailed. Mueller had gone to Paris in the last days of July 1914 to establish a common policy of the French and German socialists towards the war crisis. Now, five years later, as the German Foreign Minister he affixed his signature to the Versailles treaty, which showed no influence of the Second International but instead the heavy imprints of nationalism. Even on the German side nationalism had been galvanized into life again by the Allied demands, and German foreign policy had not been conducted with much consideration of the vital internal needs of an infant republic.

III

The actual course of German foreign policy had been finally decided by the parties and not by the old-line diplomats. Hermann Mueller was the first German parliamentarian to assume the wheel in 76 Wilhelmstrasse, and ever thereafter in pre-Hitler days the appointment of a professional diplomat to the post signified a nationalistic policy. According to the Weimar constitution, the German Foreign Office was made the sole agency for the administration of German foreign interests. The Bavarian foreign missions were abolished. Another anomaly disappeared. In the old empire the Federal Foreign Office served at the same time as the foreign ministry of Prussia that maintained legations with all the German courts. Through them the Foreign Office exercised a direct influence in German domestic affairs.

One important development was still instigated through the Prussian minister in Munich, Count von Zech, after the revolution. Relations with the Vatican under the Bismarckian constitution were reserved to the states. Since the end of the eighteenth century Prussia had sent a minister to Rome, but the Vatican had never established a legation in Berlin. The highest diplomatic representative of the Pope was the legate accredited to the Bavarian government, who, in 1919, was Eugenio Pacelli. The communist revolution in Munich in May 1919 forced him to take refuge in the Prussian legation; and, in the conversations between the young Count and the future Pope, the first steps were taken that led to an early visit of the legate to Berlin and to the establishment of a

---

[33] See, on his conversations with American representatives, *Foreign Relations: Paris Peace Conference,* XII, 124-135.

nunciatura in the capital of the German republic in 1920, an event that strengthened the republic internally and externally.

After the dissolution of the Prussian legations the Foreign Office had to gain its popular support through the parliament. The Weimar constitution did not envisage a participation of the state governments in the formulation of German foreign policy; but, since the foreign problems were closely related to those of the internal administration of the states, particularly in the occupied Rhineland, the prime ministers of the states were often consulted. The Weimar constitution had taken a leaf from the book of James Bryce[34] and instituted a special foreign affairs committee of the *Reichstag* that remained in being even between sessions and periods of legislature of the German parliament. Under German conditions the committee was not an ideal instrument for developing a foreign policy beyond individual party opinions. The German parties were profoundly divided in their views on foreign affairs. The presence of communist members, moreover, made the committee unsuitable for confidential discussions. In practice, therefore, meetings between the Minister of Foreign Affairs and leaders or foreign affairs experts of the parties forming the government assumed the functions for which the parliamentary committee had been created.[35]

The Weimar constitution had given the President of the Reich powers greater than those of the French President. In foreign affairs, they included a decisive voice in treaty-making and in the appointment of the diplomatic officers. Both Presidents, Ebert and Hindenburg, guarded these rights jealously but were anxious to avoid friction with the Foreign Office. When Brockdorff-Rantzau was made German ambassador in Moscow in 1922, he made the curious demand that he should be allowed to report to the President instead of to the Foreign Minister. This wish, though a departure from the constitution, was granted, but all reports were sent from the presidential palace to the Foreign Office. The Weimar constitution had also made an attempt to raise the position of the Chancellor above that of the other members of the Cabinet. The Chancellor was supposed to lay down the guiding principles of the policy of his Cabinet. But all the Cabinets of the 1920's were coalition governments over which the Chancellors presided as chairmen rather than as directors. Still, in certain matters, a Chancellor was able to disregard the Foreign Minister. The most important case of this sort was Chancellor Joseph

[34] See James Bryce, *Modern Democracies* (London, 1921), II, 402-420.
[35] Cf. on the Weimar constitution and foreign affairs Heinrich Pohl, *Völkerrecht und Aussenpolitik in der Reichsverfassung* (Berlin, 1929).

Wirth's approval of the independent policy of General von Seeckt in Russia. Since Wirth was simultaneously Minister of Finance, he could provide the funds for the Russian activities of the *Reichswehr*.

Even under the Weimar constitution, there remained additional agencies that were officially charged with foreign policy, or could unofficially concern themselves with it. Among the other federal ministries it was in particular the Ministry of Finance and, to a lesser degree, the Ministry of Economics which were influential in foreign affairs. The old Foreign Office had experience in the negotiation of trade agreements, but in the postwar world economic matters became so intricate and, at the same time, politically so important that members of the Ministry of Economics were brought into the international negotiations. An even more conspicuous role was assumed in all the endless conferences on reparations and loans by the Ministry of Finance. The new "financial" diplomacy was over the heads of old-time diplomats. In Germany it found its first accomplished representative in Carl Bergmann.[36]

A strong hand was needed at the helm of the Foreign Office to hold the course through various currents and to weather the storm of popular resentment and dissension. In the history of the Weimar republic Gustav Stresemann was the only statesman who, through his great ability as a parliamentary tactician and orator, as well as through his diplomatic talents, could make the office fully his own. Under him the German Foreign Office settled down to the execution of foreign policy in greater calm than in the first five years after Versailles. Immediately after the revolution, people had been unanimous in asserting that the German Foreign Office was in bitter need of a drastic reform. Count Brockdorff-Rantzau inaugurated a new internal organization which was realized under his successors.[37] The political and economic divisions of the Foreign Office were merged and then were reorganized along regional lines into three new divisions. Apart from them, four other divisions remained, dealing with legal, cultural, personnel, and press affairs. The merger of the old political and economic divisions was accompanied by the consolidation of the diplomatic and consular services into a single foreign service. Thereby, the selection for higher positions was placed on a broader basis. The change also tended to compel every member of the foreign service to acquaint himself in some measure with economic and social problems.

[36] See Sir Josiah Stamp in the foreword to the English edition of Carl Bergmann, *The History of Reparations* (Boston, 1927).

[37] The details of this organization, which was named in Germany the "Schüler reform" after the official in charge, cannot be treated here.

The German foreign service was small at the end of the war, owing to the closing of many German missions abroad and to the retirement of a good many of the old monarchists. But a substantial number of the middle-aged and younger diplomats of the imperial office remained in the service. Some, like the former ambassador in Washington Count Bernstorff, who was to represent Germany through many years at the disarmament discussions in Geneva, became members of the Democratic party; others such as Baron von Neurath, Germany's ambassador in Rome from 1921 to 1930, and in London till 1932, for the time being suppressed their displeasure with the republic. The old guard saw to it that among the young candidates a goodly number of their relatives, or members of their own elegant student fraternities were selected.

Some of the best representatives of a liberal Germany came from this group, such as Leopold von Hoesch, the greatest of the German professional diplomats of the interwar period. After the mutual recall of the ambassadors in Paris and Berlin during the Ruhr invasion, Hoesch as chargé d'affaires had impressed Poincaré so much that he asked for his appointment as German ambassador. In his eight years in Paris, and again from 1932 to 1936 in London, the sensitive and devoted man proved himself a master of his craft. Dr. Wilhelm Solf went as ambassador to Tokyo, where from 1920 to 1928 he represented a Germany without colonial ambitions and succeeded in establishing close friendly relations in the cultural and economic field.[38] On all levels of diplomatic rank, this list could be extended, and it must at least be added that in general members of this social group, whether liberal or conservative, were less easily swayed in later years by National Socialism. Some of the German nationalists, such as Admiral von Tirpitz' son-in-law, Ulrich von Hassell, even joined the conspiracy against Hitler. But, in the 1920's, these people radiated considerable ill-will toward a republican foreign policy. It is interesting to see how Baron von Neurath spread the idea that the Fascist government of Mussolini would help Germany in a revision of the Versailles treaty, or to find other German diplomats denouncing German parliamentary Ministers of Foreign Affairs as unfit to head their office. Wipert von Blücher, a member of the eastern division of the Foreign Office in the early 1920's and German minister in Finland later on, could complain even in 1951, despite all that had happened in Germany under William II and Hitler, that decisions as such to accept or reject the Versailles treaty could not be made by the discussions of a

[38] On German policy in the Far East cf. Kurt Bloch, *German Interests and Policies in the Far East* (New York, 1940).

group of people, such as the Cabinet, since "a multitude of people cannot make foreign policy, for which but a singular will is needed."[39] Ernst von Weizsäcker, a naval officer who strayed into the diplomatic service at the end of the war and within little time acquired the feeling of being a knowing professional diplomat, judged: "The old officials were accustomed from former times to work under the direction of a specialist minister. But . . . the men in charge of the Foreign Office after 1918 were changed frequently and were regarded by us as amateurs. Stresemann was indeed of a higher stature than the general run of Foreign Ministers. But in the Foreign Office he was held to be too trusting in international affairs, a field in which he was not fully at home."[40]

But in the early years of the Weimar republic, chiefly on President Ebert's insistence, an effort was made to have Germany represented in eminent diplomatic posts by men who had made their career outside of the German bureaucracy. None proved a failure; on the contrary, most of them were unusually effective diplomats. Friedrich Sthamer, a former mayor of Hamburg, was sent as ambassador to London and his absolute honesty and tactfulness helped to allay British resentment and, at least after Locarno, to give Anglo-German relations a rather cordial note. Even more successful were the three socialist ministers, a somewhat surprising fact, since the German socialists prior to 1918 had hardly a chance to acquaint themselves with diplomatic affairs and manners. All three were essentially newspapermen. The Bavarian Adolf Müller acted from 1920 to 1933 as German minister in Berne, and the relations between Switzerland and Germany prospered. His influence reached beyond that. Ebert and most republican German statesmen liked to listen to his wise counsel on foreign policy, and much was done from the German legation in Berne to prepare Germany's way to Geneva. From 1922 to 1930, the Swabian Ulrich Rauscher held the most thankless post of the German Foreign Service, the embassy in Warsaw, with extraordinary courage and circumspection. The third socialist diplomat came from Schleswig-Holstein. Adolf Köster came to the Foreign Office as successor to Hermann Mueller when the latter became Chancellor in March 1920. As German representative at the North Schleswig plebiscite, as minister in Riga from 1923 to 1928 and, until his death in 1930, in Belgrade, he proved his mettle.

[39] Wipert von Blücher, *Deutschlands Weg nach Rapallo* (Wiesbaden, 1951), pp. 47ff.
[40] Ernst von Weizsäcker, *Erinnerungen* (Munich, 1950), p. 80; English translation by John Andrews (Chicago, 1951), p. 68. Herbert von Dirksen, *Moskau, Tokio, London* (Stuttgart, 1951), pp. 44, 56-58 is more considerate and restrained in his judgment on this point. So is Erich Kordt, *Nicht aus den Akten* (Stuttgart, 1950), pp. 24-52.

A member of the Bavarian People's party, Wilhelm Mayer-Kauf-beuren, was the first German postwar ambassador in Paris; a Center parliamentarian, Maximilian Pfeiffer, became minister in Vienna; while a board member of the Krupp works, Otto Wiedfeldt, was sent to Washington.[41] It may be mentioned that, after the conclusion of the preliminary trade agreement with the Soviet Union in May 1921, for once in German history an academician was appointed the head of a German diplomatic mission. The selection of Wiedenfeld, professor of economics at Leipzig University, was, however, designed to minimize the political significance of this diplomatic exchange in the eyes of the Western Powers.[42]

In spite of the good results achieved by the appointment of public figures to diplomatic positions, this policy was abandoned after 1923. Soon after his arrival in Berlin, the British ambassador, Lord D'Abernon, who had no special prejudice against German conservatives, confided in his diary that he preferred the Germans whom democracy had brought to the fore. He disliked in the old officials what he termed "Teutonic obstinacy or dourness." At the end of his ambassadorship he wrote: "German negotiators may be, and perhaps are, difficult to deal with, slow to be persuaded, pernickety, and disposed to quibble on small points, over-careful, making an infinity of reserves and precise pre-conditions on conjunctures and developments which, in all human probability, will not arise."[43] These remarks should perhaps not be taken too literally, for there were good reasons for moving cautiously in the years after Versailles, but they point up some of the shortcomings of the old-time professional German diplomats who were soon again to set the style of the foreign service. A good many people with greater and lesser gifts had gained accession to the Foreign Office in Berlin in the early years of the republic. How long they survived the trend toward the restoration of professionalism depended largely on their party support. The Center party was especially anxious to have a number of trusted party members in the office, and, since the Center commanded a pivotal position in German politics from 1920 to 1932, it retained a certain influence on the personnel policy of the Foreign Office. The Social Democratic party never gained representation in the inner councils of the central office after 1920. The examination for admission to the foreign service was stiffened, but

---

[41] Mayer-Kaufbeuren was recalled at the time of the French Ruhr invasion and died in 1923; Pfeiffer died in 1926; Wiedfeldt resigned his post in 1925. About the events leading to his retirement, see Gustav Stresemann, *Vermächtnis* (Berlin, 1932), I, 290-293.

[42] Wipert von Blücher, *Deutschlands Weg nach Rapallo*, p. 150.

[43] Lord D'Abernon, *An Ambassador of Peace* (Boston, 1929), I, 39; III, 28.

this reform did not amount to the introduction of a merit system, since the examination could be taken on invitation only. Moreover, the candidates could not feel certain that, even after passing the entrance examination, their future career would be commensurate with their ability.

Stresemann cared about these problems, but he was not a great administrator nor quite able to see through the cunning of bureaucrats. The tremendous burden of internal and foreign problems that he carried in a continuous struggle with his failing health, forced him to leave the internal administration of the office to the Secretary of State. Carl von Schubert, a slightly gruff, methodical, and immovable *Junker*, held this position from 1924 to 1930.[44] Under him the restoration of the German professional diplomat was fully achieved. The German foreign service had acquired a somewhat broader social and political basis, but its character was determined by the conservative professional diplomat. To secure his dominance Bismarck's IA division, a division to deal with high policy question, was reintroduced in an oblique fashion. So far as the existing six divisions were not directed by old-line diplomats, a deputy director of that ilk was appointed, who received instructions from, and could directly report to, a newly created office of the minister, the *Büro Reichsminister*, which centralized all matters considered of first-class significance.[45] Thus, even in the organizational sense, the old guard, and those who wished to perpetuate the old tradition, had come back. Probably only one group had a greater influence than it used to exert in the days of the imperial office. In a time when so much of the German foreign policy was a fight over the interpretation of the Versailles treaty, the legal division under its ambitious director, Friedrich Gaus, exerted an influence on the formulation and often even the execution of German foreign policy that went far beyond the functions of legal advice.

IV

The internal development of the German Foreign Office in the five years after the revolution reflected closely the general political history of the Weimar republic. During the period from the middle of 1919 to the middle of 1920, the forces which had supplied the strength for the building of a German democracy lost what earlier had seemed an irresistible momentum. The dramatic weakening of the Democratic party in the elections has already been mentioned, but even more important

[44] On the Foreign Office at the time of Stresemann's death in 1929, see Julius Curtius, *Sechs Jahre Minister der Deutschen Republik* (Heidelberg, 1948), pp. 146-150.
[45] Dirksen, *Moskau, Tokio, London*, p. 54.

was the crisis of the Social Democratic party. In the elections of June 1920, it lost about a third of its 1919 vote, which went to the Independent Socialists instead. With the great losses which the two democratic parties had suffered, and with the doubling of the Rightist vote in favor of the German People's party and the German Nationalists, the political position of the democratic wing of the catholic Center party grew precarious. Fehrenbach, a conservative member of the Center party, became Chancellor and formed a government consisting of the Center, the Democrats, and the German People's party, with the latter exercising preponderant influence.

The attempt to have a German republic under the leadership of the German workers' movement was shattered and had no actual chance of being renewed for another twenty years or more. It has become a definite tenet of German Social Democratic "self-criticism" that their willingness to accept the Versailles treaty and to support a pacific foreign policy in the period of the Weimar republic was a major cause in the collapse of their influence on German affairs. This is not true. The German Majority Socialists lost their dominant position in German politics because they utterly failed to give their followers the feeling that they were in dead earnest about abolishing the authoritarian state in Germany, and about preparing the way to a socialist economy in accordance with what they had preached for almost a half-century. The members of the working class would have forgiven their leaders for the original delay of any decisive action in the social field, since they agreed with them that the conclusion of peace must take precedence over all other political aims. But once the peace had been signed, the socialist workers expected active leadership directed towards the goals of democratic socialism which the party had inculcated upon its following for many decades. When the Social Democratic chiefs did not take action even after the first open counterrevolutionary move, the Kapp *Putsch* of April 1920, the workers wandered to the Independent Socialist party.

Foreign policy, therefore, was not the major reason in the decline of the Majority Socialist party, and the German worker wanted nothing so much as peace then and later. But he was not easily ready to bear the suffering that the German defeat forced upon him in order to vindicate the honor of a past Germany which had denied him full citizen's rights. During the first world war and again during the resistance to the French occupation of the Ruhr, the vast majority of the German workers proved their willingness to make sacrifices for a foreign policy in which they believed. But the leadership of the Majority Socialist party was unable to formulate a program of a German foreign policy that would have defined the vital interests of a democratic nation and, at the same time, boldly sketched out the practical ideals and obligations of a worldwide society of nations. The foreign policy of the Social Democratic party appeared to many of its followers as just another version of the policy of the Right parties, while the latter could decry its pacifism as sheer supineness. The lack of a clear foreign policy on the part of the Majority Socialists, therefore, was a contributing element to the rise of the Independent Socialists and subsequently of the Communists. In this connection, it should not be forgotten that democratic socialism had been confounded everywhere by the world war and by the advent of the Third International. And both France and England emerged from the war as bourgeois states.

The direction of German foreign policy fell into the hands of the German bourgeois parties after 1920, and among them the German People's party assumed a crucial position, not only because it had startlingly increased its popular vote in the elections, but because it represented the bulk of the German industrialists, including most of the coal and iron magnates of the Ruhr district. Hugo Stinnes, who had just expanded his family holdings into one of the greatest industrial and commercial empires, was the chief political spokesman of this group. There was a streak of the gambler in his nature that appeared even in his business enterprises, which collapsed shortly after his death in 1924. In politics, he was reckless and erratic. The new constellation of German party relations made it impossible to stabilize the German currency.[46] It was asserted from now on that in any event inflation maintained high employment in Germany while on the other hand demonstrating Germany's incapacity for making large reparations. Stinnes even argued that it would be desirable to refuse outright the payment of reparations, even at the risk of an Allied occupation of the Ruhr district. He disregarded the impact that the resulting coal shortage would have on the economic life of the rest of Germany and contended that a military occupation of the Ruhr would prove, once and for all, that nobody could collect reparations from Germany with bayonets.

The policy of negotiating reparations with a stiff upper lip was temporarily defeated when, in May 1921, the Allies, through the London ultimatum, presented an exorbitant bill for reparations and a demand for immediate cash payments, which Germany up to then had not made in any considerable size. The Fehrenbach cabinet resigned and, for another

[46] Cf. C. Bresciani-Turroni, *The Economics of Inflation* (London, 1937).

year and a half, the so-called "Weimar coalition" of the Center, Democratic, and Majority Socialist parties returned to office. But they ruled largely by sufferance of the Right, which did not at yet feel ready to launch its policy of firmness and which retained sufficient power even outside of the government, since it could rely on its influence on industry, the bureaucracy, and the army. The assassination of Walter Rathenau, the Foreign Minister of the Wirth cabinet, in June 1922 was a dreadful symptom of the demoralization of the fanatic nationalists. Chancellor Wirth and Rathenau had proclaimed Germany's willingness to fulfill the terms of the London ultimatum and had hoped to be able to show through this "policy of fulfillment" the impracticability of the Allied demands. This hope proved fruitless, and, in November 1922, a government of the Right under Wilhelm Cuno took the reins again. By this time, Poincaré was set on the enforcement of French claims for reparations and he expected through the occupation of the Ruhr district to solve France's security problem, which the nonratification of the mutual assistance pact of 1919 with the United States and Great Britain had left unsettled.

The Cuno government called for passive resistance, but within a period of eight months the French administration slowly succeeded in establishing control over the occupied area, while the fantastic superinflation brought Germany to the brink of complete chaos. The danger of the loss of the Rhineland, as well as the Bolshevization of the rest of Germany, was very real. The ultra-radicals of the Right, like Hitler, would have transformed the passive into an active resistance, but the military situation was hopeless in the judgment of the chief of the German army, General von Seeckt. Thus, the *Reichswehr* marched to stamp out the supposed centers of Left socialist and communist agitation in Thuringia and Saxony. At the same time, it snuffed out the revolutionary flame that Hitler tried to kindle in Munich. The stage was thereby set for a new approach to the major political problems of Germany. Now the liberal leader of the German People's party, Gustav Stresemann, could persuade the German industrialists to assist in the stabilization of the mark and attempt to reach an understanding with the foreign Powers. This led to the Dawes plan on reparations of 1924, the Locarno treaty of 1925, and Germany's entrance into the League of Nations in 1926.

This survey of German foreign policy with regard to its most urgent questions in the years after Versailles clearly indicates how little of it was or could have been made by diplomatic action. The great decisions, as far as they were at all in German hands, were inherent in the outcome of the internal social struggle. However, to regard the reparations problem exclusively, as we have done, from a German perspective, is much too narrow a view. On the evolution of French and British thinking about reparations the Germans could exert but a moderate influence. It depended on the economic and political developments of the Western countries, and was also to be determined by the mutual political relations of the wartime allies in the postwar years. Last but not least, the future policy of the chief creditor nation of the world, the United States, was always to be considered. The size of future American capital export or, for that matter, of American imports from Europe, as well as American preparedness to draw conclusions from the practical interrelations between German reparations and inter-Allied war debts, were all contingent elements. It would be a serious error to overrate the role of German foreign policy in bringing about the Dawes plan.

In the immediate postwar years, German officials had always urged the establishment of the total German obligation, instead of accepting an interim plan of reparation payments for a number of years. It was argued that, so long as the final sum was left undetermined, Germany was not likely to receive those credits that were needed to restore the German economy and enable it to produce reparations. Obviously, the argument was self-defeating if the total sum were placed at a very high level, as happened with the 132 billion gold marks of the London ultimatum. The Dawes plan stuck officially to the London figure, but defined a payment schedule only for a limited period. This was done, however, at a time when as a result of the settlement under discussion the influx of foreign capital could be anticipated. The example illustrates the baffling complexity of the reparation question and the novel problems that it presented to modern diplomacy. It is difficult to see how the German government could have managed the reparations question without the active mediation of the British ambassador, Lord D'Abernon, sometimes referred to in those years as the lord-protector of Germany. The Dawes plan was no solution of the reparations question, as later events were to reveal. But thereafter it was impossible for France to use the reparations issue as a means to achieve political and military aims which the peace settlement of Paris had denied her. The active participation of American financiers in the discussions of reparations strengthened the belief that Europe's economic ills could be cured in spite of reparations, a faith to which Americans themselves subscribed in the form of loans and credits of which Germany became the chief beneficiary.

The solution of the reparations question was the foremost task of

German policy all through the 1920's and, even more than the military occupation, it brought German foreign policy under the predominant influence of the Western Powers. But ever since May 7, 1919, the general aim of German foreign policy was the revision of the treaty of Versailles. It was popular with every party from the extreme Right to the extreme Left and, one may say, with every individual German. Revision, however, meant all things to all men. There was, in the first place, the division of opinion on whether the revision should be sought by peaceful means alone or ultimately by military action. In the latter case, it had to be discovered how a situation of war between the major Powers might develop in which Germany could join as an ally of one party and thereby regain a role in world affairs. On the other hand, those who saw the threat of a new war to Europe and Germany took the view that bilateral understandings should only serve for diplomatic, as against military, cooperation.

All these attitudes were reflected in the actual German foreign policy, or rather policies, in the years after the first world war. The prevailing sentiment in Germany discovered the divergence of French and British foreign policies soon after the war. Lloyd George had already fought for amendments of the draft treaty of Versailles. After the signing of the treaty, British diplomacy had continued to assist in its amelioration, in the drafting of a statute for the free city of Danzig, and in foregoing the extradition of German war criminals to Allied courts.[47] British occupation policy in the Rhineland was not overbearing and, in addition, tried to resist unwarranted French schemes of oppression. Again, after the plebiscite in Upper Silesia, Lloyd George favored Germany's political wishes. To be sure, Britain insisted upon the strict execution of the disarmament provisions of the treaty and displayed no willingness to waive her own claim for German reparations, but she showed an interest in the economic recovery of Germany, and her ambassador was using suave words about German disarmament at an early moment.[48] It was clear that Britain did not wish to see France as the absolute ruler of the continent and would, therefore, back Germany as a counterbalancing force.

It became a fundamental principle of German political thought, out-

---

[47] On the history of the revisions of the Versailles Treaty, see W. E. Stephens, *Revisions of the Treaty of Versailles* (New York, 1939), and the annotated edition of the Treaty prepared at the suggestion of President Roosevelt in the State Department at the end of the second world war and published as Volume XIII of *Foreign Relations: Paris Peace Conference.*

[48] D'Abernon, *Ambassador of Peace*, I, 87, 225.

side the Communist party and a very few other small groups, that the main endeavor of German diplomacy was to be directed towards ingratiating Germany with England in order to induce her to champion the German cause vis-à-vis France. Moreover, Britain seemed to own the best key for opening some doors to American help in European affairs. Practically nobody in Germany questioned the priority of the cultivation of Anglo-German relations on the agenda of German foreign policy. Ebert and most of the ministers were convinced that Britain's support for Germany had to be won by all means. But Ebert's opinion was shared by most of the German Rightists as well. Grand-Admiral von Tirpitz led the procession of the former England-haters who confessed that, after the lost war, a new German attitude towards Britain would be in order.[49] After the acceptance of the Versailles treaty by the national assembly, Count Brockdorff-Rantzau had not joined the ranks of those who persecuted his successors with reproaches and calumnies. In July 1919, he was already warning that Germany, once she had signed the treaty, must abstain from any secret schemes to blow it up. "Where the treaty is incapable of execution, it must be proved to our opponents."[50] And Brockdorff-Rantzau, too, had his eyes on Britain.

As early as 1918 there were, as we shall see in more detail further on, some military men who thought that they could build a close Anglo-German alliance by offering German military strength to Britain for the overthrow of Bolshevism in Russia. Ludendorff and General Max Hoffmann carried this propaganda into the postwar years, accompanied by the journalistic pleas of Arnold Rechberg, a wealthy industrialist and amateur politician. Adolf Hitler's foreign program was reared in the same camp, though he placed greater emphasis upon the necessity of an internal transformation, which in his opinion would make Germany strong enough to pull Britain in the right direction.[51] But the belligerent anti-Bolshevism lost out in the practice of German foreign policy after 1920. General von Seeckt's refusal to cooperate with the group was especially important in this connection.

On one point, however, all the German schools were in agreement. The attempt at an Anglo-German rapprochement was the most promising method of working towards the diplomatic, and perhaps eventually even

---

[49] Foreword to Alfred von Tirpitz, *Politische Dokumente*, I: *Der Aufbau der deutschen Weltmacht* (Stuttgart, 1924).

[50] Brockdorff-Rantzau, *Dokumente und Gedanken*, pp. 125f.

[51] See on the "antibolshevist" school Max Hoffmann, *Aufzeichnungen*, ed. by Karl F. Nowak (Berlin, 1929), and chapters 13-15 of the second volume of Hitler's *Mein Kampf*, written after Locarno in 1926.

the military, isolation of France. The opposite idea that the most logical way to achieve an alleviation of the treaty burdens on Germany was a firm understanding with France had only a handful of advocates in Germany in the Social Democratic and Democratic parties, and it was not the official policy of either party.[52] But the political and psychological difficulties on both sides were so great that it would have been impossible to base German foreign policy upon an early Franco-German reconciliation. The economic approach, as tried by Rathenau in his negotiations with Loucheur in 1922, might have created some of the preconditions for easing the tension between the two nations, but in both countries the majority of the politically powerful industrialists opposed cooperation. In these circumstances, London acquired an even greater control over German foreign policy than could have occurred if even a remote chance for a direct Franco-German understanding had existed.

It is most doubtful whether German diplomacy could have brought such a chance into being during the years between 1919 and 1925, but there is certainly no indication that German diplomats ever thought seriously about the implications of the situation thus created. They were preoccupied with the hope that the friction between Britain and France would grow into such an antagonism as to force Britain to bury the Entente and to side with Germany. In 1922-1923 these hopes reached their highest pitch. Not only the altercations over Germany but also the clash of French and British policies in Turkey and Greece as well as in Morocco and Tangier appeared from the German perspective as definite proof of the irreconcilable nature of British and French interests. It was a bitter disappointment to these Germans when the Mediterranean and Near Eastern conflicts were composed at the time of the Lausanne conference, which wrote the new Turkish peace treaty replacing the treaty of Sèvres.[53] When British resistance to the French policy in the Ruhr remained lukewarm, it was said that the British government had acquired the oil of Mosul by giving away the Ruhr coal. But then these unhappy events showed even more clearly that Germany must not lose contact with Britain. Stresemann's decision to form a government that could end the Ruhr struggle and work out a compromise with France, under British mediation and guarantees, was greatly affected by the disappointment over British policy.

The Germans, who believed in the incompatibility of future French and British policies, made very serious errors in their appreciation of

---

[52] The main organ of this school was a socialist monthly, *Sozialistische Monatshefte.*
[53] See below, Chapter 6, § IV.

Anglo-French relations. They disregarded the imponderables entirely. Although popular anti-German feeling in Britain lost its shrill emotionalism rather quickly after June 1919, the popular British attitude towards Germany remained reserved for a good many years. It is difficult to decide how much genuine popular sympathy existed between Frenchmen and Britishers, but both knew that they had immensely benefited by the Entente cordiale; and from this practical experience stemmed the readiness to tolerate some friction and to stop it before it poisoned their relations. But even the ponderable political factors should have indicated that the British had no need to fear France. The Germans, with the French upon them, were inclined in those years to overrate the strength of France. Britain was conscious of the security that her vast naval superiority afforded her, and she was also aware of her incomparable economic preponderance over France.

There was never any panic in Britain over the political and military position that France had gained as a consequence of the Paris peace settlement. The British government was not willing to commit too much British strength on the European continent particularly after the withdrawal of the United States. If France ruled the continent within the regulations of the Paris settlement and with reasonable regard to British sensitivities in Western Europe, Britain would be content to devote herself to her own far-flung and knotty imperial problems. Poincaré, however, was unmindful of the British conception of the Anglo-French Entente. French policy became an embarrassing nuisance but not yet a dangerous threat, the less so since some soul-searching brought out past British mistakes in the treatment of the French. Outstanding among them was the gingerly way in which the British had dealt with the French demand for a British guarantee of the Rhine frontier after the draft treaty of June 28, 1919 had come to naught as the result of America's refusal to ratify. British policy would have to be more generous than in the past in order to keep France from adopting a unilateral policy in Europe that would be ruinous to the rehabilitation of the continent, to the collection of any reparations and to the restoration of European markets, which was needed for the economic recovery of Britain. In one respect, the German resistance in the Ruhr was of great consequence. The expense which the French were put led to a long-overdue crisis of their public finances and of the stability of the franc. Internally it weakened the confidence of the high bourgeoisie in the government and gave the parties of the Left fresh influence, while demonstrating how dangerous it was for France to play a singlehanded game in world affairs.[54] The moment had arrived when British diplomacy could intervene and redefine the European power relationships.

One can say that the British Foreign Office under Austen Chamberlain never intended to steer an anti-French course. On the contrary, the whole British policy was often described as a return to the Entente cordiale. Chamberlain refused to accept the Geneva Protocol that would have meant a British obligation to act in any conflict arising out of the peace settlement,[55] but in the Locarno Treaty France received a British guarantee of the Rhine frontier. On the other hand, if Germany received the same guarantee against an act of French aggression, this signified in the first place the French renunciation of a unilateral policy going beyond the Treaty of Versailles. No doubt the double-sided British guarantee of the Rhine border had, from the German point of view, a certain prestige value as seemingly joining Germany to the Great Powers on a basis of equality. In general, the British were now convinced that a stronger Germany was needed to insure not only the recovery of Europe but stricter French adherence to the general ideas of British policy. "Desiring the maintenance of the Anglo-French entente, I am compelled to desire the existence of a strong Germany," said Lord D'Abernon.[56] He might have gone a good bit farther than official British policy did or could go. For the Versailles provisions were not changed. Germany had to accept the cession of Alsace-Lorraine and, more important, to subscribe voluntarily to the demilitarization of the Rhineland. She had to do so without the evacuation of the Allied troops from the occupied western regions. It was true that the Rhineland was eventually freed of Allied occupation, five years before the final date set by the Versailles treaty. But it had already been stated by the Allied statesmen at Versailles that, once Germany fulfilled her treaty obligations, an earlier evacuation would be possible. In these circumstances, it seemed frustrating that the occupation should come to an end only five years after Locarno and after lengthy negotiations, during which the British had not exerted the harsh pressure on France for which the Germans had hoped. Nor did the British show themselves easy bargainers in reparations questions. Germany's admission to the League of Nations afforded her new political

[54] See above, Chapter 2, § II.
[55] See above, Chapter 1, § III and Chapter 4, § III.
[56] D'Abernon, *Ambassador of Peace*, II, 238-239. Cf., for the general historical analysis, Arnold Wolfers, *Britain and France Between Two Wars* (New York, 1940); W. M. Jordan, *Great Britain, France and the German Problem, 1918-1939* (London, 1943); Hajo Holborn, *The Political Collapse of Europe* (New York, 1951), pp. 124ff.

opportunities to plead her case before the world, but it was a promise on her part not to seek revision by extra-legal methods and to work in peaceful cooperation with the other League members. In this respect League membership tied Germany closely to the international system that the Western Powers represented, and it compromised her in other directions. But those Germans who criticize the courageous policy of Stresemann still have to show how Germany could otherwise have overcome the grave consequences of the lost Ruhr struggle of 1923.[57] Other gains accrued, too. The foreign loans which flowed to Germany in the second half of the 1920's enabled her to build the most modern industrial plant of any European country. Of greater significance yet was the fact that Germany was now being listened to in her new position in world affairs. By 1933 no nation, not even France, was willing to rise to the total defense of the Versailles Treaty, which had lost its moral justification in public opinion.

But the Western Powers made important concessions to Germany at the time of Locarno and of Germany's entrance into the League which in the eyes of many Germans made these events the starting point for a new German foreign policy that no longer depended exclusively on the Western Powers and that was the genuine expression of German national interests. Before we can discuss the concessions of the Western Powers to Germany in Eastern European and Russian affairs, we must briefly review German policy in the East since the armistice of November 1918. In this field, the German Foreign Office could develop a greater initiative than in Western European matters. Whereas the Western division of the Foreign Office was continuously under the pressure of the foreign Powers and domestic controversies, the Eastern division could plan and execute in an atmosphere of greater calm. However, it had a competitor or pacemaker in the German army, which was under less observation in the East than it was in the West, and which was determined to take full advantage of this situation.

At the time of the armistice German troops in the east were spread as far as to the Ukraine and the Caucasus in the south and to Finland and the Baltic provinces in the north. They flooded back to Germany in great disorder and dissolved on their march at home.[58] The hostile attitude of populations such as the Polish was a major element in this dis-

---

[57] Dirksen, *Moskau, Tokio, London*, pp. 75-76 is rather serious in his criticism, while Ernst von Weizsäcker's remarks are insipid, *Erinnerungen*, p. 69.

[58] See Forschungsanstalt für Kriegs- und Heeresgeschichte, *Darstellungen aus den Nachkriegskämpfen deutscher Truppen und Freikorps*, 1: *Die Rückführung des Ostheeres* (Berlin, 1936).

integration, as was the influence of the German revolution upon army discipline. In the Baltic provinces—called the "Baltikum" by the Germans—a somewhat different situation developed. German military and political authorities had worked closely together during the war with the German nobility, which formed a small minority in these countries but owned most of the land dearly coveted by the indigenous peasantry. But the retreat of the German troops from the northern Baltikum laid the country open to easy conquest by the Russian Bolshevists, and not only the Baltic Germans but also the democratic national movements were anxious not to lose German military protection. Some German troops remained in the Baltikum, and, beginning early in 1919, they were reinforced by a division sent by the High Command of the German army and, subsequently, by a stream of volunteers hired with the promise of land settlement in the region. In addition, Russian prisoners of war in Germany were induced to serve in the fight against the Bolshevist desecrators of the Russian empire.[59]

The German High Command under Hindenburg and Groener moved to eastern Germany in February 1919 in order to defend the old frontiers of Germany against Polish infringements and Bolshevist dangers. General von Seeckt was in command of the defense of East Prussia from January to April 1919 and was chiefly responsible for the army's decision to make the province secure by creating a protective zone in the Baltikum. His thoughts ranged beyond this immediate aim. In East Prussia and the Baltikum, it might be possible to rebuild a strong German army which would make its weight felt in the peace negotiations at Paris. But other German leaders entertained even bolder dreams, especially after the military situation in the Baltikum developed favorably and the Paris Conference entered its critical stage. Could the Baltic bastion perhaps become the military base for a decisive military action against Bolshevist Russia through the capture of Leningrad? If such a coup were successful, it could be assumed that Britain would join Germany in the anti-Bolshevist struggle. But even if Britain refused to ally herself with Germany one could expect a counter-revolutionary Russia to side with Germany.

All these dreams came to nothing. As in the past, the Germans dis-

[59] On the military events, see *ibid.*, II: *Der Feldzug im Baltikum bis zur zweiten Einnahme von Riga* (Berlin, 1937). Also Graf Rüdiger von der Goltz, *Als politischer General im Osten* (Leipzig, 1936). On the political side of the Baltikum developments in 1919, see *Foreign Relations: Paris Peace Conference*, XII, 136-227; *British Documents,* 1st series, III, 1-307; Dirksen, *Moskau, Tokio, London,* pp. 29-34; Wipert von Blücher, *Deutschlands Weg nach Rapallo,* pp. 69-86.

regarded the national movements of the Lithuanians, Letts, and Esthonians and their White Russian companions treated the Baltic countries as provinces of Russia. The Baltic peasant and middle classes waited only for the moment when they could acquire full national freedom by ridding themselves of the Germans. The hour arrived at which the Western Powers had gathered sufficient military and naval strength. Since February 1919 they had been demanding the withdrawal of the German troops; in the fall they saw to it that their orders were obeyed. The whole German Baltikum adventure had to be liquidated. For a while the German Foreign Office still endeavored to keep the White Russian troops of Colonel Bermondt in being and to relate them somehow to the Allied-supported armies of intervention. German diplomatic officials also cultivated relations with prominent Russian refugees. General von Seeckt, who became chief of the *Reichswehr* in the spring of 1920, was the leader in a revision of German policy.[60]

Already during his command in East Prussia it had dawned upon Seeckt that the German military effort in the Baltikum was doing a job for the Allied rather than the German cause. He had always lived in the Bismarck-Moltke tradition and viewed friendly German-Russian relations as the keystone of German security and France as the implacable enemy of the empire. The general, however, was also a child of the age of William II and Tirpitz and had considered the defeat of England to be the major objective of the first world war. Even after the war, he remained cool to the British, who showed no indication of giving Germany a sizable army. Considering the hostile attitude of the Western Powers, Seeckt judged that Germany could not afford to incur the enmity of Russia. Bolshevism in Germany would have to be fought relentlessly, but it was imperative to restore the natural contact between Russia and Germany. The German empire had no real interest in the new eastern European states; on the contrary, the annihilation of the new Poland and the restoration of the Russo-German frontiers of 1914 should form the main goal of German foreign policy. Thus, he welcomed the opportunity for conversations with Soviet emissaries, which were brought about by the intercession of Enver Pasha, the military leader of the Young Turkish revolution of 1908 and of the pro-German groups in Turkey during the world war. In 1920 Enver Pasha had gone

[60] Cf. Rabenau, *Seeckt, Aus seinem Leben*, pp. 251-253; 305-520; Julius Epstein, "Der Seeckt Plan," *Der Monat*, 1, No. 2 (November 1948), 42-50. Cf. also George W. F. Hallgarten "General Hans von Seeckt and Russia, 1920-1922," *Journal of Modern History*, XXI (1949), 58-71.

to Moscow, originally working for a Russo-German-Turkish alliance against the West.

Seeckt remained seemingly unmoved when the Russians approached Warsaw in the summer of 1920. He expected a total Russian victory. It is impossible to say whether Seeckt felt confident that the Russians would not cross the frontiers of 1914 into Germany or whether he hoped that, in the case of a Soviet threat to Central Europe, Germany would receive arms from the Allies. In any event, after "the miracle of the Vistula," Seeckt proceeded to set up in the War Ministry the section "R" that was charged with directing the activities of the German army with regard to the Soviet Union. The innermost concern of General Seeckt was the building up of German military strength. To all those Germans who since 1918 believed that economic recovery came before military power, he had replied that without swords plowshares were of no avail.[61] In his opinion, German diplomacy should have centered its struggle for a better peace in Paris around the retention of a German army of 300,000 men. Instead, Count Brockdorff-Rantzau appeared in sheep's clothing, inveighed against imperialism, and fought in the first place for the economic existence of Germany. The general despised the count for his cowardly policy. After June 1919, Seeckt pressed the German government to request a change of the disarmament provision of the Versailles Treaty from the Allies, an entirely hopeless demand that tended only to worsen the atmosphere in which the discussion of the reparations question had to take place.

When the Allies finally turned down the German demand for a moderation of the Allied conditions for German disarmament, and when the London ultimatum on reparations had led to the formation of the Wirth Cabinet, General von Seeckt persuaded the new Chancellor to allow the *Reichswehr* the use of whatever facilities the Russians would provide for the production of armaments forbidden to Germany under the terms of the Versailles Treaty. With public funds, though through the channels of private industry, armament factories were developed in the Soviet Union for the output of artillery, ammunition, tanks, and planes. The ominous plan of building also a factory for the production of gas weapons seems not to have been realized. But the industrial rearmament was accompanied by mutual exchanges of officers for training in staff work and the tactics of large formations. Although information on the details of the German-Russian defense cooperation is still lacking, we may well judge that it did not assume the form of a military alliance

[61] Cf. Rabenau, *Seeckt, Aus seinem Leben*, pp. 117-119.

or planned cooperation for war, but was aimed only at mutual assistance in strengthening the war potential of each nation.

The Foreign Office followed suit on the path opened by the diplomacy of the army. Among the old professional staff of the office, Baron Ago von Maltzan emerged as the most powerful member after the war. He quickly rose from chief of the Russian section to chief of the eastern division and Secretary of State in the Foreign Office. He came from Mecklenburg *Junker* stock and became related by marriage to industrial circles. With great personal means at his disposal, he made his pleasant home the center of enjoyable and interesting social gatherings in the midst of inflation-ridden Berlin. At the Maltzans' distinguished foreigners ranging from the papal nuncio to the Soviet commissar met and rubbed elbows with important Germans from all political camps. Exactly where Maltzan stood on the hard-fought issues of German domestic politics, nobody has ever found out, and he epitomized well the deflation of ideologies which was an aftermath of years of war and revolution. Maltzan used his wide connections exclusively with a view to improving the international position of Germany, and after a brief period of hesitation he accepted Seeckt's ideas on the practicability of a German-Russian rapprochement. The negotiations were carried on through the only diplomatic line that had survived the rupture of German-Russian diplomatic relations in early November 1918. Both in Moscow and Berlin commissions for the repatriation of prisoners-of-war had been created.

As a consequence of the conversations, the Soviet Union and Germany, on May 6, 1921, concluded a trade treaty which laid the foundation for extensive economic intercourse between the two countries. The treaty followed a trade agreement between Britain and Russia of March 1921 and failed to cause any remarkable international reaction. But the German-Russian treaty was in the technical diplomatic sense far-reaching. The repatriation commissions were entrusted with the execution of commercial activities and received all the rights and privileges of diplomatic missions. A bridge had been constructed over the gulf that had separated the two governments since the days of the treaty of Brest-Litovsk.

This is not the place to speculate over all the motives that induced the Soviet government to move closer to Germany. The two countries were undoubtedly pariahs among the nations at that moment, but Soviet policy was never noticeably affected by sentiment. The German talent in military organization and the engineering skill in peaceful and military industries were welcome in Russia on the eve of the inauguration of the New Economic Policy (NEP). But Germany was weak and, worst of all, poor. The centers of world politics and world finance were in the West. The Soviet Union would have liked to gain recognition by the Western Powers. In the West the impact of the postwar depression had created an appetite for new markets, and projects for the opening of the Russian market were freely discussed. Rathenau was not the first to propose such plans, but in his prolific mind the proposal for an international syndicate, supported and financed by all the Western nations and Germany, took definite shape. The expansion of European production and trade, so Rathenau thought, would make German reparations bearable. Rathenau won Lloyd George over for an international discussion of the plan which was to take place at Genoa in April 1922.[62] The idea, as Maltzan apparently felt beforehand, was much disliked in the Soviet Union. It tasted of capitalistic exploitation, which was made even less palatable by the formation of such a union of capitalistic governments.

To break up the common front of the Western Powers was the main objective of Soviet diplomacy. But, to the German delegation, this front did not seem real. They found themselves left out of the discussion and became afraid that the French might falsify the whole plan by offering the Soviet Union a share in German reparations. Article 116 of the Versailles Treaty had reserved possible Russian claims against Germany. It was a great relief to Maltzan that Chicherin offered to sign a separate treaty with Germany, in which Russia and Germany renounced all their mutual claims arising from war damages and war expenses. Beyond this, the treaty that was signed in Rapallo on the morning of Easter Sunday, April 16, was in the nature of a general treaty of friendship. It envisaged, as the most important practical step, the immediate establishment of embassies in Berlin and Moscow.

The treaty was not drafted in Genoa. So far as content went, it had been the result of negotiations in the months before. Chicherin had offered to sign the treaty in Berlin on his way to Genoa, but Rathenau did not wish to do so before the conference. There, on Russian insistence, the treaty had been consummated and turned into a demonstration against the diplomatic plans of the Western Powers. Rathenau was most reluctant to proceed behind the back of Lloyd George, and it was Maltzan's persuasiveness that dragged the minister along. Rathenau's position in reparations discussions was at least temporarily weakened, and the break-

[62] On the Genoa Conference, see, in addition to the works cited above, Chapter 1, note 56, and the memoirs of D'Abernon, Dirksen and Wipert von Blücher, Eric C. Kollman, "Walter Rathenau and German Foreign Policy," *Journal of Modern History*, xxiv (1952), 127-142.

down of the conference, though it did not inspire Poincaré's decision to use sanctions against Germany, brought the Ruhr invasion a few steps nearer.

The precipitate action of the German conference delegation made President Ebert angry. He saw in it a violation of his constitutional authority and was concerned about the reaction of the German parties. Apart from the Communists, no German party supported a Russian orientation of German foreign policy. The Social Democratic party was opposed to it; the Center party very cool; and even the German Nationalists were against close relations with the Soviet Union. Of course, this was true of the militant anti-Bolshevists, but, in addition, the agrarian interests in the party feared Russian economic competition. Genuine popular support came chiefly from a few groups in the German Nationalist, German People's and Democratic parties. But these few people, supported from the background by General von Seeckt, succeeded in getting the Rapallo Treaty easy passage through the German parliament. Public opinion was friendly, because, after so much submissive toleration of Western demands, Rapallo seemed a defiant gesture of German dissatisfaction.

Count Brockdorff-Rantzau was sent to Moscow as German ambassador. He was not in agreement with Seeckt about the aims of German policy in Russia. During the summer of 1922, the two imperious men fought a furious battle of memoranda.[63] There were many misunderstandings between them. Seeckt's critique of Brockdorff-Rantzau's opinion was an expression of unmitigated contempt for the man of 1919, who "cannot understand that ultimately every political activity rests on power." But the Count was a passionate hater, too; he was so aroused that he would have liked to challenge the general to a pistol duel. Brockdorff-Rantzau and Seeckt were in agreement that German foreign policy should aim at the isolation of France and that a British alliance was desirable. Both misjudged the state and trend of Anglo-French relations. The ambassador argued that it was dangerous to have military arrangements with the Soviet Union, since the mere suspicion of such cooperation would bring the British and French closer together. He also warned against Soviet blackmail and wanted to see German-Russian relations confined to the economic field. Seeckt, on his part, denied that the German military activities in Russia would affect the course of British policy. He believed that the clash between France and Britain would

[63] See *Der Monat*, 1, No. 2 (November 1948), 42-50; Rabenau, *Seeckt, Aus seinem Leben*, pp. 314-320.

come as the result of overseas conflicts and that a Germany strengthened by her rearmament would be more *bündnisfähig*.

Count Brockdorff-Rantzau went to Moscow in 1922 as a "Westerner." While he let his great gift for personal diplomacy work on Chicherin in many conversations in the hours after midnight, Seeckt continued to operate his own wires to Moscow. But practically, though not formally, the two German foreign policies turned into parallel directions. Brockdorff-Rantzau came to find greater value in a general cooperation between Russia and Germany.[64] When Germany was about to accept the Locarno Treaty, the German ambassador almost joined forces with Russian diplomacy in its storm against Berlin. It seems improbable that he shared the Russian fears that Germany would become in the League the tool of an anti-Russian coalition and especially a vassal of Britain. It is more likely that Brockdorff-Rantzau, in memory of Versailles, was dumbfounded by the prospect of close Franco-German cooperation. He was, therefore, little impressed by the concessions made by the Western Powers which finally made it possible to conclude the German-Russian Treaty of Berlin of April 24, 1926.[65]

Germany was exempted from participation in possible sanctions against the Soviet Union taken by the League of Nations under Article 16. Her special diplomatic situation vis-à-vis the Soviet Union was thereby officially recognized. The significance of this event was greatly heightened by the absence of a British guarantee for the postwar frontiers in Eastern Europe. Whereas Germany accepted the Rhine settlement of Versailles, she was free to press for revision in the East, though only by peaceful means. The political moderation and circumspection, as well as the strong fortitude of heart, that Gustav Stresemann had shown were the greatest single factor in achieving for Germany this new position in the world. She could feel a new sense of relative independence and at the same time of self-chosen participation in European affairs. For a short period German foreign policy was almost as largely consolidated in the hands of the Foreign Office as in the days of Bismarck. However, this influence of the Foreign Office rested as much on the balance of the domestic social and political forces as upon the gains made in the foreign field. The age in which the professional diplomat could preside over the formulation of foreign policy had passed long ago.

[64] Some interesting material on the later years of Brockdorff-Rantzau was brought together after his death in *Europäische Gespräche*, VII (1929), 1-47.
[65] Cf. Stresemann, *Vermächtnis*, II, 502-542.

THE STRUGGLE FOR
NEW POSITION

6

Turkish Diplomacy from Mudros
to Lausanne

BY RODERIC H. DAVISON

TURKEY alone of the nations defeated in 1918 was able to reverse the decision within a few years and to negotiate as an equal with the Allied Powers for a new peace treaty. She was not, like Czechoslovakia, a beneficiary of the Allied victory, nor was she, like Germany or Russia, inherently a Great Power which could be expected to grow in strength. The Turkish struggle to establish a favorable international position was unique also among Muslim peoples in successfully shaking off foreign controls.

It was not the Ottoman government of Sultan Mehmet VI at Istanbul which achieved this success, but a new nationalist government which began in Anatolia as a movement of resistance to partition and foreign occupation. The Turkish nationalists, competing for position both with the Sultan's government and with foreign Powers, were organized first as the Representative Committee of the Union for the Defense of the Rights of Anatolia and Rumelia, and then as the Government of the Grand National Assembly, before the formation of the Turkish Republic in 1923. Each change in name represented a stage in the development of the nationalist movement into an effective government, and a step forward in its international position. By the time the republic was proclaimed, the new nation-state had already created the diplomatic basis for an independent and peaceful foreign policy.

From the beginning Mustafa Kemal [Atatürk][1] was the soul and

[1] Personal names in modern Turkey offer a constant source of confusion. They will here be given in the modern Turkish spelling, with explanatory notes where necessary. A Turkish law of 1934 obliged all citizens to take family names, which few Turks heretofore possessed. The new names will be indicated in brackets wherever possible, but since these names were unknown during the period under discussion they will not be used in the text. Mustafa Kemal was given the surname Atatürk by the Assembly.

leader of the nationalist movement. He had served with distinction as an officer in the Ottoman army on several fronts, notably in the defense of Gallipoli in 1915. His wartime experience had taught him to resent the German influence over Turkey, and to oppose the domination of any foreign Power. At the time of the 1918 armistice Kemal, as commanding general on the Syrian front, tried to oppose surrender to foreign occupation of territory he regarded as geographically and ethnographically Turkish.[2] He had by this time developed a Western-style national consciousness of a sort not uncommon among educated Turks, many of them of the officer class. Not yet forty years old, he had already exhibited undoubted military and organizational ability. Since Kemal had also avoided close association with the defeated Ottoman government, and had quarreled with its military leader, Enver Pasha, he was almost ideally suited for the leadership of the new nationalist movement.

To succeed in reversing the defeat and avoiding partition, Kemal had in the first place to organize military resistance and wage war against foreign occupation. But along with the fighting went a diplomatic campaign, no less successful, which is often overlooked. The fruits of military victory in the years 1919 to 1922 could never have been gathered without an astute foreign policy which paralleled the military campaigns, aided them, and won international recognition of the results. The bases of foreign policy were simple—to create an independent and sovereign Turkey for the Turks. To Kemal and his followers this meant not only territorial unity, but complete abolition of all such extraterritorial rights in matters of justice, taxation, and economic exploitation as foreigners had enjoyed, and remarkably abused, under the Ottoman empire. The emphasis on territorial integrity, and absolute Turkish sovereignty within the state, was so constant as to appear monotonous, but Kemal's diplomacy is understandable only as the pursuit of these objectives.

His diplomacy utilized every possible advantage presented by the postwar situation. As best he could, Kemal exploited the divergence of policy between Britain, France, and Italy, and the greater chasm that separated the Western Powers from Soviet Russia. Sometimes Turkish action helped to increase the differences. Kemal would negotiate alternately with Russia or the West, or simultaneously with both; whatever advantages he won on one side increased his bargaining power on the other. At times it looked as if Kemal were the most apt pupil of the nineteenth century Ottoman diplomats who tried to find salvation by

[2] See Jean Deny, "Souvenirs du Gazi Mustafa Kemâl Pacha," *Revue des études islamiques* (1927), Cahiers 1 to 3, *passim*, on the war and early armistice periods.

playing one Power against another. There was, however, a significant difference. Ottoman diplomacy had to the end attempted to use Europe's quarrels to preserve a sprawling and heterogeneous empire. The nationalists from the start limited their aim to the preservation of control and complete sovereignty only over those areas which were predominantly Turkish in character. Nationalist diplomacy used all means possible to attain these limited but almost rigid objectives. Its workings can be understood only by following the sequence of events from the establishment of nationalist foreign policy in 1919 to the triumph of its diplomacy at Lausanne in 1923.[3]

I

When Husein Rauf [Orbay], Ottoman minister of marine, signed the Mudros armistice on October 30, 1918, most of the Arab portions of the empire were already under British and Arab control. The armistice terms[4] opened the Straits to the Allies, and permitted them further to occupy any strategic points should Allied security be threatened. The Ottoman army was to be demobilized, except for units necessary to frontier surveillance and internal order. Soon thereafter Allied warships anchored off Istanbul and Allied High Commissioners took up residence there, while British forces not only occupied Dardanelles forts, but pressed forward in the Mosul province against the vain protests of Turkish army commanders.[5] French troops later replaced the British in

[3] In view of the lack of documentary material from the Turkish archives, and of the lack of important memoirs by leading diplomats, it is not yet possible to write the full story of Turkish diplomacy, particularly in the difficult and often disorganized early years. Very little information is available on the exact processes of policy formulation, or on the correspondence between the capital and the diplomats charged with executing the policy. Various books attempt to survey the development of Turkish foreign policy in general, but none is completely satisfactory. All are lacking in diplomatic detail and documentary evidence. Among the more useful are these three theses: Frédéric Abelous, *L'évolution de la Turquie dans ses rapports avec les étrangers* (Toulouse, 1928), mostly on the capitulations and rather anti-Ankara; S. Reşat Sagay, *La nouvelle Turquie et la communauté internationale* (Strasbourg, 1936), a fairly good summary of foreign policy; Edward R. Vere-Hodge, *Turkish Foreign Policy 1918-1948* (Ambilly-Annemasse, 1950), concentrating on post-1923. Kurt Ziemke, *Die neue Türkei, 1914-1929* (Stuttgart, 1930) is perhaps the best general treatment. Arnold J. Toynbee, *The Western Question in Greece and Turkey*, 2nd ed. (London, 1923) offers a good background, though diplomacy is not its central theme. Among the most useful but most disappointing studies is Yusuf Hikmet [Bayur], *Yeni Türkiye Devletinin Harici Siyaseti* [The Foreign Policy of the New Turkish State] (Istanbul, 1934), which lists among its sources the archives of the Sublime Porte for the armistice period, and the files of the Representative Committee and of the Foreign Ministry, but cites few documents from any of these sources and gives few details on policy formulation or its execution.

[4] Text in Eliot G. Mears, *Modern Turkey* (New York, 1924), pp. 624-626.

[5] Here Turkish officers, like Kemal, tried to hold the armistice line, giving rise to a

Syria and Cilicia, while Allied armistice control officers and military units occupied various Anatolian cities. British forces were also in the Transcaucasus, where the Russian collapse had allowed Georgia, Azerbaijan, and Armenia to spring up as independent states. Ottoman armies had to retire from this region, where they had at one point in 1918 advanced as far as Baku, and where the districts of Kars, Ardahan, and Batum had voted for union with Turkey.[6]

Nominal authority over the Ottoman Empire was still exercised by the cabinet of Damad Ferid Pasha at Istanbul. To nationalist Turks, however, he appeared too Anglophile, and almost completely subservient to the High Commissioners. There was as yet no organized nationalist movement, but rather a great war-weariness in the empire which had fought the Italians, the Balkan League, and the Allies since 1911. At first the Allied control officers had little trouble with Turkish demobilization. Some of the educated Turks hoped to save their country under an American mandate. A cohesive nationalist movement did not arise until the Allies themselves provided the impetus. Toward the end of April 1919, Italian troops landed at Antalya [Adalia] in an effort to secure territory in southwest Turkey promised them by the secret treaty of St. Jean de Maurienne. This provoked far less of a nationalist reaction than the landing of Greek troops at Izmir on May 15 following.

The fateful acquiescence by Lloyd George and the Supreme Council in Paris in the desires of the Greek premier Venizelos to recapture Byzantine hegemony in those fertile areas of western Anatolia which still had a large Greek Orthodox population had explosive consequences. Ostensibly an Allied occupation, in accordance with the terms of Mudros, the landing was in fact purely Greek. To the Anatolian Turk this was the supreme indignity—that a subject and minority element, fundamentally considered second-class subjects of the Sultan, should rule him or part of his land. Knots of local nationalist resistance sprang up where there were no organized elements of the Ottoman army such as still existed in eastern Anatolia. With the arrival of Mustafa Kemal in Anatolia, four days after the Greek landing, began the painful process of incorporating such groups into a nationalist movement which produced an army, a *de facto* government, and a foreign policy. Kemal had been in Istanbul in the spring of 1919, trying to reinvigorate the Ottoman

---

seven-year controversy with Britain. Turkish documents in *La question de Mossoul de la signature du traité d'armistice de Moudros . . . au 1re* [sic] *Mars 1925* (Constantinople, 1925), pp. 8-73.

[6] Chicherin had already protested the Baku advance and the plebiscite: Degras, I, 83, 102, 109-110, 120-121.

government, when he was appointed inspector of the Third Army, stationed at Erzerum and Sivas. As rapidly as possible he left the Allied-controlled capital, never to return until long after the republic was established. His landing at Samsun on May 19, 1919 marks in Turkish hagiography the beginning of the nationalist movement.

Kemal's immediate aim was to organize military resistance to the partition of Turkey. This necessitated the creation of some unified nationalist authority in Anatolia. Kemal later said that his aim already extended to the creation of a new and independent Turkish state, since continued allegiance to the Sultan's government was unacceptable to him.[7] He could not yet announce such views publicly, but his actions soon led to a complete break with Istanbul. Disregarding an order of recall, Kemal resigned his commission. During the summer of 1919 his leadership produced the Representative Committee, the basis of a foreign policy, and the beginnings of direct though irregular contact with foreign Powers. Two nationalist congresses, one held at Erzerum in late July and the second at Sivas in early September, were the instrumentalities through which this was achieved. Though only the eastern provinces were represented at Erzerum, the Sivas congress brought together elected delegates from all Anatolia. The Union for the Defense of the Rights of Anatolia and Rumelia was formed in consequence. Each congress chose a Representative Committee with Kemal as president. The Representative Committee after Sivas began to function as the executive authority of the national will, and in its name Kemal signed telegrams and conferred with foreign representatives.

On September 9 the Sivas congress issued a declaration elaborating resolutions already passed at Erzerum which, with slight modifications, stated the foreign policy thereafter followed by the nationalists.[8] All Turkish territory inside the armistice frontiers was regarded as an indivisible whole within which no foreign intervention should be allowed, nor any independent Greek or Armenian state. The Muslim majority, "a veritable fraternity," would grant no special status to non-Muslim

---

[7] Mustafa Kemal [Atatürk], *A Speech Delivered by Ghazi Mustapha Kemal . . . October, 1927* (Leipzig, 1929), p. 17. This speech to the Peoples' Party Congress reviews the nationalist movement from 1919 to 1924, and is Kemal's self-justification, partly against the attacks of domestic opponents. It contains important information on foreign policy and its execution, though domestic matters occupy more of its 700-odd pages. Many documents are included *in extenso*.

[8] Text of Erzerum resolutions in Gotthard Jäschke, "Zur Geschichte des türkischen Nationalpakts," *Mitteilungen des Seminars für orientalischen Sprachen*, XXXVI (1933), II, 107-116; summary in Société pour l'étude de l'histoire turque, *Histoire de la république turque* (Istanbul, 1935), p. 38. Sivas declaration in Mears, *Modern Turkey*, pp. 627-628.

minorities such as the Ottoman system had permitted. No mandate or protectorate over Turkey would be considered. Foreign scientific or economic assistance would be accepted only if it were untainted with imperialism. The national will must control the Sultan's government, which should convoke a National Assembly. Though the Sivas declaration still considered the Sultan's government to be the lawful one, it rejected Istanbul's policy of acquiescence to Allied demands.

Most of these ideas were basically Kemal's, though he was no ardent supporter of the Califate and Sultanate. Defense of these institutions was mentioned in the Sivas declaration to satisfy the generally more conservative Turkish opinion, which Kemal could not afford to antagonize until his victories ended the crisis of foreign invasion. Kemal's major insistence was always on national and popular sovereignty. As early as June 3, 1919, he declared in a circular telegram to Anatolian officials that Turkey must have complete independence, and "the majority in the purely national districts of the country shall not be sacrificed in favor of the minority."[9] In August he stated that "we prefer that our negotiations and relations with foreign countries shall be conducted in the name of the nation, founded on the proceedings of the Congress."[10] Soon after, still not attacking the Sultan, he asserted that until a government with the confidence of the people should be formed, the Representative Committee would "remain in office and continue to conduct the affairs of the nation."[11]

It is a question as to how far Kemal in the early days was willing to go in accepting foreign aid of some sort. He proposed at the Erzerum congress that help be accepted from a Great Power with no imperialist interests, presumably meaning the United States, but refused to name that country when the resentment of Anatolian Turks against American support for an independent Armenia was expressed.[12] The Sivas congress debated at length a possible American mandate over all Turkey, evidently after reports by Istanbul delegates of conversations with Wilson's King-Crane commission. Kemal apparently opposed an American mandate, but was interested in possible American support for Turkish independence.[13] When the Harbord Commission in September passed through Sivas on its whirlwind trip to investigate a possible Armenian

---

[9] Kemal, *Speech*, p. 29.   [10] *ibid.*, pp. 91-92.   [11] *ibid.*, pp. 125-126.
[12] Halidé Edib [Adivar], *The Turkish Ordeal* (New York, 1928), p. 16.
[13] Kemal, *Speech*, pp. 77-100. The King-Crane commission reported that the Sivas congress was expected to declare for an American mandate: "First Publication of the King-Crane Report on the Near East," *Editor and Publisher*, LV:27, 2nd section (December 2, 1922), p. 17.

mandate, Kemal talked with General Harbord. Kemal says only that Harbord was convinced of the justice of the nationalist program.[14] But Harbord reported that Kemal said his aim was "the preservation of the Empire under a mandatory of a single disinterested power, preferably America," and wanted "the aid of an impartial foreign country."[15] Later in 1919 Kemal conferred with M. Georges Picot at Sivas, reportedly proposing to him a French economic "mandate" over Turkey if France handed back Cilicia.[16] All such ideas were undoubtedly tentative, explored as possible means to combat the Greeks and their British backers, and were abandoned as the nationalists gained momentum.

Such reports make it clear that Kemal, from the very beginning, tried to establish contact, however informal and irregular, with the Allied Powers and to win their recognition for the nationalist program. He and other nationalists saw various Allied control officers and special diplomatic agents. On many occasions in 1919 he assured his countrymen that British, French, Italian and American representatives had approved the nationalist aims, or had said that they would not interfere with the nationalist movement; that their representatives at Sivas had reported favorably to their governments; that close relations were already established.[17] Kemal exaggerated to impress the Turks and to win followers but such declarations prove his consciousness of the necessity for a nationalist diplomatic offensive. Kemal directly informed the Great

[14] Kemal, *Speech*, p. 150; Gasi Mustafa Kemal Pascha, *Die neue Türkei, 1919-1927*, III, *Die Dokumente zur Rede* (Leipzig, 1927?), no. 106.

[15] Maj.-Gen. James G. Harbord, "American Military Mission to Armenia," *International Conciliation*, CLI (June 1920), 294-295. It is perhaps significant that Kemal in October 1919, replied to all the written questions of a Turkish journalist of Istanbul except "What was your interview with General Harbord about?" Kemal, *Dokumente*, no. 144.

[16] Comte Roger de Gontaut-Biron et L. Le Révérend, *D'Angora à Lausanne* (Paris, 1924), pp. 12, 204.

[17] Kemal, *Speech*, pp. 136-137, 147-148, 151, 154, 156; Kemal, *Dokumente*, nos. 43-45, 106. A reliable account from the other side is in A. Rawlinson, *Adventures in the Near East, 1918-1922* (London, 1923), pp. 188-190, 231-232. Col. Rawlinson saw Kemal often at Erzerum in 1919, appreciated his character and aims, and reported personally to Lord Curzon on the Erzerum resolutions. Curzon naturally would accord the nationalists no recognition, but sent Rawlinson back to discover unofficially from Kemal what peace terms they might accept. Rawlinson returned ostensibly as an Allied control officer. *Ibid.*, pp. 251-252. General Harbord concluded even this early that Kemal was "no cheap political adventurer," and that his movement had to be taken seriously: Maj.-Gen. James G. Harbord, "Mustafa Kemal Pasha and His Party," *World's Work* XL (June 1920), 188. Harbord's official report included a long letter by Kemal explaining his aims, the Sivas declaration, and a letter from Kemal and Husein Rauf to the U.S. Senate asking that an American committee visit Turkey before the peace treaty was signed: U.S. American Military Mission to Armenia, *Conditions in the Near East. Report . . . by Maj.-Gen. James G. Harbord* (Washington, 1920, 66th Congress, 2nd Session, Senate Document no. 266), pp. 29-40.

Powers on September 11 that Damad Ferid's government was an illegal tyranny, and that the delegation which it had sent to Paris did not represent the nation.[18] British and French agents in Turkey in 1919 recognized that there were already, in fact, two governments in that country.[19]

Kemal refused to concede that there were two governments. Maintaining that the national will was supreme, and the Representative Committee was its spokesman, he tried to capture control of the Istanbul government for the nationalists, and thus to create and guide a unified Turkish foreign policy. This was particularly important because the Allied peace treaty with Turkey was still under discussion. Damad Ferid had led a delegation from Istanbul to Paris in June, where his carefully reasoned statement to the Supreme Council was rebuffed with biting words on the iniquities of the Turks. From Sivas Kemal reproached Damad Ferid with subservience, and set about to cause his downfall. On September 11 he cut off telegraphic communication with the Porte. "This is the last warning we shall give you," said Kemal before the Sivas congress. "The attitude that the nation will take up in the future will be explained to the representatives of the Entente through the foreign officers who are among us."[20] This pressure forced Damad Ferid out at the start of October. Ali Riza, more sympathetic to the nationalists, replaced him as grand vizier.

Thereupon Kemal tried to force his foreign policy upon the new Istanbul Cabinet. To Ali Riza he explained his foreign relations thus far as having "no official diplomatic character. They only consist of certain contacts with different political agents sent by the Allied Powers who, not finding themselves in the capital in the presence of a legitimate government resting on the confidence and strength of the nation, wanted to check the veracity or bad faith of the pronouncements made by the preceding Cabinet against the national forces. In maintaining these relations, the aim we follow is exclusively to make known the national aspirations, the extent and power of the national organizations, so as to gain the respect and confidence of foreign countries."[21] Now he demanded that Ali Riza recognize the nationalist movement, make no binding decisions until a genuine national assembly had met, and choose new delegates to the peace conference from among the nationalists.[22] Salih Pasha,

---

[18] Kemal, *Dokumente*, no. 97, annex 1.
[19] Kemal, *Speech*, p. 262; Hikmet, *Haricî Siyaseti*, p. 38.
[20] Kemal, *Speech*, p. 121.
[21] Kemal, *Dokumente*, no. 132; see also no. 143.
[22] *ibid.*, no. 128; Kemal, *Speech*, p. 168.

minister of marine in the new Cabinet, was authorized to confer with Kemal. Their three-day conference produced essential agreement. Salih accepted the main points of the Sivas declaration, and the demand that delegates to Paris be approved by the Representative Committee. Salih could not, however, persuade his Cabinet to agree, perhaps because of Allied pressure.[23] The chance for immediate coordination on foreign policy between Kemal and the Sultan's government was thus lost.

Elections for a new parliament were, however, authorized by Mehmet VI. A large nationalist majority was returned. Kemal thereupon gathered most of the deputies together at Ankara, to which he moved his headquarters from Sivas in late December 1919, to be able to use the railroad to Istanbul. The deputies subscribed to a National Pact, based on the Sivas declaration, which Kemal presented to them; it became for the future the fixed basis of nationalist foreign policy. Most of the deputies led by Rauf, a member of the Representative Committee since the beginning, left for Istanbul in early January, though Kemal did not go because of the danger to him. There the parliament met formally, voting on January 28, 1920, to confirm the National Pact. The Allies were thus notified of the Turkish demands which, in Kemal's view, had to serve as the basis for peace negotiations.[24]

The National Pact emphasized complete independence—territorial, political, judicial and economic; nothing like the capitulations would be accepted. There was no mention now of foreign assistance, as there had had been at Sivas. The territorial claims were extended to include Kurdish areas beyond the armistice lines, while plebiscites were demanded for Kars, Ardahan, Batum and Western Thrace. Only regions with an Arab majority were specifically excluded. Minorities in Turkey would have no special privileges beyond the rights commonly recognized in the minority treaties of the peace settlement. If Istanbul, seat of the Sultanate and Califate, were secure, regulations on traffic through the Bosporus could be made jointly by Turkey and other interested Powers. These principles, said the preamble, represented "the maximum of sacrifice which can be undertaken in order to achieve a just and lasting peace." It was Turkey for the Turks (and Kurds).

Though the pact lived on, the parliament which voted it was soon killed by Allied action. The Western Powers were alarmed not only by

[23] *Histoire*, pp. 42-43.

[24] Kemal, *Speech*, p. 306. Texts of the National Pact which differ slightly in translation in *Histoire*, pp. 46-47; Mears, *Modern Turkey*, pp. 629-631; H. W. V. Temperley, *A History of the Peace Conference of Paris*, VI (London, 1924), 605-606.

the Pact's demands, but by the success of nationalist troops in driving the French from Maraş [Marash], news of which burst upon an Allied conference at London in February 1920.[25] The British conceived and executed an Allied military occupation of Istanbul on March 16. Two score prominent nationalist deputies, including Rauf, were deported to Malta, the parliament was dissolved, and Ali Riza dismissed in favor of the more pliable Damad Ferid. Those deputies who could escaped to rejoin Kemal in Ankara. The nationalists jailed a few British armistice control officers as hostages. Kemal meanwhile despatched vigorous protests against the British occupation to many foreign Powers. It is significant that he did this through the Italian representative at Antalya. He was already receiving private assurances from French and Italian officials that British policy was not theirs—that Millerand and Nitti did not agree with Lloyd George.[26]

If the Greek landing of 1919 had created the nationalist movement in Turkey, the British occupation of Istanbul converted the movement into an effective separate government. The establishment of the Ankara government occurred, ironically, at the exact time when Allied statesmen at San Remo were partitioning the Ottoman empire despite the protests of Damad Ferid, whose government declared the nationalists to be rebels. Meeting on April 23, the deputies in Ankara resolved to create the Government of the Grand National Assembly and to secure independence by an honorable peace. They did not declare the Sultan deposed, but called him an Allied prisoner whose acts were therefore invalid. Mustafa Kemal was the next day elected president of the Assembly, and presided also over a council of ministers elected by the Assembly from among its members.[27] This organization was confirmed and elaborated in a law of January 20, 1921, which specifically placed in the Assembly's hands the powers of war and peace, of concluding treaties and receiving foreign diplomats.[28] Though the relations of the Ankara government to Istanbul were ill-defined—inasmuch as the Sultan

---

[25] David Lloyd George, *The Truth About the Peace Treaties* (London, 1938), II, 1285-1294. Lloyd George did not know who Kemal was.

[26] Kemal, *Speech*, pp. 353, 360-362; Kemal, *Dokumente*, no. 229. Count Sforza, Italian High Commissioner in Istanbul early in 1919, had then offered Kemal shelter in the Italian embassy from British arrest: Carlo Sforza, *Makers of Modern Europe* (Indianapolis, 1930), p. 365.

[27] In this period the nationalists used the word *vekil* for minister, which was usually translated as "commissar," "commissary," or "commissioner," probably owing to the Russian example. After Lausanne the translation "minister" became usual. The Foreign Office was often called the "commissariat."

[28] Resolutions of April 23, 1920, and of law of January 20, 1921, in *Histoire*, pp. 52-53 and 83-84 respectively.

was not deposed, Ankara not declared the capital, and the previous constitution not abrogated—the Grand National Assembly was hereafter the real government for most of Turkey. Foreign Powers were notified that it alone represented the people, and that it would "preside over the present and future destiny of Turkey" so long as the unjustified occupation of Istanbul continued.[29]

II

The Government of the Grand National Assembly set out to gain recognition abroad, to negotiate for foreign assistance or the cessation of hostilities, and to carry out by diplomacy wherever possible the stipulations of the National Pact. The task was finished only when the Lausanne treaty was signed in July 1923, but by early 1922 Ankara had won important victories in negotiation both with Russia and the West, and had passed through the first phase of its struggle for international position. Mustafa Kemal was inevitably the leader in this as in military operations, but he now had for the first time an embryonic Foreign Office and a Foreign Minister.

Ankara provided little for the ministries except a central location and a nationalist atmosphere. Space and facilities were scarce. The Foreign Office began life in a room in the agricultural school where Kemal made his headquarters. Here the credentials of the Grand National Assembly's first diplomatic mission were typed on a decrepit machine by Halide Edib [Adivar], the first Turkish woman college graduate. Soon the ministry moved to a larger building once occupied by the Ottoman Public Debt administration. More officials were added: an undersecretary for political affairs, who helped organize the office in the summer of 1920, a legal counselor and others. By November it was found advisable to have a diplomatic agent, Hamid Bey, to represent Ankara in Istanbul, and to deal there with the High Commissioners and other Western representatives.[30]

The foreign service also grew from scratch. Most of the diplomatic

---

[29] Gotthard Jäschke und Erich Pritsch, *Die Türkei seit dem Weltkriege: Geschichtskalender, 1918-1928* (Berlin, 1929), p. 32; Gaston Gaillard, *The Turks and Europe* (London, 1921), pp. 186-187. See also Donald E. Webster, *The Turkey of Atatürk* (Philadelphia, 1939), p. 86.

[30] Edib, *Turkish Ordeal*, pp. 146-147, 173-174, gives a brief account of the beginnings; she was the typist. See also Berthe Georges-Gaulis, *Angora, Constantinople, Londres* (Paris, 1922), pp. 134-135. Hamid Bey was apparently first known in Istanbul as vice-president of the Red Crescent: Hikmet, *Harici Siyaseti*, p. 83; Jäschke, *Die Türkei*, p. 41. This anomalous Foreign Office post in Istanbul continued to exist even after Ankara became capital of the new republic.

agents sent out from Ankara in the next few years were cultured men with education along Western lines, though not trained diplomats from Ottoman days; they were usually lawyers, army officers, or other professional men. One experienced diplomat who joined Kemal in 1919, Ahmed Rustem Bey, had been ambassador in Washington before 1914, but does not appear to have been employed by Ankara for important missions.[81] In these years much important negotiation both abroad and at home was handled by the Foreign Minister himself. Ankara's first official mission, to Moscow, was headed by Bekir Sami, elected Foreign Minister by the Assembly early in May 1920. Bekir Sami was a huge Circassian who had experience in a wide range of civil service posts from the time of Abdülhamid II on, including important provincial governorships. He had been, with Kemal, a member of the original Representative Committee. In May 1920, he set out to Moscow to establish treaty relationships and seek aid in the face of the British occupation of Istanbul.

Kemal later said that the first decision of the Ankara government was to send this mission.[82] He himself wrote to Chicherin, the Soviet commissar for foreign affairs, on April 26, 1920, apparently suggesting some sort of an alliance.[83] The delegation, which included Yusuf Kemal [Tengirşenk], minister of economy, spent two months in the Transcaucasus region, arriving in Moscow toward the end of July.[84] Despite the long history of Russo-Turkish antagonism, it was advantageous at the moment for each to seek support in the other. Each faced the same opponents, and the opponents controlled the Straits. Contact was easier to establish after Denikin's forces in the Caucasus collapsed in December 1919, and after the British took their troops out of the Transcaucasus region except for Batum.[85]

---

[81] Possibly because he was a Christian Pole turned Muslim. Mufty-Zade Zia, "How the Turks Feel," *Asia*, XXII:11 (November, 1922), p. 861, makes the obvious point that the nationalists no longer used Greeks and Armenians in their foreign service as the Sultans had done.

[82] Kemal, *Speech*, p. 396.

[83] Louis Fischer, *The Soviets in World Affairs* (London, 1930), I, 390. Gotthard Jäschke, "Urkunden I. Der Weg zur russisch-türkischen Freundschaft im Lichte Moskaus," *Die Welt des Islams*, xx (1938), 132, cites notes appended to the Russian translation of Kemal's *Speech* [E. F. Ludšuvejt, ed., *Put Novoi Turtsii 1919-1927*, III (Moscow, 1934)] to indicate that Kemal's letter proposed military cooperation with Russia against "imperialism," and exhibited willingness to see Turkish-speaking Azerbaijan become a Soviet republic.

[84] Hikmet, *Haricî Siyaseti*, p. 63.

[85] The first contacts between the Turkish nationalists and Soviet Russia are not yet clear from the published records. See discussion of the evidence of relations between the two while the Representative Committee guided nationalist affairs in 1919 and early

Though the immediate opponents were the same, the ultimate aims of Moscow and Ankara were quite different. Bolshevik policy conceived of the Turks as the westernmost of a string of Muslim peoples who would be natural allies against the British, and against capitalist imperialism. In December 1917, the Council of Peoples Commissars had issued an appeal for cooperation to the Muslims of Russia, India, Persia, Turkey, and Arabia, simultaneously denouncing all secret treaties partitioning Persia and the Ottoman empire.[86] When the Sivas Congress was meeting Chicherin renewed the appeal directly to the "workers and peasants of Turkey," naming the British as the enemy and denouncing "pasha landlords."[87] Kemal was interested in a national war, not a class war. Chicherin's reply to him of June 2, 1920, was therefore chiefly in terms of cooperation against "foreign imperialism."[88] Chicherin did not mention alliance or military assistance, but proposed immediate establishment of diplomatic relations. He accepted the principles of the National Pact, but tried to reinterpret two of them to Russian advantage: he noted the Assembly's decision "to allow Turkish Armenia, Kurdistan, Lusistan [Lazistan?], the Batum province . . . to decide their own destiny," and introduced the now-familiar claim that the Straits question was "to be submitted to a conference of states bordering on the Black Sea." These demands Kemal eventually succeeded in avoiding. He never accepted a class war, though in reply to Chicherin he was willing to use Bolshevik terminology like "proletarian masses."[89]

By August 24, 1920, Bekir Sami had reached sufficient agreement in Moscow to initial a draft treaty, but the formal signing was delayed for seven months by considerable friction over the Transcaucasus region. This area had for a century been the scene of Russo-Turkish conflict. Now that it was temporarily in the hands of independent Armenia (Republic of Erivan), Georgia, and Azerbaijan, both Turks and Russians sought to

1920 in Jäschke, "Der Weg zur russisch-türkischen Freundschaft," *Die Welt des Islams,* XVI (1934), 27 and note 20; *idem.,* "Urkunden I," p. 122, note 3. Several authorities assert that by April, 1920, Ankara and Moscow had already concluded a military convention, providing supplies for the Turks. None cites documents. See, for example, Harold Armstrong, *Turkey in Travail* (London, 1925), p. 116; Toynbee, *Western Question,* p. 367; John Kingsley Birge, *A Guide to Turkish Area Studies* (Washington, 1949), p. 234. Toynbee in *Survey of International Affairs, 1920-1923* (London, 1925), p. 365, mentions even earlier agreements of December 1919, and March 1920, without citing sources or indicating content. Jäschke, "Der Weg," p. 35 and note 76 discusses some of the evidence and seems to discount the likelihood of a military convention.

[86] Text in Degras, I, 15-17.   [87] Text, *ibid.,* pp. 164-167.

[88] Text, *ibid.,* pp. 187-188.

[89] Kemal to Chicherin, November 29, 1920, in V. A. Kliuchnikov and A. Sabanin, *Mezhdunarodnaya Politika noveishovo vremeni v dogovorakh, notakh i deklaratsiakh* III (Moscow, 1928), 27-28.

increase their control there, while the Transcaucasus states tried to secure their independence and their borders. Kemal complained to Chicherin in a letter of June 20, 1920, of Armenian attacks on Turkish areas, and asked assistance and mediation.[40] But while Bekir Sami was in Moscow, Russia signed a treaty with Armenia which recognized Armenian control over territory which the Turks considered theirs, involving also Armenian domination of the land route from Turkey to Russia. Chicherin then demanded that the Turks cede territory to Armenia.[41] This demand brought a suspension of Bekir Sami's negotiations. Undoubtedly Kemal was suspicious of Communist aims, and Chicherin wary of aligning Russia with a Turkish regime that still might collapse. Unofficial Bolshevik agents and propagandists had in fact appeared in Ankara and other Anatolian cities by May 1920, though their arguments and literature won few converts.[42] Despite this friction, Chicherin sent a more formal mission to Ankara in October, and the next month the Grand National Assembly authorized diplomatic and consular representation in Russia.[43] Kemal himself characteristically selected Ankara's first ambassador. Removing Ali Fuat from command of troops on the western front for alleged incompetence, he sent him to Moscow. The Assembly confirmed the appointment.[44]

Kemal was always ready to negotiate with the Western Powers as well as with Russia. The defeat of various French units in southern Anatolia had led in May to a twenty-day armistice concluded with French representatives sent to Ankara. Kemal tried to portray this as tacit French recognition of his government.[45] He became convinced that France would desert Britain and evacuate Adana. To put pressure on France, the Turks gave some encouragement to Arab opponents of French control in Syria.[46] But it was difficult to negotiate with the Western Powers in the spring and summer of 1920, when they were elaborating the Treaty of Sèvres

[40] *Hakimiyeti Milliye* (a nationalist paper in Ankara), no. 44, July 8, 1920, quoted in Jäschke, "Der Weg," p. 29.

[41] Hikmet, *Harici Siyaseti*, p. 64; Kemal, *Speech*, p. 396. Yusuf Kemal brought this demand back to Ankara, which Kemal categorically refused to grant, even in return for Soviet aid: Hikmet, p. 65; Jäschke, "Der Weg," p. 31.

[42] Edib, *Turkish Ordeal*, pp. 170-182; Rawlinson, *Adventures*, p. 295. Actually a Turkish Communist organization had already been formed in Moscow, and in June of 1920 one was started in Ankara. Kemal curbed it in about a year, and undermined it by having an "official" Communist party founded, which however proclaimed the virtues of Islam and nationalism: Gotthard Jäschke, "Kommunismus und Islam im türkischen Befreiungskriege," *Die Welt des Islams*, XX (1938), 110-117.

[43] Jäschke, *Die Türkei*, pp. 39, 41.

[44] Kemal, *Speech*, pp. 429-430, 436; Edib, *Turkish Ordeal*, pp. 224-225.

[45] Kemal, *Speech*, pp. 390-391.

[46] King Abdullah, *Memoirs*, ed. by P. P. Graves (London, 1950), pp. 190-192.

that would partition the Ottoman Empire for their own benefit and leave only a section of Anatolia to complete Turkish control. On May 11, 1920, a draft of the proposed treaty was handed to the Istanbul government. A month thereafter the Allied ministers agreed, at the Hythe conference, to a Greek offensive to prevent the Turkish nationalist forces from reaching the Straits and blocking the partition of Turkey. News of the treaty, and the Greek war, naturally spurred the nationalists to renewed opposition. Though their ill-equipped troops had to retire before the Greek drives, their deputies in the Grand National Assembly took an oath to support the National Pact in the face of the treaty, and further informed the Powers that no agreements concluded by the Istanbul government since the British occupation could be valid.[47] Damad Ferid also protested the treaty, in the name of the Sultan's government, at the Spa conference in July, but he was powerless to do more, since in Istanbul his government could not escape Allied control. The Allied ministers dismissed his protests, and obliged his representatives to sign at Sèvres on August 10, 1920. On the same day Britain, France, and Italy concluded the Tripartite Treaty, giving the latter two Powers extensive zones of influence in Anatolia.[48]

Since negotiations with Moscow were deadlocked because of Armenia, and since Sèvres created an independent Armenia and an autonomous Kurdistan in eastern Anatolia, the nationalists set out to secure their eastern frontier by force. During the fall and winter of 1920 Moscow and Ankara cooperated to exclude all Western Powers from the settlement of the area, but competed in extending their own control.[49] Azerbaijan was by then already Soviet-dominated, and the last British troops evacuated Batum in July. Ankara then sent an ultimatum to Armenia. General Kâzim Karabekir, at thirty-eight as outstanding in the nationalist military leadership as he was famous for his paternal care of hundreds of Turkish orphans, delivered an attack from Erzerum in late September that swept in six weeks through Kars to Alexandropol.[50] Moscow then engineered a coup to capture the Armenian government, which forth-

[47] *Histoire*, p. 63; Webster, *Turkey of Atatürk*, p. 86. The *Hakimiyeti Milliye* of Ankara published the terms of Sèvres under the headline "How They Tear Us Apart," and observed further that the treaty could not be constitutionally ratified because Istanbul had no parliament: Jäschke, *Die Türkei*, pp. 36, 38.

[48] Text of Sèvres in Great Britain, Treaty Series, 1920, no. 11 (Cmd. 964), and of the Tripartite Agreement, no. 12 (Cmd. 963).

[49] On events in this region see Toynbee, *Survey . . . 1920-1923*, pp. 361-376.

[50] Presumably there were Turkish-Soviet conferences during the campaign about aims in the Transcaucasus: *ibid.*, p. 368. On Kâzim Karabekir in this period: Edib, *Turkish Ordeal*, pp. 203, 400-403; Rawlinson, *Adventures*, pp. 180-181, 282-284; Berthe Georges-Gaulis, *La nouvelle Turquie* (Paris, 1924), p. 97.

with made peace to forestall any further Turkish advance. Kâzim Karabekir signed Ankara's first international treaty at Alexandropol [Gümrü] on December 2, 1920.[51] It returned the district of Kars to Turkish control, and again made possible direct land connection to Russia. Bekir Sami and Yusuf Kemal soon thereafter started for Moscow to pick up the threads of the suspended negotiations.[52]

The developing Russian-Turkish friendship meanwhile survived two potential threats. The first was the appearance of Enver Pasha in Moscow. There the former Ottoman war minister tried to pose as the real representative of Turkey, to discredit Kemal, and to win Soviet backing for his own schemes. The Bolsheviks, unwilling to lose Kemal's possible help against Britain, and suspicious of the effect on their own Turkish-speaking millions of Enver's pan-Turanian ideas, gave the latter little encouragement.[53] The second was the drive of the Comintern to dominate the Muslims of Asia, dramatically expressed in the Congress of Eastern Peoples held at Baku just as Kâzim Karabekir was about to start his offensive against Armenia, not far off. Of the nearly 2,000 delegates about a third were non-Communist, representing peoples whose anti-imperialist nationalism the Comintern hoped to exploit. Most of the 235 Turks present were of this group, many of them middle-class. Zinoviev, president of the Congress, denounced them as Calif-supporters, and criticized the "pseudo-Soviets such as are now sometimes being offered to you in Turkey." But he recognized that the Turks, like the Communists, opposed Britain. "We give patient aid," said Zinoviev, "to groups of persons who do not believe in our ideas, who are even opposed to us on some points. In the same way the Soviet government in Turkey supports Kemal. Never for one moment do we forget that the movement headed by Kemal is not a Communist movement. We know it."[54]

[51] A. Poidebard, ed., *La Transcaucase et la République d'Arménie dans les textes diplomatiques . . . 1919-1921* (Paris, 1924), pp. 56-58, giving the treaty text from an Armenian source. Gotthard Jäschke, "Die türkische-armenische Grenze und der Friedensvertrag von Gümrü (Alexandropol)," *Mitteilungen des Seminars für orientalischen Sprachen*, XXXV (1932), II, 167-171, 173-176, gives a partial text from a Turkish source. See also *Histoire*, p. 71; Kemal, *Speech*, p. 418.

[52] Hikmet, *Haricî Siyaseti*, p. 66.

[53] Fischer, *Soviets in World Affairs*, I, 384-390, on Enver in Russia. Enver was the subject of fantastic speculation and rumor, portrayed both as a Soviet tool against Kemal and a Turkish tool against Moscow. See reports in *Oriente Moderno*, I, II (1921-1923), *passim*.

[54] G. Zinoviev, "Bolshevist Aims in Asia," *Current History*, XIII, part 2, no. 3 (March 1921), 465; Michael T. Florinsky, *World Revolution and the USSR* (New York, 1933), pp. 57-62. Enver sent a message to the Congress using Communist terminology: "W," "Les relations russo-turques depuis l'avènement du Bolchévisme," *Revue du monde musulman*, LII (1922), 197, giving part of the text. Jäschke, "Der Weg," pp. 29-30,

While renewed Russo-Turkish negotiations were in prospect, opportunity came to Kemal also at the start of 1921 for conversations with the West. Turkish success against Armenia, coupled with the first victory over the Greeks at Inönü in January 1921, worried the Allied ministers, who invited the governments of Athens and Istanbul to a conference at London in February. The Ottoman delegation, they said, should include plenipotentiaries from Ankara. This was a back-handed recognition of his government which Kemal refused to accept. He asserted in a lengthy telegraphic correspondence with Tevfik, the new grand vizier in Istanbul, that only the Grand National Assembly represented Turkey, and that it demanded a direct invitation. To Tevfik's arguments that the two governments had identical aims, and that the Sultan had to maintain his government in Istanbul lest the Allies completely control the city, Kemal replied that the aims might be similar, but free Turkey could never subordinate itself to occupied Turkey.[55] In Ankara there was debate as to whether the London invitation were not merely a ruse to enable the Greeks to recover from their Inönü defeat.[56] Kemal swung the Assembly to his views, which were not those of the extremists: a delegation should set out but should not go to London unless a direct invitation was received. Italy provided a torpedo boat at Antalya to take the delegation to Brindisi. In Rome the nationalists waited until Lloyd George sent a direct invitation through Count Sforza, whose sympathy for the nationalists had frequently been expressed.[57]

Bekir Sami had just returned from Moscow when he set out as head of the new mission to London. His stay in Russia had disillusioned him. He now looked upon the Soviet government as rule by an autocratic minority, insincere in its professions of international goodwill and regard for minority rights.[58] At London his consequent desire to reach agreement with the West was quite apparent, though the demands he presented to the conference were still those of the National Pact. By agreement, Bekir Sami spoke for the Istanbul delegation as well as his own—an exhibition of harmony that astounded the Allied ministers, but reflected the relative power of the two factions. The Allies offered two schemes involving modifications of Sèvres, thereby admitting that Kemal's success so far

---

says that Bekir Sami and Yusuf Kemal attended the Congress on their return trip from Moscow; also *Oriente Moderno*, I:2 (July 1921), 87-88.

[55] Kemal, *Speech*, pp. 469-490.   [56] Edib, *Turkish Ordeal*, p. 243.

[57] Jäschke, *Die Türkei*, pp. 45-46; Kemal, *Speech*, p. 490; Count Carlo Sforza, *Diplomatic Europe Since the Treaty of Versailles* (New Haven, 1928), pp. 51-66, summarizing his Turcophil views. Ankara already had diplomatic agents in Rome and Paris.

[58] Edib, *Turkish Ordeal*, pp. 242-243.

rendered the whole treaty unenforceable. Bekir Sami accepted one scheme with reservations, on instructions from Kemal, and the other *ad referendum*. The Greeks, however, refused to consider modifications of their rights under Sèvres, and launched a new offensive against Ankara at the end of March. Ankara was thereby spared the necessity of refusing proposals which did not meet all the National Pact's demands.[59]

Bekir Sami's success at London was in widening the breach among the Allies by private negotiation with Lloyd George, Briand, and Sforza. His efforts to persuade Lloyd George to call off the Greeks were fruitless; so also his reported proposal that Britain support an anti-Bolshevik union of Turkey and the Caucasus peoples. He did arrange with Lloyd George a mutual exchange of prisoners.[60] With Briand and Sforza he was able to sign formal treaties providing for withdrawal of French and Italian troops from large sections of Anatolia in return for Turkish economic concessions. Briand also agreed to a Syrian-Turkish frontier south of that of Sèvres, while Sforza promised support at the peace settlement for Turkish possession of Izmir and Thrace.[61] France and Italy had deserted the British-backed Greeks for the Turks.

But Bekir Sami's success was also his failure. Things looked different to him than to Kemal and many other nationalists. On his return home Bekir Sami was attacked by Kemal and the Assembly for having made economic concessions which in effect paralleled the zones of the Tripartite Treaty. France and Italy were attacked in the nationalist press as still colonial-minded. Bekir Sami's attitude toward Russia was also questioned; it was important not to alienate this source of help. Kemal insisted that Bekir Sami resign as Foreign Minister, saying he had exceeded his instructions. The Assembly rejected the French treaty and did not even consider the one with Italy. A strong group in the Assembly professed themselves "Easterners," placing more hope in a Russian orientation than in negotiation with the West.[62] Despite his forced resignation, however,

---

[59] On the London conference see *Oriente Moderno*, I:7 (December 15, 1921), 390-393, including Bekir Sami's demands; Kemal, *Speech*, pp. 490-491; Toynbee, *Western Question*, pp. 93-97; Edouard Driault et Michel Lhéritier, *Histoire diplomatique de la Grèce de 1821 à nos jours*, V (Paris, 1926), 389-395.

[60] Kemal, *Speech*, pp. 497-498; Edib, *Turkish Ordeal*, pp. 254-255. A report of these conversations leaked to Krassin and Chicherin, perhaps in a British effort to block any Turkish-Russian agreement. Britain and Russia were at this time fighting for influence over Muslims from Turkey to China, and indulging in recriminations about attempts to influence the Turkish nationalists. See Degras, I, 230-233.

[61] Texts in *Oriente Moderno*, I:2 (July 15, 1921), 79-81, and II:1 (June 15, 1922), 18 respectively.

[62] Kemal, *Speech*, pp. 409-410, 498-499; *Oriente Moderno*, I:1 (June 15, 1921), 21-23; "W," in *Revue du monde musulman*, LII, 201-202; Michel Paillarès, *Le*

Bekir Sami's work was not lost. The prisoner-exchange agreement was renegotiated with Britain in the fall, the Italians began in June to evacuate forces from Antalya, and the French exhibited eagerness for new conversations. After the London conference it was obvious that Ankara spoke for the Turks, while the Istanbul government represented only the Sultan. Though the Western Powers recognized Istanbul, they had to deal with Ankara to get results.

Mustafa Kemal had in the previous fall gained the legal right to nominate ministers to the Assembly for election, thereby assuring his personal control over top-level personnel. He thus hand-picked Yusuf Kemal, minister of economy, to be Bekir Sami's successor as Foreign Minister.[63] Yusuf Kemal had been obliged in his youth to turn from medicine to law because of severe injury to his right hand. This accident gave the nationalists a successful negotiator with a lawyer's skill in settling cases out of court. Trained at the universities of Istanbul and Paris, Yusuf Kemal was at home in both French and English. He did not have the practiced finesse of the older Bekir Sami, but his direct approach, typical of the nationalist leaders, who were, like him, all about forty years old, enabled him to drive hard bargains. He was a "shirt-sleeve" diplomat, as one of his compatriots called him.[64]

When the Assembly confirmed his appointment as Foreign Minister in May 1921, Yusuf Kemal had not yet returned from Moscow, where he had successfully conducted the final negotiations for a treaty at the same time as Bekir Sami was in London. The Russo-Turkish treaty had threatened to founder on arguments over Batum, which in early 1921 was controlled by Menshevik Georgia. As Bolshevik troops advanced against this last non-Soviet Transcaucasus state, Ankara demanded territory from Georgia by ultimatum. The Georgian ambassador in Ankara, Mdivani, agreed to Turkish occupation of Batum, presumably to keep it out of Bolshevik hands. Kâzim Karabekir thereupon led Turkish troops into the city on March 11, preceding by a week the arrival of Red troops, with whom serious clashes were narrowly avoided.[65] This potential

Kémalisme devant les Alliés (Constantinople, 1922), pp. 355-356. Sforza, *Diplomatic Europe*, p. 63, confirms Kemal's analysis of the significance of the economic concessions.

[63] Kemal, *Speech*, pp. 427-428; Jäschke, *Die Türkei*, p. 49.

[64] Mufty-Zade Zia, "How the Turks Feel," p. 860; Ibrahim A. Gövsa, *Türk Meşhurlari Ansiklopedisi* [Encyclopedia of Turkish Notables] (n.p., n.d.), p. 378; Mehmet Zeki, *Encyclopédie Biographique de la Turquie* (Istanbul, 1932), pp. 37-38; Toynbee, *Western Question*, p. 178; Clair Price, "Mustafa Kemal and the Angora Government," *Current History*, XVI (1922), 794-795.

[65] Kemal, *Speech*, pp. 418-419; Fischer, *Soviets in World Affairs*, I, 392; Edib, *Turkish Ordeal*, pp. 240-241; Jäschke, *Die Türkei*, pp. 45, 47; Toynbee, *Survey . . . 1920-1923*, pp. 369-370; Hikmet, *Harici Siyaseti*, p. 66.

Fashoda was settled by compromise, which Chicherin and Yusuf Kemal agreed to make part of the treaty signed on March 16, 1921.[66]

For Chicherin this treaty may have been only one of several to secure anti-British friends; the preamble noted Turkish-Russian "solidarity in the struggle against imperialism." For Ankara, the Moscow treaty was a major victory, securing a favorable and stable eastern frontier and strengthening its hand for bargaining with the West. Yusuf Kemal had to leave Batum to Soviet Georgia, but with stipulations of broad local autonomy and free transit for Turkish goods. Kars and Ardahan were included within Turkey. Chicherin agreed that "Turkey" meant the territories specified in the National Pact, and promised that Russia would recognize no international agreements concerning Turkey not recognized by the Grand National Assembly. Each agreed to recognize no treaties imposed on the other. Russia renounced all capitulatory rights. Yusuf Kemal's greatest concession was to agree that, Istanbul being secure, the Straits regime should be determined by the littoral states of the Black Sea. So long as British warships controlled the Straits and Greek troops attacked, the concession was not surprising, though at Lausanne the Turks successfully avoided implementation of this clause.

The mutual suspicion still existing was revealed by Article 8, wherein each signatory promised to permit on its soil no group aiming at the overthrow of the other government. For Moscow, this was protection against pan-Turanian agitation among Russia's millions of Turkish subjects; for Ankara, protection against Bolshevik conspiracy based in the Caucasus or elsewhere. There was no specific provision against propaganda activity. Communist propaganda was in fact attempted in Turkey, but with little success. Kemal discouraged it by prison and other means, for which he was denounced at the third Comintern Congress in 1921 and, the next year at the second Congress of Communist Labor Unions.[67] This ideological friction did not seriously disturb governmental relations, and Moscow continued to provide military supplies to the Turks in amounts which, to this day, have not been disclosed.[68]

[66] Text in Degras, I, 237-242, from the Russian, and in *Oriente Moderno*, I:6 (November 15, 1921), 340-343, from the Turkish.

[67] *Oriente Moderno*, I:3 (August 15, 1921), 154-155 and II:8 (January 15, 1923), 472; Kemal, *Speech*, pp. 427-428; Fischer, *Soviets in World Affairs*, I, 393; "W" in *Revue du monde musulman*, LII, 193, 202; *Current History*, XV:1 (October, 1921), 144; Gotthard Jäschke, "Protest der Türkischen Volkskommunistischen Partei gegen die Regierung der Türkischen Grossen Nationalversammlung," *Die Welt des Islams*, XX (1938), 135-136.

[68] Fischer, *Soviets in World Affairs*, I, 391; Jäschke, *Die Türkei*, p. 141; *Oriente Moderno*, I:5 (October 15, 1921), 283. Kemal makes no mention of military aid, saying only that "Turkish-Russian relations developed very favorably" in 1921. *Speech*, p. 541.

Kemal was never lured by the early friendship with Russia into accepting the position of the "Easterners" in foreign policy. Nor was he a "Westerner," but sought constantly to gain advantages from both sides in carrying out the aims of the National Pact. Reviewing the international position of Turkey for the Assembly on March 1, 1921, he stressed his desire for peace and for good relations with both Orient and Occident. He was ready to negotiate with Britain, but reproached British statesmen for pretending not to understand his pacific aims.[69] A second Turkish victory over the Greeks at İnönü, shortly after the Moscow treaty was signed, led the High Commissioners in Istanbul to declare neutrality in the Greek-Turkish struggle and to deny either belligerent entrance into a neutral zone around the Straits. But the only immediate move toward peace was an Allied offer of mediation in June, which the Greeks rejected, knowing that since Constantine's return to the Greek throne France and Italy were becoming increasingly Turcophile. In July the Greeks aimed a new offensive at Ankara.[70]

Until the Greeks could be defeated, or until Kemal could negotiate agreements conforming to the National Pact, his policy was simply to maintain contact with the Western Powers. Bekir Sami was sent on a roving commission to sound out the Western capitals.[71] Meanwhile Kemal and General Harington, the British High Commissioner, were apparently willing to use their correspondence on prisoner exchange to develop a wider canvass of the situation, but as neither would see the other in the role of petitioner the projected meeting fell through.[72] The Italians began to evacuate Antalya also in June, 1921, and pressed again for an agreement like that of Bekir Sami with Sforza, but Kemal was no more willing now than before to accord the economic concessions asked by the Italian agent in Ankara, Tuozzi.[73]

It was with the French, beset by troubles enough in their Syrian mandate and at odds with Britain over many questions, that Ankara first managed to conclude a treaty on its own terms. M. Franklin-Bouillon,

[69] Text in *Asie française*, XXI:193 (June 1921), 251-252.

[70] *Oriente Moderno*, I:7 (December 15, 1921), 395-396.

[71] Jäschke, *Die Türkei*, pp. 50-52. Kemal, *Speech*, pp. 500-501 again accuses Bekir Sami of a peace-at-any-price policy.

[72] Kemal, *Speech*, pp. 541-543; Rawlinson, *Adventures*, pp. 247-248. Litvinov to Curzon, September 27, 1921, says that the Commissariat for Foreign Affairs had arranged British-Turkish conversations in Moscow: Degras, I, 260-261. Relations between the two countries in 1921 were enlivened by the public trial in Ankara of an Oxford-trained Indian Muslim accused of espionage for Britain: Edib, *Turkish Ordeal*, pp. 229-230; Georges-Gaulis, *Angora*, pp. 242-247.

[73] Hikmet, *Haricî Siyaseti*, p. 100; *Oriente Moderno*, I:3 (August 15, 1921), 183, and I:8 (January 15, 1922), 469.

president of the Senate foreign relations committee, came to Ankara in June on an "unofficial" mission, and had long talks with Kemal. Franklin-Bouillon wanted to end the hostilities in Cilicia, but only in return for economic concessions and some remnant of capitulatory privileges to protect the great interests of France in Turkish finance, economic development, and French schools and missions. To achieve this, he tried to negotiate on the basis of the abortive Bekir Sami-Briand treaty. This Kemal would not allow. The National Pact, he said, which emphasized "political, economic, legal, military and cultural" independence, must be the starting point. The French envoy was impressed by Kemal's obstinacy. His government was impressed by Kemal's victory over the Greeks in the Sakarya battle at the end of August, which repulsed the most serious military threat to Ankara. The Treaty of Ankara was therefore signed on October 20, 1921, marking as great a triumph for Turkish diplomacy as the Treaty of Moscow.[74]

The treaty provided that hostilities cease immediately, and that a new frontier between Turkey and Syria revise the line drawn at Sèvres to leave Cilicia and most of the Bagdad Railway track in Turkish hands. As he had been obliged to yield Batum to Georgia, so Yusuf Kemal's greatest concession here was to leave Alexandretta to Syria, but with guarantees of a special regime in which Turkish should be an official language, and with a promise by Franklin-Bouillon to try to arrange for a local flag incorporating the Turkish flag.[75] Yusuf Kemal avoided giving France any guarantees on economic concessions or minority rights which would limit Turkish sovereignty. By the Treaty of Ankara the Turks gained recognition of the Government of the Grand National Assembly by France and a bilateral revision of Sèvres which was essentially a separate peace with France behind Britain's back.[76] Many thousands of Turkish troops were now free to move against the Greeks, while the French turned over to Ankara quantities of military supplies.[77] Turkish-French relations were henceforth close, and Franklin-Bouillon continued to shuttle back and forth until the final armistice.

[74] Kemal, *Speech*, pp. 523-527; *Oriente Moderno*, I:3 (August 15, 1921), 152. During this period the French were suspected of encouraging the Turks to reject any Allied mediation offers: Toynbee, *Western Question*, pp. 100-101. The Turks rebuffed British attempts to frustrate the conclusion of the treaty by hinting through the Japanese High Commissioner that they were ready to recognize the National Pact: Hikmet, *Haricî Siyaseti*, p. 100.

[75] The Turks never ceased to insist that Alexandretta [the Hatay] was a special case, thus laying the basis for its eventual reincorporation into Turkey in 1939.

[76] Curzon protested such recognition and separate peace, which Paris denied was true: Turkey No. 1 (1922), Cmd. 1570.

[77] Gontaut-Biron, *D'Angora à Lausanne*, p. 98.

Not only the British, but also the Russians were worried by Kemal's success in making peace with France. Chicherin demanded explanations, and apparently threatened to use Enver from a Transcaucasus base to weaken or upset the Ankara regime.[78] But Kemal stood firm. So long as he did not also make peace with Britain, his success in negotiation with France served to increase his prestige in Russian eyes. After the Sakarya victory, and just one week before the conclusion of the Franklin-Bouillon agreement, Kâzim Karabekir signed for Turkey the Treaty of Kars with Russia, Georgia, Azerbaijan, and Armenia. Modeled on the Treaty of Moscow, this was a formal confirmation by the Transcaucasus republics under Russian pressure of the new eastern boundary of Turkey, and a declaration of friendship among the signatories.[79] In December 1921, a new Soviet mission arrived in Ankara from the Ukraine, headed by General Frunze, which led to the signing on January 2, 1922, of a Turkish-Ukrainian treaty much like that of Kars.[80] Frunze also arranged for further shipments to Ankara of military supplies, for which Kemal had asked after his Sakarya victory, and he offered military advice for campaigns against the Greeks. Soon after Frunze's three-week mission was over, a new ambassador from Moscow, Comrade Aralov, arrived to receive great acclaim both in Ankara and on a tour of the front with Kemal.[81]

In his diplomatic dealings since the Ankara government was established, Kemal had oscillated successfully between Russia and the West. He had managed also to keep on cordial terms with the Muslim world, which could give at least moral and sometimes diversionary support against the other two worlds with which he dealt. Bekir Sami had not yet left on his first mission to Moscow when the Grand National Assembly issued an appeal for the support of all Muslims.[82] But Kemal was convinced that nationalist Turkey must become essentially a secular state, and keep clear of any pan-Islamic movement. To the Assembly he said that Islamic ties had done nothing for the Ottoman sultans but extend their commitments and cause them trouble.[83] During the war of libera-

[78] Ziemke, Die neue Türkei, pp. 366-367; "W" in Revue du monde musulman, LII, 201-205; Harry N. Howard, The Partition of Turkey: A Diplomatic History, 1913-1923 (Norman, Okla., 1931), p. 268.

[79] Text in Degras, I, 263-269.

[80] Text in Kliuchnikov and Sabanin, Mezhdunarodnaya Politika, III, Pt. i, 164-165.

[81] Fischer, Soviets in World Affairs, I, 393-394. In 1922, the Soviet embassy was the best-appointed in Ankara, with a staff of 70. See Grace Ellison, An Englishwoman in Angora (London, 1923), p. 151.

[82] In the Hakimiyeti Milliye, May 9, 1920. See Jäschke, Die Türkei, p. 33.

[83] Oriente Moderno, 1:8 (January 15, 1922), 467-468; Kemal, Speech, pp. 377-378.

tion, however, Kemal accepted gracefully from influential Muslims and Muslim nations the admiration and support which they naturally accorded the Turks, who seemed to be successful in upholding the Califate against the Christian world. The new Turkey would eventually sever its ties with the house of Osman and with Islam, but the time for this step had not come.

The most important international Muslim relationship was established with Afghanistan by a treaty of March 1, 1921, negotiated in Moscow while Yusuf Kemal and the Afghan ambassador were both concluding treaties with Russia.[84] It began with the customary Muslim invocation, "In the name of God, the Merciful, the Compassionate." In its third article Afghanistan recognized the leadership of Turkey for services to Islam, and for bearing "the standard of the Califate." The two countries agreed to a formal alliance against attacks by an imperialistic Power, meaning Britain, and Turkey agreed to supply military instructors to Afghanistan. Sultan Ahmed Khan, the first Afghan ambassador, was a popular figure in Ankara after his arrival there in April 1921. "All of us other Muslims consider the Turkish cause as our own," he said to a Western visitor.[85] In the same year Kemal sent an ambassador to Bokhara, which enjoyed a tenuous independence, and received from the Bokharan ambassador in Ankara the gifts of a Koran and a sword. Kemal's speech of welcome referred to the common ties of religion, though his emphasis on this was less than that of his visitors.[86]

The leading Muslim dignitary with whom Kemal dealt was Sheikh Ahmed esh-Sherif es-Senusi, ex-leader of the influential Senusi brotherhood of Cyrenaica. Sayyid Ahmed, after fighting with the Turks against Italian, French, and British forces, had escaped to Turkey in 1918. In 1920 Kemal received him at a banquet of honor, and apparently allowed him to organize a pan-Islamic congress in Sivas and to aid the Turkish nationalists in the early days by preaching the Holy War and rallying Arabs to oppose the British and French along with the Turks. Though accepting such support tacitly for a time, Kemal never committed himself to any pan-Islamic cause. Sayyid Ahmed later found it wise to leave for Syria when Kemal opposed his ardent support of the Califate. Kemal further refused to be dragged into any attempt to reimpose Turkish

---

[84] Text in *British Foreign and State Papers*, CXVIII (1923), 10-11. This treaty was partly modeled on the Russo-Afghan treaty of the day before. See Degras, I, 233-235.

[85] Jean Schicklin, *Angora: l'aube de la Turquie nouvelle, 1919-1922* (Paris, 1922), p. 317.

[86] *Oriente Moderno*, I:9 (February 15, 1922), 545-547, and I:10 (March 15, 1922), 604-605.

control over the Arab territories which had given the sultans so many headaches.[87]

III

By the start of 1922 the Government of the Grand National Assembly was well-established. Its major task was now to drive the Greeks from western Anatolia and Thrace, and secure a peace incorporating those areas in Turkey. "We could not flatter ourselves," Kemal said later, "that there was any hope of success in a diplomatic way until we had driven the enemy out of our territory by force of arms."[88] But he was willing still to seize any chance of negotiation for a bloodless victory. For this purpose, Yusuf Kemal spent March in London and Paris, trying vainly to persuade Curzon and Poincaré that peace should be made on the basis of the National Pact.[89] The three Allied Foreign Ministers, however, met in Paris in March and proposed a further pro-Turkish modification of Sèvres, an immediate armistice, and a Greek evacuation of Anatolia after the peace.[90] The Greeks, desperate since February, accepted. Kemal was determined not to break off possible peace preliminaries but equally determined not to give the Greeks respite by an armistice to mount a new attack. The reply of April 5 which Yusuf Kemal therefore sent to the Allies, after Kemal and his ministers had conferred, accepted in principle a four-month armistice provided the Greeks began evacuation at once and completed it during the armistice period.[91] This the Greeks and Allies refused. Again on April 23 a Turkish note insisted on immediate evacuation, and tried to seize the initiative by proposing a preliminary conference on peace terms at Izmit, near Istanbul. This the Allies also rejected.[92]

[87] E. E. Evans-Pritchard, *The Sanusi of Cyrenaica* (Oxford, 1949), pp. 130-133; Jäschke, *Die Türkei*, pp. 42, 45; Georges-Gaulis, *Angora*, pp. 239-240; Sforza, *European Dictatorships*, pp. 202-203; *Oriente Moderno*, I:1 (June 15, 1921), 24, 32 and I:11 (April 15, 1922), 653. As late as January 1923, Rauf Bey, then prime minister, attended a banquet given by the Afghan ambassador in Ankara in honor of Sayyid Ahmed, and expressed the thanks of Turkey for help in an hour of danger. *Ibid.*, II:10 (March 15, 1923), 583. Kemal and the Assembly approved the idea of a pan-Islamic congress in March 1921, at exactly the same time as Bekir Sami was in London and Yusuf Kemal in Moscow, and the *Hakimiyeti Milliye* publicly endorsed the idea. France, Ministère des affaires étrangères, *Bulletin périodique de la presse turque*, XIII (April 22, 1921), 3.

[88] Kemal, *Speech*, p. 543.

[89] *ibid.*, pp. 544-545; *Oriente Moderno*, I:11 (April 15, 1922), 650.

[90] Text in *Oriente Moderno*, I:11 (April 15, 1922), 641-645, and II:5 (October 15, 1922), 266-271.

[91] Text in *Oriente Moderno*, I:11 (April 15, 1922), 650-651, where it is also reported that the Russian ambassador in Ankara tried to influence Kemal to reject the offer.

[92] Kemal, *Speech*, pp. 545-559; *Histoire*, pp. 104-108; *Oriente Moderno*, II:5 (October 15, 1922), 271-272.

While Kemal thus refused to accept the responsibility of breaking off potential peace negotiations, he attempted also to win an invitation to the Genoa economic conference in April 1922. Chicherin alone supported his demand. The Turkish ambassadors in Paris and Rome protested the exclusion; the latter went to Genoa to observe and object in person. Ankara announced that it preserved consequently complete liberty of action in economic matters.[93] In July Fethi [Okyar], minister of the interior, was given leave of absence to sound Paris and London again on the chances of a negotiated peace. Poincaré twice received him, but Lloyd George and Curzon would not.[94] Meanwhile the Greek-Turkish war was coming to its climax. To improve their situation the Greeks in July proposed to occupy Istanbul themselves. The Allies refused bluntly. Then the Greek commissioner in Izmir proclaimed there the autonomous state of Ionia, occasioning bitter Turkish protests through Hamid in Istanbul to the High Commissioners. The final Turkish answer was a drive in August which broke the Greeks, captured their commander, and resulted in a victorious entry into Izmir on September 9, as the Greeks evacuated Anatolia precipitately.[95]

Military victory at once placed the Turks in an advantageous bargaining position. They were now less dependent on Russian assistance. Kemal gave an interview to *Izvestya* saying that Turkey wanted normal relations with Britain, France, and Italy, which called forth bitter Russian comments on Turkish opportunism. The Turkish ambassador in Moscow tried to assuage feelings there with a speech of thanks which referred to the solidarity of Muslim peoples and the Russian proletariat.[96] Britain alone, now suddenly deserted by the French and Italians, faced the Turks along the Straits. Demanding that the Greeks evacuate Eastern Thrace at once, Turkish forces advanced into the Straits zone at Çanak [Chanak]. Though they came with rifles butt-forward, the appalling prospect of an Anglo-Turkish war now confronted the two governments. Peace was maintained because General Harington ignored Cabinet in-

---

[93] Degras, I, 289; *Oriente Moderno*, I:9 (February 15, 1922), 525-526, I:12 (May 15, 1922), 706, 719-721, and II:1 (June 15, 1922), 12.

[94] Edib, *Turkish Ordeal*, p. 247; Jäschke, *Die Türkei*, pp. 61-65. Presumably Fethi telegraphed Kemal from London that no peace would be forthcoming until a final attack on the Greeks.

[95] Jäschke, *Die Türkei*, pp. 63-64; *Oriente Moderno*, II:4 (September 15, 1922), 211-212; Driault et Lhéritier, *Histoire diplomatique*, V, 408-14.

[96] Ziemke, *Die neue Türkei*, pp. 367-368; *Oriente Moderno*, II:4 (September 15, 1922), 214-215. The Russians, seeing the end of the war coming, had tried in a series of notes from July to September to seize the initiative for themselves by proposing a peace conference and insisting that, by the Russo-Turkish treaty of 1921, only the Black Sea powers could deal with the Straits regime: Degras, I, 330-333, 334-336.

structions on an ultimatum to Kemal unless he withdrew, and because Kemal, so close to complete victory, chose not to provoke the British. Yusuf Kemal accepted an Allied offer of September 23 for an armistice and a peace conference on the basis of the return to Turkey of Istanbul and Eastern Thrace, including Edirne [Adrianople]. Though insisting that Thrace be evacuated at once, not after the peace, Yusuf Kemal agreed that armistice talks could begin at Mudanya. The Turks were perhaps influenced to accept the offer by Franklin-Bouillon, who saw Kemal at Izmir. That Kemal now strongly desired peace was evident from the less intransigent tone of his Foreign Minister's note of October 4 to the Allies, accepting a peace conference, though asking that it be held at Izmir, on Turkish soil.[97]

Armistice negotiations began at Mudanya, a small Marmara port, on October 3. Kemal sent Ismet [Inönü],[98] commander of the Western front against the Greeks, as his representative. Ismet provoked a crisis at Mudanya by again insisting on immediate Greek evacuation of Eastern Thrace. Curzon made another hurried trip to Paris, and the three Allied Foreign Ministers yielded. But as late as October 9 the British representative, General Harington, believed the Mudanya negotiations would break down over numerous other, though smaller, points. After repeated telephone calls from Ismet to Kemal the issues were narrowed to six, and finally to one, while Harington left hidden in his pocket two telegrams from London authorizing him to open hostilities against the Turks. The final point in dispute was settled by a maneuver which Ismet later duplicated at Lausanne. After Harington had stated the British position, he and Ismet paced on opposite sides of the room, each intractable. Ismet said he would not agree and then, suddenly, "J'accepte." He had held out as long as he could, but apparently had already been authorized to yield if necessary. "I was never so surprised in my life," said Harington later. Agreement was thus reached on October 10 seventy-five minutes before the British officers at Çanak were to start firing. Next day the formal armistice was signed by Ismet, Harington, and French and Italian generals, though the Greeks ad-

---

[97] On Chanak and the pre-armistice exchange of notes see Col. D. I. Shuttleworth, "Turkey, From the Armistice to the Peace," *Journal of the Central Asian Society*, XI:1 (1924), 61-62; Harold Nicolson, *Curzon: The Last Phase* (Boston, 1934), p. 271; *Oriente Moderno*, II:5 (October 15, 1922), 278-281, and II:6 (November 15, 1922), 338-339; Kemal, *Speech*, pp. 568-570. Kemal is said to have caused a minor crisis by declaring intemperately to the British consul-general at Izmir that the two countries were at war: Edib, *Turkish Ordeal*, pp. 385-386.

[98] Ismet later took his last name from the scene of one of his victories.

hered only three days later.[99] Refet Pasha arrived in Istanbul on October 19 to be Ankara's first governor of Eastern Thrace, thereby completing nationalist control over most of the territory claimed in the National Pact. Lloyd George, his Grecophile policy bankrupt, resigned the same day.

A formal invitation to a peace conference at Lausanne issued by the Allies on October 27 to both Turkish governments—Ankara and Istanbul—spurred the nationalists to clarify the relationship between themselves and the Sultan. This was done simply by a resolution of the Assembly on November 1 declaring the Sultanate abolished, although a Calif of the House of Osman would be chosen by the Assembly. The Istanbul cabinet resigned and Mehmet VI, declared a traitor by Ankara, fled aboard a British warship. Thereupon Abdülmecid [Medjid] was elected Calif by the Assembly. For Turkish foreign policy this meant a final break with the imperial Ottoman traditions, though for purposes of mollifying conservative sentiment at home and of retaining among Muslims abroad the prestige of the Califate, that shadowy institution was allowed two more years of existence. Istanbul no longer contained a government which could be influenced by Allied occupation; it was a provincial city only. Kemal, though not alone in his views, had forced the measure through the Assembly, using Bismarckian terms to a committee deliberating the bill. "Gentlemen," he said, "neither the sovereignty nor the right to govern can be transferred by one person to anybody else by an academic debate. Sovereignty is acquired by force, by power, and by violence.[100] Sovereignty lay with Kemal's victorious nationalists, who alone were represented at Lausanne.

IV

Ismet Pasha led the Turkish delegation to Lausanne. Kemal himself, pleased with Ismet's hard headedness at Mudanya and confident of his personal loyalty, chose him for the most important diplomatic task Ankara had yet faced. Ismet was simultaneously elected Foreign Minister by the Assembly, after Kemal had requested Yusuf Kemal's resignation.[101] The man thus chosen, now only thirty-eight, had had a purely

---

[99] On the Mudanya negotiations: *Oriente Moderno*, II:6 (November 15, 1922), 337-345; Sir Charles Harington, *Tim Harington Looks Back* (London, 1941), pp. 117-128.
[100] Kemal, *Speech*, p. 578.
[101] *ibid.*, pp. 570-572. Rauf, president of the council of ministers, was perhaps a logical choice to head the delegation, as well as Yusuf Kemal. Rauf and Kemal were divided by various arguments over domestic politics. The former, however, served as acting Foreign Minister while Ismet was at Lausanne.

military career, rising to be Under-Secretary of War before he left Istanbul in 1920 to join Kemal in Ankara. Thereafter he had served as member of the Assembly, as chief of the general staff and as commander of the Western front. Aside from his week at Mudanya he had had only slight contact with diplomacy as military adviser to the commission that negotiated peace with Bulgaria in 1913.[102] His new responsibilities weighed heavily on Ismet, and at dinner on the day he became Foreign Minister he was unwontedly somber.[103] Kemal brushed aside Ismet's plea that he was no diplomat. At Lausanne Ismet continued to have misgivings about his new role. "They have sent me, a soldier," he said to an English journalist, "to fight a Bismarck, one of your greatest statesmen."[104] Lord Curzon, who presided over most of the conference sessions, was indeed a formidable opponent, but Ismet acquitted himself well. The meetings in the Hotel du Château, where Curzon hoped to produce a treaty in a few weeks, stretched out for eight months largely because of Ismet's obstinate negotiation. The successful issue of the conference was in part due also to Ismet's sense of timing on compromise.

Ismet found himself in a difficult position at Lausanne. He represented a victorious nation which the Allied delegates tried to treat like a defeated nation. Curzon in particular employed "star chamber proceedings" and "steamroller methods."[105] But the Assembly in Turkey demanded complete equality and a diplomatic triumph. Curzon's tactics tended to make Ankara more obstinate than ever, thus increasing Ismet's difficulties in arriving at viable compromise.[106] It was generally thought by other diplomats at Lausanne that some of the Turkish delegation were there partly to see for the Assembly that Ismet did not make too many concessions in order to secure a treaty. Dr. Riza Nur, the second Turkish plenipotentiary, seemed to be a particularly intransigent watchdog.[107] During the conference Hasan [Saka], Ankara's third delegate, went back to Turkey and returned with, presumably, instructions for greater

[102] Gövsa, *Türk Meşhurlari*, pp. 188-190.

[103] Georges-Gaulis, *La nouvelle Turquie*, p. 95.

[104] Ellison, *Englishwoman in Angora*, pp. 305, 308.

[105] The judgments of the American observers: Richard Washburn Child, *A Diplomat Looks at Europe* (New York, 1925), p. 86, and Joseph Clark Grew, *Turbulent Era: A Diplomatic Record of Forty Years* (New York, 1952), Chapter 18, November 21, 1922, entry. Mr. Grew kindly permitted use of his book in proof.

[106] *Foreign Relations, 1923*, II, 901-902; Grew, *Turbulent Era*, Chapter 18, November 22, 1922, entry; Child, *Diplomat*, p. 98: "I know directly from Ismet Pasha," says Child, "that he is harassed from Angora enough as it is."

[107] Nicolson, *Curzon*, p. 346; *Foreign Relations, 1923*, II, 910; Grew, *Turbulent Era*, Chapter 19, February 4, 1923, entry.

obstinacy.[108] On territorial and political questions, where Ismet had special competence, he was able to accept solutions more often on his own authority, whereas in matters of economics and finance he was forced to rely on the expert advice of others in his delegation.[109]

At the opening session on November 20 Ismet began at once to demand for Turkey complete equality of treatment as an independent and sovereign state. Sometimes this insistence led Ismet to unnecessary extremes, but it was on most occasions his major weapon in combatting any measure of foreign control over Turkish finances, economy, justice, minorities, territory, or anything else. Ismet stood on the National Pact. Curzon grew immensely tired of Ismet's repetitious arguments, professing not to understand why Ismet insisted on undiluted sovereignty. Ismet was too sensitive on the subject, said Curzon; he should deal with realities, not phrases. The question was one of guarantees to minorities in Turkey. Thinking of Ottoman history since Kuchuk Kainarji, Ismet begged Curzon to excuse his insistence on sovereignty. "Turkey was acutely sensitive on this matter, and her fears were unfortunately well-founded, for up to the present day Turkish sovereignty had always been infringed on the plea of humanitarian considerations. The integrity of Turkey had frequently been guaranteed by means of promises from the highest authorities and also by solemn treaties, and yet Turkish sovereignty had repeatedly been violated. . . . How could Turkey help having misgivings?"[110] Ismet likewise opposed an international commission to supervise demilitarization of the Straits. "Turkey has had experience of such systems. For a state to be exposed in any way whatever to intervention in a part of the territories subject to its sovereignty is a calamity worse than death."[111] Curzon was exasperated by the same argument on the question of capitulations. "I am tired of replying to that argument," said Curzon. "Cannot the Turks realize that theirs is not the only sovereignty in the world?"[112] Curzon often assumed the role of a weary schoolmaster admonishing a stupid pupil. Ismet refused to learn. In private negotiation between Curzon and Ismet the same antithesis often developed. When the American observer brought the two men together to discuss the judicial capitulations in Turkey, Curzon shouted and beat the wall with his cane. Ismet held out for complete

---

[108] *ibid.*, January 14, 1923, entry.

[109] France, Ministère des Affaires Étrangères, *Documents Diplomatiques. Conférence de Lausanne* (Paris, 1923), II, 127-129.

[110] Great Britain, Turkey No. 1 (1923). *Lausanne Conference on Near Eastern Affairs, 1922-1923.* Cmd. 1814, p. 219. (Hereafter cited as Cmd. 1814.)

[111] *ibid.*, p. 283.   [112] *ibid.*, p. 496.

sovereignty and said that the adjustment of such matters took time. "Curzon and Ismet had about as much in common as a lion tamer and a grower of azaleas," reported Ambassador Child.[113]

Whenever he stated the Turkish position, Ismet was slow and methodical, which also annoyed Curzon. Because he was deaf, Ismet had frequently to rely on the secretary at his side for the gist of other delegates' remarks. But Ismet used his deafness to gain time to think, and he was often suspected of hearing only what he wanted to. When he did reply, he spoke indistinct French, reading from prepared statements or using notes dictated in Turkish to his secretary, and in a voice so low as to be barely audible. Ismet did not have the necessary details at his fingertips, as Curzon did. He required time to confer with his experts. He was forever reserving his right to reply, or requesting a delay to prepare an answer.[114] Curzon tried unsuccessfully to stampede Ismet into quick and injudicious statements. On the Straits question, Ismet refused to answer directly Curzon's brilliant and rather sarcastic question as to whether Chicherin's views represented the Turkish position.[115] "It must be a terrible experience," said Child, "for Curzon to turn his splendid flow of beautiful English upon this man and then find Ismet, with his little quizzical face, wholly untouched."[116] Ismet was well aware that he could not match Curzon in extemporaneous debate and analysis. He patiently conducted a siege, instead of attempting brilliant assaults. Ismet was also, of course, in constant telegraphic communication with Kemal, who followed the negotiations closely and sent instructions. A courier left each day for Ankara.[117] Even when authorized to compromise, Ismet sometimes bargained until the last possible moment. Having told Curzon point-blank one morning at 10:30 that the Greek Orthodox Patriarchate could under no circumstances remain in Istanbul, he said at 11 out of a clear sky as the two were walking together to a session, "All right, I will yield."[118]

Ismet used as best he could the differences among the Powers for Turkish advantage. Sometimes he was unsuccessful. Repeatedly he sought to strengthen his hand by suggesting to the American observers that they conclude a treaty with Turkey. They refused to do so before the Allies had completed negotiations.[119] At other times he succeeded.

[113] Grew, *Turbulent Era*, Chapter 19, January 15, 1923, entry.
[114] Grew, *Turbulent Era*, Chapters 18 and 19, *passim*; Child, *Diplomat*, p. 95; Nicolson, *Curzon*, pp. 298, 319, 333–334.
[115] Cmd. 1814, pp. 127–135. [116] Child, *Diplomat*, p. 96.
[117] Hikmet, *Haricî Siyaseti*, p. 113; Georges-Gaulis, *Nouvelle Turquie*, p. 189.
[118] Grew, *Turbulent Era*, Chapter 19, January 9, 1923, entry.
[119] *Foreign Relations*, 1923, II, 901, 970, 987, 997, 1042–1043.

Ismet had in the early stages of the conference considerable sympathy and support from the Italian and French delegations. He nevertheless made his major concessions to the British, whose warships at Istanbul and troops in Mosul offered the greatest threat. Thereafter he could oppose various French and Italian demands without fear that Britain would back them to the point of breaking up the conference and so jeopardizing her gains.

Ismet succeeded also in walking a narrow path between Russia and the Western Powers. He saw Chicherin nearly every day in the first period of the conference, and presumably received helpful advice from him.[120] After he had made concessions to Britain, he could menace the West with a return to a Russian orientation: "Turkey could look to the East and the North as well as the West."[121] But though Ismet and the Turks remained friendly to Russia, they avoided becoming dependent on her. No Rapallo resulted from Lausanne as from Genoa. The test of this was the Straits question. Chicherin was more Turkish than the Turks in arguing for their complete control over the Straits in order to close the Black Sea to vessels of other Powers. Ismet passed over Chicherin's arguments in silence. Instead he negotiated privately—"clandestinely," as Chicherin complained—with the Allies, ultimately accepting the British view that the Straits be open to all. Along the way Ismet had to made concessions to the Allies on demilitarization around the Straits, and to accept a guarantee of their security less adequate than he desired. But the final result was of inestimable advantage for Turkey. Ismet had on this point carried out the basic demand of the National Pact, but avoided applying that article of the Russo-Turkish treaty which would give a Soviet-dominated coalition of Black Sea states—Russia, Georgia, and the Ukraine—control over Turkish shores in a closed sea. He placed the new Turkey in an advantageous position between the West and Russia. Though the decision on the Straits is sometimes represented as Curzon's triumph in splitting Turkey from Russia, it was as much Ismet's triumph in avoiding dependence on Russia.[122]

By the end of January 1923, essential agreement had been reached between Ismet and the Allies on the Thracian boundary, ownership of various Aegean islands, the Straits regime, the elimination of an Armenia carved out of Turkish territory, and a compulsory exchange of Greek

---

[120] Fischer, *Soviets in World Affairs*, I, 409; *Oriente Moderno*, II:8 (January 15, 1923), 471-472.

[121] *Foreign Relations*, 1923, II, 935.

[122] Cmd. 1814, pp. 127-135, 156-173, 230-287, 447-457. See Nicolson, *Curzon*, chapters 10 and 11 for a good interpretation of Lausanne as Curzon's triumph.

and Turkish minorities.[123] The outstanding questions still in dispute concerned the Turkish-Iraq boundary in the Mosul region, the partition of the Ottoman debt, the Turkish demand for reparations from Greece, the status of foreign economic concessions in Turkey, and the possibility of some substitute regime for the capitulations which would give legal protection to Allied interests and nationals in Turkey. Ismet's strategy had been to drive a hard bargain on territorial questions, but to compromise on all of them except Mosul, whose Kurdish-Turkish majority was included in the claims of the National Pact. On all proposals tending to limit Turkish sovereignty within the boundaries thus laid down he was adamant. He successfully refused international commissions of various sorts to supervise matters as minor as the sanitary regime of the Straits. He would give no blanket validation to foreign economic concessions, nor admit any sort of foreign supervision over Turkish courts. On "Turkey for the Turks" Ismet would not compromise.[124]

The Allies presented the Turkish delegation on January 31 a draft treaty including all points on which agreement had been reached, and their draft of points still in dispute. Curzon, in skillful and forceful language, urged the Turks to accept a good offer. "We are not here to go on bargaining until we all sink into the grave, but to settle and conclude." Bompard and Garroni, for France and Italy, urged on the Turks the clauses on capitulations and finance. Ismet, in the face of this pressure, recounted the concessions he had made, accused the Allies of bringing up new points, and requested eight days to prepare his "observations" on the Allied draft. Curzon, in more of a hurry than Ismet, set a final limit of February 4 for his departure from Lausanne.[125]

There ensued four dramatic days of informal bargaining between the Turks and the Allies, during which more concessions were made by the latter.[126] Among these was an acknowledgment of Ismet's major premise, which eventually appeared in the preamble of the final treaty—that "relations must be based on respect for the independence and sovereignty

---

[123] A convention concerning the last question was actually signed by Venizelos and Ismet on January 30, 1923. See Stephen P. Ladas, *The Exchange of Minorities: Bulgaria, Greece and Turkey* (New York, 1932), pp. 335-352, 787-794.

[124] On some matters Ismet was led into extreme statements which could not stand close examination. "The present state of Turkish law is such as to meet all the requirements and necessities of modern life," he said. (Cmd. 1814, p. 489.) A few years later the Turks themselves introduced a wholesale modernization of the law Ismet had thus praised.

[125] Cmd. 1814, pp. 428-447.

[126] *ibid.*, pp. 832-837. Nicolson says that in this period Dr. Riza Nur, second Turkish plenipotentiary, proposed to him a separate Anglo-Turkish peace. (*Curzon*, pp. 345-346.) Whether Riza Nur had any such authorization is obscure.

of the States concerned." Ismet's reply to the new concessions was received by the Allied delegates at 1:45 p.m. on February 4. Ismet made a few counterconcessions, and accepted many parts of the draft treaty, but held out for the substance of sovereignty on capitulations and finance. He proposed that a treaty incorporating all agreed points be signed then, leaving the others for later negotiation.[127] Such a treaty, involving only questions on which the Turks had agreed but giving them peace, would have strengthened the Turkish position enormously. The Allied delegates met in Curzon's hotel suite and decided to offer a few more concessions. Ismet was summoned to meet them there at 5:40. He came, obviously unhappy and embarrassed; he was essentially a pleasant and agreeable man. Dire warnings and cajolery were alternately applied to Ismet as Curzon laid down post-final concessions: he would not appeal the Mosul question to the League, as he had threatened, unless after one year it remained unsolved by direct negotiation; some economic questions could be left open for six months. Ismet raised objections, saying no in unprovocative but firm tones. He would not accept the economic and judicial clauses, since they imposed "servitudes" on Turkey. Curzon's train left just after 9 that evening. Though he hoped Ismet would agree to signing before then, he had to depart disappointed.[128]

Ismet left a few days later to report to the Grand National Assembly. During a heated two weeks' debate he was both attacked for his concessions and criticized for having failed to make peace. There was general agreement that the Allied draft was unacceptable, but continued argument as to whether to resume negotiations. Mustafa Kemal defended Ismet before the Assembly, opposing the demands of some extreme nationalists that there be no resumption. Kemal's view was finally adopted on March 6, despite the opposition of the Soviet ambassador.[129] A note signed by Ismet and approved by the ministers was sent to the High Commissioners through Dr. Adnan [Adivar], now the foreign ministry's representative in Istanbul. It restated the Turkish views, with some alternative proposals, and asked that the conference be resumed at Istanbul. Along with it the Turks submitted a counterdraft of a treaty which exhibited the usual sensitivity on matters of sovereignty—as, for example, in the severe limitations with which they proposed to surround British ownership of the Anzac cemetery on Gallipoli.[130] A potential

[127] Cmd. 1814, pp. 837-841.
[128] *ibid.*, pp. 842-853; Nicolson, *Curzon*, pp. 346-348.
[129] Kemal, *Speech*, pp. 599-602; Jäschke, *Die Türkei*, pp. 71-72; Rawlinson, *Adventures*, p. 248; *Oriente Moderno*, II:10 (March 15, 1923), 589-590, 594.
[130] Texts in *Oriente Moderno*, II:11 (April 15, 1923), 643-659.

Treaty of Istanbul was no more acceptable to the Allies than a Treaty of Izmir would have been the previous September, but they were willing to meet again in Lausanne. The Turks agreed to reconvene there on April 23.[181]

During the break in the conference, Kemal lost no opportunity to bolster Ismet's negotiating position. The Turkish army was strengthened. The Turks followed increasingly a practice already begun—to treat the capitulatory rights of foreigners as if they no longer existed.[182] An elaborate economic congress at Izmir produced an Economic Pact which emphasized independence, sovereignty, and the necessity that foreign business houses observe Turkish law. Kemal, addressing the congress, said that Turkey welcomed foreign capital, but refused exploitation. "We cannot permit that this country should become as a city of slaves."[183] Kemal's effort to consolidate his political leadership within Turkey by organizing his own Peoples' party produced also a restatement of foreign policy in the party platform: the peace must assure Turkish financial, administrative, economic, and political independence.[184] A further play for American support was made when on April 9 the Grand National Assembly ratified the Chester concession, granted to the Ottoman-American Development Company. Though American economic aid might be welcome in developing nationalist Turkey, ratification was undoubtedly a maneuver to win American support at Lausanne against European economic claims. The concession involved railroad construction and the exploitation of oil and other mineral resources both in British-controlled Mosul and in regions of eastern Anatolia where the French had prior concessions. France objected to Ankara that this was an unfriendly act. Though the ratification was a diplomatic sensation at the moment, the final outcome at Lausanne was little affected thereby, despite Ismet's efforts to secure American backing on this basis.[185]

The second session of the conference required three months rather than the two weeks Ismet had hoped for. He had strenuous arguments on the Ottoman debt, Greek reparations and foreign economic concessions. In a meeting on the concessions, Ismet was reported to be "re-

---

[181] Note exchange in *Oriente Moderno*, II:11 (April 15, 1923), 659-662.

[182] *Foreign Relations*, 1923, II, 971, 1047-1049.

[183] *Oriente Moderno*, II:11 (April 15, 1923), 671-672; Mears, *Modern Turkey*, pp. 382-383.

[184] *Oriente Moderno*, II:12 (May 15, 1923), 707-709.

[185] *Foreign Relations*, 1922, II, 966-983 and 1923, II, 1198-1252; Grew, *Turbulent Era*, Chapter 20. I am indebted to Professor John De Novo of Pennsylvania State College for information on this question. The Chester concession was canceled by Ankara late in 1923 when the company remained inactive.

ceiving treatment which would make the third degree in a Harlem police station seem like a club dinner. He had deep circles under his eyes, his hair was standing on end, and he looked completely worn out, but was still holding his ground manfully in spite of all assaults."[136] Finally, Ismet obtained solutions satisfactory to him. He successfully refused any substitute regime for the capitulations. Only the Mosul question, on which Britain was as adamant as Turkey, was reserved for further bilateral negotiation or appeal to the League of Nations.

Ismet sometimes despaired of successful compromise and told Ankara he would resign. Rauf, still Prime Minister and acting Foreign Minister, differed with Ismet on matters of procedure and possible concessions. This was particularly true of Ismet's desire to renounce reparations from Greece if that country restored Kara Agaç, a vital suburb of Edirne, to Turkey. Ismet complained that Rauf did not allow him enough latitude and tried to go beyond giving him fundamental instructions to the point of prescribing negotiations in detail. This, said Ismet, would produce disaster, like the military collapse of 1877 when the Palace tried to direct the campaign against Russia. Kemal gave Ismet full support, forcing Rauf to withdraw his objections.[137] Ismet was then able to compromise the matter of Greek reparations, which had appeared to threaten a complete break and a renewed Greco-Turkish war in Thrace. At a dramatic meeting late in May, the two-hour tension suddenly changed to the hilarity of immense relief when the French chairman wrung from Ismet the admission that his instructions from Ankara, which he had thus far held in secret reserve, allowed him to accept the compromise.[138]

When the Treaty of Lausanne was signed on July 24, 1923, together with seventeen annexes and numerous letters, Ismet could pride himself on having achieved most of the nationalist aims.[139] The contrast to Sèvres was obvious. Now there were no reparations to pay. Turkey's boundaries were substantially those of the National Pact, except for the undefined Mosul frontier. No Armenia existed in eastern Anatolia, and no Greek state in the west. "Turkey for the Turks" was further assured by the population exchange with Greece, which excepted only the Greeks of Istanbul. The capitulations were abolished; foreign residents, businesses, economic concessions and schools were subject to Turkish law. The Turks

---

[136] Grew, *Turbulent Era*, Chapter 20, Speech of September 2, 1923.
[137] Exchange of telegrams between Ismet and Kemal and Rauf in Kemal, *Speech*, pp. 620-641.
[138] Grew, *Turbulent Era*, Chapter 20, speech of September 2, 1923.
[139] Texts in League of Nations, *Treaty Series*, XXVIII (1924), 11ff. and *Oriente Moderno*, III (1923), 461-550 (collated with the Turkish text).

were not completely masters of the Straits, and had accepted a demilitarized zone; their tariff rates were limited for some years; but the restrictions on complete sovereignty were so few as to leave no doubt that the Government of the Grand National Assembly represented a people victorious in diplomacy as well as in arms. Referring to the acknowledgment of sovereignty in the preamble, Ismet told the Assembly that "these are no vague words . . . (but) the result of the battles of a whole epoch."[140] Turkey's independence was more than technical, for with peace and the Straits open to all, Turkey was now balanced between the West and Russia.[141]

Some members of the Grand National Assembly, particularly those from the frontier regions, were not satisfied with the treaty, and criticized severely the cession of parts of Thrace to Greece and of Alexandretta (called by one deputy a "Turkish Alsace-Lorraine") to Syria. But 213 of 227 deputies voted for ratification on August 23, the Allied High Commissioners were at once notified, and the evacuation of British troops from Istanbul was shortly completed.[142] Kemal was proud of the Lausanne treaty, and always regarded it as the logical and necessary outcome of his leadership in the nationalist cause from 1919 on. "I was certain," he said later to his party, "that we would achieve a positive result. . . . What we demanded from the Conference was nothing more than the confirmation in a proper manner of what we had already gained. We only claimed our well-known and natural rights. In addition, we had the power to preserve and protect these rights."[143]

The conclusion of peace gave the nationalist regime the prestige and stability necessary to proclaim Ankara the capital of Turkey on October 13, and to declare formally on October 29 the existence of the Turkish Republic with Mustafa Kemal as its first President and Ismet its first Prime Minister. The peace by no means solved all Turkey's diplomatic problems, though it laid the basis for the conclusion of a host of friendship and commercial treaties in the next few years. The Califate, until its abolition in 1924, complicated Turkey's relations with Muslims outside its borders. The Mosul question brought acute tension between Turkey and Britain before its settlement in favor of Iraq in 1926 and

---

[140] Afet [Inan], "L'indépendance turque et le traité de Lausanne," *Belleten*, II:7-8 (1938), 300.

[141] Although Russia signed the Straits convention, Chicherin protested that it was a "violation of the rights and interests of the Turkish people." Degras, I, 406-408. He was still more Turkish than Ismet.

[142] *Oriente Moderno*, III:4 (September 15, 1923), 208-209; Jäschke, *Die Türkei*, pp. 75, 148.

[143] Kemal, *Speech*, pp. 586-587.

caused the Turks to sign a nonaggression treaty with Russia in 1925. The Syrian frontier produced incidents only partly solved by a Franco-Turkish treaty of 1926; a similar situation existed on the Persian border. There was friction with Greece over the population exchange and over the status of the Greek Orthodox patriarchate in Istanbul. But the diplomatic victory of 1923 allowed Ankara to negotiate with others as an equal on such matters. It is noteworthy that since 1923 Turkey has enjoyed a period of peace unparalleled in her previous history.

Turkish diplomacy rested, of course, on the military successes which allowed bargaining from a position of comparative strength. It made good use of the collapse of Allied solidarity after 1918, and of the antagonism between Russia and the West. But it could not have been successful without the severe limitation of territorial objectives, laid down in the National Pact and not increased thereafter. The heterogeneous Ottoman Empire could never have served as a basis for Kemal's diplomacy. This he emphasized again and again. "It is necessary that the State should pursue an exclusive national policy and that this policy should be in perfect agreement with our internal organization and based on it," he said of the situation in 1920.[144] These limited objectives were relentlessly pursued in the years 1919 to 1923 by comparatively able and stubborn men like Bekir Sami, Yusuf Kemal, and Ismet. Behind them stood Mustafa Kemal, who throughout the entire period kept in his own hands the control over major diplomatic appointments, the ultimate and sometimes immediate direction of all diplomatic negotiation, and the authority to make the results acceptable to the nationalists and the Grand National Assembly.

[144] *ibid.*, pp. 377-378. For an incisive discussion of the internal nationalist basis for this diplomacy see Lewis V. Thomas, "The National and International Relations of Turkey," in T. Cuyler Young, ed., *Near Eastern Culture and Society* (Princeton, 1951), pp. 167-187; also Thomas and Richard N. Frye, *The United States and Turkey and Iran* (Cambridge, Mass., 1951), pp. 38-71.

7

The Early Diplomacy of Italian
Fascism: 1922-1932

BY H. STUART HUGHES

In February 1932, in a sweeping survey of Italy's international position addressed to Dino Grandi, Italian Minister of Foreign Affairs, the ranking permanent official in the ministry, Baron Raffaele Guariglia, characterized his country's traditional policy in terms of sober realism: it was "historically constrained, for intrinsic and obvious reasons, to take its stand first on one side and then on another; to pursue the execution of its aims by cutting from the garments of its different adversaries the material necessary for its own cloak; and to take refuge on rainy days (so long as this cloak was not ready) under the ample and capacious mantle of England."[1] This was a substantially accurate statement of the modest and realistic policy to which the facts of geographic location and natural resources had condemned the Italian kingdom. For the first half century of united Italy's existence it had been pursued with fairly satisfactory consistency and success. It was the policy in which career diplomats like Guariglia had been trained and the one in which they still believed. But since 1922 they had been serving a new master whose speeches erupted defiance and praise of the heroic virtues. Between the

[1] Raffaele Guariglia, *Ricordi: 1922-1946* (Naples, 1950), p. 146. These memoirs are the most important single source for the inner history of Italian foreign policy during the decade in question. Guariglia's open admission of his ties with Fascism—and particularly his frankness about his early advocacy of a penetration of Ethiopia—suggest that his account is to be trusted. Of general histories of Italian foreign policy in this period the most thorough, penetrating, and original, despite its polemically anti-Fascist tone, is Gaetano Salvemini's *Mussolini Diplomatico*, revised edition (Rome, 1945); the most judicious and balanced is Maxwell H. H. Macartney and Paul Cremona's *Italy's Foreign and Colonial Policy: 1914-1937* (London, New York, Toronto, 1938); while Muriel Currey's *Italian Foreign Policy: 1918-1932* (London, 1932), is a pedestrian, pro-Fascist, thoroughly outdated account, valuable only for its translations *in extenso* of Mussolini's speeches on foreign policy.

old doctrine of slow and patient negotiation toward modest goals and the new program of vast ambitions and quick results, the conflict was obvious.

This conflict is the central problem in the study of Italian foreign policy during the first decade of Fascist rule. Its investigation leads us to two further aspects of the same problem: first, the extent to which the differences between Fascism and tradition were on the one hand real and deep, or, on the other hand, largely a matter of vocabulary and emphasis (i.e., big words in public and practical negotiation in private); second—and here the answer depends heavily on the one already given to the first question—the extent to which the inevitable compromises between the two policies represented something more than a merely temporary postponement of an eventual open break.

I

Italy's intervention in the first world war had been carried out in the classic manner. After carefully weighing the bids from both sides, Prime Minister Salandra and Foreign Minister Sonnino had made the proper decision—that the Entente had offered more than the Central Powers. The proposed reward, however, since it was to be carved out of the Austrian and Turkish empires, rested on certain presuppositions as to the future of those states. The former was to remain in being, the latter to collapse utterly. Actually the reverse happened. The Austrian empire vanished from the map: its southern territories joined themselves to a South Slav state totally unwilling to see a large number of its conationals pass under Italian rule. The Turkish empire—reduced to its ethnically homogeneous core—rose in resistance against the proposed partition of Anatolia. In both cases, the changed circumstances made obsolete the original Italian claims. And to these considerations of *force majeure*, the later stages of the war had added the Wilsonian doctrine of self-determination—which the American President seemed inclined to enforce with more rigor against Italy than against any other of the victorious nations.

The story of Italy's role at the Paris Peace Conference need not be retold here.[2] In retrospect, we may question whether Sonnino's literal-minded and inflexible insistence on the promises contained in the secret treaties with France and Britain was the best possible course for Italy to pursue. With a more accommodating attitude, the Italian statesman

[2] It has been told in scholarly detail by René Albrecht-Carrié in his *Italy at the Paris Peace Conference* (New York, 1938).

might actually have come away from Paris with larger territorial gains. Specifically, he might have obtained definite compensation in Africa for Italy's failure to obtain a mandate over any of Germany's former colonies. The basic significance of the Peace Conference, however, so far as Italy's future was concerned, was that it left with the whole nationalist and conservative sector of Italian public opinion the conviction that their country had been swindled of the rewards of victory. This unhappy memory was to overshadow the next two decades of Italian foreign policy.

The three years from the resignation of Sonnino in June 1919 to the advent of Mussolini in October 1922 were dominated, then, by the conflict between the indignant proponents of "sacred egoism" and those of more democratic turn of mind who wished to "renounce" the claims that had proved impossible of fulfillment. This conflict, in turn, reflected and was rendered more bitter by the internal struggle between Socialists and Fascists that was to culminate in the March on Rome. Under the circumstances, it proved impossible for a nation so deeply divided to pursue any coherent foreign policy.

Of the five Foreign Ministers who followed one another in quick succession between 1919 and 1922—Tittoni, Scialoja, Sforza, Torretta, and Schanzer—Sforza alone left a record of accomplishment. Senator Tommaso Tittoni, a politician and diplomat of the old school, had had time to do little more than preside over the final act of Italy's disappointment at Paris. His successor, Senator Vittorio Scialoja, was a man of far larger dimensions. A wit, a renowned student of Roman law, and a member of one of Italy's most distinguished Jewish families, Scialoja had consented to serve as Nitti's second Foreign Minister—as he later consented to serve under Mussolini—in a spirit of profound skepticism: to his intimates he would confess that he was "here to see that, in foreign politics at least, they do not make too many mistakes."[3] In his seven months of office, however, he was able to arrive at one permanent settlement: the agreement with Lord Milner provisionally establishing the frontier between Libya and Egypt.

Count Carlo Sforza—a curious, highly personal amalgam of aristo-

[3] In Italian the term is much stronger: *fesserie*. The anecdote is from Daniele Varè's *Laughing Diplomat* (London, 1938), p. 159. These memoirs of a half-British Italian diplomat and writer, while fairly frivolous, are not without value in tracing the backstairs aspects of Italian diplomacy. All references are to the original edition, published only in English. The Italian edition, dating from 1941, while it continues the story from 1932, where the original edition left off, to 1940, omits a good deal of the original material on the 1920's, including several references to Mussolini.

cratic attitudes and democratic sympathies—frankly and fearlessly advocated a policy of "renunciation." He argued that there existed an indissoluble "bond between the destiny of a forward-looking Italy and that of the states created by the war." And so he became the passionate advocate of an Italian understanding with Yugoslavia and Turkey—"whose resurrection Sforza was the first and for a while the only one to call inevitable."[4] His vision of a new era of international reconciliation found its embodiment in the Treaty of Rapallo with Yugoslavia, of November 12, 1920. Under its terms Italy received Istria and the Dalmatian city of Zara, while Fiume was to become a free city. The fact that this treaty could never be carried out does not diminish its historical importance. It remained through the 1920's as an inconvenient reminder of an alternative course that had never received a fair trial—the course of understanding rather than provocation toward Italy's most difficult neighbor.

Sforza had bucked the popular current. His successor, the former ambassador to London, Marchese della Torretta, passed through the Foreign Ministry leaving scarcely a trace—aside from his original declaration to the Senate that he "intended to continue the policy of his predecessor in working for peace in the eastern Mediterranean and for friendly relations with Turkey."[5] And by the beginning of 1922, when the last pre-Fascist Foreign Minister, Senator Carlo Schanzer, took office, Italy's internal situation had deteriorated to such an extent that a firm policy was no longer possible. Nor was Schanzer the man to give a clear lead. "Able, hardworking, conscientious, but timid," he was "a good Secretary of State for the Treasury, but not suited to the Consulta."[6] Before his appointment as Foreign Minister, he had played an effaced role as Italy's chief delegate to the Washington Conference (November 1921 to February 1922)—although he later took credit for having won by his own efforts the principle of naval parity with France.[7] Scarcely back from Washington and just named to the Foreign Ministry, he hurried off to Paris, where he exhibited a profound ignorance of the questions raised by the resurgence of Turkey.[8] Then—after a spring

---

[4] From the author's preface and Alberto Cappa's introduction to *Pensiero e azione di una politica estera italiana: discorsi e scritti di Carlo Sforza* (Bari, 1924), pp. 10-11, 18. On Sforza's sympathy for Turkey, see above, Chapter 6, § 11.

[5] Currey, *Italian Foreign Policy*, p. 65.

[6] Varè, *Laughing Diplomat*, p. 207.

[7] *British Documents*, 2nd series, I, 368 (Sir R. Graham to Mr. A. Henderson, May 28, 1930). The volumes of this series published to date bear on the present study only for the years 1929 to 1932, and almost exclusively in the field of naval relations.

[8] Guariglia, *Ricordi*, pp. 8-9.

interlude of futile international conferring at Genoa—he went in June to London, where, as Mussolini complained, he allowed Lloyd George to treat him in a way "of which the representative of San Marino would have been ashamed."[9] The autumn crisis over a settlement with Turkey brought further humiliation—until the advent of Mussolini, just before the opening of the Lausanne Conference, mercifully put an end to Schanzer's sufferings.

When the Fascists came to power, most of the questions of vital concern to Italy left over from the Peace Conference of 1919 were still pending: the settlements already reached with Yugoslavia and Turkey had become obsolete, and the question of colonial compensation in Africa had made little progress. But this situation was not nearly as grave as the Fascists made it out to be. It had resulted from a combination of normal delays, a lack of governmental prestige, and a too rapid succession of Foreign Ministers. All Fascist propaganda to the contrary, the governments from 1919 to 1922 had made no irrevocable mistakes, and Italy's relative standing among the Powers was just about what it had always been—last among the great or first among the little depending on how one looked at it. Italy's international difficulties were largely psychological. The comparatively shabby treatment she had received at Paris had been only natural—in view of her disappointing contribution to the Allied war effort and the changed circumstances previously alluded to. What had suffered was national pride—little else. And at the same time Italy's permanent and really pressing grievances—the handicaps under which she was laboring in her search for emigration outlets and access to raw materials—were receiving only slight attention from her statesmen. Italy might feel herself to be sick— but she was essentially a *malade imaginaire*.[10]

II

To a career diplomat anxiously pondering Mussolini's utterances for a sign as to what the new regime would do, the last weeks of 1922 brought little but uncertainty. The Duce himself had assumed the foreign portfolio—along with several others—and evidently intended to be more than a figurehead Foreign Minister. The public statements he had made before attaining power suggested that at the very least he would try to startle the diplomatic world with a series of melodramatic gestures. Yet his inexperience of foreign affairs and certain essentially conservative

[9] Varè, *Laughing Diplomat*, p. 207.
[10] Salvemini, *Mussolini Diplomatico*, p. 35.

attitudes of the Fascist movement gave hope that the permanent officials of the Consulta might be able to steer him into more moderate courses.

On the one hand, Mussolini was clearly no "renouncer." He had attacked the previous governments for their timidity toward the French and British, and he was subsequently to define Fascism as a doctrine of "education to combat and acceptance of the risks that combat implies."[11] In allying himself with the Italian Nationalists, he had taken over their whole armory of hyperbolic claims and carefully-nurtured grievances. If an opportunity arose to make a big display, his first instinct was to rush in without regard to the consequences. When, for example, Italy had at length obtained definitive title to the Dodecanese, it was all that his professional advisers could do to dissuade him from sending a naval squadron to take formal possession. Only most reluctantly and with obvious ill-humor did he silently consent to their arguments that the gesture would be both provocative and ridiculous—since, after all, the Italians had already held the islands for more than ten years.[12] With Mussolini, the threat of ridicule was to prove the most potent deterrent from rash actions.

Balanced against these dangers, the Fascist government offered distinct advantages. Primarily, it promised permanence in office and firmness in international dealings: this was doubtless what was uppermost in the minds of certain high officials of the Foreign Ministry when they had made contact with the Fascists shortly before the March on Rome.[13] Similarly the liking and respect for established hierarchies that were to become an increasingly important feature of Mussolini's program were calculated to reassure any permanent corps of functionaries. And the Fascists' own boast of the flexible and adaptable nature of their aims worked in the same direction. Mussolini had scarcely been in office two weeks when he began to exhibit a highly reassuring tendency to take up each outstanding issue in turn and to arrive at a specific, practical settlement as soon as possible. The old guard of the Consulta might well have decided that the balance had tipped in favor of their new master when, early in 1923, he disclaimed any intention of being "original" in the field of foreign policy.[14]

---

[11] From Mussolini's (actually Giovanni Gentile's) article on "The Political and Social Doctrine of Fascism," dating from 1932 and published in the *Enciclopedia Italiana*, which is the most authoritative statement on the subject. The authorized English translation can be found in *International Conciliation*, No. 306, January 1935, pp. 5-17.

[12] Guariglia, *Ricordi*, pp. 27-28.   [13] *ibid.*, p. 10.

[14] Speech to the Chamber of Deputies of February 16. For the Italian text, see *Scritti e discorsi di Benito Mussolini*, edizione definitiva (Milan, 1934), III, 59-73. Currey, *Italian Foreign Policy*, pp. 85-87, gives a slightly abridged English version.

III

Shortly after Mussolini came to power, the Italian Foreign Ministry changed quarters. From the elegant, quiet palace of the Consulta, just across the Piazza of the Quirinal from the King's own palace—a building the Foreign Ministry had occupied ever since Rome had become the capital of united Italy—it moved to the architecturally undistinguished Palazzo Chigi, located at the busiest street-corner in the city. The old officials regretted the change and feared that it presaged a new demagoguery in foreign relations.[15] Actually, within the Ministry itself, little was altered except the *décor*.

The ambassadors stayed at their posts. Sforza's abrupt withdrawal from the Paris embassy, immediately upon receiving news of Mussolini's accession to power, remained an isolated gesture.[16] Throughout the first decade of Fascist rule, most of the ambassadors continued to be men of the old type, career diplomats and frequently aristocrats. In Paris, for example, Count Sforza was succeeded by Baron Romano Avezzana, and at the turn of the decade Count Manzoni held the post.

Nor was it only the diplomats who offered the new regime a highly-appreciated contribution of permanence and respectability. Three of Mussolini's predecessors as Foreign Minister—Schanzer, Tittoni, and Scialoja—regularly supported him from their seats in the Senate. Tittoni—president of that body from 1922 to 1929—published a pro-Fascist book on foreign policy to which Mussolini was happy to contribute the preface.[17] And Scialoja served from 1921 to 1932 as Italy's representative on the Council of the League of Nations. In the latter case, however, the support was of a distinctly eccentric variety. "The position of this emaciated, refined septuagenarian, toward Mussolini and Fascism, strangely recalls that of the great aristocrats who 'rallied' to the First Consul and the Empire, a Talleyrand, for example. . . . Neither the King nor the Duce nor the institutions of the regime could escape the sarcasms . . . of this great master of the *bon mot*."[18]

Within the Ministry itself the presence of Salvatore Contarini, the experienced Secretary General (corresponding to permanent Under-Secretary) assured a continuity of administration. All witnesses agree on Contarini's ability and devotion to the state service. The Swiss Minister

---

[15] Guariglia, *Ricordi*, pp. 25-26; Varè, *Laughing Diplomat*, p. 225.

[16] For the exchange of messages between Sforza and Mussolini, see Sforza, *Pensiero e azione*, pp. 282-283.

[17] Tommaso Tittoni, *Questioni del giorno* (Milan, 1928).

[18] Arturo Carlo Jemolo, *Chiesa e Stato in Italia negli ultimi cento anni* (Turin, 1949), p. 653.

regarded him as "a man of a rare competence,"[19] and his subordinates at the Palazzo Chigi had an enormous respect for his judgment. His peculiar office hours (at meal-times only, which made him practically inaccessible), his "theory of the taps" (turn on the argument suited to each type of visitor), and his calculated rages (but never with foreign diplomats), all contributed to the growth of a kind of Contarini legend.[20] "With his exquisite political sensibility, his tact, and his way of doing business, which at first seemed confused but which was always guided by a serene and simple logic, Contarini succeeded in solving the problem" posed by the advent of Mussolini. In this endeavor he was ably supported by another career official, Giacomo Paulucci Barone, who as the Duce's *chef de cabinet*, constantly urged the counsels of prudence and moderation. It took several months of the "patient work of Contarini" to convince Mussolini that the traditional course of alignment with Britain was the correct one. But once the job was done, the Duce, "realizing his complete ignorance" in matters of foreign policy, "let himself be guided with a good deal of docility." Such at least was the conviction of the permanent officials at the Palazzo Chigi.[21]

This happy state of affairs lasted until April 1925. In that month Contarini—whose position had been growing increasingly difficult as Mussolini began to work behind his back in dealing with Yugoslavia—resigned his post as Secretary General. His successor, A. Chiaramonte-Bordonaro, remained in office less than two years. In February 1927 he left the Palazzo Chigi for the London embassy. And a month later Barone went off to Geneva. The old group of career officials was beginning to break up. Moreover, after Bordonaro's resignation from the secretary-generalship, no successor was appointed: the position was simply allowed to lapse.[22]

This change in the internal structure of the Ministry was due to the growing influence of a new figure on the scene—whom the permanent officials had at first distrusted as a Fascist and an outsider but whom they soon came to regard as an ally. In early 1925 somebody—it is unclear who—decided that the Foreign Ministry needed an Under-Secretary. This was a position that in Italy had traditionally been of little importance and had been filled only from time to time. With his customary adroitness, Contarini offered to find the proper man. His choice fell on Dino Grandi—to all appearances a strange selection. For Grandi was

---

[19] Georges Wagnière, *Dix-huit ans à Rome* (Geneva, 1944), p. 106.
[20] Varè, *Laughing Diplomat*, pp. 227-228.
[21] Guariglia, *Ricordi*, pp. 12-15, 24. [22] *ibid.*, pp. 14, 50.

known as one of the tough young men of the Fascist movement: he had been party leader of Bologna and participated in the March on Rome. But Contarini had learned that Grandi was actually both "malleable" and "understanding," and his expectations proved correct. Once in office the new Under-Secretary indicated not only that he intended to elevate his post from its traditional insignificance but that he realized the way to do it was through working with the career men against their common master, the Duce and Foreign Minister.[23]

"A few weeks . . . sufficed for Grandi to penetrate the mysteries of the Palazzo Chigi." Here, he soon realized, there offered itself a field of action and ambition far broader than the domestic sphere in which his party comrades were rapidly bogging down under Mussolini's all-controlling authority. As sole intermediary between the career officials and the Duce—as interpreter of their concept of the "inherent exigencies" of Italian foreign policy—he could eventually attain to a position of practical independence in the international field. The permanent officials soon found Grandi to be an apt scholar: he worked on his diplomatic behavior as eagerly as he took up the study of English and French. No wonder that in his first important speech in the Senate, his appearance— "measured in movement, placid and almost monotonous in voice, cordial but distant in smiling"—should have satisfied even the "old fogeys of diplomacy."[24]

Nor was it surprising that after two years in office he should have decided, by leaving vacant the position of Secretary General, to concentrate authority in his own hands. This change did not represent the threat to the career officialdom that one might imagine, for a new team was ready to take over. Baron Raffaele Guariglia—later to play an important role in the palace revolution against Mussolini of July 1943—was able to make himself a kind of substitute Secretary General, since his position of political director for Europe, the Levant, and Africa actually embraced the major areas of Italian policy. He and Augusto Rosso— who handled League of Nations affairs—became Grandi's "closest collaborators." Together they continued to uphold the thesis that relations with England were the "keystone" of Italian policy. They were satisfied that Grandi had learned his lesson well—and they believed the British to be satisfied also. "On many important occasions," they found, Grandi was able to "make Mussolini change his ideas and directives—though naturally acting with prudence and clever dissimulation so as not to offend" the Duce's "vanity." Guariglia reported only to Grandi, never

[23] *ibid.*, p. 47. [24] *ibid.*, pp. 48-50.

to Mussolini. Hence for the career men it meant no real change when in September 1929 the Duce decided to give up the foreign portfolio and to hand over sole direction of foreign policy to his former Under-Secretary.[25]

IV

The best way to judge the extent to which Grandi—and to a lesser extent Mussolini—had actually been "tamed" is to review briefly their actions in the foreign field during the first ten years of the latter's tenure of power. Two main strands of activity immediately appear—a process of liquidating the problems left over from 1919, and an incipient, if controlled, expansionism. They correspond roughly to Mussolini's two contrasting propaganda goals—to reassure foreign Powers, and particularly Britain, as to his pacific intentions, and to show his own people that he had a unique talent for chalking up points for Italy on the international scoreboard.

Mussolini's two introductory moves in the international sphere were distinctly propaganda ventures. In their unblushing amateurishness, they belong in a category by themselves. The first of these was the Duce's brief appearance at the Lausanne Conference, which was to make a final settlement with resurgent Turkey. Not yet three weeks in office, Mussolini set out for Lausanne with the resolve to do something dramatic. It occurred to him that if he had his train stopped a bit short of his destination and invited Curzon and Poincaré to come and talk with him it would give a proper impression of Italy's enhanced prestige. The representatives of Britain and France consented—Curzon with amused curiosity, Poincaré more grudgingly. After a brief huddle, the three emerged with a formula: Italy was to be treated "as an equal." Armed with this "success"—actually either meaningless or insulting to Italy, since it implied that she might *not* have been treated as a Great Power—Mussolini consented to go on to Lausanne. Here he spent only one day at the conference—a day in which he seemed ill at ease in his strange surroundings and formal attire, and in which he reportedly said nothing more important than "Je suis d'accord." The next day he returned to Italy in triumph. Actually his country, either before or after Mussolini's departure, exerted little influence at Lausanne—obtaining only the formal cession of Rhodes and the Dodecanese, which she held in any case. And the one effort that the chief Italian delegate made to black-

[25] *ibid.*, pp. 53, 60, 63-64.

mail the conference by a threatened withdrawal simply collapsed before one of Curzon's majestic attacks of rage.[26]

The Duce's second eruption on the international scene was more serious. In August 1923, in retaliation for the murder—by undisclosed assailants—of the Italian president of the commission engaged in delimiting the Greco-Albanian frontier, Mussolini ordered the bombardment and occupation of the Greek island of Corfù and presented the Greek government with a demand for an indemnity and the performance of a number of ceremonial gestures of a humiliating character. The Greeks immediately took the question to the League. Here it might have gone badly with Mussolini if the French and British had not decided to shift the case to the more friendly arena of the Conference of Ambassadors. Why they decided to do this is not entirely clear: an attack of weariness on Lord Curzon's part seems to have been largely responsible. In any case, Mussolini got his indemnity—but little else. In the general jubilation over their leader's second "success," Italians forgot that the indemnity was the only one of the Duce's original demands that the Greeks had fully met. And if Mussolini—as appears likely—had actually intended to keep Corfù, he had been obliged to give up that ambition.[27]

The lessons Mussolini drew from these two incidents were conflicting. On the one hand, he remained convinced that in the Corfù case he had scored a victory. Contarini, Guariglia, and the rest, who had tried first to restrain him and then to patch up a bad situation, found that the Corfù precedent encouraged the Duce to start on other expansionist ventures.[28] Yet his experience at Lausanne had been more sobering. It had evidently persuaded him that international conferences were not the sort of place in which his talents shone to best advantage. Between 1925 and 1937 Mussolini for the most part stayed away from them. And in the former year it was only the arguments of his professional advisers that induced him to go in person to sign the Locarno pact. He must have regretted it; for he was hurt by the massive fashion in which the foreign correspondents boycotted the reception he gave. Otherwise he found that it worked better to stay in Italy—and in this more flattering setting to dazzle his visitors. Beginning with the trip to Rome of the new British Foreign Secretary, Austen Chamberlain, in December 1924—an encounter that was to be repeated at frequent in-

---

[26] Harold Nicolson, *Curzon: The Last Phase, 1919-1925* (London, 1934), pp. 288-290, 303-304; Guariglia, *Ricordi*, pp. 17-21.

[27] Salvemini, *Mussolini Diplomatico*, pp. 61-67; Nicolson, *Curzon*, pp. 368-371.

[28] Guariglia, *Ricordi*, pp. 14, 28-31.

tervals during the next five years—a steady stream of admiring foreigners found their way to the Duce's presence. These meetings the Fascist press regularly reported as virtual "journeys to Canossa."[29]

Aside from these two introductory forays, the early years of Mussolini's rule were dominated by the first aspect—the liquidation phase—of diplomatic activity. In addition to the settlement at Lausanne with Turkey, the Duce tried to come to terms with Yugoslavia on the question of Fiume, and with Britain and France in the matter of colonial compensation. Originally, Mussolini had accepted Sforza's treaty with Yugoslavia—the Free City arrangement for Fiume evolved at Rapallo. But this was only a temporary concession. By July 1923, the Duce was suggesting to the Yugoslavs the incorporation of Fiume in Italy, and two months later, wearied by the way the negotiations were dragging, he simply took over the city. The following January, by the Pact of Rome, the Yugoslavs accepted the *de facto* situation. Although they had acted under duress—the French, fully involved in the Ruhr, had not provided the expected support—the Yugoslavs evidently decided that it was best to treat the Italian annexation of Fiume as simply the liquidation of an untenable situation. In the Pact of Rome and the subsequent Nettuno Conventions, they agreed to the friendly settlement of all pending Italian-Yugoslav questions.[30] These two documents soon became virtually a dead letter—but that story belongs to a later phase of Mussolini's diplomatic activity.

With Britain, the settlement on colonial compensation, while long delayed, was never seriously in doubt. It involved little more than the formal ratification of the pledges already made by the British in the Treaty of London of 1915 and the Milner-Scialoja accord of 1920. In July 1924, Britain ceded to Italy the region of Trans-Jubaland, adjoining Italian Somaliland, and a year and a half later, a treaty between Italy and the now independent state of Egypt finally delimited the Libyan-Egyptian frontier. But with France no such definitive solution proved possible. All through the 1920's and well into the 1930's, the question of a general accord with France held a prominent place on the Italian diplomatic agenda. But nothing substantial ever resulted. Even the boundary between Libya and French Equatorial Africa was not finally settled until 1935. Why did the question of a general understanding with France prove so peculiarly difficult?

With this question we come to the central area of Mussolini's diplo-

---

[29] *ibid.*, pp. 38-39, 99; Salvemini, *Mussolini Diplomatico*, pp. 91, 98-100.
[30] Macartney and Cremona, *Italy's Foreign Policy*, pp. 93-94, 107.

matic exertions. In the first place, in the matter of colonial compensation, Italy's claims on France were both larger and vaguer than her highly specific demands on Britain. Mussolini would speak of an extension of Libya nearly to Lake Chad, and a discussion of colonies invariably branched off into a related problem that was essentially insoluble—the status of the large Italian minority in Tunisia. Then there was the question of the two countries' relations with Germany: in the period up to about 1930 it was Mussolini who feared a Franco-German accord—later it was the French who worried over the Duce's tentative approaches to the Brüning government.[31] Nor could Mussolini resist the temptation to make a success with the crowd by violent anti-French speeches—a tendency that reached its climax in the bellicose tirades he delivered at Leghorn and Florence in May of 1930.[32] And for their part the French possessed propaganda weapons—admittedly unofficial—to which the Duce was peculiarly sensitive. The hospitality extended by the French to the *fuorusciti*, the anti-Fascist refugees, who made their headquarters in Paris, and particularly the light sentences imposed on their "subversive" activities by the French courts, regularly reduced Mussolini to impotent fury. And the attacks of the Leftist sector of the French press had the same effect: as ruler of a country where the whole educated class could read French, he rightly feared the contagion of ideas from across the Alps.[33]

Beyond all these things, however, the greatest reason for the continuation of Franco-Italian tension was the fact that beginning in 1926, Mussolini had embarked on the second phase of his diplomatic activity—the phase of expansion. The Duce's choice of an area for penetration—the new and chaotic state of Albania—implied a threat both to Yugoslavia and, more remotely, to France as Yugoslavia's protector.

In 1920 the Italians, who had occupied the Albanian port of Valona and its hinterland at the start of the first world war, withdrew to the island of Saseno, leaving the Albanians to work out their own destiny. But the following year they obtained a kind of contingent mandate over the country: the four Great Powers on the League of Nations Council declared that in the event of a threat to Albania's independence, they would recommend that Italy carry out the duty of intervention. For the next few years the Italians were too occupied with their own internal

---

[31] Guariglia, *Ricordi*, p. 123; Salvemini, *Mussolini Diplomatico*, p. 154.

[32] For the text of these speeches (slightly abridged in the case of the one delivered at Leghorn), see *Scritti e discorsi*, VII, 199-201, 203-206. In this case, Currey, *Italian Foreign Policy*, pp. 286-287, translates only extracts.

[33] Guariglia, *Ricordi*, pp. 110-111; Salvemini, *Mussolini Diplomatico*, pp. 127-128.

difficulties to take up this virtual invitation to meddle. It was rather the Yugoslavs who more successfully kept Albania in a turmoil. But by 1925, when Ahmed Bey Zogu—originally a Yugoslav protégé— had finally united and pacified the country, Mussolini decided that it was time to resume an active Albanian policy. And Zogu, in desperate need of financial aid, and realizing that the Yugoslavs were unable to supply it, was obliged to turn to Italy for help. The result was the Pact of Tirana, of November 1926, pledging Albania and Italy to mutual support and cooperation that amounted to an Italian right of intervention.

The background of this pact forms a curious chapter in the history of Mussolini's diplomatic dealings. In July 1926, Baron Aloisi, the Italian Minister to Albania, presented Zogu with a series of demands which if accepted would have made Albania virtually an Italian protectorate. Zogu, stiffened by the British Minister, Mr. Reilly, rejected them. But then Austen Chamberlain "went for a yachting cruise in the Mediterranean, met Mussolini for a long conversation off Leghorn, and not long afterwards recalled Mr. Reilly." There followed an Italian-inspired revolt in northern Albania. When Aloisi presented Zogu with a revised— and somewhat mitigated—set of demands, the new British Minister advised the Albanian President to accept. These new demands formed the basis of the Pact of Tirana.[34] They were supplemented the next year by a military alliance called—confusingly enough—the Treaty of Tirana.

The Yugoslav reaction was prompt. In November 1927, a few days before the signature of the Treaty of Tirana, the Yugoslavs concluded an alliance with the French. From this year on, Italian-Yugoslav relations were frankly bad. And they became worse as the conviction gradually spread that Mussolini was sending arms and money to dissident Croats and to Bulgarian terrorists in Macedonia. These activities cannot yet be documented; but indirect evidence strongly suggests that the Yugoslav fears were well-grounded.[35]

A second aspect of Italian expansionism—and one similarly calculated to alarm the French—was Mussolini's sporadic advocacy of revision of the Paris settlement. The idea was logical enough: it might have developed into a systematic exploitation of Italy's psychological position midway between the victorious and the defeated nations. But Mussolini never seems to have thought through exactly what he was trying to do. In his first speech as Prime Minister, on November 16, 1922, he stated

[34] Vandeleur Robinson, *Albania's Road to Freedom* (London, 1941), pp. 76-78.
[35] See, for example, Guariglia, *Ricordi*, pp. 54, 91-92, and Salvemini, *Mussolini Diplomatico*, p. 275.

his conviction that "treaties are not eternal, are not irremediable."[36] And in the following years he gave encouragement to the conservative governments of Austria and Hungary—in the latter case with shipments of arms, the discovery of one of which caused something of an international scandal. He probably also gave financial aid to Hitler's struggling National Socialist movement.[37] But at the same time he saw the danger inherent in a reviving Reich: in 1923 he tacitly endorsed Poincaré's occupation of the Ruhr. It was not until June 5, 1928—in the course of an extensive survey of Italy's relations with nearly every portion of the globe—that he clearly declared himself for revision.[38]

Certain historians have seen in this speech the beginning of revision as a "recognized instrument of Italian national policy" and the "real opening of the abyss between Italy and the Little Entente."[39] It is tempting, in the light of what occurred after 1936, to read back the events of the 1930's into an earlier period. Actually, during the whole decade we are considering, Mussolini seems to have been feeling his way. He was well aware of the possibilities inherent in revisionism—but he was not yet ready to exploit it as a fully consistent policy.

The same may be said of the whole expansionist aspect of his activity. Both anti-Fascists and Fascists, for contrasting reasons, have given him too much credit for prescience and careful planning. The former have written that the Mediterranean was "never far from . . . Mussolini's mind."[40] The latter have made much of a supposed "single program" for gradual political and cultural penetration eastward.[41] It is true that the Duce himself declared in February 1924 that the "lines of . . . Italian expansion" lay "towards the east."[42] And it is also true that every Italian government has necessarily devoted a major share of its attention to the Levant and the Balkans. But when we come to look more closely at Mussolini's eastern policy, we find that it is only bits and pieces—penetration of Albania, friendship with Bulgaria, a pact with the Yemen, the encouragement of Italian commercial and linguistic interests in the Levant. There is no clear sign of plan or considered policy. It is rather similar to the Duce's mania for signing pacts of amity with foreign coun-

---

[36] *Scritti e discorsi,* III, 9; Currey, *Italian Foreign Policy,* p. 78.

[37] Salvemini, *Mussolini Diplomatico,* pp. 81-82, 245-248, 250-252.

[38] *Scritti e discorsi,* VI, 203-205; Currey, *Italian Foreign Policy,* pp. 251-253.

[39] Macartney and Cremona, *Italy's Foreign Policy,* p. 197.

[40] *ibid.,* p. 9.

[41] Carlo Capasso, *Italia e Oriente* (Florence, 1932), p. 219; "Latinus," *L'Italia e i problemi internazionali* (Milan, 1935), pp. 395-399.

[42] Capasso, *Italia e Oriente,* p. 192. The speech is lacking in *Scritti e discorsi.* A mistranslation can be found in Currey, *Italian Foreign Policy,* p. 128.

tries of all descriptions: one can count at least eight of them between 1926 and 1930. "No country ever signed so many pacts and treaties as Mussolini's Italy; he never refused his signature to any convention that was proposed to him, even the most contrary to his ideas and purposes."[43]

Rather than a considered plan, the whole thing looks more like a random and uncoordinated striking-out in all directions in the hope of scoring points on the cheap. In the words of his admirers, Mussolini's great aim was "to prevent the crystallization of the European situation." More critically stated, this meant "to keep Europe in a constant state of uncertainty that would permit him now and then to obtain in some fashion or other some sort of advantage. His was a policy of improvisations without a definite aim."[44]

And what had been the results after ten years of this sort of activity? A hostile critic has summed them up as follows: "1) two colossal errors: granting a free hand to Poincaré in the Ruhr and the occupation of Corfù; 2) one sagacious decision: the compromise with Yugoslavia on Fiume; 3) the fulfillment of the British promises . . . [in Africa]; 4) the protectorate over Albania. . . ."[45] Whatever Mussolini had accomplished had actually been based on the work of his predecessors—Sonnino, Scialoja, and Sforza. It had been no more than what any firmly organized Italian government might have done in the same period—and doubtless with less friction. For against Mussolini's actual accomplishments one must balance off the fear and hostility that he had aroused. By antagonizing France, he had alienated the one country that offered even a partial solution to Italy's most pressing need—an outlet for emigration—a problem, incidentally, which Mussolini regularly neglected in favor of more showy issues.[46] And he had opposed every concrete effort for regrouping and coordination among the small states of Central and Eastern Europe. He had alarmed the Little Entente not only by his favors to Hungary but also by his overtures to the authoritarian government of Rumania headed by General Averescu. Likewise he had stood firm against a Yugoslav-Bulgarian rapprochement or any sort of general Balkan understanding.[47] Mussolini might have few real accomplishments to his credit—but he had at least partially succeeded in his goal of keeping Europe in a constant state of flux.

---

[43] Guariglia, *Ricordi*, p. 40. [44] Salvemini, *Mussolini Diplomatico*, p. 354.
[45] *ibid.*, p. 383.
[46] In his speech of June 5, 1928, he stated: "For the last two years the Fascist Government has followed a policy of voluntary restriction and control of emigration." *Scritti e discorsi*, VI, 183; Currey, *Italian Foreign Policy*, p. 239.
[47] See the frank admissions of Capasso, *Italia e Oriente*, pp. 237, 241.

V

Faced with this puzzling record, can we conclude that the permanent officials of the Palazzo Chigi were right in thinking that they had thoroughly domesticated Under-Secretary Grandi and had had some success in performing the same operation on his chief? The answer is half and half. We may approach it under four headings: first, the relations between the career men and the Fascist movement; second, the goals the former were pursuing; third, the elements of incoherence between the activities of Mussolini and the aims of the permanent officials; and finally, the actual satisfactions that these officials were able to derive from the Duce's rule.

It would be incorrect to picture the cleavage between Mussolini and the Palazzo Chigi as anything resembling a conflict between Fascism and democracy. Aside from a few convinced admirers of Mussolini, the Italian career diplomats—like foreign service men in all countries—were apolitical, that is, simply conservative and nationalist. Most of them had neither a strong liking for nor a strong objection to Fascism; in 1927 they accepted without protest their mass enrollment in the Fascist party. Moreover, from their standpoint, a Fascist government had definite advantages. In its internal solidity and its unpredictability, it gave them leverage for negotiation abroad; they could use it to further the permanent aims of Italian policy. Mussolini's idea was just the reverse; he tried to exploit his diplomatic successes—real or trumped-up—to consolidate his power at home.[48] This difference already represented an initial element of incoherence in the Italian diplomacy of the 1920's.

It was no fundamental opposition of political philosophy that separated Mussolini from the career men. They, like him, wanted to see Italy great and respected, substantially enlarged in territory and influence. But the methods they advocated to achieve this common goal were more patient, modest, and realistic. They well knew that the inadequacy of Italy's financial and military resources made it impossible for her to compete with the more prosperous powers in the game of building up client states, and that for this reason such small nations as Austria, Hungary, and Bulgaria could never be really reliable allies. In default of dependable satellites, then, the Palazzo Chigi continued to insist on the traditional alignment with Britain. Most of the pending questions between France and Italy, they believed, could best be approached from the British direction. Or—to regard the matter from another angle—if

<hr>

[48] Guariglia, *Ricordi*, pp. 14, 39-40, 53.

only Mussolini would proceed more cautiously in Albania and would conscientiously try to reassure the Yugoslavs, relations with France would automatically improve. The Italian professional diplomats were not particularly impressed by the League of Nations—but they would not neglect whatever advantages it offered: the main reason they had been so enthusiastic about the Locarno Pact was that it enabled Italy to place herself in a position of dignity "above the mêlée" and alongside Britain. Finally, they advocated a penetration of Ethiopia as a safety valve for Italian nationalist yearnings and a field for the exportation of Italian labor and talent. But they believed that this penetration should be preceded by a diplomatic preparation as slow and as thorough as the one that had virtually won the Tripolitan War of 1911-1912 before it was ever fought.[49] Toward this goal they had made a good start with an agreement with Britain, of December 1925, that provisionally recognized an Italian sphere of influence in eastern Ethiopia.[50]

Obviously Mussolini would never have agreed, either publicly or in private, to any such cautious definition of Italy's goals. And many of the things he did in the first decade of his rule—his Albanian-Yugoslav policy, his toying with revisionism, his provocations directed at the French, and his indiscriminate welcome to small nations seeking to sign pacts of friendship—ran directly counter to the advice of his professional counselors. With Grandi it is more difficult to tell exactly where he threw his weight. For the period of the 1920's at least, it is nearly impossible in most cases to distinguish his opinions from those of the Duce above him and those of the Palazzo Chigi career men, his technical subordinates. Usually, however, in his delicate position of middleman, Grandi seems to have sided with the professional diplomats.

Yet the curious thing about Mussolini's direction of the Foreign Ministry is that he appeared quite content to let these rather obvious situations of incoherence drag along without any clear decision. Only in the crucial case of relations with Albania and Yugoslavia did he recognize in organizational form the cleavage between his own policy and that of the permanent officialdom. We have seen how Mussolini's independent dealings with Yugoslavia had driven Contarini in early 1925 to resign his position as Secretary General. And under Guariglia's direction of the political department, the handling of Albanian and Croat affairs escaped his control entirely. The former area Mussolini assigned to a special

[49] *ibid.*, pp. 38-39, 64-66, 92, 114-115, 119, 142, 153-154, 169-170, 176.
[50] For details of this agreement, see Macartney and Cremona, *Italy's Foreign Policy*, pp. 290-294; Salvemini, *Mussolini Diplomatico*, pp. 171-173.

[227]

unit headed by Ambassador Loiacono; somewhat later, "when the contacts with certain Croat spokesmen began," these questions also were
removed from Guariglia's jurisdiction. Even "Grandi did not succeed in
this most important matter in *coordinating* . . . the activity aimed at an
Italo-Yugoslav accord (which he also *heartily* endorsed . . .), with that
into which [Mussolini's] Albanian policy had forced us, and with the
policy of favoring the Croats in order to put political pressure" on the
Yugoslav government.[51]

Otherwise, however, Mussolini seems scarcely to have realized the
extent of the existing divergence of view on Italian foreign policy. Or he
saw it simply as the inevitable and not particularly troubling gap between
what he was obliged for propaganda purposes to say in public and what
any well-run Foreign Ministry would naturally do on the official level.
In May 1930, when Grandi—now Foreign Minister—came to the Duce
in great distress to protest against the way in which his inflammatory
speeches at Leghorn and Florence had contradicted his own policy of
general pacification, the latter seemed sincerely surprised: "What does it
matter what I say to my crowds?" he queried. "Why do you think I
made you Foreign Minister except to be able to talk here exactly as I
please!"[52] This gap between public and private utterance frequently
proved extremely useful to Mussolini, and he was probably honest in
giving it as his reason for having resigned the Foreign Ministry. Under
this system, for example, it was always possible to disavow what some
Fascist propagandist had written in the newspapers—and even to get
foreign statesmen to believe that the journalist in question had spoken
without official authorization.[53]

Moreover, Mussolini similarly failed to realize (or simply chose not
to see) the contradictions inherent in his *own* policies—the incompatibility
between two lines of activity that he might be following at the same time.
We have seen how his revisionism was never strictly consistent. It was
certainly inconsistent to talk about a general revision of the Paris settlement and at the same time to oppose any move toward *Anschluss* between
Germany and Austria—as he did in the case of the proposed customs
union of 1931.[54] It was difficult to court the favor of Austria and at the

[51] Guariglia, *Ricordi*, pp. 54, 74.

[52] *British Documents*, 2nd series, I, 368.

[53] Even Sir Austen Chamberlain was apparently taken in. See Tittoni, *Questioni*, pp.
210-211.

[54] For a statement of opposition to the *Anschluss*, see Mussolini's speech to the Senate
of May 20, 1925: *Scritti e discorsi*, v, 78; Currey, *Italian Foreign Policy*, p. 150. In the
case of the customs union, Mussolini was at first in favor of it, but was subsequently
persuaded by Grandi to change his mind. Guariglia, *Ricordi*, pp. 80-81.

same time to pursue a rigorous policy of Italianization against the German-speaking inhabitants of the South Tyrol. Nor was Mussolini's support of Hungary's grievances consistent with his policy of friendship toward Italy's "Latin brothers" the Rumanians—threatened as they were with the loss of more than a third of their national territory.[55]

When everything else has been said, however, it is not too paradoxical to conclude that Mussolini, in lightheartedly dismissing all this incoherence as inevitable and unimportant, came closer to the heart of the matter than the permanent officials of the Palazzo Chigi who sighed and grumbled over his extravagances. Aside from the one great cleavage over relations with Albania and Yugoslavia, none of the questions at issue between the Duce and his professional advisers was important enough really to change in one direction or the other the main course of Italian policy. During the 1920's—under the surface of his inflammatory rhetoric—Mussolini, like the career men of the Palazzo Chigi, was essentially a believer in slow expansion based on the maintenance of the traditional alignment with Britain. And, in his curious way, he actually kept up the Anglo-Italian understanding rather well. He was certainly most successful in cultivating the good will of Austen Chamberlain and other prominent Tories, and even the change to a Labor government in June 1929 did not seriously alter his standing with the British. Moreover, Mussolini's attitude toward the League of Nations was quite similar to that of the career officials. While he had no belief in what he called the "almost mythological virtues" attributed to the League, he never seriously proposed leaving it.[56] He was "always on the verge of withdrawing without ever doing so."[57]

Thus the permanent officials of the Palazzo Chigi could take comfort in that fact that Mussolini, "despite his outbreaks of ill humor, his oratorical manifestations, and his directives to the press . . . , showed himself convinced of the necessity of not departing from . . . the fundamental lines" of traditional Italian foreign policy.[58] And the Duce offered them other satisfactions. Among the amateur diplomats of the 1920's, Mussolini was far better than average in the clarity of his aims and the precision of his utterance. His reports on foreign policy to the Senate and Chamber of Deputies were distinguished for their brevity of expression, their lucidity, and their grasp of detail. To his diplomats he usually

[55] Salvemini, *Mussolini Diplomatico*, p. 245; Guariglia, *Ricordi*, p. 75.

[56] Speech of June 5, 1928, in *Scritti e discorsi*, VI, 215; Currey, *Italian Foreign Policy*, pp. 253-254.

[57] Macartney and Cremona, *Italy's Foreign Policy*, p. 244.

[58] Guariglia, *Ricordi*, p. 106.

behaved with understanding and generosity. One of his first acts on becoming Foreign Minister was "to put an end to the lingering paralysis" that had descended on their careers since the end of the first world war.[59] With Mussolini in power, promotions began again, and the diplomats could rest assured that their chief was taking a personal interest in the internal reorganization of the Italian foreign service.[60] Abroad, they enjoyed a fair degree of independence—provided, of course, they followed major instructions and did not openly criticize the Fascist regime. A German representative at Geneva noted that the Italians there—Scialoja, Rosso, and the rest—"were not much bothered by what the Party had prescribed in Rome. They did what Italian foreign policy seemed to demand, and in this they were supported by the authorities at home."[61] Provided he had a certain dose of skepticism about his country's international role and his own activities—and such an attitude was not totally foreign to Mussolini himself—the Italian diplomat of the 1920's could ride comfortably along with scarcely a thought for the noisy vagaries of the Fascist party.

And so for a certain time in Italian foreign relations the traditions of the old diplomacy and the impatience of the new came to a kind of happy compromise. But this was a special and peculiar case. It was possible only because Italy was a lesser Power and most of the international issues in which she was involved were relatively unimportant. During the 1920's, after all, it was France and Britain that were really making the great decisions. Italy remained on the fringes of major diplomacy. So long as she stayed there, the divergences of view between Mussolini and his professional advisers could be compromised or glossed over. But once there should come a radical change in European alignments and Italy could succeed in forcing her way into the main stream of international negotiation, the fragile compromise between Fascism and tradition could scarcely fail to collapse.

VI

The year 1929 marked the high point of Mussolini's diplomatic prestige—and of the accompanying sense of qualified satisfaction in the Palazzo Chigi. In that year, Italy's relations with nearly all the nations of Europe were in a state of happy tranquility. The British were demonstrating their customary reserved friendliness, the French were giving

[59] Varè, *Laughing Diplomat,* p. 215.

[60] See the statements in his speech of June 5, 1928: *Scritti e discorsi,* VI, 217-227.

[61] Ernst von Weizsäcker, *Erinnerungen* (Munich 1950), p. 89; Eng. Trans. by John Andrews, *Memoirs of Ernst von Weizsäcker* (Chicago, 1951), pp. 74-75.

few signs of alarm, and the Austrians were settling into a relationship of amity with their protector south of the Alps that the Italian professional diplomats could characterize as answering "the purposes of sound policy." Even the Yugoslavs were enjoying a sense of precarious *détente*: in the autumn of 1928 they had at length ratified the long-pending Conventions of Nettuno. And the following winter, in February 1929, Mussolini scored the most substantial success of his whole career—the signature of the accords with the Vatican. This amicable settlement of the vexed Roman question, although based, like nearly all the Duce's diplomatic triumphs, on the less showy work of his predecessors, had enormous repercussions throughout Europe and the Catholic world: the thesis that Mussolini was essentially a moderate and constructive statesman now seemed to have found irrefutable confirmation. The Duce had conducted the whole negotiation himself. The Palazzo Chigi—apparently even Grandi—were kept in ignorance of what was going on. But when they heard the news, the professional diplomats were delighted.[62] Seven months later, Mussolini turned over the Foreign Ministry to Grandi. And the latter, convinced that international conciliation had now become the accepted goal of Italian policy, began to devote his major attention to preparations for the London Naval Conference that was to meet in January 1930, and more particularly to the crucial question of a naval agreement with the French.

The Naval Conference, however, failed to arrive at a general Franco-Italian understanding. After its adjournment in April, Grandi continued the negotiations on a two-Power basis, with the British and Americans as interested mediators. These supplementary negotiations were to drag along for a year and three-quarters, finally to end in total failure in January 1932. As they pursued their tortuous course, Grandi began to succumb to a sense of bewilderment and frustration. The "admirals and naval party," he knew, were systematically hampering his work with their insistence on a building program that would give Italy parity with the French in all major classes of warships.[63] What he did not know was that Mussolini himself had turned against his new Foreign Minister and was beginning to undermine the whole policy of conciliation.

In May 1930, the Duce emerged from an exclusive concentration on internal questions that had made him "almost inaccessible to foreign

[62] Guariglia, *Ricordi*, pp. 107-108.

[63] For details of these negotiations, see *British Documents*, 2nd series, I, 354-472, and particularly Doc. No. 198 (Sir R. Graham to Mr. A. Henderson, May 3, 1930). Other details, *ibid.*, II, 383-434.

representatives,"[64] and went on an extended speaking tour of northern Italy. His stops along the way—Leghorn, Florence, Milan—witnessed those provocative oratorical displays whose disturbing effect on the French we have already noted. Five months later, on October 27, in an address to the provincial directors of the Fascist party, he made a number of statements that were widely interpreted as an abandonment of the idea that Fascism was not a product for export. "Yesterday," he declared, "it was Italy, today it is the world, because everywhere there are people fighting for or against Fascism." And he added a more categorical endorsement of treaty revision than he had ever given in earlier years.[65]

From now on—this time in earnest—revisionism was to be a dominant element in Mussolini's foreign policy. The insistent and increasingly successful demand for international equality on the part of the German government headed by Chancellor Brüning had at length opened that crack in the post-Versailles alignment of European diplomacy for which the Duce had been waiting. Now he was ready to offer his friendship to a resurgent Reich. In 1931, the semi-official Fascist propagandists began to warn the French against the dangers and pitfalls of a Franco-German understanding.[66] And in August of that year, Brüning and his Foreign Minister, Julius Curtius, paid a visit to Rome: their reception was warm, and the exchange of toasts strongly suggested that in the forthcoming general Disarmament Conference Italy would take a pro-German line. This assumption proved correct. When the Conference opened, in February 1932, the initial Italian proposal—to consider as aggressive arms all weapons forbidden to the conquered countries by the peace treaties—was close to the German demand for complete equality.[67]

Meantime, the Palazzo Chigi had taken alarm. Guariglia, who had begun to worry about Mussolini's revisionism as early as 1928 and had been insisting for some time on the urgency of coming to an understanding with France, was pleased when he was asked to accompany Grandi on the latter's journey to Berlin to return Brüning's visit: at least it would give him a chance to caution his chief and to assess on the spot the strength of the German nationalist resurgence.[68] But Grandi was becoming a feeble support to lean on. He also was beginning to feel the ground slipping from beneath his feet. Back in March 1930, at the time of the

[64] *ibid.*, I, 379 (Sir R. Graham to Mr. A. Henderson, June 27, 1930).
[65] *Scritti e discorsi*, VII, 225-228; Currey, *Italian Foreign Policy*, pp. 295-297.
[66] See, for example, Arrigo Solmi, *Italia e Francia nei problemi attuali della politica europea* (Milan, 1931), pp. 120, 132.
[67] Macartney and Cremona, *Italy's Foreign Policy*, pp. 161, 269.
[68] Guariglia, *Ricordi*, pp. 129-131.

London Naval Conference, he had confessed to Prime Minister Mac-Donald that he detected in a recent declaration of the Grand Council of Fascism "a veiled admonition against himself for having gone as far as he had" toward a compromise with the French.[69] The following June he had complained to the French Ambassador of the activities of the "strong party . . . which wished to throw Italy into the arms of Germany" and had characterized his own position as "one of extreme difficulty."[70] Part of this lament, of course, had been for effect—to induce the French to come closer to the Italian viewpoint. But the distress had been real. Grandi had proved his sincerity nine months later, in March 1931, when, faced with a new and totally discouraging turn in the two-party naval negotiations, he had "placed his resignation in Signor Mussolini's hands in case the latter thought somebody more suitable could be found."[71]

This time the Duce had refused to accept his Foreign Minister's resignation. But a year later he was ready to do so. On June 16, 1932—just as the Conference on Disarmament at Geneva was beginning to adjourn its inconclusive labors—Mussolini gave an interview to the *Daily Express*, in which he voiced his pessimism about the League of Nations and about the Conference itself.[72] To the initiated it was a clear indication that Grandi's time had come. Five weeks later, on July 21, Mussolini, in effect, simply fired his Foreign Minister—with none of the usual "internal or external preparation" and "without any reason given."[73]

As a consolation prize Grandi received the London embassy. And he was allowed to find suitable positions for his two close collaborators, Guariglia and Rosso: the former went as ambassador to Madrid, the latter to Washington. The professionals in the Palazzo Chigi had now lost their adopted leader. They were left to the tender mercies of the Duce himself and, subsequently, to those of his son-in-law, Count Ciano.

---

[69] *British Documents*, 2nd series, I, 275 (record of an interview between Mr. MacDonald and Signor Grandi, March 24, 1930).

[70] *ibid.*, I, 377 (Sir R. Graham to Mr. A. Henderson, June 25, 1930).

[71] *ibid.*, II, 392-393 (Graham to Henderson, March 28, 1931).

[72] Salvemini, *Mussolini Diplomatico*, p. 376.

[73] Guariglia, *Ricordi*, pp. 176-178.

Soviet Diplomacy: G. V. Chicherin, Peoples Commissar for Foreign Affairs, 1918-1930

BY THEODORE H. VON LAUE

IN 1923, five years after the humiliating treaty of Brest-Litovsk, the government of Soviet Russia, according to its new federal constitution, considered itself the nucleus of a global association of Soviet socialist republics. To an observer unencumbered by ideology and judging international relations by prewar standards, the millennial goal of the new regime might have seemed preposterous. With the resources of imperial Russia, which had been so recently found wanting and which were further reduced by loss of territory and civil war, the Bolsheviks tried to sustain a political ambition far exceeding the boldest aspirations of the Tsars. The discrepancy between a weakness so recently demonstrated and an ambition so boldly proclaimed would have forever discredited the Soviet leaders, had they not developed, at ferocious cost, two novel sources of power: a totalitarian dictatorship to expand Russia's military and industrial potential; and a totalitarian type of foreign relations. With their new plenitude of controls the Bolshevik leaders were able to manipulate every phase of the relations between Soviet Russia and the outside world; they could fit every point of contact between Soviet citizens and foreign nationals into their central scheme of foreign relations. The new regime thus evolved an armory of foreign policy instruments exceptionally complete for that time. It had at its disposal the Comintern, Profintern, the secret police and military intelligence, as well as the traditional channels of diplomacy, the foreign trade agencies, the Society for Cultural Relations with Foreign Countries (voks), Intourist, and a host of other organs. This multitude and variety of agencies with contacts abroad helped Soviet foreign policy to offset the weakness of Soviet Russia and gave the Soviet impact on other countries an unusual intensity.

Through these channels the Bolsheviks made bold to transmit their techniques of class warfare and social disintegratión into the struggle between states. And by the example of their intentions, properly interpreted by Bolshevik ideology, they also claimed the leadership of all "progressive" causes. In short, they arrogated to their rule as universal a significance as was implicit in the cultural preeminence of the Great Powers of the West; and, in doing so, they issued a profound challenge to the world order inherited from the nineteenth century.

It was understandable that the role of diplomacy, the traditional tool of international relations, should be changed under an avowedly revolutionary regime, for it found itself in an alien milieu. In the competition for power, in which the Bolsheviks, after their revolution, joined with such seemingly unlimited aims, diplomacy had to accommodate itself to an inferior role. It was the tragedy of Chicherin, who assumed the post of Peoples Commissar for Foreign Affairs after Trotsky's resignation in March 1918 and who carried the burden of office longer than any contemporary Foreign Minister, that he was placed in the center of the turbulent confluence of diplomacy and social revolution. In order to be intelligible, Soviet diplomacy, and Chicherin's role in it, must therefore be viewed not in isolation but as a fragment, and a rather unrepresentative one, of Bolshevik policy in world affairs. This chapter will deal, above all, with the relationship between the two seemingly discordant instruments of Bolshevik foreign relations, between diplomacy and revolution, leaving out the other less important agencies of policy and treating the main lines of Soviet foreign policy proper in a necessarily summary fashion.

I

Strictly speaking, Soviet diplomacy did not begin with Chicherin, but with Trotsky; and Trotsky began by abolishing diplomacy. Named Peoples Commissar for Foreign Affairs after the seizure of power, he took an optimistic view of his tasks at the Foreign Office, now renamed Peoples Commissariat for Foreign Affairs (Narkomindel): "I will issue some revolutionary proclamations to the peoples and then close up the joint."[1] Admittedly he exaggerated, but not without reason. Diplomacy— if one may extend Trotsky's unspoken thought—was part of the capitalist superstructure, like the national state. The revolutionaries of all countries would know how to deal more simply and honestly among themselves; and the advanced national states, now locked in ferocious imperialist

---

[1] L. Trotsky, *Mein Leben* (Berlin, 1930), p. 327. See also Lenin's startled comment: "What, are we going to have foreign relations?" *Ibid.*

war, would disappear in the world revolution which had begun in Petrograd. What was needed most at this historic moment in the foreign relations of the new regime were stimulants to set the sluggish masses of Europe and the European dependencies throughout the world into revolutionary motion, primarily to assist in the revolution at home, and perhaps, in a series of chain reactions, to spread and even complete the world revolution.

From the first, Bolshevik foreign policy aimed at world revolution. Asked early in the world war what he would do if he should come to power, Lenin gave the daring answer: "We would propose peace to all the belligerents, the liberation of all colonies and all dependencies, all the oppressed, and those peoples who do not have equal rights. Neither Germany nor England and France would accept these conditions with their present governments. Then we would have to prepare and conduct a revolutionary war: i.e. not only would we carry through our whole minimum program with decisive means, but we would at once systematically start to incite rebellion among all the peoples now oppressed by the Great Russians, all the colonies and dependent countries of Asia (India, China, Persia, and others). And we would also raise in rebellion the socialist proletariat of Europe against their governments. . . . There is no doubt that the victory of the proletariat in Russia would create very favorable conditions for the development of the revolution in Asia and Europe."[2]

Having seized power in Petrograd, Lenin proceeded at once to put that master strategy into effect. The opening act of the new regime was its Proclamation on Peace, the starting-point of Soviet foreign relations, which outlined a revolution in international relations no less drastic than that accomplished in civil society. First of all, by its peace proposal the Bolshevik regime eliminated itself from the traditional European system. As a socialist government, it considered itself outside the pale of "capitalist" nations. Bent upon liquidating the most Westernized elements in its population (and later, by the same token, in the Bolshevik party), and following an ideology which, in strict theory at least, permitted no dealings with "capitalism," Soviet Russia lapsed into profound isolation. A citadel of suspicion and hostility, she lived henceforth as though in a different world, which remained obscure to the outside and, in turn, permitted only a distorted picture of the alien realities of Western democracy. Secondly, in calling for world revolution, Lenin's Proclamation on Peace envisaged a global, rather than a European, system of

[2] Quoted from D. Shub, *Lenin* (New York, 1948), p. 144.

international politics. Although, in its special appeal to the workers of England, France, and Germany, it obliquely recognized the traditional preponderance of Europe, it counted more on the nationalist and anti-Western stirrings of the non-European, and particularly the Asiatic, world; for the new regime was dedicated to the overthrow of the global balance of power inherited from the nineteenth century. Finally, in preferring revolutionary agitation to traditional diplomacy, Lenin's Proclamation introduced a new dimension into the field of power politics, the dimension of social revolution. What was the use of armament factories, of imposing armies and navies, and of strategic strongpoints, if the social structure was crumbling underneath them? Thus, cohesion again took its place as a factor of political power, and subversion became a potent weapon of power politics. As for the Bolsheviks, who in the months after November 1917 commanded practically none of the traditional weapons, revolutionary agitation was almost the sole effective instrument at their disposal. Besides, from their own upbringing, it was one especially dear to them; they were superior to all statesmen of the liberal tradition in handling it. Circumstances in due time apprenticed them in the use of the traditional tools as well, even of diplomacy; but to this day revolutionary agitations remain closest to the revolutionary core of the party.

The attempts which Lenin made before the foundation of the Communist International to exploit war-born and war-nurtured unrest in Europe and Asia may be studied in Merle Fainsod's *International Socialism during the War*. With the formation of the Comintern in March 1919, the preliminary, experimental phase of these efforts was ended. Henceforth, revolutionary agitation became institutionalized as a permanent feature of Soviet foreign relations. To be sure, the Comintern, with its related agencies, was not a flawless tool of Soviet policy; it could not be as freely wielded as was sometimes assumed. But, at a time when they possessed few other resources, it brought great advantages to the Soviet leaders. Through it, they could extend the techniques of revolutionary agitation into the realm of international relations. The conditions for admission into the Comintern were such as to mold its members in the Bolshevik pattern. They were ordered to establish an underground organization beside their legal party apparatus and to infiltrate not only into every proletarian organization but also into the armed forces of their country. And above all, they were commanded to observe Bolshevik discipline, which made them subject to the decisions of the Comintern Executive, dominated in turn by the Russian Communists. Lenin himself was the chief Russian delegate; Trotsky, Bukharin, and Zinoviev were his associates on the Executive Committee.[3] This revolutionary organization, which soon had its own information service and intelligence center in Moscow, followed closely Lenin's original aim: the immediate preparation for the dictatorship of the proletariat.

In the center of that struggle, as the guiding policy of the Comintern stated,[4] stood the Soviet Republic. It was surrounded and protected by the proletarian vanguard of all countries and the liberation movements of the colonial and suppressed peoples—the revolutionary *glacis*. Beyond lay the hostile capitalist world, doomed by the very laws of its existence to be reborn into Soviet socialist society. It was the task of the Comintern to hasten the dialectical development, with the active assistance of the Soviet Republic. How far that active assistance might go was made clear by events. In March 1919 Lenin dispatched troops to help Bela Kun, although he had to recall them almost immediately because of the advance of Denikin's White Armies; and in the following year, during the offensive against Poland, he undertook to "break the crust of the Polish bourgeoisie with the bayonet." Soviet Russia's weakness again interfered, and for the next two decades its revolutionary agitation abroad was carried forward with minimum effort and without the active assistance of the Red army. But, according to the main strand of Bolshevik theory, revolutionary war remained part of the revolutionary outward thrust, as it was part of the domestic attack. As Stalin expressed it in 1924: "The victorious proletariat of one country should stand up against the remaining capitalist world, attracting to itself the oppressed classes of other countries, raising revolts in those countries against the capitalists, in the event of necessity coming out even with armed force against the exploiting class and their governments."[5]

The policies of the Soviet regime or its novel techniques of agitation and organization within the framework of the Comintern may be studied elsewhere. The record is clear: between 1919 and 1930 Soviet domination increased until it amounted to tightest possible control. Through the far-flung activities of international communism, the Politburo manipulated to a considerable extent the revolutionary forces of Europe and Asia in order to suit its own ends according to its interpretation of world affairs.

[3] The close ties between the Comintern and the Politburo were inadvertently revealed by Zinoviev at the Twelfth Party Congress, when he spoke of immediate consultation with the Politburo on a matter of Comintern policy. See P. Miliukov, *La Politique Extérieure des Soviets* (2nd ed. Paris, 1935), p. 135.

[4] Lenin, Theses on the Nationality and Colonial Question, submitted at the Second Comintern Congress, July 1920.

[5] In "The October Revolution and the Tactics of the Russian Communists," quoted by Historicus, "Stalin on Revolution," *Foreign Affairs*, Jan. 1949.

Through the Communist parties it reached into the center of domestic politics in other countries where, at least in the recent history of the sovereign state, no foreign Power had ventured in such strength.

But while the Bolsheviks perfected their revolutionary instruments of foreign relations, they were confronted with new situations in which these instruments were patently inadequate, or even harmful to their interests. Even at the time of the foundation of the Comintern, revolutionary agitation, in which Trotsky had put such hope, had ceased to be the sole tool of Soviet foreign relations. What, in the eyes of the faithful, had been intended to do away permanently with power politics had become merely another dimension of the same old evil. For, contrary to Trotsky's prediction, the Narkomindel had not yet closed shop. Almost from the beginning, its diplomatic activities were expanding, with aims that were eventually to differ radically from those of the Comintern. Diplomacy, indeed, had been implicit in Lenin's Peace Proclamation (which, in regard to the relation between revolution and diplomacy, maintained a revealing ambiguity). And when the Central Powers, who alone among the belligerents had accepted the Soviet proposal for peace negotiations, pressed home their ruthless terms, and when the German revolution did not come to the rescue, the Bolshevik leaders were forced to resort to the traditional forms of international relations. "The given relation of forces in the world arena," read a party resolution of March 1918, left no choice except negotiating with the Central Powers and signing the Treaty of Brest-Litovsk. In its precarious position, both at home and abroad, the Soviet government was thus compelled to recognize the existence of capitalist governments and to adapt itself, for the time being, to the conditions of capitalist encirclement. While the international revolutionary movement gained momentum, with active Soviet assistance but still far too slowly, "we must . . . stick to our tactics of waiting," Lenin reported to the party on May 14, 1918, "taking advantage of the conflict and antagonisms among the imperialists and of slowly accumulating strength. . . ." He promised "everything diplomacy can do," in the execution of that policy. On July 4, 1918, before the Fifth All-Russian Congress of Soviets, Chicherin reported on the new situation in yet greater detail. After the revolutionary offensive which had followed immediately upon the seizure of power, he explained, a radical change had come over Soviet policy. It was now on the defensive, trying to gain time while the international revolution matured and Soviet institutions took hold at home. There were certain assets upon which Soviet foreign policy could draw: the split among the capitalist Powers just then fighting the fiercest battles of the war, and disagreements within each capitalist Power between military and industrial groups, and between those who favored intervention in order to restore the Russian front and those who wanted thereby to overthrow the Bolshevik regime. Bolshevik diplomacy, he claimed, had already been maneuvering among these forces.

The record of Soviet diplomacy in the two years after the seizure of power (which need not be told here) substantiated Chicherin's analysis.[6] But, of course, while there was still a chance for a White victory in the civil war, Soviet diplomacy could make little headway among the "capitalist" Powers. The only direction in which it could move with greater assurance was Asia. But even on that continent, its actions were rather in the nature of gestures; and, despite their enthusiastic reception, particularly in China, they brought no immediate relief to the hard-pressed Soviet regime. The full opportunity for Soviet diplomacy inevitably lay in the West.

When at last in 1920 the struggle between the White armies assisted by foreign intervention and the Bolshevik outward thrust for revolutionary penetration had been fought to a stalemate, Soviet diplomacy came into its own. Peaceful coexistence between capitalism and socialism, proclaimed by the Narkomindel long before capitalist stabilization was conceded by the Comintern, demanded machinery for formal relations. The New Economic Policy, a reluctant retreat on the home front, called even for capitalist assistance in the construction of socialism in Soviet Russia. At the Genoa Economic Conference in April 1922 (a time of famine in Russia), the Soviet delegation, headed by Chicherin, officially made its debut in European diplomatic circles. The old-time diplomats noticed with pleasure that the Soviet representatives, in frock coats and striped trousers, behaved exactly as diplomats were expected to behave. Chicherin even went to a royal reception and exchanged toasts with an archbishop. Henceforth, Soviet diplomats became known as sticklers for diplomatic etiquette.

Soviet diplomacy, indeed, had come a long way in the five years since Trotsky's casual repudiation of diplomacy. It now occupied a legitimate place in the Soviet scheme of government, helping the revolutionary

---

[6] The length to which Soviet diplomacy would go in this period in order to attract attention and aid might be seen in Litvinov's and Vorovskii's letter to the Norwegian lawyer Ludwig Meyer, in which they offered the reinstatement of the political emigrés, reconsideration of the repudiation of the Tsarist debt, and cessation of all propaganda. These promises, needless to say, would never have been honored by Lenin. See Degras, I, 133.

regime to adjust itself to its capitalist environment and even to derive a limited benefit from it. On this unrevolutionary plane of its policy, the Soviet republic was merely one state among others. It had to be informed of the plans of other governments so as to know how to cope with their presumably hostile designs, to exploit their separate needs, and to support within each of them the groups most favorable to itself. For that reason it had to maintain normal relations, and to cultivate at least a minimum of goodwill. Thus, by the logic of survival in a capitalist world, diplomacy was foisted upon a revolutionary regime. But it was tainted from the start with defense, retreat, concessions, insincerity, and the weakness of revolutionary Russia in general.[7]

II

Needless to say, in the process of evolution these two almost antithetical planes of Soviet policy—the revolutionary one close to the Bolshevik core and the more peripheral one of diplomacy—became only gradually differentiated. At the very beginning, of course, diplomacy and revolutionary agitation were almost indistinguishable. Even after Trotsky's resignation, the Narkomindel, barred from formal relations with other governments, continued in his spirit. It was the first Foreign Office to put the "new diplomacy" into effect. All diplomatic correspondence was conducted in the open with an eye to its publicity value both in revolutionary and nonrevolutionary circles. In July 1918 Chicherin frankly admitted that assistance to non-Russian revolutionary movements was a recognized function of revolutionary diplomacy,[8] and in the following January the invitation to the first Congress of the Comintern went out through his Commissariat; moreover, he attended it in person. In his more strictly diplomatic utterances he tried to mobilize Western labor unions over the heads of their governments on behalf of Soviet interests. In the inner councils of the Narkomindel he, Karakhan (its eastern expert), and Radek functioned as a triumvirate, joined for a time by Kamenev. Radek was in charge of the central European department, whose main function consisted of agitation among German prisoners of war; he founded the Karl Liebknecht brigade from their ranks. But, as a brilliant journalist,

[7] One can detect a defensive note even in Chicherin's formal and informal analyses of Soviet diplomacy. Particularly in the early years he constantly stressed the complexity of international relations, as if to justify his work as a necessary and autonomous field of government activity.

[8] Quoted by Bruce Hopper, "Narkomindel and Comintern," *Foreign Affairs*, July 1941. Chicherin had told Bruce Lockhart already in the spring of 1918 of the coming Third International.

Radek was also the commissariat's chief publicist. Only later, when diplomacy and revolution had become divorced, did he drift into work with the Comintern in order to stay nearer the center of revolutionary power. (He remained, however, always closer to diplomacy than Zinoviev.) Among the Soviet plenipotentiaries abroad the identity of revolutionary action and diplomacy was still more prominent. Joffe, who was sent to Germany after the Treaty of Brest-Litovsk, at once formed close relations with the Independent Socialists and worked to the utmost to strengthen the revolutionary movement. A few days before the revolution in Germany he was expelled for his machinations—his baggage had burst open (not entirely by accident) in a Berlin railway station and was found stuffed with revolutionary propaganda. Lenin at the time fully conceded that the Soviet embassy in Berlin was "a carrier of the revolutionary contagion";[9] and Chicherin, in his annual report to the Seventh All-Russian Congress of Soviets in December 1919 commented upon the incident in a telling formulation, saying that "the rising revolutionary wave in Germany [had] gradually forced the technical diplomatic work into the background."[10]

Even the very paraphernalia of diplomacy were affected by the original association with revolution. The first Soviet delegation to the Brest-Litovsk negotiations was distinguished by the presence of a worker, a peasant, and a soldier; the proletarian touch was even preserved, although in a far more dignified manner and for more concrete reasons as well, in the Genoa delegations which contained top representatives of Soviet trade unions. A further revolutionary note was carried into diplomacy in June 1918, when it became clear that diplomacy was here to stay: all diplomatic ranks as established by the Congress of Vienna were declared abolished, and equality was decreed between diplomatic and consular agents. Henceforth the heads of Soviet missions abroad were to be known simply as "plenipotentiary representatives." In this connection the old distinction between small and Great Powers, another hangover from the capitalist system, was also considered dropped. Unfortunately, when formal relations were later established with capitalist countries, it proved rather difficult to determine the exact position of a "plenipotentiary

[9] Speech on the anniversary of the October Revolution, November 6, 1918; also the following day before the Extraordinary All-Russian Congress of Soviets.

[10] Quoted by T. A. Taracouzio, *War and Peace in Soviet Diplomacy* (New York, 1940), p. 76, note 40. Later when the Soviet government began to insist upon the fiction of the complete separation of the two spheres, the incident was fiercely denied and the blame cast upon White agents, who were accused of having smuggled the compromising material into Joffe's suitcase.

representative" in the diplomatic corps of a foreign capital; and the Soviet government had to recognize the old titles, albeit in an indirect way. In the same year (1924) the government also prescribed for all Soviet diplomats abroad "the simplicity of form and the economy of expenditures fitting the ideals of the Soviet regime."[11]

After the formation of the Comintern and the end of the civil war, the separation of the two spheres of Soviet foreign relations proceeded apace. If the Soviet government wanted to deal with capitalist governments it had to conform to their standards of diplomacy. The issue of revolutionary propaganda cropped up at once as an almost insurmountable obstacle to diplomatic recognition and even to the resumption of trade relations. The result was a strict outward separation of the two spheres.[12] The Soviet government denied any complicity whatever with the activities of the Comintern; it always protested any contrary view as an unfriendly act.

Underneath the fictional separation, however, the relationship between the two spheres was always a troublesome problem. In most areas of the East, where from the Leninist point of view national and revolutionary movements tended to coincide, there were far fewer sources of conflict.[13] But where, as in the West or in Japan, there was a sharp distinction between the established government and the revolutionary movement, the two branches of Soviet policy were bound to collide. One strained its utmost to overthrow the governments with which the other tried to

[11] T. A. Taracouzio, *The Soviet Union and International Law* (New York, 1935), app. viii. This regulation, incidentally, did not prevent Rakovsky from wearing silk breeches in his audience with the King of England. How far Soviet diplomats would go in submitting to capitalist or feudal ceremonial practices depended to a large extent upon the current political situation. If the Politburo desired good relations, its diplomats could conveniently drop their Bolshevik simplicity. There seemed to be almost no end to Soviet adaptability: in 1926, at the death of the Mikado, the Soviet representative deposited the official wreath with the Soviet insignia, but without the inscription: "Proletarians of all countries unite," which was part of it. See Bessedovsky, *Den Klauen der Tscheka Entronnen* (Leipzig, 1930), p. 99.

[12] The clearest formulation of this separation was given by Chicherin in 1922: "The Communist party stands at the head of a great government. As a government it enters into relations with all other governments and establishes close friendly relations, guarding the political and economic interests of its republic. . . . Speaking in the name of the government organs we leave [party policy] on the side. The fate of the communist movement, the successes and experiences of communist parties belong in the realm of other organs. Our attention is given to the fate of the Soviet government." "Za piat liet," *Mezhdunarodnaia Zhizn,* 1922, No. 15. There is, of course, much discussion of this point in Soviet literature on international law, which obscures rather than clarifies the relationship.

[13] After the Congress of the Peoples of the East in September 1920 no more revolutionary congresses were held. In relations with the Near and Middle East, the Comintern did not seem to have played an active part. Thus, communications with the Indian communists were maintained, according to M. N. Roy, through diplomatic channels.

maintain friendly relations. Which branch would prevail in the conflict depended upon circumstances. According to Chicherin's felicitous phrase, a rising revolutionary wave would always force "the technical diplomatic work" into the background; in that respect diplomacy was forever inferior to revolution. But in the uncertain setting of the 1920's a twilight zone developed, with revolution and diplomacy holding each other in balance. In the end, the relative success of each branch determined to a large extent its standing in regard to the other. Insofar as the revolutionary ventures of the Comintern and its chief, Zinoviev, collapsed, diplomacy gained;[14] and, insofar as diplomacy failed, revolutionary agitation again advanced. The two branches were in constant adjustment to each other through most of the 1920's for reasons of foreign as well as domestic policy. The period ended, however, with a net gain for diplomacy.

While the prevailing impression is thus one of considerable friction, there is no doubt that the two branches also supplemented each other. The members of the Comintern were always bound, unless otherwise instructed, to support the diplomacy of the Soviet government in their own countries, often much to their chagrin.[15] And without the diplomatic immunity which Comintern agents enjoyed as members of a Soviet foreign mission, they could not have done their work either. Despite their friction, then, a degree of cooperation was indispensable to both.

At the top level of the Politburo, foreign relations, of course, appeared again as one. All disputes between the two main instruments of foreign policy were submitted to it, and it chose the tool, or more commonly the combination of tools, that seemed best to fit the particular occasion. Sometimes diplomacy won an outright victory, as in the case of the Soviet Union's friendly relations with Mussolini in the mid-1920's. Sometimes the Politburo seemed to pursue two seemingly contradictory policies, as in regard to the Kellogg-Briand Pact, which it supported on the diplomatic level while the Comintern denounced it. Sometimes again, as in relations with Germany in the fall of 1923, the revolutionary impulse gained the upper hand without, however, depriving diplomacy of its

[14] This may be the point to comment on *Pravda's* famous cartoon, showing Zinoviev haranguing a revolutionary crowd while Chicherin, in the background, held his head in despair. This cartoon appeared before the Fifth Congress of the Comintern in June 1924, when a new equilibrium between diplomacy and revolution was in the making. But the pictorial design of the cartoon still leaves no doubt of Zinoviev's superiority. (See illustrations).

[15] At the Fourth Congress of the Comintern in 1923, Bukharin found it necessary to justify the ways of Soviet diplomacy to the members of the Comintern. See B. Moore, *Soviet Politics: The Dilemma of Power* (Cambridge, Mass., 1950), p. 208.

usefulness. One might say then that each of the two main branches of Soviet policy had an area of maximum effectiveness, with a relatively small area of friction separating them. In the case of the divided attitude towards the Kellogg-Briand Pact, the Soviet leadership tried to make the most of each dimension of its foreign relations, the contradiction not really being as prominent as one might expect (except in the eyes of a few intellectuals) because both dimensions were usually kept apart also in the life of most contemporaries.

The Politburo's analysis of the basic factors of Soviet strength in world affairs likewise counted on the two dimensions. As Stalin put it in the Political Report to the Fifteenth Party Congress, the position of the Soviet Union depended upon three interrelated elements: the inner strength of the Soviet Union; the strength and weakness of the capitalist states; and the strength and weakness of the suppressed classes all over the world and of their revolutionary movements. The first element, the only one entirely under Soviet control, remained, of course, uncomfortably insufficient from the Politburo's point of view, despite all strenuous effort to build up Russia's internal security, her army, and—above all—her industrial potential. All the more significant were the other two, in which the Soviets operated as much as their preoccupation with their internal reconstruction permitted. Their joint significance was also revealed in the chief party documents. In the Political Reports of the Central Committee, particularly in Stalin's methodical rendition from 1925 on, one is apt to find a passage dealing with the world situation in general, analyzed in Marxist terminology, followed by a section on the tasks of the party in the international revolutionary movement and another one on the tasks of diplomacy.[16]

In assessing the scope of Soviet foreign relations, one cannot overstress the fact that from the beginning the Soviet leaders insisted in their dealings with capitalist countries upon the combination of revolutionary activity, with all its illegal components, and traditional diplomacy. The Soviet regime had reverted permanently and wholeheartedly to a more brutal interpretation of the nature of international relations than had become customary in the West. As with diplomats in the age of royal absolutism, Soviet foreign missions were designed to spy, to lie, and to intrigue abroad for the welfare of their masters. But while the Machiavellian diplomat combined the legitimate with the illegitimate business

[16] The fact that the spokesman of the Central Committee gave a Leninist analysis of the world situation, from which Soviet diplomacy in its official reports was barred, showed again the relative inferiority of that branch of government.

in his own person, the Soviet regime, recognizing that the standards of diplomacy had been raised in a liberal age, relieved its diplomats[17] of the more unsavory functions. It created a number of separate agencies for spying and subversion, for which, in the eyes of the gullible, it need not assume responsibility. The advance over the days of cabinet policy lay in the vastly improved technique of socio-political agitation, the chief contribution of Leninism. To be sure, in the period under consideration, much of its revolutionary agitation in Europe and Asia remained an idle boast and an act of self-deception. The revolutionary tide had receded and the bulk of Soviet effort came to be concentrated at home. But, for the conduct of Soviet foreign relations, the combination of diplomacy with revolution remained standard practice. In an age of almost universal social and political crisis the Soviets had opened up, for better or worse, the cohesion of society as a new field of power politics, which demanded new instruments, new organizations, and new concepts of theoretical analysis. The Soviets thus started their career with a more comprehensive grasp and control of the factors of power in the twentieth century than their liberal-democratic opponents were to possess for another generation.

And to ask the Soviet regime in its weakness to refrain from making use of its revolutionary tools was as futile as to ask the British Empire to scrap its fleet.

III

One can imagine the difficulties of Chicherin as Soviet Russia's chief diplomat in such a setting. The Soviet Foreign Office had lost the monopoly over the conduct of foreign relations. In the Comintern, it always had a jealous rival and one which was closer to the ears of its superiors.[18] Traditionally, the Foreign Minister had always enjoyed a leading position in the government, and the Foreign Office was an honored branch of the government. There had been notable exceptions to the undisputed monopoly of foreign relations in the hands of Foreign Offices, but never had diplomacy fallen to such a humble and suspect position as it now did. In an avowedly revolutionary society, diplomacy was an anomaly, a standing contradiction to the essential spirit of the regime. Its imitation of the formalities practised by other states was—even while patently insincere—disconcerting and unpleasant to the hard-bitten professional revolutionaries who dominated the government. No

---

[17] Except Joffe, who on all his foreign assignments (in Berlin and Vienna, and on his trip to the Far East) combined the two elements.

[18] For a long time Radek (and never Chicherin) was the Politburo's rapporteur on foreign affairs. See Bessedovsky, *Revelations of a Soviet Diplomat* (London, 1931), p. 62.

one, for instance, could have been unhappier than Kalinin, when he was forced, in his capacity as Chairman of the Presidium of the all-Union Congress of Soviets, to receive King Amanullah of Afghanistan.[19] It is not surprising that the Narkomindel was often by-passed. When something really important seemed in the offing, as for instance the revolutionary upsurge in Germany after July 1923, the Politburo took over, acting through the Comintern; and, for the promotion of the Chinese revolution, it appointed a special Chinese Affairs Commission, in which the Narkomindel was represented by a Far Eastern expert only.[20] In short, at the slightest pretext the Politburo was always inclined to deal directly with all matters within the jurisdiction of the Narkomindel, thus reducing its significance. In many ways, an early uncomplimentary characterization of the Narkomindel as "just a diplomatic chancellery attached to the Central Committee"[21] stated the simple truth. And as a true clerk it was not necessarily admitted into the secret purposes of its masters.

Chicherin's low position in the Communist party, the center of Soviet power, also reflected the inferior status of his office. A former Menshevik, admitted into the party in January 1918, Chicherin could not expect to be heard in the inner councils. Even foreigners knew how much he depended upon Lenin in all major decisions.[22] An early tiff with Stalin over the nationality question, in which he lost out, may have also shown him his powerlessness.[23] His timidity towards the chief leaders increased with the years; rarely did he dare to assert himself. Party distrust was also expressed in the appointment of Litvinov, an old Bolshevik, who in April 1919 joined the *collegium* of the Narkomindel as an informal party guardian over his chief. Joffe, Krestinsky, Rakovsky, Krassin, and others who in the 1920's represented the Soviet government abroad, stood

---

[19] A. Barmine, *Memoirs of a Soviet Diplomat* (London, 1938), p. 221.

[20] Bessedovsky, *Revelations*, p. 122. This commission was headed by Unschlicht, the head of foreign military intelligence.

[21] Ascribed by Bessedovsky to the acting head of the Ukrainian Narkomindel, Yakovlev, in 1920. *Revelations*, p. 20. Important notes were drafted by members of the Politburo themselves; so Trotsky drew up the reply to the Curzon Ultimatum in May 1923. It is significant also that the official *History of the Communist Party* barely mentions Soviet diplomacy in the period under discussion.

[22] Lenin's private opinion of Chicherin may be gathered from his letter to Trotsky after Chicherin had suggested that substantial concessions be made at the Genoa Conference: "Send Chicherin at once to a sanitarium." Trotsky, *Mein Leben*, p. 455.

[23] At the Tenth Congress (March 1921) Stalin attacked Chicherin over a series of articles in *Pravda* written by the latter, entitled: "Against Stalin's Theses." Although nominated to the Committee on the National Question at that Congress, Chicherin was not elected to it. See the stenographic protocols of the Tenth Congress (ed. N. N. Popov, 1933).

higher in the party than their official chief. Until the Fourteenth Party Congress in 1925, the Narkomindel had not even a voice in the Central Committee, while its rival, the Comintern, had from the beginning several spokesmen in the Politburo, not to mention Radek on the Central Committee. At the Party Congress of 1925, because of the changing balance of power in the party and the successes of Soviet diplomacy in the previous year, Chicherin was promoted to the Central Committee, but by that time this body had lost its original significance; and in 1930, at the Sixteenth Congress, he was deprived of this preferment without his successor Litvinov at once being elected in his place.[24] Obviously, the Narkomindel was left very much on the outer fringes of the party.

Under these circumstances it was not easy to organize and operate an efficient foreign service. Soviet diplomacy, to discuss briefly its internal organization, was handicapped from the outset because, unlike most other branches of the Soviet government and unlike its foreign equivalents, it had to start entirely from scratch. The Narkomindel's historian has described the tense scene when Trotsky took over the Foreign Office.[25] Upon his arrival he ordered the entire staff inherited from the previous regime to assemble and announced to them curtly: "Those for us go to the left, those against us go to the right." The *chinovniks*, after deliberating among themselves, went right to a man. Only the menials remained to shake hands with the new Commissar. Shortly thereafter all Foreign Office personnel abroad was recalled or repudiated. Within two months, however, the personnel of the Narkomindel already numbered about two hundred, including the revolutionary guards from the Siemens-Schuckert works and a nearby pipe-rolling mill. But even after the arrival of Chicherin, the organization and routine of the new Peoples Commissariat reflected for some time the shiftlessness of that hectic phase of Soviet rule. By 1921 it had at last achieved some stability. Its internal organization was sanctioned by a decree of the Council of Commissars; and the treaties with Soviet Russia's neighbors, the trade negotiations with England, and expanding relations with the outside world in general provided its officials with a steadily growing volume of business. But for a long time it had a reputation for amazing inefficiency.[26]

The top personnel, constituting the *collegium*, which ran the Narkomindel in the mid-1920's, was a remarkable body in the annals of

[24] Litvinov was elected in 1934, at the Seventeenth Congress.
[25] See the Narkomindel's publication *Desiat Liet Sovietskoi Diplomatiia* [*Ten Years of Soviet Diplomacy*] (Moscow, 1927), p. 4.
[26] See O. Blum, *Russische Köpfe* (Berlin, 1923), p. 406.

diplomacy. Georgii Chicherin himself, his country's chief diplomat, was considered rather an oddity.[27] A shy, timid little man with an intelligent and gentle glance, utterly negligent of dress, an aesthete and hypochondriac, he had little of the outward polish of the diplomat, despite his aristocratic birth. Those who knew him closely called him a visionary who had shut out all reality and who lived with his job twenty-four hours a day—although occasionally he would lock himself up in a room adjoining his study and for hours play Mozart on the piano. They praised him as a man above pettiness and party intrigue, almost too fragile for the rude hurly-burly of Bolshevik politics. The foreign correspondents discussed his unorthodox methods of work, his custom of receiving foreign diplomats and other callers in the small hours of the morning, his dislike of modern office equipment. The gossipers traded stories of how, because he was unable to delegate work, he drafted, wrote, typed, sealed, and posted diplomatic notes himself; or how, in his absent-mindedness, he mislaid important documents, for which then the whole department had to search. In such an event, they related, he even routed his colleagues from bed or the ballet. But everyone who knew Chicherin respected his abilities as diplomat: his brilliant mind, his sharp repartee, and that amazing memory which made foreign diplomats wince.

Only revolution could have placed such an unusual man in charge of Russian diplomacy; but even among the revolutionaries he remained a stranger. Among the matter-of-fact life stories of Old Bolsheviks, Chicherin's authorized biography (which only he himself could have written) reads like a chapter from Dostoievsky.[28] There were no revolutionary deeds in the underground to record; there was only the tortuous metamorphosis of a Russian aristocrat into a Menshevik, who during the world war found himself in agreement with Lenin's revolutionary internationalism rather than the "social chauvinism" of the bulk of European socialists.[29] In his case the making of a Menshevik consisted of a series of inner crises: the adjustment problems of an only child reared in an emotionally surcharged and highly religious atmosphere; the sufferings and inhibitions of a poor relation in the fast and superficial northern capital; the tensions which led to his final break

---

[27] Characterizations of Chicherin's personality can be found in Louis Fischer, *Men and Politics*; Bruce Lockhart, *Memoirs*; Lincoln Steffens, *Autobiography*; Louise Bryant, *Mirrors of Moscow*; G. Bessedovsky, *Revelations*; O. Blum, *Russische Köpfe*; E. Cerruti, *Visti da Vicino*; etc.

[28] Printed in *Entsiklopedicheskii Slovar Russkago Bibliograficheskago Instituta Granat* (hereinafter cited as *Granat*), XLI, part III, 215ff.

[29] See Trotsky, *Mein Leben*, p. 334, for Chicherin's initial leanings towards patriotism.

with his aristocratic past. His intense spiritual struggles, which he later described with introspective detail, carried him from bourgeois respectability, Nietzschean yearning for the superman, and tortured compulsions towards self-destruction to the optimistic collectivism of Marxism. They left his physique undermined from an early age; he was not fit for active revolutionary duty. But there was also a more stable side to his development: his interest in foreign policy.

Diplomacy had been in the family. His father, before he took up pietism and retired to his estate in the province, had been secretary to the Piedmont legation in 1859 and, shortly thereafter, counselor at the Paris embassy. His maternal grandfather, Count Stakelberg, had been the Russian ambassador at Vienna, at the time of the Congress of Vienna; hence the self-avowed Metternich touch in Chicherin's diplomacy.[30] This tradition compelled the young Chicherin to join the Tsarist Foreign Office. He entered, however, not as an active diplomat, but as an archivist and scholar, who was set to work on Russian foreign policy between the Crimean war and the Congress of Berlin, a fact which may account for his special interest in the Near and Middle East and for his anti-British bias in later years.

After 1904 the two strands of his life interests, diplomacy and social justice, separated to be united again only after the revolution. Quietly giving up his position at the Foreign Office, he left Russia and studied the social-democratic movement in Germany, where he became a close friend of Karl Liebknecht. It was indicative of his ability that, within three years, he assumed an important post in the revolutionary movement by becoming secretary of the foreign bureau of the Russian Social-Democratic party, which tried to coordinate the work of the various Marxist emigré centers. At the same time he took a deep interest in the socialist youth movement. After the outbreak of the war, he shifted from Paris to Brussels and London, where he worked for the relief of Russian political refugees and took a hand in the antiwar agitation of the Independent Labor party. After the March Revolution, he headed a committee for the repatriation of political exiles, was arrested after the Bolshevik coup for his propaganda activities, and was finally exchanged in January 1918 for Sir George Buchanan, the British ambassador to Russia. Upon his return he joined the Bolshevik party. As he was the only comrade with Foreign Office experience, an excellent linguist, and otherwise well-qualified except perhaps in party staunchness, Lenin assigned him at once to the Peoples Commissariat for Foreign Affairs, and, even before

---

[30] See his biography, cited in note 28 above.

Trotsky's resignation as Commissar in March 1918, he assumed control. Thus, at the age of 45, "a new page of his life," as he wrote, began for him. It was not to be an altogether happy one, for, as he confessed in his autobiography, the revolutionary and the aesthete did not always blend in him, either before or after the revolution.

Next in importance in the Narkomindel, and eventually to replace his chief, came M. M. Litvinov, Vice-Commissar, whose work will be evaluated in a subsequent chapter of this book. Beside Litvinov stood L. M. Karakhan, also Vice-Commissar and specialist for Far Eastern affairs.[31] His background was rather undistinguished both from a revolutionary or intellectual point of view. Born in the Transcaucasus (his name indicates Armenian origin) and trained in the law, he joined the Russian Social-Democratic Workers party in 1904, and worked for a while in its Far Eastern organization. Later he went to the capital where he became a permanent member of the international committee. He was said to have proved himself a competent agitator, propagandist, and organizer, who remained outside the factional strife. A "defeatist" during the war, he was banished to Tomsk, where he continued his revolutionary work and extended it into eastern Siberia. He joined the Bolsheviks after the March revolution and appeared for the first time in the limelight as a member of the Brest-Litovsk delegation, owing his selection to Lenin. His background in Asiatic Russia seemed to fit him particularly for Soviet relations with the East; in 1925 he was Soviet ambassador in Peking. He was generally described as an able, but by no means outstanding person, who impressed some of the younger Bolsheviks like Barmine as the department's diplomatic dandy.[32]

A fourth member of the *collegium*, who joined it in 1923, was V. L. Kopp, who, like Karakhan and Litvinov, stemmed from petty bourgeois background. He had studied engineering but had soon followed the revolutionary call and became a member of the "transport administration" which received and distributed revolutionary materials within Russia. After organization work among St. Petersburg metal workers in 1905, he had gone into foreign exile and newspaper work with Trotsky and the German Social Democratic party. After the outbreak of the

---

[31] The following biographies are based on *Granat*, XLI. It should be noted, however, that these official biographical sketches are by no means reliable. All revolutionaries had to censor their *curricula vitae* both before and after the revolution. See also Bessedovsky's characterization of Karakhan as "the ass with the classical profile."

[32] Barmine, *Memoirs*, p. 155. Maybe Trotsky's quip was directed at him (or was it Litvinov?): "I absolutely cannot understand those revolutionaries who like to become ambassadors and swim in their new role like a fish in water." Trotsky, *Mein Leben*, p. 348.

war, he served in the Russian army—an unusual turn for a future Bolshevik commissar—but was captured by the Germans in 1915. Joffe obtained his release in the fall of 1918 and made him counselor at the Berlin embassy. He then served as Soviet representative in Berlin until his promotion to the *collegium*. In 1925 he was Soviet ambassador in Japan, where he proved quite susceptible to the geopolitical teachings of Haushofer.

The *collegium* of the Narkomindel, in which the Commissar was *primus inter pares* rather than undisputed chief, was far from a unanimous body. Litvinov, the Old Bolshevik, had been set to watch over Chicherin. In the ensuing jockeying for power, which divided the Commissariat ever more deeply towards the end of the 1920's, Karakhan sided with Chicherin, Kopp with Litvinov. It was said that a fifth member, T. A. Rothstein, was appointed to break the deadlock. Rothstein, however, who had been an editor of the London *Daily News* and had his sons educated at Oxford, proved unequal to the task. More of a scholar than a diplomat, he was put in charge of publicity and press affairs. At times other men also joined the *collegium*—Rakovsky as Ukrainian delegate and Vice-Commissar, and after him the party economist Schlichter. As a body, the *collegium* may be said to have been made up of the least revolutionary type of Bolsheviks, most of whom had fairly extensive knowledge and experience of western European life. They were "halfway men," making their career in the twilight zone between the outside world and the Bolshevik core. But, apart from Chicherin, its chief members would have hardly qualified for Sir Ernest Satow's characterization of a diplomat as an "educated gentleman." The *collegium* was apparently not a congenial environment for profitable common work. Bessedovsky, a minor diplomat, found it shot through with intrigue and scandalmongering.

Under the *collegium* there operated, besides the numerous secretariat, the various geographical and functional departments.[38] The latter dealt with administrative and personnel affairs, the press, economic and legal matters. As to the geography of its foreign relations, the Narkomindel knew only East and West, the Eastern Department being divided into Near East (including Africa), Middle East, and Far East, and the Western, according to the decree of November 12, 1923, into Central Europe, the Baltic limitrophes and Poland, Scandinavia, Anglo-Roman

---

[38] *Desiat Liet*, p. 19. They were organized under the *Sovnarkom* decree of November 12, 1923. This decree is reprinted in French in the Yearbook of the Narkomindel for 1929.

(Britain, France, Italy, Spain, United States, and Latin America), and the Balkans. In 1927, as an economy measure, the Balkan division was dissolved and its countries assigned either to the Anglo-Roman or Central European divisions.[34] Altogether, between 450 and 550 men and women seem to have been employed at the central offices during the mid-1920's,[35] a number roughly comparable to the personnel of the central offices of the Comintern.[36] Paul Scheffer, the German correspondent, found the department overworked and somewhat neglected.[37] Indeed, a position in the Narkomindel was not considered an easy berth, particularly in the early 1920's, not only because of Chicherin's unusual hours but because of the low pay scale. Other government departments paid their officials three to four times as much[38]—a further indication of the relative unimportance of the Narkomindel in the Soviet scheme. By comparison the experts of the Comintern, mostly pampered foreign comrades, lived like kings.

The Narkomindel as part of the formal government structure was subordinate to the Council of Peoples Commissars and through it responsible to the all-Russian Congress of Soviets and its Central Executive Committee (VTSIK).[39] Occasionally Chicherin or Litvinov reported before these bodies on the state of international relations, and their Commissariat submitted its annual report to them. One may assume that the few public discussions on foreign affairs in these bodies,[40] prepared beforehand, were no problem to the Narkomindel; at least Soviet diplomacy was spared the worry over parliamentary pressure groups or public opinion. The relations of the Narkomindel with other executive agencies, however, were more complicated. Within its extensive bureaucracy the Soviet government found it difficult to coordinate all its formal foreign relations. In 1927, for instance, the Naphtha Trust was discovered negotiating on its own with the Spanish government[41] (which had not yet recognized the Soviet Union), despite the recent decree of *Sovnarkom* that all business between the branches of the Soviet government and

[34] *Desiat Liet*, p. 23.
[35] *ibid.*, p. 17. For 1924 the number of "responsible workers" (corresponding roughly to the Tsarist *chinovniki*) was given as 484, 376 of them being party members.
[36] P. Scheffer, *Sieben Jahre Soviet Union* (Leipzig, 1930), p. 286.
[37] *ibid.*, p. 416.
[38] *Desiat Liet*, p. 12.
[39] For the place of the Narkomindel in the constitutional structure of the USSR, see J. Towster, *Political Power in the USSR, 1917-1947* (New York, 1948).
[40] See, for instance, the debates of the Third All-Union Congress of Soviets in May 1925, and the analysis of them in Towster, *Political Power*, pp. 217ff.
[41] Bessedovsky, *Revelations*, p. 205.

foreign governments be conducted through the Narkomindel.[42] Under that decree only strictly nonpolitical matters could be handled directly; otherwise the Narkomindel was to be informed immediately. Military and naval authorities were to arrange with the Commissariat their modes of communication with their attachés (who were outside the jurisdiction of the Narkomindel). That decree incidentally suggests that, even within the relatively narrow legitimate sphere of foreign relations, the Narkomindel had found it difficult to enforce its monopoly. The very size of government in the twentieth century—the Soviet government took the lead in "big government"—created new problems for the conduct of diplomacy.[43]

The Narkomindel's relations with other government departments, however, were far less of a problem to it than its relations with the Comintern, the OGPU, and the party, i.e. with those interlacing agencies which by their nature were closer to the Bolshevik core. The full extent of the domestic pressures bearing down upon the Narkomindel will probably never be known with certainty; but the few available glimpses into that fluid and carefully hidden realm of internal Soviet politics, although to be interpreted with caution, tell their own story. There is no evidence of any routine liaison between the Narkomindel and the central office of the Comintern (the OMS—International Liaison Section) headed by O. A. Piatnitsky. But there were two indirect ties, one through the Politburo acting as arbiter between the two agencies; the other through the foreign missions. If Bessedovsky's case was at all typical, a Soviet diplomat about to assume a new post abroad was briefed not only by the Narkomindel but also by the Comintern and the Politburo—not to mention the OGPU and military intelligence.[44] In his embassy then he would have to shift back to the position of mere diplomat. There his job was to come to some working relationship with the Comintern agents and other nondiplomatic personnel who were part of his suite and enjoyed full diplomatic privileges no matter how subversive their real concerns.[45]

[42] Joint decree of *Vtsik* and *Sovnarkom*, August 27, 1926, reaffirming an earlier one of 1921. See Taracouzio, *Soviet Union*, Appendix x.

[43] There is no room here to discuss the federal aspects in the organization of the Narkomindel. There is no reason to assume, however, that they were of any special concern either to Chicherin or Soviet diplomats in general.

[44] Bessedovsky, *Revelations*, pp. 127ff.

[45] As the presence of Comintern agents in Soviet diplomatic missions was public knowledge, it was the desire of all governments to limit the size and number of Soviet missions in their territory; hence the protracted negotiations over the status of Soviet trade delegations in England and other countries.

Inevitably, the relation between revolution and diplomacy within the walls of a Soviet foreign mission were often stormy. Nowhere else was their rivalry so keen and so intimate. Naturally the Narkomindel wished to rid its embassies of their most compromising members, or at least curtail their powers.[46] And many times it carried the dispute over the disciplinary rights of its diplomats to the Politburo.[47] Over the years the position and influence of the subversive agents in Soviet embassies and trade delegations was reduced. After the failure of the German revolution in 1923 the Comintern agents were given more subordinate functions as translators or press agents, and their work was organized separately to reduce friction with the diplomatic staff. But individual Comintern agents with strong backing in Moscow occasionally defied these regulations. And while the Narkomindel succeeded in limiting the power of the Comintern in its foreign missions, it never could eliminate it altogether; diplomatic immunity was too essential for its work. Sometimes it would even occur that a diplomat was asked to aid directly in some Comintern transaction, which he was apt to refuse if he was worth his salt.[48] But while individual diplomats might resist such compromising orders at some risk to their careers, diplomatic mail pouches would unfeelingly carry dynamite, weapons, propaganda, or money for revolutionary purposes. And the couriers of the Narkomindel were all said to be OGPU men.[49]

The Narkomindel's relations with the secret police resembled somewhat its relations with the Comintern. As part of the subversive machinery abroad and closely related to the Comintern at the center,[50] the police agents constituted an equally compromising part of foreign missions. In the home office in Moscow, the presence of a Cheka man was reported in the early 1920's.[51] In 1927 Chicherin confessed to Bessedovsky that his office (like most others in the government) was wired with hidden microphones by the OGPU.[52] That agency also interfered in matters of policy. Paul Scheffer, the German correspondent, reported that after 1927 the OGPU, staffed ever since Dzerzhinsky's days with Poles, manufactured anti-German incidents to the embarrassment of

---

[46] The second secretary of the mission was usually the Comintern agent, the third secretary the OGPU man (or woman). Miliukov, *Politique extérieure*, p. 136.

[47] Bessedovsky, *Revelations*, pp. 69ff.

[48] *ibid.*, p. 166.

[49] Krivitsky, *In Stalin's Secret Service* (New York, 1939), p. 38.

[50] Piatnitsky, the head of the OMS, was a close friend of Trillisser, in charge of the foreign section of the OGPU. G. Agabekov, *OGPU* (New York, 1931), p. 269.

[51] Louise Bryant, *Mirrors of Moscow* (New York, 1923), p. 191.

[52] Bessedovsky, *Revelations*, p. 196.

Chicherin.[53] It meddled furthermore in the censorship exercised by Roth-stein of the Narkomindel's press department over foreign correspondents, often stopping dispatches previously passed by him.[54] Litvinov, who could afford to be bolder than his chief, took a vigorous stand against OGPU penetration, with scant success.[55] Here, still more than in the case of its struggle with the Comintern, Soviet diplomacy had its hands tied. This does not mean that harmony prevailed between the agencies closer to the core of the party—there was some friction also between the OGPU and the Comintern; but the two were apt to present a common front against diplomacy. And yet, no doubt, Soviet diplomacy also benefited from the code cracking and espionage services of the OGPU.

The link between the Narkomindel and the party was kept fairly well out of sight, for obvious reasons. Of course, all its chief officials were party members and thus under party discipline. Lenin commented proudly on the close penetration of the Narkomindel by the party. Chicherin's speeches, and still more Litvinov's, although adapted to diplomatic non-Marxist parlance, reflected the official line. At party congresses, Chicherin after 1921, and later Litvinov and Karakhan, appeared only as nonvoting delegates for their department; they took no part in the discussion. The report on foreign policy, as part of the Political Report, was entirely in the hands of the leading member of the Politburo, Lenin, Zinoviev, or Stalin.[56] But while Soviet diplomacy was silent at party congresses, the head of the Comintern submitted a lengthy and fully publicized report. As to the attitude of the Politburo towards the Narkomindel, it was what would be expected: tolerance because of a limited usefulness but not respect. In public, Lenin had treated Chicherin and his work with a certain friendly solicitude; even Zinoviev in delivering the Central Committee's report in 1923 found a few good words for him, but Stalin was cool. Only after 1928 was he said to have taken a greater interest in the department, when Chicherin was already

---

[53] P. Scheffer, *Sieben Jahre*, p. 441. [54] *ibid.*, p. 421.
[55] Agabekov, *OGPU*, p. 269.
[56] Litvinov once spoke, at the Fifteenth Party Congress in December 1927, reporting on the Preparatory Committee on Disarmament of the League of Nations, in whose work he had recently participated. But his speech was an exception prompted by a very special reason. At that congress Stalin played a difficult and ambiguous game. On one hand he had been forced to set a sharp Left course, which implied bitter hostility to the League. On the other hand, he had already determined upon a policy of cautious rapprochement with the Western Powers. It was left to Litvinov, just back from Geneva, to reconcile the two incompatible policies by giving a strongly Left interpretation to Soviet policy at Geneva. Judging by the hilarious reception of his speech, he acquitted himself successfully of his difficult task.

See also Towster, *Political Power*, on the discussion of foreign policy at party congresses.

on his way out. Bessedovsky reports many instances when Stalin ignored the views of the department; he also tells of Stalin's private correspondence with diplomats over the heads of their chief and of errands on which he sent them contrary to official diplomatic policy.[57] Needless to say, the fact that the Politburo was occasionally divided in itself on foreign policy was another source of complications to Chicherin.[58] Of cordiality between the Narkomindel and the chief figures in the party there was no trace; Chicherin disliked Stalin, and both he and Litvinov disliked Molotov.

While Soviet diplomacy at the center was hampered by internal friction and hostile crosscurrents, Soviet diplomatic missions abroad operated on the whole—if one may trust Bessedovsky or Barmine—no more efficiently or harmoniously. And yet they did not lack able diplomats. During its first ten years the Soviet government drew on the services of Krassin, who in the past had followed an unusual, but successful, career as an electrical engineer, big businessman, and revolutionary, and who was also its Commissar for Foreign Trade;[59] of Joffe, who as a young man of means had given his time to studies and revolutionary underground work until he was exiled to the Siberian *taiga* to rise after his return to the inner circles of the party;[60] of Krestinsky, who had been a lawyer, a Bolshevik candidate for the Fourth Duma, and later chairman of the Ural committee of the Communist party before he was made secretary of the Central Committee; and finally of Rakovsky, the Ukrainian communist who for years had practiced medicine in France before he became chairman of the Ukrainian Council of Peoples Commissars and its Commissar for Foreign Affairs.[61] To be sure, Krestinsky and Rakovsky were sent to their foreign posts as a form of political exile; they had become *personae non gratae* in Moscow. In the years of Stalin's rise, assignment to the diplomatic service became a favorite method of isolating potential opponents, a practice which reflects again the relatively inferior position of diplomacy. During the

[57] Bessedovsky, *Revelations*, p. 210. The issue here was Bessarabia.

[58] As in the Ghilan affair. See L. Fischer, *The Soviets in World Affairs* (new ed., Princeton, 1951), I, xv. (Not to mention the party division over the Chinese revolution.)

[59] His biography in Lubov Krassin, *Leonid Krassin, His Life and Work*; and more revealingly in Simon Liberman, *Working for Lenin's Russia*, which contains interesting glimpses of Soviet diplomacy in the early years.

[60] *Granat*, XLI. Also for the following.

[61] One might also mention Vorovsky, who was of Polish noble background and had received a scientific education. He was the Bolshevik representative among the Polish Social Democrats and lived in Stockholm, as a contact man, during the war. After the February revolution he became a member of the foreign bureau of the Bolshevik Central Committee, to be sent back to Scandinavia after the seizure of power.

struggle against the "left deviation," Kamenev thus became ambassador in Rome, and Mme. Kollontai, the Soviets' first woman diplomat (and much advertised as such), minister to Norway and later ambassador to Mexico. Unfortunately, no study of the background of Soviet diplomats in the 1920's is available. It appears, however, that not only Bolsheviks secured diplomatic assignment. Bessedovsky, a career diplomat, had been a Ukrainian Social Revolutionary and forestry expert; Leonid Obolensky, Soviet plenipotentiary in Warsaw until 1925, an aristocrat and Tsarist tax collector in Siberia.[62] In the subordinate positions, at least in the first years after the revolution, all sorts of revolutionary riffraff could be found. In general, the conditions were such that the Narkomindel was forced from an early time to undertake the training of suitable Bolshevik cadres to make the most of the opportunities for distinction which Soviet diplomacy afforded.

The position of Soviet diplomats in foreign capitals, indeed, was a very challenging one, although not without obvious physical dangers.[63] Their job was twofold: to overcome the often extreme hostility against the Soviet regime—a feeling so intense on occasion that Litvinov, upon his first arrival in Copenhagen for negotiations with the British over the return of prisoners of war, was unable to secure lodging in any respectable hotel—and to make a position for themselves which would enable them to wield at least some political influence. Their situation was not unlike that of the diplomats of an earlier period, when, in the absence of instantaneous communication with their home office, they had to rely upon their own resources. The Soviet diplomat, of course, could always resort to the telegraph. But as his success depended upon adaptation to a very alien scene, the home office could not always assist him. This suggests, incidentally, that it was not only modern communications but also the increased uniformity of conditions and diplomatic practices among the Western governments that deprived diplomats in general of their former independence. Where there was little common ground between governments, as between the Soviet Union and the outside world, the diplomat—at least potentially—had a chance to regain his former stature. That was true, not only of Soviet diplomats with spirit and boldness, such as Rakovsky in Paris, but also of foreign diplomats in Moscow, when political circumstances favored their assignment, as was

---

[62] Bessedovsky, *Revelations*, p. 40. He was appointed, it seems, because he had done a favor to a Bolshevik exile in Siberia.

[63] Two Soviet diplomats, Vorovsky and Voisky, and a courier, Nette, were assassinated in the 1920's. Throughout, Soviet embassies lived in fear of attack.

the case with Brockdorff-Rantzau. The independence enjoyed by these men, however, could not last. Rakovsky's attempts to manipulate French domestic politics (entirely without recourse to revolutionary forces) finally led to a demand for his recall;[64] and the tightening control of the Stalinist regime soon limited whatever opportunity existed for Soviet diplomats abroad or Western diplomats in Moscow. What Stalin expected of his diplomats may be gathered from his admonition to Bessedovsky as he set out for Tokyo: "Talk to the Japanese as little as possible and telegraph us as often as possible. And don't think yourself the cleverest of us all."[65]

Here, in short, was the constant dilemma of Soviet diplomats. They had to attempt to bridge the profound gap between the core of the revolutionary regime, with its Leninist-Stalinist sense of reality, and the "capitalist" governments to which they were accredited. If they played too much the professional revolutionary or kept too much to themselves, they could not hope to make their way abroad and to be of maximum usefulness to their government. If, on the other hand, they made their way too well, they laid themselves open to the charge of submitting to capitalist influences. Few members of the Soviet foreign service knew how to strike a balance acceptable to their masters and true to their craft. Some, like Krassin, found their influence increasingly limited; others, like Bessedovsky, Solomon, and Dimitrievsky, fled from Soviet service when the disparity between the Soviet Union and the outside world, between the Stalinist regime and their political ideas, became too uncomfortable. These dramatic defections were followed by the adoption of greater security measures. But, as the later examples of Barmine and Kravchenko show, the loyalty problem was never completely solved, despite very strict supervision within Soviet missions abroad.

Apart from the supervision of the diplomats by the agents of the secret police and the Comintern within their mission, there was the scrutiny by the party cell, the secretary of which reported directly to party headquarters. In appointments to foreign posts, loyalty checks played a great part by 1930, with the chief of the foreign section of the OGPU and the members of the Central Committee in charge of party cells abroad conferring with the Narkomindel or the Commissariat for Foreign Trade on every candidate.[66] The activities of the party cells in

---

[64] The official reason was that he had signed a manifesto of the Left opposition which encouraged foreign soldiers to desert to the Red Army in case of war with the Soviet Union.

[65] Bessedovsky, *Revelations*, p. 131.

[66] Agabekov, *OGPU*, p. 269. The penalties for desertion were further increased in the 1930's.

foreign missions often descended to a rather unpleasant personal level. Relatively idle and almost completely isolated from "capitalist" society, Soviet missions abroad, particularly the lesser ones, often stagnated in their own sordid little messes. A touch of scandal or insurmountable personal animosity often led to the transfer of personnel from one post to another. These circumstances may have contributed in part to the low esteem in which diplomats were held in inner party circles.[67]

Nor could they, on the whole, make a good impression abroad on grounds of their professional integrity or competency. How could a Soviet diplomat fulfill the conditions which Lord Balfour set for the good diplomat?[68] As a party member and representative of the Soviet government, he could not expect to gain the confidence of the government to which he was accredited. Nor could he honestly and clearly convey the policies of the Politburo to that foreign government, for he voiced only the surface segment of Soviet foreign relations. And again, if he reported to his Soviet superiors accurately and understandingly on the intentions and policies of foreign governments, and particularly on general conditions abroad, he always ran the danger of being accused of lacking in revolutionary rectitude. The safest procedure for a Soviet diplomat under the circumstances was to forget professional standards and, as a diplomatic technician, adapt himself to the outlook demanded of him, at whatever cost to Soviet interests or world peace.[69]

The individual diplomat's dilemma, however, only reflected the larger quandary of Soviet diplomacy. In all countries the Diplomatic Service must mediate between foreign reality and domestic pressures; for that reason, it is bound to encounter hostility at home. Particularly in countries where social cohesion is insufficient for the purposes of government, those who urge the need for adjustment to the nature and the needs of foreign peoples are under suspicion, for they introduce an alien element into a society which fears any challenge to its orthodoxy. In Soviet Russia, the Bolshevik norm was increasingly narrowly defined; hence the professional handicaps of diplomacy increased during the 1920's. In order to win successes abroad, Soviet diplomacy was forced to indulge

[67] That is the picture conveyed by Bessedovsky, and to a lesser extent by Barmine. There was, however, also the example of Iureniev, Soviet representative in Rome, who conducted his embassy according to the best Bolshevik ideals. See Barmine, *Memoirs*, p. 206.

[68] Lockhart, *Memoirs*, p. 271.

[69] The effects upon diplomatic negotiations resulting from such close supervision of diplomats may be seen in Philip E. Mosely, "Some Soviet Techniques of Negotiation," in *Negotiating with the Russians*, ed. Raymond Dennett and Joseph E. Johnson (New York, 1952).

in a degree of adaptation to "capitalist" environment; by its very nature, then, it had a bias towards the "right deviation"—just as, in the case of capitalist countries dealing with socialist governments, the conscientious diplomat is apt to be accused of Leftist sympathy. No wonder, then, that Soviet diplomats were put under very strict observation.

What, then, was the outward appearance of Soviet diplomacy as a halfway station between the revolutionary core and the capitalist world? As the legitimate segment of Soviet policy it had to serve as a shield of the revolutionary core; its task in carrying out its assignments was to explain away, to conceal, to deny, or to ignore the revolution. For all its actions, it had to find nonrevolutionary motives. And here Soviet diplomacy, which was to be "open diplomacy," presumably averse to all secrecy or camouflage, found itself often in another insoluble dilemma, from which it escaped only by employing the most preposterous lies, half-truths, or arguments which, in strict theory, were incompatible with Soviet ideology.

Among the outright falsehoods frequently employed was the contention that the Soviet government had nothing to do with the Comintern. In his speech to the Central Executive Committee of the all-Russian Congress of Soviets on March 4, 1925, to quote but one example, Chicherin rejected a German protest that a member of the presidium of that body had signed a revolutionary appeal to the German Communist party: "We have already been forced once before to advise the German government formally that our government is not responsible for the activities of the Comintern and has nothing in common with it." The German government, bound to Soviet Russia by political necessity, did not pursue the point further. In 1921 and 1922, the British government under Curzon had disputed the same Soviet assertion and had been met with a series of evasions[70] and claims that British information about the connection between the Comintern and the Soviet government was false (it was in form, although not in substance); that it was fabricated by White agents (who, indeed, were active forgers in that period); and that the British, too, were employing subversive agents against Soviet influence (which presumably was also true but beside the point); and that members of the British Cabinet were also members of international organizations (which again was irrelevant). If Soviet diplomacy admitted the existence of the Comintern at all, it argued—and this was another

---

[70] See the documents in Degras, I, 209, and Krassin, *Leonid Krassin*, pp. 135ff.

half-truth—that capitalist and colonial conditions inevitably made for revolution, regardless of Soviet propaganda.[71]

When Soviet diplomacy was not rubbed so hard against uncomfortable verities, it resorted to more congenial subterfuges. It took a line which might be called homeopathic revolution; it would be progressive, anti-capitalist, even proletarian, but without the Bolshevik sting. Chicherin's speech at the opening session of the Genoa Conference, carefully prepared with Lenin's help, may serve as an illustration of this mode. He said that the Russian delegation came in the interest of peace and the economic reconstruction of Europe and recognized, without surrendering their Communist principles, the parallel existence of the old and the new order in the present historical period. He even put the economic opportunities for foreign business under the NEP in a rather favorable light. But then he introduced issues not on the agenda: various measures of disarmament; a better League of Nations, in which the distinction between small and Great Powers, between the victorious and the vanquished, was abolished; and even a plea for planned global distribution of industrial resources. In short, he presented a picture of the Soviet government as the leader in progressive reforms of international relations, advocating drastic but not necessarily revolutionary measures for an admittedly bleak postwar world. On other occasions, Soviet diplomacy harped on the foibles of capitalist international relations in general, the brutal character of the Versailles settlement, the shortcomings of the League, the friction between the Great Powers, and the high cost of power politics in general; it delighted in pointing out the injustices of the existing balance of power and the hypocrisy of all capitalist diplomacy (as it was quick, in retaliation, to show up the dirt in the politics of any other government). In the 1920's, the climax of this propaganda policy without the revolutionary corollary was of course Litvinov's famous first performance before the Preparatory Commission on Disarmament in November 1927. While Chicherin did not approve of Litvinov's policy, he himself had many times sung a similar gloating tune on other issues; it was the *basso continuo* of Soviet diplomacy. The closest Soviet diplomacy came to admitting an interest in revolution—and it did this only in the early 1920's—was to claim that it represented the foreign policy of the international proletariat.

Another motif of Soviet revolutionary not-so-revolutionary diplomacy,

[71] In Chicherin's circular to Soviet representatives abroad (September 10, 1920) concerning a note from the American Secretary of State Bainbridge Colby to the Italian ambassador in Washington. Degras, I, 210. Also Stalin, Political Report to Sixteenth Congress.

in which Chicherin, the Metternich pupil, felt particularly at home, was its frank *Realpolitik*. It sought to exploit the "contradictions" among the capitalist powers. These "contradictions" were always listed in any Soviet survey of the foreign situation and often much exaggerated, particularly in the case of Anglo-American relations. Soviet diplomacy tried to aggravate these cleavages and thus sided with the revisionist powers and with the weaker against the stronger, like any practitioner of the traditional balance of power policy. At the same time—and here it reverted somewhat to Marxist analysis—it made much of the divisions among capitalist groups within a given country, attempting particularly to bait certain commercial and industrial interests with concessions in Russia. On this level of its diplomacy, social revolution played no part whatever; any traditional practitioner of power politics might have acted likewise.[72]

Considering Chicherin's background (and also the fact that the Bolshevik revolution represented a strong upwelling of Russian national feeling), the strong trace of nationalism in the rationalizations of Soviet diplomacy should not cause surprise; it again helped to obscure the revolutionary segment of Soviet foreign relations. In many cases, the same policy could be equally interpreted from a revolutionary or from a nationalist point of view, as was true, for instance, of the monopoly of foreign trade. Justified on grounds of socialist theory, this was equally acceptable to non-Bolshevik Russian mercantilists.[73] Similarly, the revolutionary fear of contamination through contact with the West reappeared in diplomatic talk as the nationalist fear of Western economic and political penetration, which had been quite widespread in Russia before and during the war. In the same category, also, belongs Chicherin's championship of the protection of Russian boundaries, shores, and access to its shores, his claim to Bessarabia, his clash with Curzon over the Straits, and his demand for Soviet participation in all diplomatic arrangements involving traditional Russian interests like the Aaland Islands and Spitzbergen. In September 1926, he even pressed for Soviet participation in the current Tangiers negotiations, because Tsarist Russia, he argued, had been a signatory to the Algeciras Treaty,[74] (although the foreign debts of the regime had been repudiated, it will be remembered, precisely because they had been contracted by that government). And

---

[72] How much Chicherin was at home in the intellectual milieu of *Realpolitik* may be gathered from his articles, signed *postscriptum*, in *Mezhdunarodnaia Zhizn*, the Narkomindel's organ.

[73] Krassin, *Leonid Krassin*, p. 167.

[74] Reported in *Osteuropa*, I (1926), 697.

who could not hear the voice of traditional Russia in Chicherin's impassioned fulmination against Curzon at the Lausanne Conference in 1923: "The Russian revolution has transformed the Russian people into a nation whose entire energy is concentrated in its government to a degree hitherto unknown in history; and if war is forced upon that nation it will not capitulate. You are uneasy because our horsemen have reappeared on the heights of the Pamirs and because you no longer have to deal with the half-witted Tsar who ceded you the ridge of the Hindukush in 1895. But it is not war that we offer but peace. . . ."[75]

England, with whom Russia had clashed so often in the past, was also the main enemy of Soviet Russia in Chicherin's eyes. Hoetzsch, the German observer, was right in saying that the second Commissar for Foreign Affairs had always at his heart the *Staatsgedanke* of Russia; it was enshrined by him at the Narkomindel.

No further illustration is needed to show Chicherin's efforts to motivate and conduct Soviet diplomacy as if it were the sole instrument of Soviet foreign policy, and a nonrevolutionary one at that. Those familiar with the discussions of Soviet foreign relations on the Politburo level will be amazed how much Chicherin's conception of foreign policy differed from his masters'. But it must be remembered that, quite apart from the Soviet leadership's ability to accommodate itself to halfway stations, Bolshevik theory permitted any conceivable expedient in the relations with the capitalist world.[76] And no matter how unrepresentative the stated motivations of Soviet diplomacy—to take a view above the quarrels and disabilities from which it suffered at home, and to see it from the perspective of the Politburo—its successes aided the revolution, too, at least indirectly. In the security of its boundaries, its prestige in the world (even a "capitalist" world), in the matter of foreign economic assistance and loans, national and revolutionary interests overlapped or coincided. The only conflict on this higher level arose perhaps from a difference of emphasis. A diplomatic course which represented the *Staatsgedanke* of Russia was apt to consume prematurely the national

---

[75] Degras, I, 348. Chicherin, indeed, often interpreted the Bolshevik revolution as a source of renewed unity and energy in Russian foreign policy.

[76] The variability of Soviet attitude towards the western world goes probably far deeper than mere expediency. Soviet foreign relations in the first decade show the same "variability in depth" that can be found in the personal attitudes of the revolutionary leaders. They could range from the surface level of polite and seemingly sincere compliance with western standards, the give-and-take with foreign visitors through a whole gamut of intermediary moods to the raw revolutionary inner core of relentless hate. Under Stalin, however, this variability, born of the prerevolutionary contact between Russia and the West, has been greatly reduced.

resources which Bolshevik leadership wanted to husband for the further domestic development of the revolution. There prevailed in this period, from the Treaty of Brest-Litovsk to Stalin's willingness to surrender the Russian claim to Bessarabia and the sale of the Chinese Eastern Railway, a considerable inclination at the revolutionary center (not shared by the Narkomindel) to make territorial concessions for the sake of strengthening the revolution at home. But there was no reason why the territorial and strategic viewpoint should not again come to the fore and be justified in Leninist-Stalinist terms, once "the given relation of forces in the world arena" had changed in favor of the Soviet government.

IV

In conclusion, the analysis set forth in the previous pages will be illustrated by a brief and necessarily casual survey of Soviet foreign relations in the crucial period between 1921 and 1928. The following sketch will change the observer's vantage point from the Narkomindel to the Politburo and cast into bold relief what appears so flat from a survey of Soviet foreign policy premised on the fiction of the Narkomindel's effective monopoly of foreign affairs. As seen from the Kremlin, foreign relations stretched over a broad and deep front, with the revolutionary detachments of the Comintern and Profintern deployed on the left flank, along with the OGPU and military intelligence, with its various organizations for foreign cultural contact and foreign trade arrayed in the center, and with diplomacy engaged on the right flank. Unfortunately no picture of the fascinating complexity of interaction along this extended phalanx, of its coordinated maneuvers, sallies, feints, and ambushes, can here be given. Only the barest outline of the chief ventures on both flanks, the diplomatic and revolutionary, in their interplay and common relation to domestic conditions, is possible.[77]

[77] No history of Soviet foreign relations in the Chicherin period has yet been written from the Politburo point of view, covering the entire foreign policy phalanx and coordinating its actions with domestic development. Most existing texts suffer from an overemphasis upon Soviet diplomacy. Louis Fischer's indispensable volumes were conceived largely from the Narkomindel's point of view (in unusually close collaboration with Chicherin himself). P. Miliukov, *La Politique Extérieure des Soviets*, does far greater justice to the complexity of the subject. I. Deutscher's account of "Foreign Policy and Comintern I" in his biography of Stalin gives the best general background to the study of Soviet foreign policy in the Chicherin period, without devoting, however, much space to Chicherin's work. The essays by Boris Nikolaievskii, "Vneshnaia Politika Moskvy"; "Sovietskoie IAponskoie Soglashenie 1925 g"; "Revoliutsia v Kitaie, IAponia i Stalin" (in *Novyi Zhurnal*, 1942-1944); and "Russia, Japan, and the Pan-Asiatic Movement to 1925" in *The Far Eastern Quarterly*, VIII (May 1949), no. 3, show by far the greatest insight into the problems encountered in a detailed study of Soviet policy in this period. Least helpful, of course, from the point of view here taken is the official

As the Soviet government considered itself the spatial nucleus around which other Soviet Socialist republics might eventually gather, its relations with its immediate neighbors assumed special significance. In the West, the postwar settlement, based on Soviet weakness, had surrounded Russia with a *cordon sanitaire* of buffer states. A barrier had thus been established separating the Soviet regime from other countries with a revolutionary potential, such as Germany. While communist parties were forbidden by law in all of these border countries, the Bolsheviks maintained the usual underground organizations with the help of whatever local communist forces they could rally. The establishment of White Russia as a Union Republic and the creation of an autonomous Moldavian Republic were, at the same time, designed to create pro-Soviet sympathy among the Russian minorities in Poland and Rumania respectively.

In Soviet relations with all the border states, diplomacy necessarily stood in the foreground. In a series of treaties in 1920 and 1921, the Soviet government recognized the existence of these states with stipulations safeguarding Russia from attack through their territories; only relations with Rumania, which had seized Bessarabia in 1918, remained unsettled. Chicherin succeeded also, by playing Lithuania off against Poland, in preventing the creation of a Baltic bloc under Polish leadership. It seems in the last analysis, however, that it was the obvious threat of Russian power which discouraged dangerous adventures on the part of the border states. As things stood, they continued to be unfriendly to the Soviet Union, and they effectively blocked her revolutionary outward thrust; but, at the same time, by their very existence, they afforded the Soviet government a measure of protection against foreign intervention.

In the Near and Middle East, Soviet Russia faced an entirely different situation. Lenin had stressed the revolutionary importance of anti-western nationalism in colonial and semicolonial countries. In accordance with this, Soviet policy towards Turkey and Persia at once repudiated the Tsarist heritage and supported the national aims of the new governments. Thus, Soviet Russia supported Kemalist Turkey in her struggle with the Western Powers, helped the rise of Riza Khan in Persia and granted assistance to King Amanullah in Afghanistan. In their relations

---

version of Soviet diplomacy in V. V. Potemkin's volumes: *Istoriia Diplomatii.* On the other hand, the introductory paragraphs of the article on "Soviet Foreign Policy" in the official *Diplomatic Dictionary* (II, 650ff.) confirm, although in general terms, the tenor of Soviet foreign relations as viewed in this chapter.

with Turkey, the men of the Politburo appear to have played a straight-forward game, although the sincere friendship which Chicherin displayed toward Kemal's government was probably no more than mere expediency to Stalin.[78] In the vast territory stretching from Azerbaijan to Manchuria, however, Soviet policy and Tsarist expansion tended to coincide, despite Soviet professions to the contrary. In repudiating imperialism, the Bolshevik leaders were careful to hold on to the many concrete advantages they had inherited, such as the fishery rights in the Southern Caspian, the domination of Outer Mongolia, the operation of the Chinese Eastern Railway, and the disposition of the Russian share in the Boxer indemnity.

In the long run, the Politburo counted on the natural dissemination of its ideals and accomplishments in the Asiatic hinterland. Its agents were not only its diplomats, consuls, trade officials, OGPU and Red army men, but also its telegraphs, railways, tractors, and the example of Uzbek and Turkmen autonomy. It was as though Soviet Russia had attached a series of suction cups[79] to adjacent territories. How successfully and quickly these cups would work depended on local circumstances and the world balance of power.

In the last analysis, however, the important question was not that of Soviet Russia's relations with the border states, but rather of her relations with the three great capitalist Powers of the West, Great Britain, France and the United States. Germany and Japan, which—in Stalin's mind—occupied somewhat analogous positions, were more ambiguous factors; they were capitalist Powers which nonetheless contained strong anti-Western elements. Finally, there was a lesser Power, Italy, and the host of the small ones, which, apart from certain propaganda and nuisance aspects, counted for little. It was towards the centers of world power that the Politburo directed its diversified foreign policy instruments.

In 1920, Lenin had confidently set them all to work in order to break the blockade that had been imposed upon Soviet Russia. He had built up the Comintern to intensify the revolutionary pressure; he appealed to labor organizations and humanitarian groups for political and economic assistance; he held out the promise of concessions to foreign businessmen, trying to draw rival business groups into competition for Soviet favor; through his diplomats, he shouted peace to the victorious Allies

---

[78] Bessedovsky, *Revelations*, p. 187. On Soviet policy with regard to Turkey, see above, Chapter 6, §11.
[79] Scheffer, *Sieben Jahre*, p. 355.

and whispered consolation to the wounded nationalism of the defeated; and he tried to stir up the colonial peoples of the East. The question was: on what part of his broad foreign policy front the first breakthrough would occur and which foreign policy instruments would be the most effective in the long run. The first opening—there never was a break-through—occurred on the diplomatic flank, in relations with Great Britain. Lloyd George, in an attempt to secure the Russian market for British business, met the Soviet offer for a trade agreement, and thus *de facto* established relations. The Soviet government, through Krassin, proved most accommodating and even curtailed its anti-imperialist propaganda in the East. Yet trade relations nevertheless developed rather slowly. At the same time, Lenin directed his special attention towards Germany. As early as 1919, Radek, from his prison cell in Berlin—(he had been caught while organizing the revolutionary underground in Germany)—had negotiated with German industrialists and militarists; and in the next two years, against a backdrop of retreating revolutionary waves in Germany and Soviet threats of a rapprochement with France, the groundwork for future nonrevolutionary German-Soviet collaboration was laid.[80]

A still more satisfying gain was made, again on the economic-diplomatic wing (but with the support of the revolutionary wing),[81] in 1922 at the Genoa Conference, the first European diplomatic gathering to which the Soviet government was invited. The invitation was made possible by a widespread anxiety among European business groups to overcome the postwar depression by restoring the prewar economic ties between Russia and Europe. The danger for Soviet Russia in this juncture lay in the creation of a European consortium strong enough to force a breach in the Soviet monopoly of foreign trade. The Politburo, however, succeeded in dealing separately with interested parties, selecting one, the Urquhart interests, as proof that it was possible to do business with Russia (but repudiating the contract the moment the demonstration had outlasted its usefulness). Despite these maneuvers, the Politburo (acting through Chicherin and Krassin) could not create such competition among Western economic interests for the Russian trade as to weaken their demands for a prior settlement of the Tsarist debt and for concessions limiting its monopoly of foreign trade. The Genoa Conference thus failed, as did the subsequent Hague Conference. But at the same

[80] See Wipert von Blücher, *Deutschlands Weg nach Rapallo* (Wiesbaden, 1951), p. 155.

[81] The Comintern had been instructed to agitate everywhere for economic relations and political recognition.

time a more important matter than economic relations was decided: a course of German-Soviet collaboration.

The Rapallo Treaty, skillfully brought forward at Genoa by Chicherin at a time when the Germans were feeling their isolation most keenly, signified that with Soviet help Germany would try to pursue an independent national policy; it sanctioned a major split among the capitalist Powers. Through Radek, the Politburo had made a strong bid to enlist on its side the anti-Western elements of German nationalism and had succeeded. This tie not only weakened the force of capitalist encirclement but, through the influx of a variety of German experts, directly assisted the socialist reconstruction of Russia. This guarantee of a Soviet-induced and partly Soviet-controlled division of the capitalist world remained one of the major features of Soviet diplomacy, as well as of Politburo policy, throughout the Chicherin period.

It cannot be claimed, however, that at the time even the combined power of Germany and Soviet Russia altered the political situation appreciably. In the following year the French occupied the Ruhr, and Russian diplomacy, unable to prevent an adverse settlement of the Straits question, had also to back down before the Curzon Ultimatum, by which the British Government, in terms so peremptory as to suggest an imminent rupture of relations, demanded compensation for outrages against British subjects and a cessation of anti-British activities in the Middle East. Obviously, it was more difficult than Lenin had anticipated to raise Soviet Russia's position in the world. And he had to face the fact that the concrete gains (such as they were) had been won by diplomacy rather than revolutionary measures.

In 1923 revolution, however, seemed to be in the ascendancy. In that year the entire front of Soviet foreign policy was on the move, with revolution and diplomacy in close interaction. The Ruhr occupation—to concentrate upon the events in Germany—had set the stage for intensified revolutionary agitation and incited the hopes of Soviet leaders. For half a year after the French had moved, Soviet policy still stuck to the spirit of the Rapallo agreement. Chicherin vigorously protested against the Ruhr occupation, branding it a crime; protest demonstrations were held in Soviet cities; and the Red Army forwarded munitions to the *Reichswehr*. Through the Comintern, Radek preached the Schlageter line: communist cooperation with German nationalism. In thus supporting the German government's policy of passive resistance, the Soviet leaders hoped, at best, for a national war of the defeated against the victors. In mid-August, however, the Politburo abruptly changed its tune from diplomatic alliance to social revolution. What had happened to cause this sudden shift of initiative from the right flank of the Soviet foreign policy front to the left?

For one thing, seven months of French occupation had increased the likelihood of a genuine revolution in Germany. On August 12, a series of bitter strikes broke out throughout the country. Secondly, faced with such turmoil, the German government, now headed by Stresemann, decided to abandon passive resistance. With British mediation it now pursued a more moderate course of fulfilment and worked for pacification at home. At this point of Stresemann's retreat—which seemed also a retreat from Rapallo—the Politburo began to play for revolution through the Comintern.[82] Its agents had been ready since the beginning of the year; now they set up the necessary organizations. Thousands of Russian party members with a knowledge of German were alerted and the government of the new Soviet Socialist Germany was actually designated.[83]

But in preparing the German revolution, the Politburo faced two major decisions: how much direct aid could it give to the Germans, and what was it to do if a revolutionary victory should be followed by foreign intervention in Germany? Considering the unprepared state of her army and the conditions of the country in general, Soviet Russia was in no position to face war. Territorially separated from Germany, its leaders—at the time of Lenin's illness divided among themselves— could not send armed force without provoking a major international conflict. They dispatched, therefore, a variety of experts, but kept their material contributions at a minimum. The German communists thus had to fend for themselves, the Politburo staking all on their native strength and determination, although it gave serious thought to what would follow a communist victory.

Unable to prevent French meddling, as the French were already in occupation of the Ruhr, the Bolsheviks at least set out to neutralize hostile intervention from the east. They did this on the diplomatic front by sending Kopp to Poland and the Baltic limitrophes to arrange with them an agreement keeping them neutral and permitting the Soviet government to transship grain and other supplies to Germany. Kopp went so far as to threaten the Poles with an attack from the rear if their army should move against Germany. On the revolutionary side, the

---

[82] See Ruth Fischer, *Stalin and the German Revolution* (Cambridge, Mass., 1951), pp. 300ff.
[83] Bessedovsky, *Revelations*, pp. 46ff.

Politburo's program called for diversionary sabotage in Poland, not to mention aid to the German workers enjoined upon all communists through the Comintern. The risk taken by the Politburo thus included war only in case of Polish intervention in Germany, and it was assumed that the Russian threat would in itself prevent the emergency creating that risk. During these months diplomatic, economic and military relations with the German government of course continued as before, as though nothing had been changed. And after the failure of the German revolution in November 1923, the Politburo conveniently fell back upon its formal ties and the Rapallo policy, having lost very little ground in its unsuccessful revolutionary offensive.

The setback in Germany (and a simultaneous failure in Bulgaria), however, prepared the regrouping of units in the Soviet foreign policy phalanx resulting in greater freedom of action for the diplomats, particularly as the failure on the revolutionary flank was followed by further gains on their sector of the front. Early in 1924 both Great Britain and Italy granted *de jure* recognition to the Soviet government; later in the year France followed suit. The "objective circumstances" seemed to favor the diplomats. The change of government in England and France and the more relaxed atmosphere of international relations raised the position of the Soviet Union as a state among others in the comity of nations. It was in this new situation, calmer than any Soviet Russia had yet experienced, that Lenin's death occurred and the problem of the succession became acute. For the next four years—highly complex years in Soviet foreign relations—Soviet foreign policy was conditioned not only by the changes in world politics but more than ever by the changing internal scene.

At the time of Lenin's death, Soviet policy was determined by the "troika" of Zinoviev, Kamenev, and Stalin, who still followed the basic directives evolved by Lenin. Zinoviev, as head of the Comintern, naturally wielded a dominant influence over foreign relations, which meant continued strong emphasis upon revolutionary agitation. The failures of 1923 weakened his standing in the party, but during 1924 the Left course represented by him still prevailed. For that reason the Politburo remained cool, even hostile, towards the friendly overtures of the Mac-Donald government. Nor could it share the optimism welling up in Western Europe. The new calm in the international sphere began to reduce communist voting strength abroad; and this made the revolutionary weapons of Soviet foreign relations less effective. Furthermore, under the Dawes Plan, Germany was drawn into economic cooperation with

Western countries, which portended a weakening of the Rapallo policy. Finally, there were signs of outright hostility, such as the raid upon the Berlin trade delegation in April, and the reaction of the British public to the Zinoviev letter in the elections of October. In the face of such facts, Soviet leaders were divided. The old policy seemed no longer adequate; the direct incitement of revolution became increasingly ineffectual and even ridiculous. Zinoviev's miserable Reval putsch in December 1924 was the last expression of that policy. What new line should be taken?

Considering the unsettled situation in the party, it is not surprising that the answer came from domestic politics. While Zinoviev's policy still prevailed, a new trend based on internal considerations gained ground in the party. A group called "the economists," eager to rebuild Russian prosperity, even with foreign assistance, advocated less revolution and more foreign trade, which could be obtained only with the help of diplomacy. Zinoviev himself, in delivering the Central Committee's report at the Thirteenth Party Congress in May 1924, alluded to this trend, saying that now more than ever foreign policy stood in close relation to domestic policy. More than that, he even played up Chicherin's significance. There existed, indeed, an intimate connection between Soviet diplomacy and the Russian peasants. The more plentiful the supply of foreign capital for industrial development and the better Soviet Russia's standing with the capitalist Powers, the less sacrifices were demanded of the peasantry. For that reason, as Zinoviev put it, the Narkomindel should be one of the most popular Peoples Commissariats in the villages. In this manner a right turn in Soviet domestic policy meant also a promotion for Soviet diplomacy.

Such a turn took place in the spring of 1925. The uprising in Georgia, a minor Kronstadt, had demonstrated the necessity for greater concessions to the peasants; and the trend abroad was patently against revolution and for diplomacy. At the Fourteenth Party Conference, the new line in domestic as well as foreign policy was proclaimed; as to the latter, its aims were now to be based on the assumption of capitalist stabilization. The Fourteenth Party Congress confirmed the new orientation and also accepted the implicit corollary that, at a time of capitalist consolidation in the world, Soviet socialism would have to advance first of all within Russia. The new status of diplomacy, however, did not mean surrender of the revolutionary flank of the Soviet foreign policy front. But the previous direct incitement of violent revolution wherever possible was now replaced, under Bukharin's guidance,[84] by a more peaceful policy of gradual transition. Communists everywhere were instructed to cooperate with socialists; a link between Soviet trade unions and the British Trade Union Council was established in the form of the Anglo-Russian Trade Union Committee. Bukharin himself admitted, at the time of the English general strike, that revolution in England might not conform to the Bolshevik prototype. In China, too, Borodin was committed to a policy of cooperation with the Kuomintang rather than to outright sovietization. In the mid-1920's, in short, Soviet foreign policy, somewhat in line with the spirit of the times, had moved towards greater moderation. The original predominance of revolutionary agitation was ended; diplomacy had risen to equal rank. But the extreme hopes of some Soviet diplomats for a return by their government to pre-revolutionary power politics and a settlement of spheres of influence with the leading colonial powers, were not fulfilled; although with clipped claws, revolutionary agitation continued. And furthermore, the preferment of diplomacy did not imply greater tractability on the part of the Soviet masters. It only meant a partial shift back to European standards in the choice of foreign policy instruments. The total effect of the change upon foreign capitals was thus bound to be negligible, as was fully revealed in 1927.

While diplomacy now enjoyed greater prestige with the Politburo, it did not become more conciliatory and cooperative in its relations with Western governments. Its elevation coincided with the conclusion of the Locarno agreements and the preparation for Germany's entry into the League of Nations. In order to offset such capitalist solidarity under League auspices Chicherin undertook in 1925 and 1926 a vigorous diplomatic offensive. He strengthened Soviet ties with Turkey, secured the continued adherence of Germany to the Rapallo policy (with a commercial treaty and a 300 million mark credit added) and then set out to construct an anti-League of Soviet Russia's neighbors through non-aggression pacts, not all of which, however, could be concluded even after protracted negotiation. Only Lithuania, Turkey, Afghanistan, and Persia responded favorably. After a while the diplomatic offensive bogged down amidst signs of mounting British hostility. Chicherin's diplomatic weapons could not provide an effective antidote to determined British counteraction against the revolutionary wing of Soviet foreign

[84] See B. Nikolaievskii, *Novyi Zhurnal*, no. IV, 1943, pp. 302ff., for an analysis of Bukharin's views. Zinoviev, incidentally, was dropped from the Presidium of the Comintern Executive Committee in 1926.

policy; and, in May 1927, disaster overtook him in the rupture of diplomatic relations by that country.

The chief activities on the revolutionary wing of Soviet foreign policy under the new course, which had so provoked the British conservatives and caused Chicherin's failure, had been the offer of extensive Soviet financial support to the British strikers (who rejected it) and particularly Borodin's energetic promotion of the Chinese revolution. From the summer of 1926 on, the events in China claimed the intense attention of the men in the Politburo, who again set to work all the foreign policy instruments to attain their end. Only a few features of an extremely complex situation can here be mentioned.

Formal Soviet relations with the Far East were established in the spring of 1923, after the Japanese evacuation of Siberia and the absorption of the Far Eastern Republic by the Soviets. In a short time the Politburo negotiated with the chief authorities in China: to wit, the official government in Peking, Chang Tso Lin, the *tuchun* of Manchuria, and Sun Yat Sen in the south, dealing with each in their own terms. Most promising from the Soviet point of view was the incipient nationalist movement of Sun Yat Sen. The Politburo at once dispatched Borodin, an acquaintance of Sun's, together with military advisors, arms and money, to help organize the Kuomintang as a militant mass party with a progressive social and strongly anti-imperialist program. It was clear to the Politburo that the success of such a movement in China with its 400 million population would create a valuable ally and have immense repercussions through eastern and southeastern Asia and affect even the balance of power in the Pacific. In support of the Kuomintang, the Politburo also enlisted the help of Soviet diplomacy: for a time Karakhan was stationed in Peking; in Manchuria the Soviet officials of the Chinese-Eastern railroad defended Soviet interests against Chang Tso Lin, an enemy of the Kuomintang. In 1925 a settlement with Tokyo was negotiated, stabilizing Soviet-Japanese relations and creating a new *point d'appui* in the Tokyo embassy. In addition, Comintern agents were busy in all major cities of China, among the Korean nationalists, and in the Japanese Communist party. Finally, there was the Red Army, a far more active and influential agent in the Far East than in Europe, stationed along the Manchurian border.

After June 1926, with the Kuomintang striking north to the Yangtse, a decisive period was reached. Would the left or the right wing of the Kuomintang prevail? If the right wing under Chiang Kai-shek won out, the Kuomintang would be lost to Soviet Russia, as the seaboard cities with their Western orientation would determine its foreign policy. The Politburo, therefore, supported the left wing, without, however, advocating an all-out Bolshevik social policy. There were bitter disputes in and around the Politburo as to how far to the left the course ought to be set, with Stalin taking a relatively moderate view. The diplomats at the Narkomindel, on the other hand, worried about English reaction and, uninitiated into the projects of the Politburo, stood vigorously opposed to any revolutionary venture, even to the extent of Stalin's commitment.[85] They argued that China was not ready for more than a Kemalist revolution and they warned of Japanese hostility to a Soviet China. The clash between diplomacy and revolution assumed here a novel form, that of a conflict between an Eastern and Western orientation. The Politburo, having been repeatedly disappointed in its revolutionary expectations in Europe, had now turned to the East; for the present it braved British hostility and staked all upon success in China. The diplomats, considering the European scene with its global repercussions of greater importance, sought to minimize first of all friction with the British conservatives whom they greatly feared. In this dispute, the position of Japan also had to be considered, not only because of the extensive Japanese interests in northern and eastern China, but because Chinese nationalism was also anti-Japanese. In order not to antagonize Japan it seems that Stalin, through Comintern agents, tried to stifle the anti-Japanese agitation in the Kuomintang, while through his diplomats he cultivated friendly relations with the Japanese government. He valued the anti-Western potentialities of Japanese nationalism as highly as he did those of German nationalism.[86] During the height of the Chinese crisis in the spring of 1927 and the sharply rising British reaction, he even put his diplomatic representative in Tokyo under unusual pressure to wrest, in a sort of Far Eastern Rapallo, from the Japanese government a Soviet-Japanese nonaggression pact, in order to forestall active British intervention in China (which he thought possible only with Japanese help).[87] Yet even Japanese neutrality could not save the revolutionary venture in China.

The final crisis in the relations between the right and left wings of the Kuomintang merged with a general crisis in Soviet foreign relations and domestic politics. While at home the left opposition prepared its final demonstration, the foreign situation went from bad to worse. In

---

[85] Bessedovsky, *Revelations*, pp. 120ff.
[86] Nikolaievskii, *Novyi Zhurnal*, no. III, pp. 205ff.
[87] Bessedovky, *Revelations*, pp. 156ff.

April the Soviet embassy in Peking was raided; elsewhere in China consulates were searched. At the end of May the British government, after the Arcos raid, broke off diplomatic relations. British hostility radiated into other quarters. In June the Soviet ambassador in Warsaw was assassinated. In the same month Borodin was ordered home and the Chinese revolution, for all practical purposes, written off. In October the French government demanded Rakovsky's recall, after which Franco-Soviet relations reached a low point. Even in Germany the former enthusiasm for the Rapallo policy had waned. The trend of adversity even extended to Russia's hitherto reliable mid-eastern auxiliaries. In Persia and Afghanistan Great Britain won back lost ground; Turkey grew cooler as her relations with the Western Powers improved. Obviously the anti-imperialist shibboleths of the immediate postwar years no longer carried their old weight. At the end of the year the Soviets had lost all ground in China, and in Japan Count Tanaka, the protagonist of an active Manchurian policy, had been made Prime Minister. The crisis extended throughout the entire length of the Soviet foreign policy front. It was a defeat of diplomacy as much as of revolution; it affected Chicherin as adversely as Bukharin and the Comintern, not to speak of Stalin, who in the eyes of the left opposition was also responsible for the alarming turn of events. And yet, in the end, it helped to thrust the party's General Secretary, whose hand had been noticeable here and there even during the period of Bukharin's greatest influence, to the fore in a field in which he had hitherto held back. With his rise, the confusion and uncertainty in Soviet foreign relations dating from Lenin's last days began to disappear. Soviet foreign relations were reconstituted around a new set of convictions, Stalin's convictions.

The serious setback in the tenth year of the revolution on both the diplomatic and revolutionary flanks of the Soviet foreign policy front brought into sharper focus again the old bleak assumptions about the incompatibility of socialism and capitalism and the isolation of revolutionary Russia. A different leader might have chosen the other alternative and abandoned all revolutionary agitation and reverted to the traditional scope of power politics; and this would have also been the inclination of Chicherin. With Stalin there was no chance of such a course. His ascendancy deepened the distrust of the outside world. The former optimism about the imminence of world revolution or of universal formal recognition by "capitalist" governments—both had been conspicuous earlier, despite their contradictory nature—had gone. The "objective circumstances" of the world situation that had seemed to favor the Soviet regime in earlier years had changed. The instruments of international revolution designed to draw strength from these favorable constellations for the Soviet regime therewith also lost much of their reliability. The failures of 1927 thus put the naked fact of Soviet weakness back into bold relief: Soviet Russia could not play the part of a Great Power without the internal resources of a Great Power. In 1927, therefore, Stalin put the course of domestic politics again to the left: he answered the failure in foreign relations with terror at home and increased antiforeign agitation; he fabricated a war-scare that would justify the drastic measures to come, particularly the policy of rapid industrialization at all costs, out of Russian resources and at the expense of the Russian peasant. Only through the fastest possible development of Russian industries could he provide Soviet Russia with the means for victorious participation in the intensified struggle for world power which he saw ahead. At the Fifteenth Party Congress in December 1927 and the Sixth Congress of the Comintern in 1928, which ended Bukharin's uncertain influence over Soviet foreign policy, the ideological foundation for the new line (for which, of course, there was much cause from purely domestic considerations) was laid down. The brief era of capitalist stabilization was declared ended. Instead Stalin envisaged a new period of capitalist disintegration with attendant wars and crises, which would require that Russia be ready, not only to repel any capitalist attack, but to throw in her weight for the ultimate decision which would decide the fate of the world. In terms of practical politics, Stalin's policy, which he presented as a continuation of the old Left course, meant a drastic break with it. Now, the order of the day was concentration upon the domestic tasks of the First Five Year Plan. Foreign policy, despite the revolutionary flourishes of the Fifteenth Congress, was relegated, for a long time to come, to second place. Its sole task was to work relentlessly for peace and Soviet security in the period of socialist industrialization. No realignment of its forces was needed; the foreign policy phalanx remained roughly in the order in which it had been cast in 1925. But the freedom of the diplomats was sharply curtailed and the units on the revolutionary wing were reorganized. The Comintern was thoroughly "Bolshevized," i.e. transformed into a pliant tool for extensive foreign espionage and underground work. All along the policy front, the aggressive tactics of the earlier years gave way to a new defensive quiescence. The millennial hopes of the early period, although not forgotten, were replaced by ruthlessly realistic aims for the immediate future.

In Soviet diplomacy the change became obvious even before the break with England. Even in the latter part of 1926, foreign observers had noticed increased anxiety and uncertainty in Soviet foreign policy, fore-shadowing a change of course.[88] In the following spring the new policy emerged as the crisis of Soviet foreign policy deepened. A renewed but fruitless effort was made to win American recognition. As to Europe, the Narkomindel in a sharp reversal gave up its former unconditional hos-tility towards the League and dispatched a delegation under Sokolnikov to the World Economic Conference in Geneva, where it stoutly main-tained the possibility of peaceful coexistence and cooperation between the two systems.[89] Even more significant was Litvinov's participation, after November 1927, in the work of the preparatory Commission on Disarma-ment, not to speak of Soviet support of the Kellogg-Briand pact in the following year. Soviet weakness drove the regime to seek closer diplo-matic ties with the League of Nations, thus dimly foreshadowing a reac-tion which, in the 1930's, led to membership in it.

The new turn of Soviet foreign relations also affected Chicherin's posi-tion[90] and aggravated the physical ills that had always plagued him. Quite apart from the incompatibility between his temperament and that of Stalin, their political differences made further cooperation difficult. Chicherin, who had much in common with the Right opposition, refused to concede the necessity for the change in Soviet diplomacy dictated by Stalin. He had always opposed the League and did not agree now with the Stalin-Litvinov policy of cautious rapprochement; nor did he accept the necessity for the anti-German agitation that was part of the domestic course. He could not share the dictator's apprehension about the immi-nence of capitalist attack. And finally he who had always stood for the defense of Soviet state power in critical border areas, as well as in the world in general, could not willingly consent to such a far-reaching sub-ordination of foreign relations to domestic reconstruction. For that reason, he spent much time away from his desk, ill and grumbling, leav-ing most of his business to Litvinov, who was better adjusted to the totalitarian spirit of the Stalinist regime and found the new policy more congenial to his talents. After an absence of a year and a half, the ailing Commissar was finally released from his position by the Sixteenth Party Congress in July 1930, to die six years later in utter obscurity. As

[88] See P. Scheffer, *Sieben Jahre*, p. 304. Also O. Hoetzsch in *Osteuropa*, II, 397.

[89] In order to make Soviet attendance possible, the Narkomindel, after having rejected the original invitation, suddenly asked for another invitation. See Nikolaievskii, *Novyi Zhurnal*, no. VIII, p. 376.

[90] On Chicherin's position in the late 1920's, see L. Fischer, *Men and Politics*; and Bessedovsky, P. Scheffer, and O. Hoetzsch in the books previously quoted.

Chicherin disappeared from the scene, Stalin abandoned for the time being any intention to engage in competition for new power abroad and rallied all his energies to the single task of strengthening his home base. He drew the line which he was prepared to hold with his foreign policy phalanx in his report to the Sixteenth Party Congress, insisting that: "We do not seek a single foot of foreign territory, but we will not surrender a single inch of our territory either." By this statement, it is safe to say, he also implied: We will not seek any foreign revolution even during the tempting opportunities of a world depression.

In summary, then, what were the aims of Soviet policy in world affairs as they evolved during the first dozen years of capitalist encirclement? The principal one, which overshadowed all others, was to guarantee the absolute independence and security of the revolutionary development within its world base, Soviet Russia. This, incidentally, implied a far stricter interpretation of sovereignty (manifested in an extreme reluctance to enter binding political, economic, or even technical arrangements with non-Soviet governments) than prevailed in Western countries. From the first aim followed the second: to make the Soviet government as strong as possible through the planned organization of its human and material resources. Throughout the Chicherin period (and for at least a decade afterwards) Soviet Russia was, despite her often pathetic attempts to exaggerate her significance in world politics, if a Great Power at all, certainly a very weak one. Consequently, her main energies as well as her chief domestic controversies were concerned with the best and quickest ways of overcoming that weakness. The aims and means of her relations with other countries in turn were all conditioned by that weakness. From its narrow base of yet undeveloped strength, the Politburo conducted what might be called "negative" power politics; it counted less on the determining force of its material power than upon the opportunities provided by unrest and disunity among its opponents. The greatest desideratum of Soviet foreign relations was foreign revolution fomented by propaganda and local organization, not alliance or territorial gain. In the absence of such revolution (which, to be sure, in a country like Germany might have made all the difference), the position of Soviet Russia in the world depended to an amazing extent upon the minor ups and downs of parliamentary politics in the West, the turn of the business cycle, local, social and economic conditions, and still other factors not normally controlled by foreign governments. No wonder then that, given its soaring political ambition, the Soviet regime perfected its revolutionary techniques so as to gain at least some measure of control over these hitherto so elusive and hence neglected factors of power politics; no wonder that it strove to intensify its impact abroad by manipulating all phases of its foreign contact and by putting to maximum use every shred of sympathy and loyalty which it could find. Such dependence upon foreign conditions also made the Soviet regime unusually sensitive to regional and national differences; it was forced at the risk of being contradictory to identify itself very closely with local circumstances and the political forces there at play. In other words, it had, in its weakness, to seek for sources of power where the powerful countries had hitherto not yet penetrated, because their traditional resources of strength seemed still adequate.

In the new dimensions of international relations thus opened up by the Bolsheviks, Chicherin and the Narkomindel could play only a limited part. Social agitation was a highly specialized field which called for an experience and a mental outlook far different from those required in the conduct of strait-laced diplomacy. As a result, Soviet diplomacy was excluded from a large share of Soviet foreign relations. And Chicherin faced in acute form many of the difficulties which sooner or later beset diplomats everywhere when their governments are driven to cope with the instability of state and society in vital areas of the world. Within his restricted sphere of activity, he proved a very able craftsman, who justly earned the respect of his critics. His tactical skill in the negotiations at Genoa and Rapallo and his sallies against Curzon at Lausanne raised his prestige even in party circles. But his major successes, like Rapallo, and his failures, like the breach with Britain in 1927, were not of his own making. They were caused by the policies and actions of the Politburo, over which Chicherin had very little control. He was, after all, Foreign Minister in name only. His importance was exaggerated by foreign journalists who were guided in their interpretations by the example of Western governments, where Foreign Ministers enjoyed a large measure of influence in foreign relations, and who failed to realize that this was not true in Russia. Chicherin succeeded, however, in giving credence to their fiction, largely, one suspects, because it was his ambition to make it a reality. Whether unintentionally or by design, he thus effectively camouflaged the real politics of his masters.

Chicherin's main contribution, however, should be sought, not so much in the history of international relations in the 1920's, as in the changing formulations of Soviet foreign policy among the inner circles of the party. He stood for a continued validity of *Realpolitik* in the tradition of Metternich and Bismarck at a time when the professional revolutionaries were all but throwing diplomacy overboard. In his efforts to preserve the *Staatsgedanke* of Russia, he carried over into the new regime the heritage of Tsarist diplomacy. He was responsible for the element of continuity which links Tsarist and Soviet foreign policy and which, despite the great contributions of Leninism, seems to grow stronger as the years go by.

9

The Department of State and
American Public Opinion

BY DEXTER PERKINS

THE emphasis in the essays in this volume is placed upon the role of distinctive personalities in the evolution of foreign policy, and this emphasis is an eminently proper one. The study of social history, highly desirable and fruitful, has led in some instances to a distorted concentration on trends and movements, and to an undue minimization of the part played by highly individual decisions. In American foreign policy, as elsewhere, the importance of resolutions taken *in camera* by a few persons is not to be disregarded. Yet in a fundamental sense, the diplomatic history of the United States does not resemble the diplomatic history of Europe. Essentially, the professional diplomat has always played a subordinate role. There are few Légers, few Vansittarts, few Holsteins in the record of American action. Occasionally, we have a House, or a Hopkins, or a Harriman—a non-professional—who plays a significant role; and, in the 1930's, a career diplomat, Sumner Welles, had great influence. But, for the most part (and the longer the perspective the truer is the generalization), men of this type are rare. The elements in the formation of policy are at once more subtle and more complex than they are in many other states. We may, therefore, before describing the diplomacy of the 1920's, properly examine the various factors that enter into it.

In a sense that is true in no such degree in other nations, American diplomatic action has been determined by the people. There were ardent debates on foreign policy in the first days of our national history. There have been such debates ever since. Uninstructed though the average citizen may be in the facts of international life, he still has an opinion with regard to them. If he does not know, he thinks he knows. And this conviction on his part is one that cannot be disregarded. Nor do those who conduct our affairs in the main desire to disregard it. The democratic tradition is deeply rooted in our history. The men who stand at the levers of control are almost always men with substantial political experience. Their habits, their prepossessions, their convictions all lead them to pay heed to the voice of the great body of citizens, to shape their decisions with that voice in mind.

This does not mean that the minutiae of diplomatic action can be determined by the masses. Nor does it mean, if we are careful in our use of terms, that "public opinion," in the sense of a carefully thought-out view of a specific problem, is the fundamental factor. It means, rather, that the general sentiment of the people lies at the root of every great issue. There have been times when the mood of the American people was essentially militant. The government has responded to this militancy. There have been times when the mood was essentially one of withdrawal, of *reculement* as the French would put it. The government has responded to this mood likewise. Presidents have been powerless to withstand these deep-seated feelings. President McKinley was a man of peace, yet he was swept into war. President Franklin D. Roosevelt was certainly by conviction no isolationist, yet his first administration was essentially isolationist in spirit. This overmastering popular emotion rationalized, perhaps, into convenient slogans, often influences policy. To say this is not to praise or condemn. It is simply to state a fact. One may believe, if one is a convinced democrat, that in the main the popular instincts are sound. Or one may be cynical enough to distrust them. The important thing is to recognize that they exist.

But once this essential generalization has been made, there are others that need to be added to it. So far as individuals make policy, the balance of influence in the United States is always tipping, now this way or that, now to the executive, now to the legislature, and rarely to the professional diplomat. For example, there have been many Presidents of the United States who have exercised a remarkable personal influence on diplomatic action. This was true of Polk, of Theodore Roosevelt, of Woodrow Wilson, of Franklin D. Roosevelt, to mention only a few. But there have also been Presidents who delegated a large part of their power to their Secretaries of State. Except perhaps at the beginning of his administration, Lincoln did so. Grant did so. Harding and Coolidge did so. The role of the Chief Executive in foreign policy is a shifting thing, now great, now small, depending upon the type of individual happening to hold the office.

It is the same way with Secretaries of State. Some have been strong personalities, the true makers of policy. Others have recorded the views of Presidents, or depended upon their professional staffs. The one thing that is certain is that no definite and fixed role can be assigned to the Secretary under our constitutional system.

But we cannot end here. The conduct of American diplomacy is substantially affected by our constitutional forms. It is not, of course, merely that the legislative body, through the treaty-making power, participates in the formation of policy. In other states some control of foreign affairs can be exerted by the law-making power. What is more important is that, under our type of government, there is no certainty of harmony between the executive and the legislature. Under the parliamentary system with cabinet responsibility there naturally exists between the government of the day and its majority in parliament an intimate and cooperative relationship. But in the United States the Congress does not feel bound to pay any very extraordinary deference to the views of the executive, and its attitude is all the more likely to be critical if the Congressional majority is, as it may be under our system, of a different political complexion from that of the executive. Furthermore, the chairmen of the great committees, especially the chairman of the Senate Committee on Foreign Relations, may be veterans in political life, and men of strong convictions who feel no obligation to take their views from the other end of Pennsylvania Avenue. They may insist not only on being consulted but on being heeded.

Let us look for a moment at the manner in which these generalizations apply to the period under examination in this essay. It is the period of the Harding, Coolidge, and Hoover administrations, from 1921 to 1933. First, as to the mood of the American people. When the Harding administration entered power, the country had just emerged from a great war. There had been much disillusionment and a severe letdown from the mood of exaltation induced by the leadership of Woodrow Wilson. The question of the role of the United States in world affairs had been under constant and vigorous debate. On the whole, I think it fair to say, the country had reacted against a policy of extensive commitments in the world at large. In the struggle over the League, there was so much pettiness and partisanship that it is difficult to discover its essential meaning. Yet it seems reasonable to say that between the President and his opponents there was a real issue involved and that this issue centered upon that part of the Covenant which projected the United States most deeply into the international scene. Article 10, with its pledge of territorial sovereignty and political independence, may or may not have been, as Wilson claimed, the heart of the whole matter. But, if one reads the

Senate reservation to that article,[1] one becomes convinced that there was a real and fundamental question at stake, the question whether the United States should participate in the fullest sense in the development of a system of collective security for the maintenance of peace. And the answer that the American people gave, with the election of Harding to the Presidency, was that they did not care much about the matter. This renunciation must not be understood as implying that the withdrawal of the United States from world affairs was to be anything like total, or that there was not much devotion to the peace ideal as an abstraction. It merely means that the American mood was not one in which a sense of world responsibility played a dominant part.

Moreover, the mood of 1920 was the mood of virtually all of the period we shall consider. The immense prosperity of the United States, and the profound reaction from that prosperity, both concentrated American attention upon domestic rather than foreign matters. Those who conducted the foreign affairs of the nation, while often far ahead of public opinion in the breadth of their vision and in their sense of the large role which the country ought to play, had to take account of that essential fact.

As to the role of the Executive, neither President Harding nor President Coolidge was fitted to assume the function of leadership in the field of foreign affairs. Harding was an easygoing man of very mediocre intellectual gifts, if the word gifts may be used at all, and when he thought at all he thought in stereotypes. Coolidge was congenitally cautious, incapable of powerful or effective leadership, essentially the exponent of the laissez-faire philosophy. Neither exercised any really powerful influence on the diplomacy of the period. The same thing cannot be said of Herbert Hoover. Few Presidents were more conscious of their responsibilities than he, and, as we shall see, in some essential matters the opinion of the Chief Executive was of great significance during his administration.

The Secretaries of the period we are examining present an interesting

---

[1] The Senate reservation reads as follows: "The United States assumes no obligation to preserve the territorial integrity or political independence of any other country by the employment of its military or naval forces, its resources, or any form of economic discrimination, or to interfere in any way in controversies between nations, including all controversies relating to territorial integrity or political idependence, whether members of the League or not, under the provisions of Article 10, or to employ the military or naval forces of the United States, under any article of the treaty for any purpose, unless in any particular case the Congress, which, under the Constitution, has the sole power to declare war or authorize the employment of the military or naval forces of the United States, shall, in the exercise of full liberty of action, by act or joint resolution so provide." D. F. Fleming, *The United States and the League of Nations* (New York, 1932), p. 433.

picture, and interesting contrasts. Charles Evans Hughes, Secretary from 1921 to 1925, was undoubtedly one of the ablest men who ever held that office. His personal role in the formation of policy was a most important one. Secretary Kellogg, on the other hand, was much less disposed to initiate action of any kind, much more conscious of the limits imposed upon him by public opinion and by the Congress. Henry L. Stimson, Hoover's Secretary of State, was a man of powerful and strongly-held convictions, but was compelled in some matters, as we shall see, to defer to his chief.

All three Secretaries had to consider the legislative branch. The great concentration of powers inevitable to the waging of the first world war had inevitably led to a reaction, and the Congresses of the 1920's were in many respects jealous of their own position, and none too disposed to defer to the Executive. Despite the obstacles thrown in his way, Hughes often succeeded in by-passing the legislators, and in shaping policy by his own personal force. Kellogg was exceedingly deferential to Senators, and he had to deal with a man of great force, and of capacity superior to his own, in William E. Borah, chairman of the Senate Committee on Foreign Relations. Stimson was, on the whole, on good terms with the Senate, and was more confined by the views of his chief than by the opposition of the legislature. Yet on some questions, as we shall see, he could make little headway over Congressional resistance. The pattern, in other words, changed with each Secretary of State.

As for the permanent personnel of the Department, it is not easy to estimate its role. But it seems fair to say that Hughes dominated his department, Kellogg was often much influenced by his professional advisers, and Stimson, like Hughes, had strong views of his own. From all of which it can be understood how difficult it would be to write the diplomatic history of this period in terms of any single personality.[2]

Since the personal interpretation of American foreign policy is denied to us by the facts of the American scene, it seems wise to center our examination of the 1920's about certain key ideas. The emphasis, as in all these essays, is on Europe, and much, therefore, will be omitted that is not relevant to the European picture. Such emphasis is wholly justified. For whatever may have been the case before 1914, the relations of the United States with the great communities of the West are, in the period with which we are dealing, of great significance to the world as a whole.

---

[2] It is relevant to remark that in the brief period between 1921 and 1933 there were no less than six Under-Secretaries of State. No single fact indicates more strikingly the contrast between the American and the European diplomatic scene.

II

Let us choose, as the first theme for our examination, the attitude of the United States towards the idea of collective security, as it was reflected in the three administrations from 1921 to 1933. First of all, it is necessary to reiterate that the opposition to the famous Article 10 of the Covenant was nothing more or less than opposition to the collective security idea. That article was designed by its framers to prevent physical aggression on the part of one state against another. The members of the League agree, it read, "to respect and preserve as against external aggression the territorial integrity and existing political independence of all members of the League." This was not, as has sometimes been said, a freezing of the *status quo*. It was a prohibition on the alteration of the *status quo* by force. But it involved, and involved very deeply, the notion of common action against an aggressor, and it became the focus of the most fundamental attacks upon the Covenant itself. While the materials for a judgment are not so satisfactory as we might desire, it seems clear that a majority of the Senate were not ready to accept such an obligation, and when President Wilson attempted to make an issue of the matter in the election of 1920, he utterly failed. The great vote for Harding in that year showed, so it seems to me, that the mass of the people, to put it mildly, attached no very great positive importance to this central idea— if, indeed, they apprehended it at all clearly.

It seems clear, too, that Mr. Hughes, soon to become Secretary of State, was not enamored of the collective security idea, either. He was not a foe of the League idea in general but, as his correspondence shows, he thought of it in quite a different way from Wilson. "There is plain need for a league of nations," he wrote, "in order to provide for the development of international law, for creating and maintaining organs of international justice and machinery of conciliation and conference, and for giving effect to measures of international cooperation which may from time to time be agreed upon."[3] There is not a word in this interesting statement with regard to the machinery of coercion. It is, moreover, abundantly clear that he was opposed to Article 10. Indeed, he expressed such opposition as early as March of 1919, and this position he consistently maintained. Whether or not the treaty was to be ratified by the new administration, there seems no reason to believe that Hughes was ready to fight for the principle of common action against aggression. In point of fact, however, the question was never discussed in the early

[3] C. E. Hughes to Senator Hale, July 24, 1919, quoted in M. J. Pusey, *Charles Evans Hughes* (2 vols., New York, 1951), I, 397.

days of the Harding regime. For so bitter was the opposition of the irreconcilable Republicans to the whole Wilsonian edifice that Hughes, despite his own desire to see the Versailles pact ratified with reservations, was obliged to abandon this idea, and to abandon it even in the face of the assurances that he had offered to the American people in the campaign of 1920 that a vote for Harding was a vote for entry into the League under reasonable conditions.[4]

Despite the rebuff administered by the new administration to the idea of collective security, the idea itself showed a remarkable vitality. This is not to say that it was ever close to general acceptance in the 1920's; such a proposition, I think, cannot be maintained. But there were important discussions of the problem, and we should understand these discussions before we can examine the American attitude with regard to them.

First of the attempts to strengthen the machinery of the Covenant was the Draft Treaty of Mutual Assistance of 1923. This treaty gave to the Council considerably greater power than that conceded in the League constitution itself. It permitted that body, for example, in case of the outbreak of hostilities to designate the aggressor nation, and bound the contracting parties to furnish each other mutual assistance against the nation so designated, on a basis determined by the Council itself. It assumed that both military and financial aid would be accorded the aggressed state, and implied that an international force would be created to give effect to the obligations of the treaty. It sought at the same time to limit the operation of sanctions by declaring that in principle no state in a continent other than that in which the operations would take place would be required to cooperate in military, naval, or air operations.[5] The draft treaty was transmitted to the various governments by the Fourth Assembly, and comment invited.

There is little reason to believe that there was ever much chance of the adoption of this ambitious scheme, even by the members of the League. Indeed, the opposition to more extensive commitments than those of the Covenant had been expressed by not a few states in the deliberations which preceded the drafting of this instrument, and in the Fourth Assembly itself. In the debates at Geneva, indeed, it is possible to discern a distinct reaction against the idea of collective security, a reaction by no means wholly due—perhaps not even chiefly due—to the

[4] For a discussion of this point see Pusey, *Charles Evans Hughes*, II, 431-434.

[5] For a scholarly discussion of the mutual assistance treaty, see B. S. Williams, *State Security and the League of Nations* (Baltimore, 1927), pp. 151-182. See also Chapters 1, § III and 4, § III above and Chapter 10, § I below.

attitude of the United States. Nevertheless, it is interesting to observe the extremely cold tone in which Mr. Hughes replied to the note of January 9, 1924, in which the Draft Treaty was presented to the American government. Delaying his answer until June 16, and expressing a "keen and sympathetic interest" in "every endeavor" for the reduction of armaments, an end towards which the treaty was directed, he pointed out that wide powers were given to the Council of the League of Nations. "In view of the constitutional organization of this government," he declared, "and in view of the fact that the United States is not a member of the League of Nations, this Government would find it impossible to give its adherence."[6]

The reference in this note to the constitutional obligations of the United States deserves a word of comment. What Hughes is talking about is perfectly clear. Obviously effective action under any agreement looking to the application of collective measures for the maintenance of peace can, under our form of government, only be taken by the Congress of the United States. But this is not to say that the Executive cannot enter into an engagement which would bind Congress to act. Many another treaty, and not merely a treaty of the type we have been discussing, can be made effective only by affirmative action of the legislative branch. The question is not constitutional but moral. When an obligation is incurred, it is morally imperative that the Congress should carry it out. It should not be incurred, of course, unless there is good reason to believe that it would be honored. But it is quite unnecessary to speak, as did Mr. Hughes, as if our governmental forms prevented the signature by the United States of agreements for the maintenance of peace.

Practically speaking, we repeat, the Hughes note was not of very great importance. The Draft Treaty was probably doomed from its inception. The point to be made is that in this instance the Secretary showed no enthusiasm for—indeed no interest in—the idea of collective security.

The Secretary was to take a still more drastic stand with regard to the Geneva Protocol.[7] In 1924 the European diplomats tried their hand once again at the problem which the Treaty of Mutual Assistance had failed to solve. The result was the Geneva Protocol for the Pacific Settlement of International Disputes. This Protocol erected an elaborate system for the solution of international difficulties, first by extending the compul-

---

[6] *Foreign Relations*, 1924, I, 79.

[7] For a discussion of the Protocol, see Williams, *State Security and the League*, pp. 182-205, also D. H. Miller, *The Geneva Protocol* (New York, 1925), and P. J. Noel Baker, *The Geneva Protocol for the Pacific Settlement of International Disputes* (London, 1925); and Chapters 1, §III and 4, §III above and Chapter 10, §I below.

sory jurisdiction of the Court of International Justice, and, second, by providing for the settlement, either by the Council of the League or by compulsory arbitration, of all disputes which did not fall within the jurisdiction of the Court. At the same time it made it possible to define an aggressor with more precision than was possible in the Covenant, and bound the signatories to participate loyally and effectively in the application of sanctions, but with the proviso that aid should be given by each state "in the degree which its geographical position and particular situation as regards armament allows." It is important to note that the Geneva Protocol was unanimously approved by the Fifth Assembly of the League on October 2, 1924.

The Geneva Protocol has a far greater significance than the Draft Treaty. The leaders of the greatest states of Europe were at the meetings of that famous Assembly of 1924, Ramsay MacDonald for Great Britain, Eduard Herriot for France. The Protocol was launched at a favorable moment and under favorable auspices, with the end of a period of tension in the relations of France and Germany, and in an atmosphere favorable to constructive achievement. It is true that the position was somewhat altered by the fall of the Labor government in November of 1924. Still, without overstressing the matter, it is possible to say that, on the mere basis of the significance of the instrument, the attitude of the United States towards the Protocol was bound to be of considerable importance.

The Foreign Relations of the United States for 1925 contain a very remarkable account of conversations on the subject between the Secretary and the British ambassador in Washington. The first occurred on January 5, 1925. It is important to quote this document, recorded in a memorandum by Mr. Hughes himself. It was Sir Esmé Howard who opened the conversation. Declaring that "it was a cardinal point in British policy to maintain friendly relations with the United States, and to cooperate with this Government wherever possible," he added that "there might be interference with this policy if contingencies should arise in which through the operation of the Protocol the British Government was brought into opposition to the interests of the United States." "On the other hand," he continued, "it seemed to the British Government that it would not be well to throw out the Protocol entirely. . . ." "The only alternative to such a competition in armament with all its possible consequences would seem to be the adoption in some form of such an arrangement as the Geneva Protocol proposed."[8]

In reply to these observations the Secretary took what can only be

[8] *Foreign Relations*, 1925, I, 16-17.

described as a rather high tone. "There were," he remarked, "two aspects, at least, of the Geneva Protocol which might give concern to this Government." "If the Protocol were taken as having practical value and actually of portending what it set forth," said Hughes, "there would appear to be a proposal of a concert against the United States, when the Powers joining in the Protocol considered that the United States had committed some act of aggression, although the United States might believe itself to be entirely justified in its action, and in fact be acting in accordance with its traditional policies. The Secretary said that he did not believe that such a concert would actually become effective but he supposed that the Protocol must be taken as it is written and in this view the United States would be compelled to view it with disfavor. The Secretary said there was another class of cases where the action of the United States itself might not be involved but that of some other country with which the United States had trade relations, and the action of the Powers who had joined in the Protocol might turn out to be inimical to the interests of the United States in such relations with the country in question." Alluding still further to the possibility of collective action against some other nation, Mr. Hughes went on to remark that "there was one thing he believed could be depended upon, and that was that this Government from its very beginning had been insistent upon the rights of neutrals and would continue to maintain them." He "did not believe that any Administration, short of a treaty concluded and ratified, could commit the country against assertion of its neutral rights in case there should be occasion to demand their recognition."[9]

All this could hardly be described as encouraging. But Mr. Hughes went further. He declined at one and the same time to approve or to disapprove the Protocol. He intimated that the British sounding was a mere maneuver and excuse for inaction, and expressed the hope that if other governments did not approve of the Protocol, they should deal with the matter from the point of view of their own interests and not put the responsibility on the United States. To the suggestion that the matter might be handled by a reservation on the part of the British, he declared that he would not wish anything to be said that might imply that this way of dealing with the problem might be satisfactory to the United States.

It is difficult to describe this commentary of Mr. Hughes as other than a dash of cold water thrown in the face of Sir Esmé. Indeed, it is hard to see how the tone could have been much more intransigent and un-

[9] *Foreign Relations*, 1925, I, 17.

conciliatory. Nor was the effect of this interview diminished three days later when the British ambassador returned to the State Department and was told that the Secretary had consulted with the President and that the Chief Executive approved the point of view previously expressed.[10] And it is worth noting that the position then assumed was in no sense due to any particular political pressure. The date, it will be noted, was January 1925. The presidential elections were over, and the Republican party had been brilliantly victorious. It may be that Mr. Hughes believed that he was expressing the mood and temper of the American people. It is certain that he was not acting on the basis of any particular exigency of the moment.

On the other hand, it is by no means clear that the action taken by the Secretary was a determining factor in the final collapse of the effort to strengthen the League through the Protocol. The British elections of November 1924 brought the Conservatives into power with an overwhelming majority, and the new Secretary of State for Foreign Affairs was not an enthusiast for the arrangements that had been worked out at Geneva. The Dominions, when consulted, also were disposed to avoid the rather sweeping commitments contained in the League proposals.[11] True, the position of the United States afforded an excellent argument against these new commitments, and the British government made a good deal of this argument in its memorandum of March 1925.[12] But the most that can probably be said is that the position assumed by Mr. Hughes reinforced a point of view that the London government might have assumed in any event. It is useless to speculate, of course, on what would have been the course of events in the 1920's if the United States had wholeheartedly accepted the engagements of the Convenant itself.

The dislike of the League idea, it must be stressed, did not, in the secretariat of Mr. Hughes, prevent the taking of steps which expressed American interest in the idea of peace. There was, for example, in 1923, a proposal put forward by the administration for American adhesion to the protocol creating the Court of International Justice.[13] Such a proposal was consonant with American traditional thinking, which connected peace, not with power, but with orderly process. But this proposal got nowhere. When the United States Senate in 1926 voted to adhere to the protocol,

[10] *Foreign Relations*, 1925, I, 19.

[11] See some of their comments in Williams, *State Security and the League*, pp. 310-320. See also Chapter 1, note 91, above.

[12] Williams, *State Security and the League*, p. 306.

[13] On the World Court question, see D. F. Fleming, *The United States and the World Court* (Garden City, 1945).

it did so with reservations that created new problems and that carried the whole controversy with regard to the Court over into the Roosevelt administration.[14]

But let us return to the movement for collective security. The failure of the Protocol was followed by the very significant negotiations, lasting through a great part of 1925, that finally resulted in the treaties of Locarno. By these treaties specific agreements strengthening the principles of collective security were approved in place of generalized understanding. Thus the French, British, Italian, Belgian, and German governments entered into engagements by which the territorial *status quo* with regard to the frontiers between France and Germany and Belgium and Germany were guaranteed, and by which the countries concerned mutually undertook in no case to attack each other or resort to war against each other. They also agreed to settle all disputes arising between them by resort to arbitration, and to extend mutual assistance to one another against any one of their number which resorted to war in violation of the pact. The Eastern frontier settlements of Versailles, that is, the frontier between Germany and Poland and Germany and Czechoslovakia, were not similarly guaranteed. But treaties of arbitration were drawn up between Germany and Poland and Germany and Czechoslovakia, and these treaties were buttressed by antecedent agreements between France and Poland and France and Czechoslovakia to give each other immediate aid and assistance in case of an unprovoked recourse to arms. The Locarno agreements, signed at the end of 1925, represent the high-water mark of the movement for collective guarantees in the period between the wars.[15]

By the time the Locarno treaties were under discussion, Secretary Hughes had laid down his charge at the State Department and had been succeeded by Secretary Kellogg. The new director of American foreign policy was a man of far less force than his predecessor, far less likely to adopt any initiative in the field of foreign policy. Yet the very fact that the Locarno agreements were regional in their character was calculated to relieve the United States of any embarrassment with regard to them. To such partial understandings the American government could have no such objections as pertained to the strengthening of the Covenant. Mr. Kellogg, of course, when informed of what was going on, firmly declined to have anything to do with any guarantee.[16] But Presi-

---

[14] *ibid.*
[15] For a convenient summary see Williams, *State Security and the League*, pp. 206-226. See also G. Glasgow, *From Dawes to Locarno* (New York, 1926).
[16] *Foreign Relations*, 1925, I, 21.

dent Coolidge speaking in July of 1925 gave the negotiations his bless-ing,[17] and in his message of December 1925, the cautious Chief Executive declared that the recent agreements "represent the success of the policy on which this country has been insisting . . . of having European coun-tries settle their own political problems without involving this country," and went on to suggest that the way was now clear for the reduction of land armaments, while underlining the fact that this was primarily a European problem.[18]

III

The question of American participation in the movement for the reduction of land armaments was, in due course, to take another turn. In no little time the American government began to participate in dis-cussions at Geneva looking to such reduction. But, since the climactic moves in this discussion came in the early 1930's, it will be convenient to postpone discussion of this subject for a moment, and to examine first that remarkable movement which culminated in the famous Kellogg Pact, or the Pact of Paris, for the maintenance of peace.[19] This pact, finally signed on August 28, 1928, was a simple pledge on the part of the contracting parties "not to have recourse to war as an instrument of national policy, and to settle all disputes arising between them by peace-ful means." At first blush this compact looks like a denial of the very principle of collective security, a substitution of peace by promises for peace by common action. But whoever studies the background of the Kellogg Pact in detail will, I think, come to a somewhat different con-clusion. For the friends of the Pact were by no means always clear on the matter of sanctions. Mr. S. O. Levinson of Chicago, who very early espoused the idea of the outlawry of war and who was one of those who pressed it most tenaciously throughout the 1920's, though certainly not depending on force as the essential element in his own view of the prob-lem, at one time seems to have believed that in flagrant violations of a no-war pledge force might be used.[20] Senator Borah, who had a great deal to do with the promotion of the Kellogg Pact, on one occasion de-

---

[17] See the *New York Times*, July 4, 1925.

[18] The *New York Times*, December 9, 1925.

[19] On the Kellogg Pact, see the full discussion in *Foreign Relations*, 1928, I, 1-234. See also J. T. Shotwell, *War as an Instrument of National Policy and its Renunciation in the Pact of Paris* (New York, 1928), D. H. Miller, *The Peace Pact of Paris. A Study of the Briand-Kellogg Treaty* (New York, 1928), and D. P. Myers, *Origins and Con-clusion of the Paris Pact; the renunciation of war as an instrument of national policy* (Boston, 1929).

[20] See J. E. Sloner, *S. O. Levinson and the Pact of Paris: A study in the techniques of influence* (Chicago, 1943), esp. pp. 27 and 185.

clared that it was "quite inconceivable that this country would stand idly by in case of a grave breach of a multilateral treaty to which it was a party."[21] Statements such as these ought not, it is true, to be given an exaggerated importance. They certainly do not represent the prevailing mood or conviction of the two men just mentioned, both of whom seem to have had a naive faith in the power of public opinion. But neither can they be entirely disregarded. To this fact must be added another. Some of the friends of the pact were quite clear as to what they hoped would flow from it. Believing in the principle of collective action against aggression, they took the view that once the treaty was ratified there would arise, almost inevitably, a demand that it be "implemented." And this demand, they hoped, would in due course lead the United States into closer relations with the League of Nations. If once the principle that war was inherently illegal, as well as immoral, were accepted, a way would be found by which the American people would take action in support of the principle they had affirmed. This point of view appears most clearly in Professor Shotwell's interesting book on *War as an Instrument of National Policy*.[22] But one can find it in many other pronouncements of the period as well.[23]

Perhaps the most interesting thing about the Pact of Paris, however, is the illustration it affords of the way in which American foreign policy on occasion comes up from the grass roots rather than down from the State Department or its Secretary. It is a well-known fact that the initial step in the negotiations that led to the pact came from a proposal of the French Foreign Minister Aristide Briand, made on April 6, 1927, to enter into a bilateral treaty for the renunciation of war. This proposal, incited by Professor Shotwell on a visit to Paris, passed almost unnoticed at the time, and was indeed completely ignored by Secretary Kellogg. The situation was in some degree changed when Nicholas Murray Butler, then president of Columbia University, in a letter to the *New York Times*, called attention to the significance of the Briand offer, and when Professor Shotwell and Professor Chamberlain put the idea in the form of a draft treaty. In June of 1927, the French government presented a formal proposal to the United States.[24] Still the administration hesitated, indeed the State Department declared that no such compact was necessary, and that it would not even be desirable.[25] But the outlawry of war

[21] See Shotwell, *War as an Instrument of National Policy*, p. 224.

[22] *ibid.*, pp. 254ff.

[23] See, for example, Miller, *The Peace Pact of Paris*, and J. B. Whitton, *What Follows the Pact of Paris* (New York, 1932).

[24] Shotwell, *War as an Instrument of National Policy*, p. 72.   [25] *ibid.*

proposal aroused an increasing interest, and the crucial factor in securing official consideration for it was doubtless the attitude of Senator Borah, the powerful chairman of the Senate Committee on Foreign Relations. On December 27, 1927, Borah introduced a resolution calling for the outlawry of war, the establishment of an international code, and of an international court by the decisions of which the nations of the world should be bound to abide.[26] On the very next day, Secretary Kellogg, in a note to the French government, proposed that "the two governments, instead of contenting themselves with a bilateral declaration of the nature suggested by M. Briand, might make a more signal contribution to world peace by joining in an effort to obtain the adherence of all of the principal powers of the world to a declaration renouncing war as an instrument of national policy."[27] Thus were initiated the negotiations that finally led to the Pact of Paris.

I do not think it desirable to trace these negotiations in detail. There were substantial obstacles to be overcome. The French were by no means enthusiastic about the alteration of their original proposal, and they feared that the proposed agreement might weaken the structure of the League of Nations, and the machinery of sanctions embodied in the Covenant. Other difficulties soon arose. The British, in particular, seemed to fear that their freedom of action in certain parts of the world might be limited by the proposed engagement. Matters ended happily, however. By making it clear, as he did in a speech of April 28, 1928, that the Pact did not affect the right of self-defense, Mr. Kellogg calmed the apprehensions of the critics, and at the same time (having regard to the flexibility of the term self-defense itself) whittled away some of the significance of the Pact itself.[28] By the spring of 1928, with a Presidential election coming on, there was only one course of action to be followed, and that was to press matters to a conclusion. And so the Pact was signed.

What effect did the Pact have on American diplomacy in the years that followed? The first attempt to invoke it concerned a dispute between China and Russia in 1929 and need not concern us here save to remark that the appeal made by the American government exposed the United States to a severe rebuff from the Soviet Union.[29]

The fiasco which resulted in this particular case led Mr. Stimson to

[26] The resolution is found most easily in Shotwell, *War as an Instrument of National Policy,* pp. 108-109.
[27] *Foreign Relations,* 1927, II, 626-627.
[28] The speech is in the *New York Times,* April 29, 1928.
[29] The voluminous correspondence is in *Foreign Relations,* 1929, II, 186-435.

meditate on possible means by which the Kellogg Pact might be made more effective. Thus arose the idea of consultation, or of a consultative pact.[80] This idea was discussed with the French ambassador in the fall of 1929.[81] It also came up at the London naval conference of 1930. At that conference the French again brought it forward and threw out the hint that the reduction of their own naval armament might be facilitated by some understanding on the matter. The Secretary was at first cold to the suggestion since it smacked of a diplomatic bargain, and President Hoover was still more opposed. But, as the conference proceeded, it appeared possible that the French and the British might agree on some strengthening of their association under the Covenant of the League, and Stimson played with the idea of encouraging such a strengthening by some agreement for consultation. On March 25 he issued a somewhat cryptic statement to the press on the matter, intimating that some positive step might be taken. He seems at this moment to have had the support of the American delegation of which he was the head. There was, however, less enthusiasm in Washington; the President was distinctly nervous with regard to the matter and feared the reaction in the Senate. He was, indeed, strongly opposed to any generalized engagement to consult. Though he gave his approval to a watered-down version of a consultative clause in the naval treaty, the project was, in the last analysis, abandoned.[82]

But Stimson was tenacious of the general objective. When the Manchurian crisis broke in the fall of 1931, he maintained close contact with the League, even to the extent of permitting the American representative at Geneva to sit in on meetings of the Council, and of sending General Dawes to Paris to participate at arm's length in the League deliberations. There was an American member on the commission which the League appointed to investigate the situation and make recommendations, and the League and the United States cooperated in the winter of 1932 in proclaiming the so-called Stimson doctrine by which it was declared that there could be no recognition of an illegal situation arising out of the violation of the Kellogg Pact. In the course of the year 1932, moreover, both party nominating conventions declared in favor of the principle of consultation,[83] and Stimson underlined the desirability of

[80] For this whole matter of consultation, see R. M. Cooper, *American Consultation in World Affairs for the Preservation of Peace* (New York, 1934).
[81] See *Foreign Relations*, 1929, I, 59-64.
[82] See *Foreign Relations*, 1930, II, *passim*, esp. pp. 36-92.
[83] Cooper, *American Consultation in World Affairs*, p. 58.

accepting this principle in a speech of August 8.[34] Nonetheless, no formal engagements were entered into during any part of the period which we are reviewing.

Taken all in all, however, it cannot be said that the American government, between 1921 and the advent of the Roosevelt administration, had gone very far towards the acceptance of the idea of collective security. There was very distinctly a difference between the attitude of Hughes and the attitude of Stimson,[35] but the difference was by no means so wide as practically to affect the policies of the European nations. On the whole, the dogma of freedom of action dominated American policy during the period, and none was more deeply attached to it, it should be said, than was President Hoover.[36] It seems likely that in this respect he expressed the dominant opinion of the nation.

Interesting as it is to speculate on "what might have been," in summarizing the attitude of the United States in the years under review, all that can really be said is that the general line of policy was unfavorable towards common action against an aggressor, but that the Kellogg-Briand Pact, by branding war as immoral, reflected something of the sentiment of the American people, and may have provided a basis for the more active diplomacy of the United States at a later period.

IV

The dislike of the administrations of this period for the League idea is well illustrated in the manner in which they dealt with the problem of reduction of armaments. There was, at the end of the war, an immense sentiment for such reduction, and Mr. Hughes, in the very first year of his administration of the State Department, boldly capitalized on such sentiment. The Washington Arms Conference of 1921-1922 was, in many ways, a great diplomatic achievement. Though the British would have liked the credit for calling it, Mr. Hughes insisted on garnering that credit for himself. He electrified all observers when, at the very outset, he laid down a plan for the scrapping of a substantial part of existing building programs and for the establishment of fixed ratios in capital ships and aircraft carriers. He secured that parity with the British which American opinion (for no very clear reason, it must be conceded) demanded, and he persuaded the Japanese to accept a subordinate position. He brought about these striking results without what the enemies

[34] *ibid.*, p. 59.

[35] Stimson was disposed to acquiesce in sanctions against Japan in 1931.

[36] See President Hoover's recent article in *Colliers, The National Weekly*, for April 19, 1952, p. 57.

of the League would have described as "entanglement." The nearest approach to such an entanglement, indeed, was a Four Power pact, consultative in nature, with regard to "the regions of the Pacific." (Somehow or other, such a pact could, even in 1922, be regarded as innocent if it applied to the Orient.) In the course of the negotiations, moreover, assisted by the pressure exercised by the Dominions, and especially by Canada, he broke up the Anglo-Japanese alliance which had existed since 1902. But this story is not for us to tell here in detail.[37] The point is that the American theory with regard to arms reduction was essentially different from the thesis upheld by many influential Europeans, and especially by the French. To the latter, the building of a system of external security was a condition precedent to the reduction of armaments, and it was only under very heavy pressure that the Quai d'Orsay yielded even on the partial limitation of naval armaments at Washington. But American statesmanship stoutly insisted that there was no necessary connection between the curtailment of armed forces and a network of treaties to punish aggression. It succeeded, in this particular instance, in making its point of view prevail by giving up, in the face of Japanese pressure, the right to fortify Guam and the Philippines. In other words, it abdicated so far as the use of force in the Far East was concerned. No doubt, as was frequently maintained at the time, because of the state of American public opinion, it would have been impossible to secure funds for such fortifications in any case. But however this may be, the significant thing is that the American outlook on the whole question of armaments was so very different from that involved in acceptance of the League.

The success of the Washington Conference in the field of naval armament was to be repeated and extended in the administration of President Hoover. For a time after 1922 it seemed as if the rivalry of the United States and Great Britain, partially exorcised so far as capital ships were concerned, was to break out in new construction of vessels of inferior tonnage. An attempt to come to an agreement in 1927 in a conference at Geneva aborted, largely because the preparations for the conference were inadequate and because the admirals were allowed a very important, if not a central, role in the negotiations. But at London in 1930, the three Great Powers, the United States, Great Britain, and Japan, came to an agreement which limited ships of every kind and which was, indeed, a remarkable achievement.[38] It ought, perhaps, to be

[37] The best brief account of the Conference is in A. W. Griswold, *The Far Eastern Policy of the United States* (New York, 1937), pp. 269-332.

[38] The London negotiations are given in much detail in *Foreign Relations*, 1930, I, 1-186.

said parenthetically, that one of the reasons for the success of both the Washington and London conferences was the appointment of influential Senators as members of the American delegations. This specific is not infallible, but it has frequently proved efficacious in smoothing the way to successful negotiation.

The naval agreements of the period seemed at the time to be remarkable achievements. In the short run they were rightly so regarded. But they did not survive the tensions of the 1930's, and their long-time effects were certainly not entirely happy. The United States was for a time lulled into a false security and neglected its naval establishment, failing to build up to the agreed quotas. The British were compelled at London, or in the negotiations preceding London, to reduce their cruiser strength in order to propitiate the American government, and this was to be a serious handicap in the 1940's. Naval disarmament was an expression of the temper of the 1920's and of a distinctively American point of view. But it was very far from affording a long-time guarantee of peace, and it contributed little to the stabilization of Europe. It is for this reason that I have dealt with it so summarily.

Let us turn to examine the American role in the effort carried on from 1925 to 1933 to reduce land armaments. As early as 1925, eschewing the very cautious view of the matter expressed by Secretary Hughes, and responding, no doubt, to the pressure of powerful elements in American opinion, Secretary Kellogg permitted the United States to take part in the deliberations of the Preparatory Commission on Disarmament that assembled at Geneva. For years a long discussion went on in this Commission which finally culminated in the Geneva Conference of 1932. In this conference bold proposals were put forward for the curtailment of land armaments as well as sea armaments, and in June of 1932 President Hoover presented a sweeping program which laid the emphasis on the abolition of "offensive weapons."[39]

But firmly, at all times, the United States adhered to its idea of no entanglement, of making no engagements that might tie its hands. And, equally firmly, the French insisted that such engagements were essential to any understanding. Thus the arms conference was to end in a fiasco; the way was blocked to any concrete accomplishment, and though the attitude was slightly changed when the Roosevelt administration came into power, the advent of Hitler in Germany dimmed the prospects of any accord. The world, instead, was to march down the long road to war.

[39] See *Foreign Relations*, 1932, I, 180-182.

Let us summarize at this point the policies of the United States with regard to peace and security as they relate to Europe. We shall have to begin by saying once again that these policies were narrowly circumscribed by public opinion. There are those who believe that if the American government had been able to take part wholeheartedly in a program of military guarantees the catastrophes of the 1930's might have been avoided. Certainly, in this year of grace 1953, the assumptions of American diplomacy are based on the idea of such guarantees. But different times, different manners. Neither Secretary Hughes nor Secretary Kellogg ever believed in the principle of collective action, and Stimson, believing in it more, had to contend with a President who was deeply set against any such conception. It is easy, if one will, to bewail the situation. But it is perhaps more judicious merely to recognize the fact that in democratic countries it is not possible to proceed in defiance of, or in opposition to, a powerful body of opinion.

V

Let us turn from the questions of politics to the principal economic problems that vexed the administrations of the 1920's. And here the two principal matters to be considered are the war debts[40] and reparations. On the former a position had been taken at Paris by President Wilson from which it was impossible at any time in the next fifteen years to depart. This position was that the cancelation of the debts could not be considered. It is obvious that, in assuming this position, Wilson was interpreting American opinion. It would have been impossible to take any other course. In the wave of postwar nationalism most Americans saw only that they had come to the rescue of the Western democracies in a great war, that they had played a decisive part in the winning of that war, and that the United States had little to show, in the way of material gain, for the immense sums of money that had been expended and for the loss of American lives. The suggestion that they should now forgive borrowings which had been understood to be such at the time they were made was hardly to be tolerated.

Accordingly, the Harding and Coolidge administrations were bound to base their own policy on the position assumed by the previous administration, and to turn a deaf ear to European appeals for a scaling down of both the war loans and reparations. The American attitude was first defined in an explicit manner, that is, by legislation, in the winter of

---

[40] On the war debts, see especially H. G. Moulton and L. Pasvolsky, *War Debts and World Prosperity* (Washington, D.C., 1932).

1922. The act of February 9 of that year created a special War Debt Commission to preside over the liquidation of these debts into long-term obligations. The Secretary of State, the Secretary of the Treasury, and members of both Houses of Congress were to constitute this commission. The original act narrowly confined the Commission as to the terms on which refunding could take place. No new bonds were to be issued the date of maturity of which was later than June 15, 1947, and the rate of interest was not to be fixed at less than 4¼ per cent.

The legislation of 1922 produced no great enthusiasm in the breasts of our European debtors for refunding, and it was indeed fundamentally vulnerable. For as the rate of interest fell in the United States so that the American government could borrow at a rate substantially lower that that of the war years, it seemed unreasonable to exact a high rate from other governments. It was also apparent, as time went on, that if interest payments were to be added to principal, there was little chance of arriving at agreements which stipulated for the complete discharge of the debt by 1947. The Congress was therefore obliged to enact a much more flexible statute in the winter of 1923, which gave far more latitude to the Commission. It was undoubtedly influenced to that end by the negotiations with Great Britain which took place in January of the same year. Secretary Mellon was chairman of the Debt Commission, and it does not appear that the American Secretary of State took the leading part in the discussions. The first of these discussions, carried on for the British by Stanley Baldwin, who came to America for that purpose, ended in a deadlock. The problem was complicated, moreover, by the wholly unauthorized assurances of George Harvey, our ambassador in London, as to the rate of interest that the United States would demand, and as to the possibility of floating a tax-free loan in the United States.[41] Hughes had good reason to lament the good old American custom which confided the charge of the most important embassies to political supporters of the administration. But, in due course, an arrangement was arrived at, the rate of interest reduced, and the period of payments extended to 62 years, and this agreement was approved by the Congress. The method adopted, that is, legislative approval instead of the negotiation of a treaty, undoubtedly made easier the arrival at an accord, and is an interesting example of a method, which was to be more and more employed in the future, of circumventing the Senate.

Other debt agreements followed. It was the French who were the most obdurate in negotiation, and who were particularly insistent that

[41] Pusey, *Charles Evans Hughes*, II, 585.

the war debt problem be linked up to the question of reparations. Against any such proposition the War Debt Commission and the State Department alike took a very strong and unyielding stand. No connection between the two subjects was admitted, though it was obvious, of course, that if Germany defaulted on reparations, the burden of repayment of the debts would fall squarely upon the taxpayers of the debtor nations, and would, to some extent, at least, create a new situation. The first flurry with the French took place in 1925. When the French went home without an agreement, and in a good deal of a huff, the Italian government, nicely calculating the moment for a deal, took up the thread of its own negotiations, and, for reasons that are somewhat obscure, emerged with a settlement that reduced the average rate of interest on the Italian obligations to something like .4 of one per cent. A new effort at dealing with the French was undertaken in 1927, and in a much more favorable climate of opinion. Though the French continued to press for a recognition of the relationship between debts and reparations, an agreement was signed and payments began to be made.

In these negotiations for debt refunding, the principal burden was borne by the Treasury. But it was not so with reparations. Here the State Department played an important role, and this was particularly true under Secretary Hughes.

At Paris in 1919, it was impossible to arrive at any settlement with regard to Germany's payments to the victors. The problem was, at best, a very complicated one, and it was rendered more complex by the strong public feeling in both France and Great Britain. The exaggerated hopes of the mass of people had been encouraged by the politicians, and economic realism flew out the window. Accordingly, what was done was virtually to adjourn the settlement of the matter, to entrust the determination of Germany's indebtedness to a Reparations Commission set up by the treaty, which should by May 1, 1921, following certain principles laid down in treaty, determine the facts of the situation. In the meantime Germany was compelled to make certain types of payment, which we do not need to examine in detail.

Originally, it was expected that the United States would be one of the five nations represented on the Commission, and that the American member would be chairman. But the treaty of Versailles failed in the Senate, and when a separate treaty was negotiated with Germany, the Senate tacked on a reservation by which the representation on any of the numerous bodies functioning under the pact was forbidden, unless the explicit consent of Congress had been given. Mr. Hughes thus found himself in a most embarrassing situation. He could, of course, and did, appoint "unofficial" representatives to the Commission. But these individuals could wield very little authority; they could not vote on any issue. As a consequence, the control of the Commission gravitated into the hands of the French, and the attitude assumed became more and more rigorous. On a problem where the relatively objective attitude of the United States might have been of very great value, it became of almost no value at all.

The hamstringing of the State Department did not prevent Mr. Hughes from taking an active interest in the reparations question. At the outset of his term of office he was approached by the German government and asked to mediate the reparations question, and to fix the sum to be paid by Germany to the Allies.[42] This hot potato the Secretary naturally laid down hastily enough, but he urged that the German government itself formulate proposals that would form a proper basis for discussion. This suggestion was promptly accepted, and an offer made to pay a sum of 50,000,000,000 gold marks, present value, which would have amounted to something like four times this sum in annuities. The very afternoon it was received, the German proposition was submitted to the British and French ambassadors, and in the conversation that ensued Mr. Hughes raised the question whether a point had not been reached where it was better to take the proposal as a basis for further negotiations.[43] But the various European governments concerned remained obdurate. And on May 2 the word went forth to Berlin that the United States "finds itself unable to reach the conclusion that the proposals afford a basis for discussion acceptable to the Allied Governments."[44] The first American effort at a solution of the reparations question had met with failure.

As is well known, the reparations question became more and more aggravated in 1922, and the French government in particular manifested a more and more rigid point of view. The situation was shaping up towards sanctions and military pressure on Germany in the fall of the year. Very obviously, this development the Secretary profoundly deplored. Indeed, in December of 1922, he held a long conversation with Jusserand in which, in none too gentle a tone, he pointed out the difficulties to which further coercive measures by France would surely lead.[45] Moreover, there was germinating in his mind as early as September a proposal that the reparations question be taken out of the field of

---

[42] *Foreign Relations*, 1921, II, 41.　　[43] *Foreign Relations*, 1921, II, 48.
[44] *Foreign Relations*, 1921, II, 54.　　[45] *Foreign Relations*, 1922, II, 187ff.

emotional debate, and submitted to the examination of financial experts, and this idea, too, he presented to Jusserand. On the other hand, he rejected as impracticable a proposal that came from Ambassador Houghton in Berlin, and which looked towards easing the general international tension by canceling the war debts in exchange for measures of disarmament, and a pledge on the part of the great nations of Europe not to go to war without a public referendum.[46] At the end of December, in a step only less remarkable than the dramatic proposal for arms reduction at the Washington Conference in November 1921, he laid bare to the public his views on the reparations question, in a speech before the American Historical Association at New Haven. The speech, it is true, indicated no concessions on the part of the United States. But it contained a key idea, which the Secretary stated as follows, "Why should they (the Allies) not invite men of the highest authority in finance in their respective countries—men of such prestige, honor and experience that their agreement upon the amount to be paid (by Germany), and upon a financial plan for working out the payments, would be accepted throughout the world as the most authoritative expression obtainable. I have no doubt that distinguished Americans would be willing to serve on such a commission."[47]

At the time that it was pronounced, the New Haven speech produced no effect whatever. On January 2, Britain dissenting, the Reparations Commission declared Germany to be in default, and authorized sanctions against her. Not many days later the French moved into the Ruhr, and there began one of the most disastrous political moves of the postwar decade.

During the summer and early fall of 1923 the situation in the Reich deteriorated in sensational fashion. There was, in Hughes' opinion, nothing that the United States could do that would not make the situation worse; any suggestion in favor of Germany would, he felt, irritate the French and weaken the force of the suggestion that he had made at New Haven. Only experience could alter the situation and provide a means of settlement. And experience did precisely that. Slowly the French, in the face of British and American criticism and German passive resistance, yielded ground. They haggled over terms of reference to be laid down for the committees of experts and sought to limit the conclusions of the inquiry in time. But Hughes stood his ground, and at last he had his way. On November 23, 1923, the Reparations Commission approved of an inquiry of the type the Secretary had suggested,

---

[46] *Foreign Relations*, 1922, II, 181.   [47] *Foreign Relations*, 1922, II, 199-202.

and two committees of experts were appointed to consider means of balancing the budget and stabilizing the currency and to investigate the amount of German capital that had been exported abroad. Since the Commission itself appointed the members of the committees, the limitation that the Senate had appended to the treaty of peace with Germany with regard to official representation on international bodies was of no effect, and that body was neatly outflanked.

The deliberations of these committees, appointed in November 1923, resulted, of course, in the Dawes plan. It is not possible to analyze that plan here. But it is important to note the part which Hughes played in seeing that its recommendations were carried into effect. Ostensibly going to Europe as President of the American Bar Association (a camouflage that seems a bit ineffective), he visited the various capitals of Europe and lent his influence to persuading the governments concerned to accept the program that General Dawes and his associates had laid down. He appears to have had his greatest difficulties in France, where Premier Herriot, himself not unfavorable to the plan, was mortally afraid of the hostile influence of Raymond Poincaré. But he saw both Herriot and Poincaré and made it clear that rejection of the scheme would have a very unfortunate effect.[48] Whether his role was decisive it is not possible to say. But, at any rate, the Dawes plan was put into effect.

Of course the new arrangements did not last long. They had to be revised in 1929 when the same technique of committees of experts was again employed. And then came the depression of 1929, forcing still further readjustments.

These readjustments we must for a moment examine if only for the light they throw on the character of American foreign policy in general. As the depression deepened, it became increasingly clear that the whole structure of international indebtedness erected in the postwar years rested on a flimsy foundation. The crisis came in 1931, with the collapse of the Austrian bank, the Credit-Anstalt, and a serious deterioration in the economic situation of Germany. Though Congress was not in session, and though his only recourse was to telegraph Congressional leaders in both Houses, the President came forward with a proposal for a year's moratorium on reparations and war debts alike. In his recent memoirs Mr. Hoover declares that this proposal was his own.[49] Certainly there have been few examples of more forthright action on the part of the

[48] Pusey, *Charles Evans Hughes*, II, 591-592.
[49] *Collier's*, May 10, 1952, p. 72.

Chief Executive, and no one will deny that the decision took political courage. Even so, it was necessary to attenuate its effects by declaring that no question of cancelation was involved, and by stating (somewhat illogically, it must be confessed) that the question of German reparations was a "strictly European problem."

The President's bold initiative did not alter the fundamentals of the situation. It was accepted by the French only after some diplomatic haggling, and it did not prevent an increasing agitation for the reduction of German reparations. The European conference which met at Lausanne in the summer of 1932 reduced the obligations of the Reich to a minimum, while at the same time drawing up a "gentleman's agreement" which stipulated that these reductions would not go into effect if the United States persisted in maintaining its attitude with regard to the war debts. What followed is no part of our story, except to say that both reparations and war debt payments had broken down entirely by 1934. The essence of the matter is that here was a problem that the diplomats simply could not settle, one in which the prejudices and resistances of the masses were more powerful than any appeal to intelligence could be. And outside the gesture of the Hoover moratorium, it is to be stated that American statesmanship in the last years of the debt question was never ready to face up to explaining to the American people the cold realities of the situation.

There is a peripheral aspect of this question of war debts and reparations that deserves a word of attention. The tariff attitude of the United States in the 1920's and early 1930's was in glaring contrast with its position on the refunding of the war obligations. It is an extraordinary commentary on the architects of American policy that they seem to have been so oblivious of the fact that if Europe were to pay up, it would be necessary to tear down, or at least to lower, customs barriers. Yet Secretary Hughes appears to have been little interested in the tariff act of 1922, and Secretary Stimson, though apparently more clearly aware of the problem, offered no effective resistance to the still higher tariff bill of 1930. The coordination of economic and political factors in the evolution of American diplomacy would, in any case, have been difficult; but in this one phase, at any rate, it does not seem even to have been attempted.

It is further to be noted that the edifice erected in the 1920's, the edifice of the naval treaties, of the Kellogg Pact, of the Dawes plan and the Young plan, was virtually completely to collapse in the 1930's, and here again the principal reasons were economic. When economic collapse came, and economic collapse for which the uncontrolled inflation in the United States must be regarded as a heavy contributing cause, the diplomats found their work in large degree undone. In the face of popular pressures based on economic discontent, they were powerless to prevent the deterioration of the general international situation in the 1930's.

The central question raised by this essay is, then, the question as to where, in the last analysis so far as America is concerned, foreign policy is made. And the conclusion is one suggested by the first pages of this text. It is made by the people, to no inconsiderable degree. It functions only within a frame of reference which they prescribe. Today, we seem to have embarked upon courses of action entirely antithetic to those of the 1920's. Then the thought was all of keeping American freedom of action, of avoiding Leagues and treaties which implied commitments. Today we think in terms of massing collective strength against a new menace, of alliances, of common action, and warning to aggressors that aggression will meet with punishment. Such policies are today dictated by the public mood, or are at least consistent with it. But the statesmen of the 1920's labored in a different climate of opinion, and were circumscribed by the prejudices which were typical of that climate. In the long run, they failed to erect a structure of peace. Will the formulas of the 1950's make success possible where it was not possible three decades ago? That is a question, not for the historian but for the prophets.

INDEX

LIST OF CONTRIBUTORS

RICHARD D. CHALLENER is Associate Professor of History at Princeton University. He is author of *The French Theory of the Nation in Arms 1866-1939;* editor (with Gordon B. Turner) of *National Security in the Nuclear Age.*

GORDON A. CRAIG is Professor of History at Stanford University. He is author of *Politics of the Prussian Army, 1640-1945; From Bismarck to Adenauer; Europe Since 1815.* He was collaborating editor of and contributor to *Makers of Modern Strategy: Military Thought from Machiavelli to Hitler.*

RODERIC H. DAVISON is Professor of History at the George Washington University. He is author of *The Near and Middle East.*

FELIX GILBERT is Professor in the School of Historical Studies at The Institute for Advanced Study, Princeton. He is author of *To the Farewell Address: Ideas of Early American Foreign Policy* and was collaborating editor of and contributor to *Makers of Modern Strategy;* editor of *Hitler Directs His War.*

HAJO HOLBORN is Sterling Professor of History at Yale University. He is author of *The Political Collapse of Modern Europe; A History of Modern Germany;* and other historical books.

H. STUART HUGHES is Professor of History at Harvard University. He is author of *An Essay for our Time; Spengler; The United States and Italy; Consciousness and Society; Contemporary Europe: A History; Approach to Peace;* and other historical books.

THEODORE H. VON LAUE is Professor of History at the University of California, Riverside. He is author of *Leopold Ranke: The Formative Years.*

ERIK LONNROTH is Professor of History at the University of Gothenburg, Sweden, and a Member of the Swedish Academy.

DEXTER PERKINS is Professor of History Emeritus at Cornell University and the University of Rochester, Mellon Professor of History at the University of Pittsburgh. He is author of *American Approach to Foreign Policy; America's Quest for Peace; History of the Monroe Doctrine; The New Age of Franklin Roosevelt; The United States and Latin America;* (with Glyndon Van Deusen) *The United States of America;* and other historical books.

PAUL E. ZINNER is Professor of Political Science at the University of California, Davis. He is author of *Revolution in Hungary.* He was editor of *Documents on American Foreign Relations* and *National Communism and Popular Revolt in Eastern Europe.*

Atheneum Paperbacks

Atheneum Paperbacks

GOVERNMENT AND PUBLIC AFFAIRS

ECONOMICS AND BUSINESS

HISTORY AND SOCIETAL STUDIES